Citizenship in a Global World

At the beginning of a new millennium Turkey finds itself at a critical juncture in its democratic evolution. This momentous event has been precipitated by its desire to enter into the European Union and the recent governing crisis it has faced, both of which have fueled the need for the creation of a strong, democratic Turkey.

This book combines an analysis of social, political and economic determinants of Turkish politics with an exploration of the different dimensions of the republican model of Turkish citizenship; thus providing the reader with a comprehensive account of Turkish modernity and democracy.

Consisting of a collection of innovative and influential essays written by prominent scholars, this book will supply the reader with an historical and sociological understanding of Turkey, and add a new dimension to the ongoing discussion surrounding global citizenship and global identity.

Citizenship in a Global World will prove to be invaluable to students studying political economy, comparative politics, globalization, democracy and civil society, European studies, the sociology of modernity and Turkish politics.

E. Fuat Keyman is Professor of International Relations at Koç University, Istanbul, Turkey.

Ahmet İçduygu is Associate Professor of International Relations at Koç University, Istanbul, Turkey.

Routledge Studies in Governance and Change in the Global Era

1 **New Socialisms**
Futures Beyond Globalization
Edited by Robert Albritton, John Bell, Shannon Bell and Richard Westra

2 **International Crisis Management**
The Approach of European States
Marc Houben

3 **Citizenship in a Global World**
European Questions and Turkish Experiences
Edited by E. Fuat Keyman and Ahmet İçduygu

4 **The New Economy in Transatlantic Perspective**
Spaces of Innovation
Edited by Kurt Huebner

5 **Worlds of Capitalism**
Institutions, Governance, and Economic Change in the Era of Globalization
Edited by Max Miller

Other titles in this series include:

States Against Markets
Edited by Robert Boyer and Daniel Drache

Political Ecology
Edited by David Bell, Lessa Fawcett, Roger Keil and Peter Penz

Health Reform
Edited by Daniel Drache and Terry Sullivan

Democracy, Citizenship and the Global City
Edited by Engin F. Isin

Between the Market and the Public Domain
Redrawing the Line
Edited by Daniel Drache

Citizenship in a Global World

European questions and Turkish experiences

Edited by E. Fuat Keyman and Ahmet İçduygu

Routledge
Taylor & Francis Group
LONDON AND NEW YORK

First published 2005
by Routledge
2 Park Square, Milton Park, Abingdon, Oxfordshire OX14 4RN

Simultaneously published in the USA and Canada
by Routledge
711 Third Avenue, New York, NY 10017

Routledge is an imprint of the Taylor & Francis Group

First issued in paperback 2012

Typeset in Times by
Taylor & Francis Books

British Library Cataloguing in Publication Data
A catalogue record for this book is available from the British Library

Library of Congress Cataloging in Publication Data
A catalog record for this book has been requested

ISBN 978-0-415-35456-1 (hbk)
ISBN 978-0-415-64665-9 (pbk)

To the memory of our fathers

Ahmet Nazif Keyman (1924–2004)

Mehmet Hamdi İçduygu (1914–1992)

Contents

Contributors

Feyzi Baban, Assistant Professor, Department of Political Science, Trent University, Toronto, Canada.

Yılmaz Çolak, Assistant Professor, Department of Political Science, Eastern Mediterranean University, Gazimagusa, Cyprus.

Ahmet İçduygu, Associate Professor, Department of International Relations, Koç University, Istanbul, Turkey.

Engin F. Isin, Professor, Department of Political Science, York University, Toronto, Canada.

Ayşe Kadıoğlu, Associate Professor, Faculty of Arts and Social Sciences, Sabancı University, Istanbul, Turkey.

Hasan Bülent Kahraman, Assistant Professor, Faculty of Arts and Social Sciences, Sabancı University, Istanbul, Turkey.

Ayhan Kaya, Associate Professor, Department of International Relations, Istanbul Bilgi University, Istanbul, Turkey.

E. Fuat Keyman, Professor, Department of International Relations, Koç University, Istanbul, Turkey.

Ziya Öniş, Professor, Department of International Relations, Koç University, Istanbul, Turkey.

Nükhet Sirman, Professor, Department of Sociology, Bosphorus University, Istanbul, Turkey.

B. Ali Soner, Ph.D., Department of Political Science, Bilkent University, Ankara, Turkey.

Nalan Soyarık-Şentürk, Assistant Professor, Department of International Relations, Başkent University, Ankara, Turkey.

Deniz Vardar, Associate Professor, Department of Political Science and International Relations, Marmara University, Istanbul, Turkey.

Preface

Every book has its own history, and this book does not constitute an exception. On the contrary, the idea of putting together a volume which deals historically and theoretically with the question of citizenship in Turkey started in an international conference on "Citizenship, State, and Identity in a Globalizing World," held at Bilkent University in Ankara on 2–5 June 2000. The aim of the conference was to compare Turkey and Europe on the basis of different citizenship regimes and discourses. Although, at the outset, our intention was to publish a book consisting of a number of case studies analyzing the changing nature of citizenship in Turkey and Europe, the very stimulating and knowledge-generating discussions that had been produced during the conference led us to believe that it was necessary and timely to focus exclusively on the Turkish experience of modern citizenship. This is mainly due to the fact that as Turkey-EU relations have become more certain and deep, more information, explanation and understanding of Turkey is needed. We believe that rather than focusing solely on political parties, state elites and political leaders, which conventional studies on Turkish politics tend to do, a focus on citizenship would enable a more comprehensive account of Turkish modernity and democracy.

Thus, we have decided to put together a book on Turkey which attempts to analyze critically both the historical and discursive construction of the state-centric modernity in Turkey, and more importantly its recent transformation in which Turkey's integration into the European Union has played a crucial and positive role. Such an analysis takes as its methodological and analytical focus "Turkish republican citizenship," its crucial role in Turkish modernity, and its recent deconstruction by various claims to identity/difference and new demands for differential citizenship rights.

Producing a book on Turkey may be justified on the following grounds. First, given that the Turkish experience of modern citizenship has to a large extent remained unknown outside the borders of Turkey, it seemed necessary to provide a detailed and comprehensive account of the complexities and peculiarities embedded in the Turkish republican model of citizenship. In fact, the present volume is the first attempt of this kind. Second, since the full accession of Turkey into the European Union appears to be the most difficult and challenging question the process of European enlargement is facing today, and insofar as Turkey's success in articulating a largely Muslim identity with secular democracy/modernity has the potential to reshape European multicultural identity, a detailed and comprehensive analysis of the modern Turkish experience from the perspective of citizenship would be timely. Third, in producing the present volume, we also hope to contribute to the existing theoretical discussions about (global) citizenship which mostly appear to have remained limited within the epistemological and philosophical boundaries of Western modernity.

In this context, *Citizenship in a Global World: European Questions and Turkish Experiences* should not be read only as a specific case-study, that is, citizenship in Turkey. Instead, it should be viewed both as a comprehensive account of contemporary Turkey from the perspective of citizenship and as a contribution to the recent debates on European citizenship, as well as advancing our understanding of citizenship in a global world. Of course, achieving such a task requires a collective effort. We have been extremely lucky in receiving valuable support from a large number of colleagues and friends, as well as institutions. We should state from the outset, however, that this book would not be possible without the most valuable intellectual input and personal commitment of our dear friend Engin F. Isin in our project. Thanking him here would not be enough to show our appreciation for his true friendship and his contribution to this book. We are also very grateful to Daniel Drache for his valuable support and editorial suggestions.

In the course of producing this book, we have benefited immensely from the intellectual support of the following scholars and friends: special thanks go to Ayşe Çağlar, Gerard Delanty, Thomas Faist, Güliz Ger, Nilüfer Göle, Metin Heper, Thomas Hammar, Banu Helvacıoğlu, Cara Murphy Keyman, Kemal Kirişçi, Lauren McLaren, Jan Nederveen Pieterse, John Rex, Jeremy Salt, Bobby Said, Isador Ryan, Bryan Turner, Galip Yalman, and Arus Yumul. Furthermore, for their valuable assistance in preparing the manuscript for publication, our thanks are especially due to Fadime Boztaş, Evren Tok, A. Biriz Karaçay and Nazan Albayrak.

We also thank the Bilkent University Center for Research on Transitional Societies and Koç University President Professor Dr Atilla Aşkar for their financial support. And last but not least, our special thanks go to Rob Langham, Mike Wendling and Terry Clague at Routledge for their careful editorial suggestions and contributions, as well as to the anonymous readers for their helpful comments on the manuscript.

Finally, we would like to emphasize that we bear sole responsibility of any possible shortcomings of our book.

E. Fuat Keyman and Ahmet İçduygu
Koç University, Istanbul, May 2004

Introduction

Citizenship, identity, and the question of democracy in Turkey

E. Fuat Keyman and Ahmet İçduygu

On the eve of a new millennium Turkey finds itself at a critical disjuncture. As a country whose economy has been going through a severe crisis and whose state-centric politics has been facing a strong legitimacy and governing crisis, and whose social and cultural life has been generating identity-based conflict, Turkey has to make a crucial decision about its future. These crisis-ridden historical changes are forcing Turkey to decide either to shake itself radically in a way to alter its state-society relations in a democratic and liberal form or to decide once again to hide behind the illusionary walls of state-centricism and nationalism by maintaining the privileged status of the Carl Schmittian understanding of politics as governing society on the basis of "the friend and foe relationship." Although the latter choice has been the dominant tendency in the state-centering political culture of Turkey during the 1990s, today there is a strong societal will and demand, and even a realistic possibility for the creation of an economically stable, democratically governed and culturally pluralistic Turkey.

A number of recent historical events, namely those of the 3 November 2002 national election, the Copenhagen Summit (12–14 December 2002) and the war on Iraq, all have indicated that the possibility of the creation of a different, strong and democratic Turkey is not a naive optimism. On the contrary, it constitutes an achievable reality, as long as the strong societal will and demand for democratization and economic stability can be transformed into a political will to restructure state-society relations in a democratic, liberal and pluralist way. The war on Iraq and its post-war reconstruction has indicated that a democratically and economically strong Turkey has the potential not only to promote multilateralism *vis-à-vis* the security-based and unilateral hegemonic operations of American foreign policy in the Middle East, but also to aid the creation of a peaceful and stable solution to the tragic and human-costly problems of the region. As the American occupation of Iraq continues, it is likely that the more Turkey achieves its democratization and economic stabilization, the more it will play an important role in the possibility of creating a peaceful Middle East. However, the end result of the US-led attempt to reconstruct Iraq still remains to be seen.

In this context, insofar as the democratization and economic stabilization of Turkey entails a strong political will to structure its domestic state-society relations in a democratic mode, we suggest that rather than the war on Iraq, the November 3rd national election and the recent deepening of Turkey-EU relations should be seen as key to the possibility of creating a strong and democratic Turkey.[1] The November 3rd national election has resulted in the emergence of a single party majority government that has created a widespread societal hope for the long-waited efficient and stable governing of society and economy. Additionally, the Copenhagen Summit declared that the negotiations between the European Union (hereafter the EU) and Turkey for full-membership status will start without delay on the condition that Turkey succeeds in the application of what are known as "the Copenhagen political criteria" in its state-society relations before the Helsinki Summit of December 2004. This has yielded an external pressure on Turkey to achieve the possibility of democratization and economic stability within a given time. In this sense, whether or not Turkey is able to render such democratization and economic stability as an achieved reality depends on the political will of the government to deal effectively and democratically with the problems and demands of society in such a way that also makes Turkey strong enough to begin its full-accession to the EU.

It should be pointed out, however, that creating a strong and fully democratic Turkey is not an easy process. It cannot be achieved only through the set of legal and constitutional changes that Turkey initiated in 2002, regarding the abolishment of capital punishment and the question of human rights and group rights, even if these changes are of utmost importance to Turkey-EU relations. Nor can it be achieved only with a set of partial political and administrative changes that will establish a more transparent and accountable governing system in Turkey, even if the creation of efficient governance is of utmost importance in the elimination of the problems of clientalism and corruption, whose negative consequences for Turkish society have recently become obvious and devastating as a result of the total collapse of the Turkish economy in 2001. In fact, the creation of a strong and fully democratic Turkey requires a radical change and transformation in state-society relations whose scope, content and affectivity go much beyond these superstructural changes. As the decision of the Copenhagen Summit regarding Turkey indicates, a strong and democratic Turkey can be achieved, if and only if Turkey realizes the "full application" of these superstructural changes in such a way that substantial democracy with an emphasis on the normative primacy of individual rights and freedoms becomes the defining feature of the way in which the state attempts to regulate societal relations.

It is here that citizenship becomes an extremely important issue, insofar as (a) it constitutes "a significant sociological and normative ground" on which we can analyze the changing nature of Turkish modernity which has given rise to the recent impasse of the state-centric structure of Turkish politics. We can also explore possible ways in which such an impasse can be overcome; (b) more specifically, it functions as "an adequate criterion" to measure the degree to which the superstructural changes, initiated by the state in 2002 as a necessary step for the full accession of Turkey into the EU, are being applied concretely to the way in which the state governs its society; and (c) more importantly, it enables us to see that the creation of a strong and democratic Turkey cannot be achieved fully without the successful implementation and dissemination of "the language of rights" throughout society.

This book is an attempt to provide a detailed and comprehensive analysis of Turkish modernity in a historical way. In doing so, it aims at demonstrating in a convincing fashion that a liberal democratic reconstruction of Turkish modernity on the basis of the insertion of "the language of rights" into Turkish citizenship constitutes a necessary condition for the realization of a further democratization of Turkish politics and the possibility of Turkey's full accession into the EU. In this sense, as opposed to the conventional analysis of Turkish politics that tends to focus exclusively on political parties and their interactions with the state without paying enough attention to economic, social and cultural factors or processes, this book employs a historical and critical analysis of Turkish modernity which focuses on state-society interactions and their changing nature over time, pays attention to the role of sociological and political-economic determinants of Turkish politics and its recent impasse, and more importantly aims at developing a democratic vision necessary for the creation of a different and strong Turkey. We argue that the question of citizenship constitutes an adequate ground not only for a historical and critical analysis of the recent crisis of Turkish modernity and its state-centric *modus vivendi*, but also for its democratic reconstruction. This is so, for, as the chapters of this book will indicate in their own contexts, the crisis of Turkish modernity is also a crisis of the republican model of Turkish citizenship on which it has initiated its state-centric operation; and in the same vein, a democratic reconstruction of Turkish modernity is also a multicultural, differentiated and constitutional reconstruction of Turkish citizenship on the basis of the language of rights. In this context, we propose first that a discussion of both the different dimensions of the republican model of Turkish citizenship and especially the recent challenges to it provides a more comprehensive and detailed analysis of Turkish politics. We also propose that citizenship, understood not only as a legal status but also as a "practice" through which individual and group demands are made for the expansion of the scope of existing rights, should be taken seriously as a significant site for the further democratization of state-society relations in Turkey.

A critical analysis of Turkish modernity, in which the question of citizenship is the main focus, is timely and necessary. It is timely, for the radical changes and transformations that have been occurring and generating important impacts on state-society relations in Turkey are forcing us to go beyond the conventional understanding of Turkish politics, whose explanatory power is limited to an analysis of political parties and their relations to the state. It is necessary, for since these changes and transformations involve serious challenges not only to the state and political parties, but also, and more significantly, to the state-centric nature of Turkish modernity and its constitutive elements such as strong-state traditions, national developmentalism, an organic vision of society and a republican model of citizenship, they are forcing us to focus on state-society relations in our search for feasible solutions to these challenges. Four historical processes are of utmost importance for an adequate understanding of the emergence of the radical changes and transformations in Turkish society that have made a critical analysis of Turkish modernity timely and necessary. These processes are those of "the changing nature of Turkish modernity and its legitimacy crisis," "the process of Turkey's full accession into the EU and the question of liberal democracy," "the recent economic crisis, Turkey-IMF relations and the question of economic restructuring," and "the impasse of Turkish politics and the November 3rd national election." In what follows, we will briefly look at these processes, insofar as they together constitute a historical context for our argument that citizenship provides us with a significant site for a critical analysis of Turkish modernity, as well as for the possibility of its democratic reconstruction.

Turkish modernity, change and legitimacy

Although displaying certain continuities with its Ottoman past, Turkey was in fact "made" in the image of the Kemalist elite as a modern republic. In the process of "making," the primary aim of the Kemalist elite was to "reach the contemporary level of civilization" by establishing its political, economic, and ideological prerequisites, such as the creation of an independent nation-state, the fostering of industrialization, and the construction of a secular and modern national identity. The Kemalist elite thus accepted the universal validity of Western modernity as *the* way of constructing a modern Turkey and attempts to "reach the level of civilization," which it sees as the process of building a modern nation-state in its fullest form. The conceptualization of the Turkish Republic as nation-state was regarded by Mustafa Kemal Atatürk and his followers as the precondition for the possibility that "Turkey would live as an advanced and civilized nation in the midst of contemporary civilization" (Ahmad 1993: 53).

In the process of building a modern Turkey, the idea of the state employed by the Kemalist elite was by no means abstract: rather it was derived from a reaction to two fundamental problems which they saw as the key to the decline of the Ottoman Empire. First, the Ottoman state was identified with the personal rule of the sultan, which eventually led to its inability to compete with the European nation-state system (Heper 1985: 49). Second, the Islamic basis of the Ottoman state was regarded as the primary obstacle to progress in Ottoman society. For the Kemalist elite, there was therefore a need to create a nation-state distinct from the person of the sultan and secular enough to reduce Islam to the realm of individual faith. The state is thus viewed as not an arbitrary institution nor an expression of class interest, but as an active agent that, while taking its inspiration from the genuine feelings and desires of the nation, shapes and reshapes it to "elevate the people to the level of contemporary (Western) civilization" (Heper 1985: 50). In this context, Gellner considered the Kemalist idea of the state to be a commitment to "political modernity," which sees "the modernization of the polity and society" as "linked to the state." This commitment "constitutes its legitimation and is itself in turn justified by the strength which it bestows on the state" (1994: 83).

However, for Kemalism modernization was not just a question of acquiring technology, but something that could not be absorbed without a dense network of cultural practices (see Chapter 12 by Keyman). Thus, political modernity could be supplemented with a set of cultural practices, *imposed from above* to "enlighten the people and help them make progress" (Heper 1985: 51). Republicanism, nationalism, statism, secularism, populism, and revolutionism-reformism (from above) were the six principles by which the state was to govern its society by creating a unitary nation as an organic totality.

In the light of the above (synoptic) analysis, we could state that the process of the making of Turkey constitutes a "state-centric modernity." There are four defining elements of the state-centric operation of Turkish modernity, and since the 1980s and especially during the 1990s we have witnessed the increasing legitimacy crisis of such an operation, whose manifestations have been observed in each of these elements. The four elements can be described in the following way:

1 *The strong-state tradition*: since the beginning of the Turkish Republic, modernity has been defined by the dominant role that the state has played in various ways in the production and reproduction of societal affairs as a whole. The state in Turkish modernity has acted as the privileged and sovereign subject operating almost completely independently from society and assuming the capacity to transform society from above. In this process, it has been the state, not the government, that has constituted the primary context of politics, defined its boundaries, and decided who can or cannot participate in it. In doing so, the state was the basic site at which national interest was formulated by the state elite in such a way that it was identified as state interest. Thus, the strong-state tradition meant a state-centric way of governing society from above by assuming a unity between state and nation, as well as between national interest and state interest.
2 *National developmentalism*: one of the main ideologies of the strong-state tradition was the ideology of national developmentalism which, in

its anti-liberal and state-centric modes of operation, involved a "planned, import-substituting industrialization" as the "proper prescription for development (Keyder 1997: 40). National developmentalism defined the state as the dominant economic actor whose basic aim was to regulate the economy in such a way that the rapid economic modernization of what was regarded by the Kemalist elite as a backward society could be achieved. In doing so, the state acted as the developmental state, creating a state-directed economy and taking substantial decisions for the regulation of economic activities for industrialization. In this context, as Keyder (1997: 41) points out, the state in its national developmentalist intervention into society assumed potential autonomy and the administrative characteristic of having no transparency or accountability to society.

3 *The organic vision of society*: if national developmentalism established the economic dimension of the state-centric Turkish modernity, its sociological grounding was created through an organic vision of society that defines society not with reference to such categories as class or individual, but on the basis of the "duties and services" of different occupation groups to the state. Thus, in its attempt to modernize Turkey, the Kemalist elite did not approach its society in terms of individual rights and freedoms, nor did it see society as containing individualism, pluralism, participation and claims to difference. Instead, society had to be organic, in that societal affairs were organized in a homogeneous and monolithic way to serve the national interest, that is, for the making of Turkey as a civilized and modern nation.

4 *The republican model of citizenship*: in governing society through the ideologies of national developmentalism and organic society, how could the state activate the masses toward modernity? The Kemalist elite answered this question on the basis of the republican model of citizenship, which, while giving the masses political rights, demanded at the same time that they accord normative primacy to the national interest over individual freedoms, to duties over rights, and to state sovereignty over individual autonomy. Thus, the making of modern Turkey involved the transformation of the masses into citizens, but prevented the language of rights from entering into the process of the construction of secular national identity. For the Kemalist elite, citizenship was not a liberal category framed by the language of rights, but refers to a morally-loaded category aimed at creating a secular and rational national identity compatible with the project of modernity as civilization. In this way, the republican model of citizenship serves for the state, first as a "link" between state and society on the basis of the principle of national unity, second as an "articulatory principle" that connects people with different religious, ethnic and cultural origins under the rubric of modernity as civilization, and third as an effective ideological device by which the state attempted to disseminate its will to civilization throughout society.

The strong-state tradition, national developmentalism, an organic vision of society and the republican model of citizenship together established the foundational basis for the state-centric mode of operation of Turkish modernity. To the extent that the will to civilization entailed primarily the construction of Turkey as a modern nation-state, Turkish modernity in fact was successful in its state-centric operation. It was successful in economic development, industrialization, urbanization, education and social welfare. Although since 1945 Turkish politics has been characterized by formal democracy as a multi-party parliamentary system of rule, the material success of Turkish modernity has not gone hand-in-hand with democratization and the development of the language of rights and freedoms. Nor has it led to the promotion of individual autonomy or the recognition of cultural differences.

Since the 1980s and especially during the 1990s, it has become apparent that both in a world-historical context and due to the radical changes and transformations that have been occurring in Turkish society, Turkish modernity and its state-centric governing of society from above "is in serious crisis: the legitimacy it once enjoyed has been withdrawn" (Keyder 1997: 47). Likewise, its democratic deficit has been steadily increasing. The sources of this crisis are many, and most of them will be analyzed in the following chapters of this book. However, we shall highlight briefly these changes and transformations. First, in a world-historical context and in parallel to the changes in the world economy, framed to a large extent by the emergence and subsequent consolidation of the neoliberal discourse of free market rationality, the era of national developmentalism came to an end. The replacement of import-substitution industrialization with export-promotion industrialization in the 1980s, and then the increasing exposure of the Turkish economy to economic globalization, especially in the 1990s, together indicated that national developmentalism was no longer an effective ideological device to be used by the strong-state to dictate the rules of the economic sphere in its regulation of the economy. On the contrary, since the 1980s, the Turkish economy has been radically transformed both ideologically and institutionally. Ideologically, the free market-based economic rationality has begun to play an extremely significant role in the increasing societal dissatisfaction with the strong-state tradition. Rather than national developmentalism, the regulation of state-economy relations has become increasingly dictated by the neoliberal discourse of individualism, the free market and the minimal state. Institutionally, free-market ideology has given rise to the emergence of a multiplicity of economic actors and economic pressure groups accepting the rules and norms of economic globalization and demanding a minimum state intervention. These ideological and institutional changes have radically transformed state-bourgeoisie relations in such a way that calls for autonomy, civil rights, democracy, European integration and economic efficiency have become the main discourse of the Turkish bourgeoisie (Özbudun and Keyman 2002: 296–319).

Second, since the 1980s we have witnessed both the collapse of the organic vision of society and the concomitant development of what has come to be known as the politics of identity. The three sets of developments are of utmost importance in this context, insofar as they have paved the way for the strong critiques of state-centric Turkish modernity and its homogenizing and monolithic political culture. These developments are the resurgence of Islam, the "Kurdish question," and the emergence of civil society, all of which have initiated in their own ways a strong challenge to the organic vision of society, and thus have contributed to the process of the fragmentation of political culture in Turkey. As we will see later in the book, the resurgence of Islam as a strong political, economic and cultural actor has challenged the secular foundation of organic society and national identity. In doing so, it has brought claims for the recognition of religious identity to the center of Turkish politics. Similarly, the Kurdish question, articulated as a language of ethnic difference and a claim to recognition, has forced us to rethink our understanding of modernity, national identity, and democratic subjectivity. Thus, in the form of ethnic violence, terrorism and identity politics, the Kurdish question has shaken the foundations of the assumed unity between state and nation, which was constructed on the basis of the organic vision of society. In addition, since the 1980s there has been a steady increase in the qualitative and quantitative development of civil society organizations, and a call to democratize state-society relations in Turkey. Civil society organizations have been extremely important in introducing to Turkish society the language of rights and freedoms, the discourse of individualism and the idea of participatory democracy. All of these developments havc resulted in the collapse of the organic vision of society on which the secular and homogeneous Turkish national identity was constructed, a collapse that can no longer be prevented by further strong-state interventions into society.

Third, as a consequence of the crisis of national developmentalism and the organic vision of society, during the 1990s the republican model of citizenship has been challenged by the language of rights and freedoms which involved both individual and group-based claims to autonomy, pluralism and democracy. The societal calls and demands for the expansion of the state-controlled space of rights, which were voiced on the basis of both the politics of identity/recognition and the language of individual rights and freedoms, have revealed that the potential for the further democratization of Turkey lies in the implementation and consolidation of a more liberal, democratic and civic understanding of citizenship as a democratic link between state and society. This meant the replacement of the republican model of citizenship that had privileged the duties and services of the citizens to the state with the active, democratic and liberal understanding of citizenship speaking in the language of rights.

By the end of the 1990s it had became very clear that the crisis of the main ideologies of state-centric Turkish modernity, namely those of national developmentalism, an organic vision of society and a republican model of citizenship, had created an increasing "gap" between the strong-state tradition and the changing society. It is this gap that has given rise to the changing nature of Turkish modernity and the legitimacy crisis. Moreover, it is also this gap that constituted the sociological basis of the current impasse in Turkish politics. What has marked the nature of state-society relations in Turkey during the 1990s have been the mutual efforts of the strong-state tradition and the societal calls for democratization to eliminate each other in their own attempts to define the future of Turkey (Kramer 2000). It is in this sense that Turkey has found itself at a critical juncture, where it must decide between partial democracy in favor of the state and full democracy in favor of society in determining its future. The first option is the preferable one for the strong-state tradition which thinks that it can solve its legitimacy crisis through a partial democratization of its governing of society and by including in its state-centric discourse some of the demands of civil society for the protection of individual rights and freedoms, as long as they do not pose a serious challenge to its primary position in Turkish politics.

Economic crisis, European integration and citizenship

However, the scenario of partial democracy has recently been challenged by the two significant historical processes that have created crucial turning-points in Turkey in 2001 and 2002. These processes concern, first, Turkey's recent financial crisis and its relations to the IMF, and second, Turkey's full accession to the EU which has taken a new form via the Copenhagen Summit. Both processes have generated powerful impacts on the strong-state tradition, and have indicated in their own right that Turkey needs an efficient and effective governing whose realization requires both a radical transformation of the institutional structure of the strong-state and a full democratization of state-society relations. It is in this context that the second option, that is, the creation of a different, strong and democratic Turkey, has become a possibility that can be realized.

On 19 February 2001, when at a National Security Council meeting the president of the Turkish Republic, Ahmet Necdet Sezer, threw a copy of the Turkish Constitution at the prime minister, Bülent Ecevit, during their heated debate on the problem of corruption, neither of them realized that their quarrel had the potential to trigger the worst and the deepest economic crisis ever faced by Turkey in its modern history. The next morning, the *Financial Times* declared that the "Turkish economy collapsed." The crisis negatively and very strongly affected every segment of Turkish society by giving rise to the contraction of the national economy by 9.4 percent, causing Turkey an approximate loss of $53 billion in its gross national product, creating more than one million unemployed and reducing the gross national income per capita from $2,986 to $2,160. Thus, the political economy of Turkish capitalism in the 1990s, which had been organized around the clientalist and populist ties between the government and its constituencies, and which was also structurally conducive to the problems of high inflation, increasing internal and external debts, corruption and illegal accumulation of wealth, totally collapsed. This economic and financial collapse was also the collapse of the strong-state into its worst legitimacy and governing crisis.

The economic crisis was also a new turn in IMF-Turkey relations, insofar as it created a complete dependency relation between Turkey and the IMF. In order for the state to receive financial assistance, it had to accept the harsh conditionality principles, embedded in the IMF's structural adjustment program. As a result, Kemal Derviş, who had been working for many years as a World Bank executive, was brought to Turkey as the state minister responsible for, and in charge of, economic affairs. Over the year 2001 and until the November 3rd national election in 2002, the Turkish economy was radically restructured on the basis of the "strong economy program" prepared by Derviş. This program entailed a number of legal, constitutional and institutional changes with the aim of creating a strong financial sector and macro-economic stability, both of which were necessary for economic growth on a free-market basis. However, the economic crisis has made it very clear that a strong economic program cannot be initiated effectively without changing the clientalist and corruption-generating structure of the strong-state tradition which became crystallized during the 1990s. For this reason, the strong economy program initiated a set of institutional changes, such as the independent Central Bank and the establishment of the autonomous regulatory institutions, in order to create a new governmental rationality capable of yielding a sound political development management that will make the state more efficient and accountable in the mode in which it governs its society. In this sense, the primary aim of the program was in fact to "restructure the state to achieve the elimination of structural distortions caused by clientalism and populism" (Derviş 2001: 4). It was only in this way that the efficient and accountable state could initiate the sound macroeconomic and political management necessary to eradicate high inflation, to eliminate corruption and so strengthen the financial sector, and thus to make a significant contribution to economic growth.

Within the limited scope of this introductory chapter, we cannot provide a detailed analysis of the multi-dimensional impacts of the economic crisis and the IMF-led structural adjustment program on Turkey. Yet it is clear that the economic crisis has indicated that the strong-state tradition is unable to govern society through clientalism and populism. Nor can it maintain its undemocratic structure that has operated as unaccountable to and detached from society and societal demands. Instead, the long-term solution to the economic crisis has required the radical restructuring of the state to make it more efficient, transparent and accountable, so that it becomes compatible with the new economic rationality. Moreover, the economic crisis has also indicated that an active civil society, consisting of effective economic pressure groups demanding the expansion of the limited space of civil and social rights, is necessary for the creation of an economically sound and strong Turkey. Thus, the economic crisis, while causing an increasing societal distrust for the strong-state tradition, has also activated in civil society calls for full democratization, the need for an effective state and the protection of individual rights.

A reason for more active civil society organizations and their demands for democratization is also, and more importantly, related to the process of European integration. During the economic crisis, Turkey had to prepare for the Copenhagen Summit of December 2002, where the decision on Turkey's full accession to the EU was to be taken. Turkey has had a long association with the EU, and in order to gain full membership status, it had to implement a set of radical changes and transformations in its state structure, in its partial democracy and in its state-centric modernity. All these changes and transformations were concerned directly with the problem of democracy and the lack of the language of rights in Turkey. Also, as a candidate country, its success in implementing these changes and transformations would give Turkey powers of negotiation to secure a definite date for its accession at the Copenhagen Summit. In other words, while going through a severe economic crisis and implementing the strong economic program necessary to overcome it, Turkey found itself in a situation where it could deal effectively with its problem of the democratic deficit, which was the central concern in its relations with the EU. For Turkey, the economic crisis was also the time for democratization, and in this sense in 2002, the need for development overlapped with the need for democracy. Moreover, as opposed to the previous decades, in which the strong-state tradition had constantly deferred democracy in the name of modernity and development, this time there was no chance for the strong-state to do so, simply because the Copenhagen Summit was to decide the boundaries of the enlarged and "new" Europe. In this context, the summit was extremely crucial for Turkey, insofar as it was to determine the future place of Turkey in the new Europe.

In the long, crisis-ridden process of European integration, the Helsinki Summit of December 1999 constituted an important turning-point for Turkey. The summit declared the inclusion of Turkey into the process of enlargement. Thus, Turkey's long association with the EU has finally produced a certain level of certainty, as the decision to include Turkey also meant that Turkey had a chance to find a place in the enlarged Europe as a full member. In this sense, although the Helsinki Summit did not give Turkey any definitive timetable for beginning the accession negotiations, it indicated that the EU took seriously Turkey's attempt to become a full member. At the same time, the decision taken at the Helsinki Summit made it clear that the main condition for beginning the accession negotiations was the full implementation and application of what have come to be known as the Copenhagen criteria, adopted by the European Council in its Copenhagen Summit of June 1993. The Copenhagen criteria involved:

> (a) stability of institutions guaranteeing democracy, the rule of law, human rights and respect for and protection of minorities; – these criteria are integrated into the Charter of Fundamental Rights, adopted in the 2000 Nice Summit of the European Council; (b) the existence of a functioning market economy and the capacity to cope with competitive pressure and market forces within the Union; and (c) the ability to take on the obligations of membership including adherence to the aims of political, economic and monetary union, in other words the ability to adopt the EU's acquis communautaire.
>
> (in Müftüler-Baç 2002: 10)

These criteria must be fully satisfied by any candidate country. The Helsinki Summit was an important turning-point for Turkey-EU relations, for it defined what Turkey, as a candidate country, should do in order to qualify as a full-member, even if it did not give Turkey a specific date to start accession negotiations. Since then, Turkey has made certain legal and constitutional changes to alter its legal system in accordance with the Copenhagen criteria. However, these changes were not enough for the EU to give Turkey a definite date at the recent Copenhagen Summit of December 2002. Instead, the summit has decided on 2004 as a conditional date, which indicated that if Turkey achieves the full application of the Copenhagen criteria the decision for the beginning of "the accession negotiations without a delay" will be taken at the Helsinki Summit of December 2004. However conditional, the decision of the Copenhagen Summit for Turkey has reinforced the degree of certainty established in 1999 regarding Turkey's accession to the EU. Furthermore, the Copenhagen Summit has also clarified once again that it is the application of the Copenhagen criteria that will constitute the objective basis for the decision about Turkey.

It should be pointed out that by giving a conditional date to Turkey, the Copenhagen Summit has pushed the strong-state into the position of being the main actor that will determine the future of Turkey. Yet, at the same time, it has declared that partial democratization will not be enough for Turkey to become a full member of the EU. Instead, full democratization, which will radically alter the nature of the state-centric Turkish modernity and its constituting elements (ideologies), is what is required as an objective criterion for its full membership. For the full implementation and application of the Copenhagen criteria to state-society relations in Turkey means the radical reconstruction of the strong-state tradition in a liberal democratic way. Moreover, it entails the insertion of the language of rights in the republican model of citizenship. More specifically, it requires granting rights to minorities and ethnic identities. In this sense, when applied fully, the Copenhagen criteria would force the strong-state to approach its society by accepting that it consists of individuals as right-holders.

Having provided a brief account of the impact that the economic crisis and European integration have generated on Turkish modernity, we now come to the fourth source for the possibility of full democratization in Turkey. This source is the November 3rd national election of 2002, which took place in a historical context dictated by the impasse in Turkish politics. The November 3rd national election was an election in which the changing nature of Turkish modernity and its legitimacy crisis, the 19 February economic crisis and the Copenhagen Summit of December 2002 together played an influential role in the determination of voters' choices and preferences. It was also an election that, as we will see in the following section, has created an earthquake in Turkish politics.

The November 3rd national election

On the evening of 3 November 2002, as the election results were becoming known, an earthquake shook Turkish politics. The three governing parties that had formed the coalition government after the 1999 national election, as well as the two opposition parties, all failed to pass the 10 percent national threshold and found themselves thrown out of parliament as the thorough losers of the election. At a time when Turkey was going through its deepest economic crisis, generating the severe problems of unemployment, poverty and insecurity, the November 3rd national election resulted in the electoral punishment of both the governing parties and the opposition parties, so much so that the winner of the 1999 election, the Democratic Left Party (DLP) lost almost all of its electoral support, and thus its leader Bülent Ecevit has completed his long political career with a tragic but deserved end. The other governing parties, the Nationalist Action Party (NAP) and the Mother Land Party (MLP) lost more than half of their electoral support. The leaders of these parties announced their resignations. The opposition parties, the True Path Party (TPP) and the Felicity Party (FP) were also subject to electoral punishment, in that rather than gaining any electoral support, both were thrown out of parliament. It can be argued, therefore, that the November 3rd national election has created a political earthquake in Turkey. The election took the form of social unrest, meaning that it created a suitable platform for the democratic expression of the deep anger that Turkish people have been feeling since the 1990s toward the existing political system and its parties, whose *modus vivendi* was characterized by economic populism, clientalism, corruption and democratic deficit.

The winners of the election were the Justice and Development Party (JDP) and the Republican People's Party (RPP). By receiving 34.2 percent of the popular vote and with the aid of the undemocratic 10 percent national threshold, the JDP gained 66 percent of the parliamentary seats (that is, 363 of 550 seats) and thus constituted a single-party majority government. With its 19.4 percent of the popular vote, the RPP became the main and single opposition party and gained 178 seats. In the near future, Turkey will be ruled by a single-party majority government with a very strong executive structure, and a two party system-based parliamentary democracy. After having had a series of extremely problematic coalition governments, the general public mood before the 2002 election in Turkey was one which called for an end to the existing ineffective, undemocratic and ungoverning governing structure, that is the strong-state tradition, that had been operating totally detached from society and societal needs. In this context, this new governing structure has been welcomed by the different segments of society in the name of political stability and effective governing. Thus, although the JDP was created as one of the two parties that emerged from within the constitutionally-banned Virtue Party, whose Islamic identity and discourse has been seen by the Supreme Court as a threat to the secular foundation of the Turkish Republic, its electoral success leading to its strong single-party majority government has been received very well by a large part of Turkish society longing for political stability and effective governing.

The way in which the JDP gained an electoral victory sufficient to form a single-party majority government consisted of a three-pronged electoral strategy. It is through this strategy that the JDP has established a successful organic linkage with the different segments of society. First, by understanding very well that the November 3rd national election was a society-centered election in which the economy was the dominant issue, the JDP presented itself not as an Islamic party but as a "center-right" party, claiming to have a strong will to govern effectively on the basis of well-prepared and efficient policies to overcome the economic crisis. In doing so, the JDP attempted to convince the Turkish electorate that it had changed from an ideology-based party whose constituency was limited to Islamic identity, to a center-right party concerned about the problems of society at large. Second, the JDP argued that in its attempt to create a new impetus for economic change by cleaning up "the cronyism and corruption that have hobbled Turkey's banking and financial system for decades," it would act in the service of society at large by listening caringly to the needs and demands of different social groups, especially those that directly faced the problems of unemployment, poverty and insecurity. Thus, as opposed to the RPP's economic program, prepared by Kemal Derviş in accordance with an unquestioned acceptance of the IMF's structural adjustment program, the JDP presented itself as a center-right party which would put the deep problem of "social and distributive injustice" at the top of its immediate economic agenda, even if this should create a conflictual relationship with the IMF. Third, in establishing its organic linkage with society at large, the JDP insistently and repeatedly argued that democracy constitutes the fundamental and effective basis for the long-term solution to Turkey's problems. This heavy and special emphasis placed on democracy has been maintained and voiced strongly in the JDP's discourse on the protection of individual rights and freedoms, as well as in its full support for Turkey's integration into the EU as a full member.

This three-dimensional electoral strategy also enabled the JDP to present itself not as Islamic but as a center-right party whose primary aim is both to overcome the economic crisis and to work for the further democratization of state-society relations in Turkey. Thus, the JDP created a suitable ground on which to differentiate itself from the other parties in the following (and convincing) ways: (a) it distanced itself from the parties of the coalition government (the DLP, the NAP and the MLP) by claiming that as opposed to the state-centric nature of these parties, it will work for society, and in doing so it will listen to societal actors such as economic pressure groups and civil society organizations; (b) it distanced itself also from the FP and its Islamic nature by arguing that in governing society the JDP would be democratic, and in doing so it would represent a moderate Islamic discourse which respects the secular foundation of the Turkish Republic and sees religious affairs within the context of pluralism and the language of rights; and (c) finally, it differentiated itself from its main competitor, the RPP, by suggesting that the economic program it would initiate to overcome the crisis was more humanistic than that proposed by the RPP and Kemal Derviş, in that not only would it pay more attention to the problem of social and distributive injustice, but also it would support the medium and small-scale industrialists in order to revitalize the production-side of the Turkish economy.

It should be noted at this point that what determined the attitude and the orientation of the Turkish electorate in the 2002 election was the economic crisis and the immediate need to solve the problems of unemployment, poverty and economic growth. In this sense, the majority of the Turkish electorate chose the JDP because of its claim that its economic program was both different to that of the other parties and more suited to providing effective solutions to the severe economic problems. The JDP's economic program was a *communitarian-liberal synthesis* operating on the basis of three principles:

(a) *an effective and post-developmental state* which is democratic, transparent and accountable in its interaction with society, but at the same time "caring" and assuming a supervisory role in its relation to the economy. In this context, the JDP claims that in its governing, it will change the existing state structure, which is detached from society, blind to its needs and demands and therefore functions as a closed, ineffective and undemocratic system of rule, and create an effective and post-developmental state;
(b) *a regulated free market* which is not destructive and corrupted, but enriching, contributing to economic development and socially just. The JDP argues that it promotes a free-market economy and sees it as the basis for growth, to the extent that it will contribute to the further industrialization of the Turkish economy and its consolidation on the basis of financial stability and a strong real economy; and
(c) *social justice*, which is to be established both in terms of the distribution of wealth and welfare services and with respect to the domain of

> recognition in which social segments will not be discriminated in terms of their different cultural practices. At this level, The JDP's economic program differentiated itself from the RPP's economic liberal economic program, which saw the question of social justice as an indirect problem at best. In doing so, the JDP argued that a strong, stable and trust-based economy cannot be established without solving the problem of social justice in distribution and recognition.

Working on the basis of these principles, the communitarian-liberal synthesis means, at the very general level, an articulation of the free market with communitarian values, which promotes religious values, societal norms and local characteristics. More concretely, the communitarian-liberal synthesis calls for a just society not organized on the basis of pure egotistical individualism, but as a democratic regulation of state-society relations in which free-market rationality is backed by, in the words of Prime Minister Abdullah Gül, "a moderate and democratic Muslim society." The success of the communitarian-liberal synthesis in the November 3rd national election should be taken seriously, for it has created for Turkey a chance, maybe the last chance, to have a strong and stable government, one which (a) can establish a reciprocal and democratic relationship between state and society, so that the main problem of the 1990s, i.e. the disjuncture and the widened gap between the ineffective strong-state and a changing society, can be solved; (b) can cope effectively with the severe economic problems to create a better quality of life, financial stability, job security and sustainable economic development; and (c) can prepare Turkey as a strong and democratic country for its integration into the European Union.

However, whether or not the JDP can create this chance is open to question. There are challenges ahead for its government. These challenges are focused on the question of democracy and economic stability. Moreover, they have both international and domestic dimensions, and it is almost impossible to separate these dimensions in post-November 3rd Turkey, where global actors such as the EU and the IMF play a very important role in the process of shaping and reshaping Turkish politics. In this context, the first challenge to the JDP occurred immediately after the election, as it found itself facing the very difficult job of obtaining a definite date for Turkey's full accession to the EU at the Copenhagen Summit. The JDP also had to convince the EU that it is not an Islamic party, but a center-right party which strongly supports Turkey's accession to the EU. Although successful in this respect, the JDP received a conditional date for full-membership negotiations in December 2004. As noted before, the conditional date meant that if Turkey achieves a successful realization of the application of the Copenhagen criteria, then negotiations between the EU and Turkey will start "without delay." Of course, the application of the Copenhagen criteria is not limited to the realization of certain constitutional and institutional changes aimed at creating a democratic, transparent and accountable state. The process of application entails and requires a radical transformation of state-society relations on the basis of the language of rights.

It is in here that the JDP faces a difficult task, for such a radical transformation requires the state to govern its society democratically, to regard its citizens as having rights and freedoms, and to conceive of societal relations on the basis of the principle of difference rather than that of sameness. This means a reconstruction of Turkish citizenship in such a way as to make it democratic, liberal, multicultural and constitutional. This also means that the state deal with societal demands for democratization, recognition and pluralism through a new understanding of Turkish citizenship that is in accordance with post-national values embedded in the EU, that provides a democratic solution to the recent identity-based challenges to Turkish modernity, and that constitutes an adequate normative and political ground for the creation of a different, democratic and economically strong Turkey. We believe that it is through this democratic and liberal understanding of citizenship that Turkey will respond effectively, efficiently and democratically to the European questions concerning the problems of democracy, human rights and freedoms.

Articulating citizenship and identity

Of course, the construction of a democratic and liberal Turkish citizenship requires not only the political and social will to make Turkey a democratic society compatible with post-national values, but also a theoretical and discursive effort that locates citizenship at the center of the academic and public debates in Turkey as a useful heuristic device by which we can deal effectively and democratically with the deep problems of Turkish politics that have given rise to the politics of identity/recognition and the civil society-based calls for individual rights and freedoms. In other words, although the possibility of creating a democratic and economically strong Turkey requires mainly a political and social will, it is also equally important to employ a theoretically sound understanding of citizenship as an adequate and effective heuristic device for strengthening such a will discursively.

This book does not aim to construct a general theory of citizenship. Much has been written on the question of how to reconstruct modern citizenship in a way that it becomes a solution to the problems of our late-modern times (Isin and Wood 1999; Heater 1999; Kymlicka and Wayne 2000; Junonski 1998). Nor does this book aim to provide a theoretical approach to the question of citizenship in a non-Western setting (Ong 1999). However, by relying on the existing literature on modern citizenship, we argue in this book that a feasible and effective solution to the deep problems of Turkish politics should be sought not in "identity terms," but by exploring "with an emphasis on the practice of democracy" (Isin and Wood 1999: 4) possible ways of articulating identity-claims to citizenship rights. Of course, such an articulation requires first abandoning a false dichotomy drawn between identity and citizenship, second an attempt to go beyond the purely legal-universal conception of citizenship, and finally, by following Isin and Wood, approaching citizenship and identity "from a perspective that sees modern citizenship not only as a legal and political membership in a nation-state but also as an articulating principle for the recognition of group rights" (1999: 4).

Seen in this way, citizenship involves not only legal obligations and entitlements which frame the boundary of the "membership-based relations" of individuals with their states, but also "the practices through which individuals and groups formulate and claim new rights or struggle to expand or maintain existing rights." Therefore, as Isin and Wood correctly point out (1999: 4–5), citizenship is neither purely sociological nor purely legalistic, but refers to a "relationship" whose discursive and political conditions of existence are constituted sociologically and legalistically by a set of practices which makes the claims of individuals or groups for new rights both possible and limited to the existing regime of modernity in a given country. In this sense, citizenship contains in itself both an enabling and conditioning relationship between individuals/groups and their states, in that it provides a ground for the possibility of new right-claims to challenge and expand the existing model of citizenship in a given country, but at the same time acts as a conditioning practice by framing, situating and limiting those claims within the regime of modernity. This implies first that there is no need to think of identity-claims and citizenship-rights as necessarily antagonistic or incommensurable: instead they should be seen as sociologically interlinked claims involving possible tensions, conflicts and antinomies. Second, it should be pointed out here that, as Turner (2000: 23) has suggested, citizenship could be both "(1) an inclusionary principle for the distribution and allocation of entitlements, and (2) an exclusionary basis for building solidarity and maintaining identity." In other words, the conditioning and limiting practice that citizenship exercises on new right-claims could generate both negative (exclusionary) and positive (inclusionary) results, for it might be used as a practice of silencing and limiting right-claims, but at the same time it might function as a solution to the politics of identity by preventing its transformation into ethnonationalism or religious fundamentalism.

As for the deep problems of Turkish politics, articulating identity-claims to citizenship rights means then trying to seek democratic solutions to societal demands not in terms of the politics of recognition, initiated by ethnic claims for group rights, but by attempting to reconstruct the republican model of Turkish citizenship in such a way as to make it more flexible, differentiated and constitutional. In so doing, it becomes possible to transform the claims to particularism, essentialism and communitarianism into "claims for group rights as a challenge to the *modern* (and republican) interpretation of universal citizenship, which is itself a form of group identity"

(Isin and Wood 1999: 4). In this way, we recognize the omnipotence of claims to identity/difference as a social and historical fact "that cannot be wished away, that cannot be phantasmatically made to disappear" (Yeatman 2000: 103). Thus, we become able to attempt both sociologically and historically to articulate identity-claims to citizenship rights as a solution to the deep problems of Turkish politics and its strong-state tradition within the context of democratic, liberal, constitutional and multicultural citizenship. In doing so, we think of citizenship "not only as a legal and political membership in a nation-state but also as an articulating principle for the recognition of group rights." Thus, as will be discussed throughout the book, we become able to create the conditions for Turkey's full accession into the EU by responding effectively to the requirements of the Copenhagen criteria.

The content of the book

Under the title *Citizenship in a Global World: European Questions and Turkish Experiences*, the essays collected in this volume provide in their contexts a historical and theoretical analysis of the republican model of citizenship, its crisis and its possible transformation into a democratic and liberal model as a solution to the recent impasse in Turkish politics. In doing so, these essays together also offer a comprehensive and detailed account of Turkish modernity and its changing nature, which constitutes the foundation for a thorough understanding of Turkish politics.

In this introductory chapter we have sought to establish a thematic analysis of Turkish modernity which constitutes a general ground for the arguments that the chapters of this book make in their own analysis of their subject-matter.

Part I presents a theoretical and contextual approach to Turkish modernity and its republican model of citizenship.

In Chapter 1, Isin provides us with a fascinating historical analysis that contemplates the significance and relevance of investigating Ottoman citizenship for an understanding of the problems embedded in the accession of Turkey to the EU. In this context, he makes two important suggestions: avoiding Orientalism in investigating (Ottoman) citizenship, and constituting it as an object of analysis. Isin suggests that one should avoid Orientalist and Occidentalist approaches in approaching the question of Ottoman citizenship, so that it becomes possible to understand it within the context of what has come to be known as "a generalized problem of otherness." This attempt also makes a significant contribution to advancing our understanding of Turkish citizenship in terms of its past and contemporary figurations. Isin questions the debate about the compatibility between the European tradition of citizenship rights and Turkish republicanism. He argues that the problems of convergence, divergence and approximation, as well as distortion, which occur in the process of analyzing the relationship between Turkish and European citizenship rights, need to be considered in a different context, that is, the relationship between Orientalism and citizenship. Isin's chapter not only examines the roots of the notion of citizenship in Turkey, but also makes an important theoretical intervention which enlarges our thinking space about modern citizenship.

Feyzi Baban, in Chapter 2, stresses the importance of the concept of universal citizenship for modernity despite the fact that there are variations between the ways that modern societies organize their citizenship regimes. While the citizenship regime in Turkey claims to contain the main premises of universal citizenship under civic republicanism, it in fact carries the communitarian notion of the republican tradition and consequently denies the primacy of the individual and of diversity. According to Baban, what really defines the two competing political projects of our times in Turkey, the republican citizenship regime and its critique by Islamists, is their perception of the Ottoman tradition of community. Both are communitarian projects, which refuse the dynamic characteristics of identity positions and are intended to limit the boundaries of identity politics. In this context, Baban highlights the risk of ahistorical approaches. He focuses on the universal variations in citizenship regimes by giving the examples of Britain, the United States, and France. Then, drawing parallels between the French and Ottoman/Turkish cases, he points out that the contemporary debate around citizenship in Turkey becomes meaningful only when it is historically grounded.

In the contribution by Kahraman (Chapter 3), modernity is again central to the study of citizenship in Turkey. He discusses the cultural foundations of Turkish citizenship by looking at the various phases of the history of Turkish modernity. Defining Turkish modernity as the process of Westernization since the Ottoman empire of the nineteenth century, he elaborates three successive periods in which both discourses and practices of citizenship in Turkey have evolved: 1839–1908, 1908/1923–1980, and post-1980. Since the *Gülhane Verdict* in 1839, which could be seen as the starting point of the reformation of the Ottoman empire, "the question of 'identity and citizenship' as the two offsprings of modernity," as argued by Kahraman, falls into the broad context of Westernization that is the political and social perception of modernity. While citizenship had been seen almost as a tool of survival and of imitation and implementation of Western social and political institutions in the early stages of Turkish modernity, in the nineteenth century, as a natural articulation of the other offspring of modernity, it also involved references to notions of nationalism and democracy. Kahraman demonstrates in a historical fashion that the same kinds of causes and consequences of citizenship debates still prevail in Turkey in the late twentieth and early twenty-first centuries, especially within the wider context of Turkish-European relations. Thus, approaching Turkish citizenship as an epistemological problematic, Kahraman relates the dynamics of the realm of identity and citizenship to the various dichotomies dominating the political reasoning and practices in the country: civilization/culture, gemeinschaft/gesellchaft, political reason/reasons of state, and individual/community.

Considering the fact that the Turkey-EU membership issue is not only a question of the application of the Copenhagen criteria but also a matter of the identity problem inherited both in Turkey's European-ness (as a cultural problem) and in the process of European enlargement (as a problem of territoriality), Vardar (Chapter 4) rightly points out that notions of citizenship and democracy are essential subjects in the context of Turkey-EU relations. Vardar first examines the nature of the EU identity, looking at its political construction and its citizenship context, and then provides a historical analysis of Turkey's long association with Europe. This analysis enables Vardar to argue that, as the Copenhagen Summit of December 2002 indicates in terms of its decision on Turkey, Turkey's full accession to the EU depends on its attempt to transform the republican model of citizenship into a more liberal, democratic and constitutional understanding of citizenship that is compatible with the post-national values of the new Europe. Of course, as Vardar correctly warns, Turkey's accession also depends on the EU maintaining and reinforcing its commitment to a multicultural Europe based on a political rather than culturalist definition of European citizenship.

Part II considers how notions of state and democracy are articulated into the citizenship debate in Turkey.

In Chapter 5, Kadıoğlu presents the distinction between a view of citizenship as membership (either of a nation or a state) and a view of citizenship as a position (as an empty space or as non-membership) "in the set of formal relations defined by democratic sovereignty" (Donald 1996: 174). She argues that as the modern notion of citizenship that involves membership of a nation-state is inapt in responding to the demands of diverse societal groups, it often creates a serious obstacle to the democratization efforts of modern nation-states. Hence, Kadıoğlu argues for the adequacy of envisioning citizenship as "a position" which enables us to see citizenship as detached from the notion of identity. However, taking into consideration the argument that "the citizen precedes the individual in Turkey," she suggests that Turkish modernity makes it very difficult for us to approach citizenship as non-membership. According to her, evolving within the civic republican tradition, citizenship in Turkey is heavily embedded in national identity and defined in relation to duties rather than rights. Trapped in the mission of various social and political projects such as Kemalism, Socialism, and Islamism, Turkish citizenship is unable to situate individual rights and freedoms prior to duties and services to the nation.

In Chapter 6, Soyarık-Şentürk focuses on the legal and constitutional foundations of citizenship in Turkey. In doing so, she emphasizes that these legal and constitutional arrangements have stood out as political phenomena in Turkish modernity since the early twentieth century. In this context, in analyzing the evolution of Turkish citizenship, she focuses on the constitutions of 1924, 1961 and 1982, as well as on a set of citizenship laws enacted by the state. Her analysis demonstrates clearly that these three constitutions are directly reflective of the state-centric operation of the republican model of citizenship and its exclusionary mode, especially with respect to individual and group rights. Soyarık's analysis also makes it clear that the ongoing debates and negotiations between the European Union and Turkey concerning legal and constitutional reforms are directly related to citizenship issues. In this sense, Soyarık reminds us that constitutional and legal reforms are necessary and essential components of transforming Turkish citizenship into a liberal and democratic one compatible with the post-national values of the EU.

Part III considers three particular instances of Turkish modernity where serious challenges have been posed to the republican model of citizenship during the 1990s: gender, entrepreneurship, and migration.

Vital to any consideration and systematic analysis of the relationship between gender and citizenship in Turkey is a critical assessment of the various dimensions of gendered citizenship. In this context, Sirman (Chapter 7) provides a gendered perspective to issues of citizenship and sovereignty in the Turkish post-colonial context. Sirman elaborates the conditions and discourses through which citizenship was instituted in Turkey around the problem of realizing national sovereignty. She argues that the building of a national sovereign state is usually the product of discourses of the identity of the nation in the process of constituting the nation-state as a specific kind of polity. Focusing on these discourses in the country, Sirman points out that the particular form of citizenship that was produced can best be described as familial citizenship. What becomes clear in this framework is a gendered discourse in which the ideal citizen is inscribed as a sovereign husband and his dependent wife or mother rather than as an individual, with the result that his/her position within a familial discourse provides that person with status within the polity. According to Sirman, it was through the forms of intimacy pertaining to the nuclear family that the morality of the proper citizen was to be produced and citizens turned into the subjects of the modern nation-state.

Focusing on the case of TÜSİAD, a voluntary interest association representing big business and large conglomerates in Turkey, Öniş in Chapter 8 explores the key role played by business leaders and business associations in the emergence of societal calls for democratization and citizenship rights, particularly with reference to Turkey's potential membership of the EU. Öniş emphasizes the radical shift in the business-democracy relationship, which changed from a relatively authoritarian stance to a clearly pro-democratization position. In the course of neoliberal globalization, two main routes of democratization and two main understandings of democracy have been classified by Öniş. The first, which is narrower in its scope, sees democratization as a way of "good governance," and citizenship rights as "market-centered" rights. The second, which is more liberal, concerns the necessity of improving and enlarging the scope of civil and human rights. It is clear that the latter approach promotes a more comprehensive understanding of democracy on the basis of the extension of citizenship rights. In his chapter, Öniş poses the question of how the Turkish business community positions itself in relation to the second and broader understanding of democracy and citizenship. Taking the example of TÜSİAD, he argues that the interest of the business community in supporting this kind of democratization agenda stems from their awareness that the dynamics of the second or third wave of democracies in the context of neoliberal globalization require economic actors to act not only as economic pressure groups but also as civil society organizations concerned for larger societal problems. According to Öniş, this awareness amongst the Turkish business community can be clearly observed in Turkey-EU relations in which TÜSİAD has become an important actor promoting and actively supporting Turkey's full accession.

Chapter 9, İçduygu's contribution, draws our attention to the linkage between international migration and citizenship issues in Turkey. İçduygu argues that as far as individual citizens are concerned, international migration has become a new aspect of Turkish citizenship. Thus, the demand for a personhood-based understanding of citizenship was initiated against the state-based one. İçduygu's historical analysis of international migration suggests that in order to better understand the personhood-based conception of citizenship, one must consider not only the notions of membership and belonging, but also the concept of "attachment to the state." İçduygu argues in this sense that we have to recognize the fact that citizens seek a secure bond of attachment to the state in the context of the international migration-citizenship puzzle. This recognition enables us to consider citizenship in terms of the following three ways in which attachment to the state occurs: legal status, identity, and civic virtue. Thus, İçduygu's important analysis demonstrates that each of these elements are conceptually and empirically linked to the other and are affected by the experience of international migration. İçduygu concludes that if international migration has the potential to make the interrelatedness of these three elements of citizenship more complicated and multi-dimensional, then attention should be paid to an adequate model of citizenship. This model should accommodate not only the membership, belonging and attachment aspects of citizenship, but also the status, identity and virtue elements.

One of the important sites at which international migration generates its impacts on citizenship is the question of diasporic citizenship of which the case of German-Turks provides an illustrative example. In Chapter 10, Kaya presents a historical analysis of German-Turks and their struggle to gain citizenship rights. In doing so, Kaya explores how the German state might meet the demands of Turkish immigrant workers for citizenship rights. Kaya argues that the idea of a shared German citizenship is necessary in order to recognize and protect the transnational position of the German-Turkish identity. After presenting some details of the migratory process of Turkish migrants in Germany, Kaya addresses various legal and political aspects of citizenship laws in Germany and relates them to the notion of "hyphenated" German-Turkish identity. He suggests in this context that in Germany, there are two antithetical notions of culture, the holistic versus the syncretic, that have played a key role in determining the position of diasporic identities in the realm of citizenship. After a discussion of the multiplicities of membership and identity that German-Turks, or Turkish Germans, themselves experience, Kaya argues that we need to go beyond these two antithetical notions of culture and promote a third space in which diasporic identity claims can be articulated to citizenship rights. This third space is the space of hybridity, as a resistance to cultural essentialism and as a way of constructing a multicultural and democratic community.

Part IV discusses the politics of identity and the claims for recognition that have emerged in the last decade in Turkey, but whose roots can be traced to the early period of the Republic in the twentieth century, and even to the late Ottoman period in the nineteenth century.

In this context, Çolak, in Chapter 11, examines the role of secularism in the formation of Turkish citizenship and the problematic place of Islam in it. Çolak argues that Kemalist secularism, which has operated on the basis of a "specific interpretation of Islam," has been an important element in the making of Turkish citizenship. He suggests that Islamic groups have tended to expand the scope of Turkish citizenship in such a way that their cultural claims can be included in the public sphere. By utilizing the ideology of secularism, the Turkish state has always repelled these demands. After presenting a selection of historical developments and current events, Çolak's analysis draws our attention to the period of the 1990s, in which Islamic demands for various civil, political, and cultural rights have challenged the Turkish state's conventional idea of secular citizenship. In this challenge, Islamic discourses claim that Turkish secularism employs an exclusionary understanding of citizenship, which prevents not only the Islamic presence in formal politics but also the symbolic and ritualistic practices of Islamic identity in the public sphere. Çolak argues that such citizenship-related policies and practices have set the limits of equitable rights, access and opportunities, which are essential to the modern notion of citizenship. For instance, as in the case of the headscarf issue, the state has initiated strict policies aiming at limiting the right of religious women to education. Çolak suggests in this sense that we need a new regime of rights to provide a secure political and social ground for increasing pluralism and diversity in Turkey. This new regime of rights and freedoms, according to Çolak, leads to the emergence of "cultural citizenship" which accepts the secular foundation of the Turkish state but at the same time recognizes the practice of cultural rights in a pluralist society, to the extent that they are exercised democratically.

In Chapter 12, Keyman evaluates the Kurdish question in Turkey by locating it in Turkish modernity as "a hegemonic ground for the construction of a secular and homogeneous discourse of national identity." This enables him to suggest that one should not seek a solution to the Kurdish question in "ethnic terms." Instead an attempt should be made to articulate ethnic claims to citizenship-right debates within the context of the practice of democracy. According to Keyman, this approach helps to abandon a false dichotomy drawn between identity and citizenship. Additionally, it enlarges the purely legal-universal conception of citizenship. Finally, it sees modern citizenship within the context of recognition of group rights in addition to the legal and political membership of a nation-state. He argues that seeing dynamic linkages between identity claims and citizenship rights enables us to shift from ethnonationalist assertiveness to the area of citizenship. This move provides a chance for egalitarianism, an inclusive political culture, and the construction of societal consensus in Turkey. As a solution to the Kurdish problem, Keyman calls for a new form of citizenship, promoting post-national, multicultural and constitutional values, which in turn makes an important contribution to creating "a possibility of coping effectively with the recent legitimacy, representation and governing crisis of Turkish modernity by democratizing its state-centric operation."

In addition to the cases of religious and ethnic identity-claims, the position of non-Muslim minorities poses a serious challenge to the republican model of citizenship. In Chapter 13, Soner attempts to provide a historical analysis of the minority question in Turkey. In doing so, he refers to the distinction between the notions of state-membership (citizenship) and ethno-cultural membership (nationality) that in fact reflects a tension between the principle of sameness and that of difference. In the context of non-Muslim minorities, Turkish citizenship excludes difference in the name of sameness. Soner indicates therefore that the Turkish state officially recognizes the minority status of the non-Muslim religious identity in Turkey. In doing so, the state enables the non-Muslim identity to have certain group rights integrated into their citizenship status. However, the minority question occurs as the concrete practice of how these rights have been seriously limited by the mono-culturalist construction of Turkish society. Soner's very detailed historical analysis concludes that a solution to the minority question in Turkey requires a system of substantive equality tolerant to the ethno-linguistic, religious and sectarian differences of both Muslim and non-Muslim members of the Turkish citizenry. However, in order for this system of substantive equality to be operative, there is an essential need to consolidate and deepen the process of democratization in Turkey.

Having read the chapters to come, we hope that the reader will have an understanding of Turkey which goes well beyond the existing simplistic and Orientalist visions that tend to reduce the complex history of Turkish modernity either to a portrait of a traditional Muslim society striving for modernization and democratization or to a story of an authoritarian state and its state-centric political actors. In this book, we aim to provide the reader with a substantial, comprehensive and detailed analysis of Turkey and its changing modernity through a sociological, cultural, political and multi-dimensional reading of Turkish citizenship. In doing so, we take seriously the recent societal challenges to the strong-state tradition and its republican model of citizenship, and argue that the possibility of democracy in Turkey lies in the reconstruction of state-society relations in such a way that these challenges and their demands, articulated in different discourses of identity, self and difference, can be negotiated in a democratic platform of public deliberation. Of course, to achieve this possibility of democracy is also to achieve the possibility of creating a new Turkey where citizens define themselves as right-holders, give their loyalties to post-national values, and participate actively in the process of the consolidation and deepening of Turkish democracy. In this way, we believe that a democratic Turkey as a full member of Europe will become an achievable reality.

Note

1 See Larrabee and Lesser (2003) for further information.

References

Ahmad, F. (1993) *The Making of Modern Turkey*, London and New York: Routledge.

Derviş, K. (2001) "Turkey's crises: causes, consequences and solutions," *Insight Turkey*, 3 (2): 3–10.

Donald, J. (1996) "The Citizen and the Man About Town," in S. Hall and P. du Gay (eds) *Questions of Cultural Identity*, London: Sage.

Heater, D. (1999) *What is Citizenship?*, Cambridge: Polity Press.

Heper, M. (1985) *The State Tradition in Turkey*, North Humberside: The Eothen Press.

Gellner, E. (1994) *Encountering Nationalism*, London: Routledge.

Isin, E. F. and Wood, P. K. (1999) *Citizenship and Identity*, London: Sage.

Junonski, T. (1998) *Citizenship and Civil Society*, Cambridge: Cambridge University Press.

Keyder, Ç. (1997) "Whither the Project of Modernity?," in S. Bozdoğan and R. Kasaba (eds) *Rethinking Modernity and National Identity in Turkey*, London: University of Washington Press.

Kramer, H. (2000) *A Changing Turkey*, Washington DC: Brookings Institution Press.

Kymlicka, W. and Wayne, N. (eds) (2000) *Citizenship in Diverse Societies*, Oxford: Oxford University Press.

Larrabee, F. S. and Lesser, I. O. (2003) *Turkish Foreign Policy in an Age of Uncertainity*, Santa Monica: RAND.

Müftüler-Baç, M. (2002) *Enlarging the European Union: Where does Turkey Stand?*, Istanbul: TESEV Publications.

Ong, A. (1999) *Flexible Citizenship*, Durham NC: Duke University Press.

Özbudun, E. and Keyman, E. F. (2002) "Cultural Globalization in Turkey," in P. L. Berger and S. P. Huntington (eds) *Many Globalizations*, Oxford: Oxford University Press.

Turner, B. (2000) "Liberal Citizenship and Cosmopolitan Virtue," in Vandenberg, A. (ed.) *Citizenship and Democracy in a Global Era*, New York: St Martin's Press.

Yeatman, A. (2000) "The Subject of Democratic Theory and the Challenge of Co-existence," in Vandenberg, A. (ed.) *Citizenship and Democracy in a Global Era*, New York: St Martin's Press.

Part I

Citizenship and modernity

Theoretical and historical context

1 Citizenship after orientalism

Ottoman citizenship

Engin F. Isin

Introduction

This chapter offers some thoughts about investigating citizenship after orientalism and reflects on the possibilities of exploring "Ottoman citizenship" under different terms as neither an oriental nor occidental institution. I address three distinct but interrelated issues. First, I discuss the relationship between orientalism and citizenship. While orientalism has received considerable attention in the last three decades, the debate has remained focused on representations of the Orient in occidental art and literature. The focus has been much less on how orientalism mobilized both imperial and local groups to organize political and legal practices. As I have argued elsewhere (Isin 2002a; 2002b) and will briefly discuss below, one of the building blocks of orientalism has been making an ontological difference between the orient and occident on the question of the political in general and citizenship in particular. In a nutshell, the occidental tradition has constituted the Orient as those times and places where peoples have been unable to constitute themselves as political precisely because they have been unable to invent that identity the occident named as the citizen. The figure of the citizen that dominated the occidental tradition is the figure of that sovereign man (and much later woman) who is capable of judgment and being judged, transcending his (and much later her) tribal, kinship, and other primordial loyalties and belongingness. The figure represents an unencumbered and sovereign self in a direct contractual relationship with the city (and much later the state). By contrast, the Orient never invented that figure and mimetically reproduced it with only limited success. I critique this particular variant of orientalism – political orientalism – as a condition for rethinking citizenship.

Second, I explore the theoretical and intellectual options available after the critique of political orientalism and its claims to occidental uniqueness for citizenship. I address the question of possibilities for rethinking citizenship after illustrating what orientalism has mobilized and justified. There have been roughly two approaches to address that question. I am critical and skeptical of both. There has been a tendency to reverse arguments of political orientalism to demonstrate that indeed those things that it deemed as lacking in the Orient were actually present. As I will illustrate, for example, if political orientalism claimed that corporate organization of the city was lacking in the Orient, the tendency has been to demonstrate that indeed it was not lacking and that various oriental cities were organized as corporations. There are several difficulties with this approach, which we might call "reverse orientalism." The most obvious is, of course, that using the definition by political orientalism as given and trying to demonstrate that there is some veridical deficit in orientalism misses its strategic orientation: in its effects, orientalism is less about the Orient and more about provoking various assemblages of meaning that make possible various actions upon the Orient. Understood this way, orientalism as an assemblage of claims always operates dynamically and relationally rather than remaining static. In other words, before the ink dries on those arguments that attempt to illustrate the existence of occidental institutions in the Orient, new claims are assembled to illustrate the inferiority of oriental ways of being and the absence there of various political and legal institutions. The veridical rectification of political orientalism is a losing battle. In the truth game that produces the Occident and Orient as ontologically distinct blocs, the Orient can never win because it is already socially constituted to demonstrate the superiority of the Occident.

Perhaps as a result of the difficulties arising from rethinking citizenship without orientalism, some scholars abandon making comparisons altogether and refute the existence of citizenship practices in the Orient. The difficulty with this approach, which might be called "occidentalism," is that the interpenetration and intertwining of the Orient and Occident has gone on for too long to assume that a practice that exists in one will not exist in the other. Moreover, such categorical denials reinforce an ostensible ontological difference between Occident and Orient by leaving the constitution of citizenship to occidentalist claims.

This leads me to my third discussion, which I call "Ottoman citizenship." It should be clear by now that when I use the term "Ottoman citizenship," I do not have in mind a citizenship practice in the way in which the occidental tradition has organized it during the last two centuries by reference to a cluster of absences or presences in the Orient. If that were the case, Ottoman citizenship would be a contradiction in terms since the Ottoman politics and government as instances of oriental culture would be defined precisely by their lack of citizenship. According to this view, Ottomans were imperial subjects and Turks were republican citizens. The history of citizenship, however, cannot only begin with the self-conscious Westernization of the Ottoman Empire in the nineteenth century and culminate in the Turkish Republic in the twentieth. Yet, following the argument outlined earlier, it also does not mean to make claims about the existence of citizenship in the Ottoman Empire defined by a series of presences. In other words, I do not have in mind a nostalgic Ottoman citizenship that through its millet system "accommodated" and "recognized" minorities and enabled certain autonomous institutions as an example of tolerance, etc. As important as it is to understand Ottoman institutions in those terms, it is both anachronistic and dangerous to create an Ottoman Empire that is somehow more authentic and originary than Europe by using the contemporary language of European sociology and thought. What Ottoman citizenship might possibly mean, therefore, can neither be constituted by references to absences nor presences, whether these be defined as corporate cities, tolerance, accommodation, or recognition. Exploring Ottoman citizenship after orientalism is indeed a very complicated task and I do not wish to simplify it. This chapter is, then, more an invitation to explore this complicated issue than a conclusive set of arguments.

I wish to conclude these opening remarks by reflecting on the importance of reconsidering or even constituting an object called "Ottoman citizenship." The immediate political question is of course the new wave of Europeanization or Westernization of the Turkish Republic occasioned by its theoretically imminent accession to the European Union. Arguably, this wave began much earlier, going back to the 1830s and the final decades of the Ottoman Empire (Timur 1998). But there is certainly a new sense of urgency brought on by broader geopolitical shifts and realignments as well as institutional transformations associated with the enlargement of the European Union. As is well known, the difficulties of accepting the Turkish Republic into the European Union have centered upon a small set of claims which, while phrased in different ways, one may call the question of compatibility between the European tradition of citizenship rights – civil, political and economic – and Turkish republicanism. This has exacerbated the question of Turkish modernity, which has been a fundamental question since at least the 1830s. As other chapters in this volume illustrate, the debate over the formation of the Turkish Republic and the extent to which it converged toward or diverged from the European civic republican tradition is currently in full swing (İçduygu *et al.* 1999; Keyman 2000). As is the question of whether Turkish citizenship approximated or distorted European citizenship by attempting to create an ethnicized and racialized Turkish nation (Yeğen 2002). These questions of convergence, divergence, approximation, and distortion as a relationship and compatibility between Turkish and European citizenship rights need to be considered within a canvas of the relationship between orientalism and citizenship that I attempt to sketch in this chapter.

Orientalism and citizenship

The relationship between orientalism and citizenship has not received the attention it deserves in either postcolonial or citizenship studies. It is well known that orientalism involves dividing the world into two "civilizational" blocs, one having rationalized and secularized and hence modernized, the other having remained "irrational," religious and traditional. Some scholars demonstrated how the Orient has been produced as representation in especially occidental art and literature. Others have argued that what was produced was not only representation but also the Orient itself, materializing through orientalizing discourses. Some scholars have argued that indeed Said (1978) was ambiguous on the difference between the Orient as representation and the Orient as real, sometimes assuming that the Orient was simply the former, sometimes assuming that it was a distorted version of the latter (Yeğenoğlu 1998: 15–20). What concerns me is that for orientalizing discourses the ostensible ontological difference between the Occident and the Orient can be directly attributed to citizenship understood as a contractual arrangement amongst unencumbered and sovereign citizens, associated with each other and capable of acting collectively. In other words, I am not concerned with how the Orient was "merely" represented, but how it was produced through orientalizing practices involving both occidental and oriental subjects and spaces. It is this relationship that has not occasioned a sustained discussion. That Said did not concern himself with orientalism in the social sciences may have contributed to this (Turner 2000: 6). Be that as it may, the images of citizenship that dominated occidental thought essentially invoked citizenship as a contract. The contractual images of citizenship are not merely representations. These images constantly organize our political thoughts and practises. An occidental tradition where the origins of "city," "democracy" and "citizenship" are always traced to the "Greek," "Roman" and "medieval" histories, for example, generates such images through which it gradually becomes impossible to imagine that these institutions may have existed elsewhere. An entire tradition reminds us that polis, politics and polity, civitas, citizenship and civility, and demos and democracy have "common roots." We are always provided with images of virtuous Greek citizens debating in the Agora or the Pnyx, austere Roman citizens deliberating in the republican senate, and "European" citizens receiving their charter as a symbol of contract in front of the guildhall. Moreover, the modern European nation-state claimed inheritance of this invented tradition. As Weber would claim, "the modern state is the first to have the concept of the *citizen of the state*" according to which "the individual, for once, is *not*, as he is everywhere else, considered in terms of the particular professional and family position he occupies, not in relation to differences of material and social situation, but purely and simply *as a citizen*" (Weber 1917: 103, original emphases). This is, of course, a normative ideal as Weber saw the meaning and purpose of modern citizenship as a "counterbalance to the social *inequalities* which are *neither* rooted in natural differences nor created by natural qualities but are produced, rather, by social conditions (which are often severely at variance with nature) and above all, inevitably, by the *purse*" (Weber 1917: 103, original emphases). But this universal ideal of citizenship has been effectively and widely critiqued (Isin and Wood 1999; Young 1989; Yuval-Davis 1997).

What these images mobilize and provoke is an invented tradition: that the West is somehow an *inheritor* of a tradition that is different and superior from an oriental tradition. As we shall see below, when Weber says "everywhere else," he has in mind a very specific space than that broad term may suggest: the Orient. These images, then, do not just invent one but two traditions: a superior way of being political as "simple and pure citizen" and an inferior tradition that never sorted out the contractual state or the citizen. All the same, these images provoke and assemble "natural" ways of seeing and perceiving the political. For the occidental imagination some images are now such ways of seeing: that democracy was invented in the Greek polis; that Roman republican tradition bequeathed its legacy to Europe and that Europe Christianized and civilized these traditions. The image of the virtuous citizen is ineluctably linked with the occidental tradition, whether it is told through canonical thinkers such as Aristotle, Cicero, St Augustine, Locke and Rousseau, or through narrating epic battles where citizenship virtues were discovered. While in the late eighteenth and early nineteenth centuries this narrative was told as a seamless web, constituting an occidental tradition of citizenship, for much of the twentieth century its seamlessness was called into question, liberalism, republicanism or communitarianism claiming different strands as their own. Yet, until the present, this narrative has held its sway: liberalism, republicanism and communitarianism are really different ways of telling the same occidental narrative. Many representations of orientalism either rely upon or reproduce this one essential difference between the Occident and the Orient.

I would like to return to Weber to highlight the way in which he emphasized citizenship as *the* unique foundation of occidental tradition. I have provided closer readings of his argument elsewhere, so here I will limit myself to essentials (Isin 2002a; 2002b). The return to Weber is for two crucial reasons. Weber elaborated upon citizenship as a unique occidental invention with more insistence than any other twentieth-century scholar. His influence has been extraordinary. At the outset, what concerns me is that the overemphasis on Weber's interpretation of the origins of capitalism in the Protestant ethic has impeded what, in my view, is his more significant and broader interpretation that citizenship made capitalism possible. For Weber capitalism was uniquely an occidental phenomenon precisely because citizenship was an occidental invention. That for Weber the absence of autonomous cities and citizenship was decisive for the failure of oriental societies to develop capitalism, and that this was connected with "synoecism," is the connection to which I wish to draw attention. For Weber, what made the occidental city unique was that it arose from the establishment of a confraternity, a brotherhood-in-arms for mutual aid and protection, and the usurpation of political power (Weber 1927b: 319). In this regard, Weber always drew parallels between the medieval "communes" and ancient "synoecism." Thus for Weber

> The polis is always the product of such a confraternity or synoecism, not always an actual settlement in proximity but a definite oath of brotherhood which signified that a common ritualistic meal is established and a ritualistic union formed and that only those had a part in this ritualistic group who buried their dead on the acropolis and had their dwellings in the city.
>
> (Weber 1927b: 320)

While Weber consistently emphasized that some of these characteristics emerged in China, Japan, the Near East, India and Egypt, he insisted that it was only in the occident that all were present and appeared regularly. From this he concluded that "Most importantly, the associational character of the city and the concept of a burgher (as contrasted to the man from the countryside) never developed [in the Orient] at all and existed only in rudiments" (Weber 1921: 1227). Therefore "a special status of the town dweller as a 'citizen', in the ancient medieval sense, did not exist and a corporate character of the city was unknown" (Weber 1921: 1227). He was convinced that

> in strong contrast to the medieval and ancient Occident, we never find the phenomenon in the Orient that the autonomy and the participation of the inhabitants in the affairs of local administration would be more strongly developed in the city ... than in the countryside. In fact, as a rule the very opposite would be true.
>
> (Weber 1921: 1228)

For him this difference was decisive:

> All safely founded information about Asian and oriental settlements which had the economic characteristics of "cities" seems to indicate that normally only the clan associations, and sometimes also the occupational associations, were the vehicle of organized action, but never the collective of urban citizens as such.
>
> (Weber 1921: 1233)

Above all, for Weber only "in the Occident is found the concept of *citizen* (*civis Romanus*, *citoyens*, *bourgeois*) because only in the Occident does the *city* exist in the specific sense of the word" (Weber 1927b: 232). For Weber, citizenship was crucial in explaining why capitalism emerged only in the occident precisely because the city existed as such and that the citizen as a special status stood above any other identity. It was this combination that made possible the contractual man, the foundation of capitalism (Holton 1986).

Broadly speaking, Weber provided two reasons why the city as confraternity (a contractual organization) arose only in the occident. First, since the occidental city originally emerged as a war machine, the group that owned the means of warfare dominated the city. For Weber, whether a group owned the means of warfare or was furnished by an overlord was as fundamental as whether the means of production were the property of the worker or the capitalist (Weber 1927a: 320). Everywhere in the Orient the development of the city as brotherhood-in-arms was prevented by the fact that the army of the prince or overlord dominated the city from outside (Weber 1918: 280). Why? That was because the question of irrigation was crucial for India, China, the Near East, Egypt and Asia. "The water question conditioned the existence of the bureaucracy, the compulsory service of the dependent classes, and the dependence of subject classes upon the functioning of the bureaucracy of the king" (Weber 1927a: 321). That the king expressed his power in the form of a military monopoly was the basis of the distinction between the Orient and the Occident. "The forms of religious brotherhood and self equipment for war made possible the origin and existence of the city" (Weber 1927a: 321). While elements of analogous developments occur in India, China, Mesopotamia and Egypt, the necessity of water regulation, which led to the formation of kingship monopoly over the means of warfare, stifled these beginnings. The reader will recognize the well-known "oriental despotism" thesis here that can be traced back to Montesquieu (1721) and forward to Wittfogel (1957). The second obstacle which prevented the development of the city in the Orient, was the persistence of magic in oriental religions. These religions did not allow the formation of "rational" communities and hence the city. By contrast, the magical barriers between clans, tribes, and peoples, which were still known in the ancient polis, were eventually abolished and so the establishment of the occidental city was made possible (Weber 1927a: 322–3). What makes the occidental city unique is that it allowed the association or formation of groups based on bonds and ties other than lineage or kinship, the basis of which were contract and secularism.

As Springborg (1987) convincingly argued, this contractual and secularist interpretation of the superiority of the occident has older and deeper roots than Weber. What Weber accomplished, in my view, was his essential linking of contractualism and citizenship. Springborg (1987: 402) sees the formation of the theories of oriental despotism and the articulation of contractualism as civic republicanism in two historical moments: a classical phase that coincides with the period in which the polis was the dominant political formation, and an early modern phase, coincident with the formation of the modern European state. I am skeptical whether the first moment should be considered as a moment at all, since our understanding of the Greeks is so much more intertwined with and influenced by the later moment that it is doubtful if the Greeks are accessible to us in a way that enables us to make that kind of claim. I would also suggest breaking her more homogeneous moment "early modern" into an earlier civic humanist moment and a later absolutist moment. Moreover, I would also add the nineteenth-century modern appropriation of both the Greco-Romans and civic humanists as part of an occidental tradition. Nonetheless, the significance of Springborg's argument is her insistence on interpreting this tradition as a gradual and fitful invention. I would therefore agree that the formation of this occidental tradition has achieved two strategic aims. First, it has created a seamless web between the Greek polis and the modern state as one history, including the absolutist European monarchies. Second, it has created an ontological difference between the Occident and the Orient, the latter being constituted as its despotic other. Springborg (1986; 1987), however, goes even further and argues that the formation of an occidental tradition has also masked the fact that the polis may well have derived from earlier "oriental" civilizations, and that this latter achievement is an extraordinary inversion, rendering monarchical, absolutist regimes of the early modern Europe essentially democratic and oriental regimes as essentially despotic. This argument has considerable merit, and is useful in understanding some of the outstanding gaps in Weber's work concerning the early modern monarchies and absolutist states.

Yet, ultimately, I suggest that Springborg falls into a trap of reverse orientalism in the sense that she takes Weber's argument as given and attempts to demonstrate that the features of citizenship and contractualism were not lacking in the Orient but were present. She, for example, argues that

> A preponderance of the evidence from ancient and medieval Iraq, Persia, Syria and Egypt over a long period and under successive empires, Babylonian, Assyrian, Achaemenid, Parthian, Sasanian, Hellenistic, Roman, Byzantine, Umayyad, Abbasid, Fatimid, Mamluk and Ottoman, suggests that these were societies based on a loose federation of autocephalous communities enjoying a fair degree of autonomy, within which unusually democratic conditions prevailed, and between which conditions of religious toleration and economic co-operation were typical.
>
> (Springborg 1987: 401)

What Springborg argues here is that oriental societies exhibited features of citizenship and contractualism but they were either willfully or unintentionally omitted from orientalist scholarship. Thus,

> Far from being the victims of oriental despotism, the average citizens in these communities enjoyed a degree of legal and economic freedom, personal and corporate rights and immunities, which compares favorably with those of the citizen in the modern "democratic" state. It is fair to claim that the contours of the classical polis are far more faithfully reflected in the cities of the medieval and modern oriental world than in the structures and institutions of the Northern European nation states, so widely assumed to be its legitimate heir.
>
> (Springborg 1987: 401)

Throughout her argument a resistance to overcome negative representations of oriental cities lacking citizenship is accompanied by positive attempts to transform oriental cities into cities just like their occidental counterparts: that "ancient society was explicitly contractual" (398); that "recent scholarship has shown a considerable degree of corporate autonomy on the part of Mesopotamian cities vis-à-vis the royal authority, at a time at which the Germanic and Celtic tribes were still in the bush, so to speak" (411); that

> Citizenship in Mesopotamian cities, like that of Athens, depended on the twin criteria of birth to free parents and ownership of municipal land. Citizenship brought with it rights and duties: economic, social, legal and religious privileges, but [also] the duties of taxation and military service.
>
> (Springborg 1987: 412)

and that "the legal definition of relations between citizens in contractual terms does not belong to the Western historical tradition to anything like the extent that it belongs to that of the East" (1987: 421).

As relevant and significant as it is, there are two problems with her argument. First, of course, it is problematic to take the Weberian theses on the uniqueness and superiority of ostensibly occidental contractualism and citizenship and attempt to demonstrate that indeed oriental cities were more occidental than occidental cities, when these categories of the political were originally produced by reference to a lack or absence in oriental cities in the first place. This is more than a logical problem where the referent is missing from the reference. It results in a theoretical problem of having to always demonstrate the presence of citizenship in oriental cities with reference to occidental cities. Second, while this argument intends to call into question an ontological difference between the occidental and oriental cities, it in fact contributes to creating even a deeper wedge between them by making them essential terms of discourse. Either way, and this is generally true for critics of orientalism as representation, the will to truth underlying this view to correct orientalism misses the fact that orientalism operates as a strategic orientation that mobilizes and organizes various practices.

Springborg is not alone in falling in the trap of reverse orientalism. Throughout the twentieth century a veritable discourse on oriental cities emerged, taking Weberian theses as their starting point and attempting to either falsify or corroborate them. Whether it was about the generic notion of the Islamic city (Goldberg 1991; Hourani 1970; Lapidus 1969; Stern 1970) or studies of specific Muslim cities (Auld *et al.* 2000; Çelik 1999; Goitein 1969; İnalcık 1990; Lebon 1970; Leeuwen 1999; Ze'evi 1996), or the Ottoman city (Eldem *et al.* 1999; Faroqhi 1984; 1994), historical scholarship developed under the shadow of an orientalist Weber in attempts to refute, corroborate, modify or at least to respond to his theses. I suggest that since

Weber drew his conclusions on contractualism and citizenship from his interpretations of oriental cities, to explore the possibilities of rethinking citizenship after (or without) orientalism, the literature on the Islamic city or the Ottoman city as a genus in that species, while indispensable, poses considerable challenges and imposes perhaps insurmountable limits.

Citizenship after orientalism

The question that this analysis raises is how one might approach citizenship without orientalism. Approaching citizenship without orientalism will require overcoming fundamental assumptions about synoecism and an ontological difference between Occident and Orient mobilized by presences and absences (Isin 2002a). Moreover, it will require abandoning teleological, historicist and presentist ways of interpreting histories of citizenship (Isin 1995; 1997). I have suggested a way of investigating citizenship historically as a generalized problem of otherness (Isin 2002a; 2002b; 2002c). Appropriating various strands of thought that range from legal and sociological thought to psychoanalysis and social psychology, I have argued that it is possible to rethink occidental citizenship from the perspective of an analysis of the formation of groups as a generalized question of otherness and of the ways of being political without any appeal to an ontological difference between the Occident and the Orient. Such an analysis requires critically transforming some of the fundamental categories of occidental social and political thought. Briefly, this analysis regards the formation of groups as fundamental but dynamic processes through which beings articulate themselves. Through *orientations*, *strategies* and *technologies* as forms of being political, beings develop *solidaristic*, *agonistic* and *alienating* relationships. I maintain that these *forms* and *modes* constitute ontological ways of being political in the sense that being thrown into them is not *necessarily* a matter of conscious choice or contract (Isin 2002c: 13). It is through these forms and modes that beings articulate themselves as *citizens*, *strangers*, *outsiders* and *aliens* as possible ways of being rather than identities or differences. It is therefore impossible to investigate "citizenship," as that name that citizens – as distinguished from strangers, outsiders and aliens – have given themselves, without investigating the specific constellation or figuration of orientations, strategies and technologies that are available for deployment in producing solidaristic, agonistic and alienating multiplicities.

I maintain that each figuration is a moment that should not be understood as merely a temporal unit but as a spatio-temporal way of being political. Each moment is constituted as a consequence of analysis and does not exist as such, but only through this analysis. Each moment crystallizes itself as that space which is called the city. I have argued that the city should not be imagined as merely a material or physical place, but as a force field that works as a difference machine. The city is not just simply a place or space but a figuration. I have called this figuration a "difference machine."

The city is a difference machine because the groups are not formed outside the machine and encounter each within the city, but the city assembles, generates, distributes, and differentiates these differences, incorporates them within strategies and technologies, and elicits, interpellates, adjures, and incites them.

> The city is not a container where differences encounter each other; the city generates differences and assembles identities. The city is a difference machine insofar as it is understood as that space which is constituted by the dialogical encounter of groups formed and generated immanently in the process of taking up positions, orienting themselves for and against each other, inventing and assembling strategies and technologies, mobilizing various forms of capital, and making claims to that space that is objectified as "the city." The city is a crucial condition of citizenship in the sense that being a citizen is inextricably associated with being *of* the city.
>
> (Isin 2002a: 283)

Therefore I maintain that

> The city is neither a background to these struggles *against which* groups wager, nor is it a foreground *for which* groups struggle for hegemony. Rather, the city is the battleground *through which* groups define their identity, stake their claims, wage their battles, and articulate citizenship rights, obligations, and principles.
>
> (Isin 2002a: 283–4)

Admittedly, this summary is indeed very condensed. But it aims to highlight two issues regarding theorizing the city and citizenship relationship. First, while many critics of Weber emphasized lacunae in his interpretation of the oriental city, the astounding assumption is that his account of the occidental city is fundamentally correct. I argue that the unification that Weber attributes to the occidental city and its ostensible expression, citizenship, is questionable. I called this "synoecism" and argued that we must begin interpreting the history of occidental citizenship itself differently, and accept that that history itself was articulated as an invented tradition that needs to be interrupted. Second, the constitution of the occidental city has not been without reference to the ostensible features of the oriental city. That "orientalism" is not merely a representation but a strategic orientation that has mobilized various practices as a result of which some cities have been constituted as the bedrock of citizenship and some cities with their lack, should be an object of critical analysis. I doubt that remaining within the terms of discourse that dominated our senses of being political on the basis of an orientalist – if not imperialist, racist and colonialist – difference between cultures and nations for at least two centuries, will we be capable of articulating new understandings of the ways in which humans become political beings. Whether we like it or not, citizenship has institutionalized specific ways of being political in world history, and leaving its investigations to either occidentalist or orientalist forms of thought is not an attractive option.

Ottoman citizenship

Approaching citizenship without orientalism potentially opens up new ways of investigating the ways in which at various moments in world history distinct groups articulated themselves by mobilizing distinct orientations, assembling strategies and technologies and producing different forms of otherness through which different ways of being political are rendered possible. Approaching citizenship this way interrupts the burden of comparing and contrasting various cultures or civilizations with a view to establishing the superiority or inferiority of one over the other. Weber focused incessantly on Judea, China, India and Islam to compare corporate organization, contractualism, and so forth with the ostensibly occidental institutions. As I have argued, the aim of approaching citizenship without orientalism is not to abandon a difference between and amongst various world historical moments, but to refuse to reduce them to fundamental ontological differences along the axis of inferiority or superiority (Isin 2002a: 22ff). Nor is it simply about abandoning occidental ways of thought. Rather, it is about revealing the multiple and critical traditions of both occidental and oriental thoughts and appropriating them for alternative and critical interpretations.

Without these caveats, the notion of "Ottoman citizenship" would be an apparent oxymoron. When citizenship is defined by its arbitrary designation in a given moment, as was articulated during the eighteenth and nineteenth centuries in Europe, perhaps the only moment that one can claim that Ottoman citizenship can be legitimately named would be during and after the reform period in the 1830s known as the *Tanzimat*. It can further be argued, specifically until the promulgation of the 1869 "citizenship" law, and 1876, when a new Ottoman constitution was drawn up, that citizenship had not been institutionalized in the imperial governing order (Ünsal 1998). One may even further argue that these were proto-moments of citizenship and that properly modern citizenship did not emerge until the new Turkish Republic was formed in the 1920s, and clearly adopted and articulated citizenship laws (Aybay 1998). Clearly, I would reject these arguments. To limit the analysis of citizenship in the Ottoman Empire to only those moments when "it" was imported from Europe during Westernization and Europeanization is to accept political orientalism. Whatever reasons one gives to limit analysis of Ottoman citizenship to its Western incarnations, one should not approach it with an always already-defined and understood notion of citizenship and look for its traces, development and emergence.

This clearly converges toward either orientalist or reverse orientalist modes of thought that grant the existence of citizenship only on condition of being found in a particular form in the occident. Besides, when this approach is followed faithfully, one can argue, as the recent European Union documents have done, that even Turkish citizenship can be said not to have arrived yet since it still does not conform to its European counterpart (CEC 2002a, 2002b).

Yet, the constitution of the Turkish republican citizenship began much earlier than the 1920s and was indeed a European project. It is well known that a Turkish identity and citizenship founded on a racialized and ethnicized Turkishness became prevalent in the late Ottoman Empire and the early Turkish Republic (Deringil 1993; Kadıoğlu 1998; Yeğen 2002). This must, however, be understood in the context of a broader movement toward Westernization that incorporated the racist and nationalist discourse in the West on the purity of Aryan races and their ostensible superiority (Davison 1973; 1990; Timur 1994: 121–43). The European discourse on race began in the late eighteenth century and continued well into the 1940s, which was a crucial moment of transformation of the Ottoman Empire into the Turkish Republic. The discourse itself was not only implicated in various European projects of imperialism, colonialism and orientalism, but also provided direct justification for them. It is often argued that the Ottomans did not use race or nation as operative concepts with which to organize their practices of belonging, identity and difference (Makdisi 2002; Mardin 1962; Timur 1994). But when the Ottomans were faced with the new question of national identities in the nineteenth century, they were implicated in Western theories of race, identity and nation. Western anthropology, archeology, philology, and psychology were not only the sources the Ottoman intellectuals and intelligentsia drew upon but also became ways of seeing and thinking that enabled Ottomans to conceive themselves as modernizing and Westernizing forces (Timur 1994: 139–40). Just as many European intellectuals and intelligentsia constituted European nations as *sui generis* and authentic polities with racial and ethnic purity and homogeneity, so did their Ottoman counterparts in their quest to define a nation emerging from the fragments of an empire. While the intellectuals and intelligentsia of the early republic attempted to differentiate themselves from the Ottoman legacies, they nonetheless inherited the fundamental assumptions of the late Ottoman search for Turkish origins and, in some ways, intensified and deepened it (Timur 1994: 144–8). Thus it would be a mistake to consider the birth of republican citizenship without a broader context in which orientalism and nationalism played a crucial role. To take orientalist and nationalist assumptions about citizenship as given and deploy them in analyses in interpreting various ways in which citizenship was used in republican institutions leads to orientalism and reverse orientalism.

An opposite danger is to find in Ottoman institutions more progressive and developed conceptions of "the art of living together" that avoided the racism of modern European citizenship. In recent years there has been a development in this direction, which interprets certain Ottoman institutions from the point of view of tolerance and difference (Armağan 2000). The well-known system by which the Ottomans allocated certain rights to minorities – the millet system – has now increasingly been interpreted as a sign of Ottoman tolerance and accommodation for difference (Braude and Lewis 1980; Reppetto 1970; Stefanov 1997). The problem with these arguments is not their plausibility or implausibility. It may well be that Ottoman institutions that were overlooked by orientalist interpreters did indeed involve certain forms of tolerance and accommodation that were alien to the emerging nineteenth-century nationalist and racist forms of constituting modern otherness. Yet, discovering forms of tolerance, pluralism and accommodation in the Ottoman Empire in terms understood in the late twentieth and early twenty-first centuries generates more problems than it solves. First, it serves as yet another form of orientalism where Ottoman institutions once again are justified by using ostensibly European standards, albeit from its contemporary rather than historical figurations. Second, it also serves as an apologetic yet irredentist Islamization that finds justification in ostensibly progressive Ottoman institutions, which becomes mired in occidentalism.

I suggest that investigating Ottoman citizenship must avoid orientalist, reverse orientalist and occidentalist approaches. Understanding citizenship as a generalized problem of otherness would generate more useful theses by which to evaluate citizenship and to rethink its contemporary figurations. The question that these suggestions raise is what kinds of investigation can one undertake concerning Ottoman citizenship without orientalism? There is a cluster of problems that suggest themselves for investigation. The first is, of course, the formation of Turkish citizenship during the long nineteenth century between the 1830s and 1920s. The debate over Westernization of the Ottoman Empire in that period and the role of military-intellectual cadres known as Young Ottomans and later Young Turks is extensive. But the limited debate over the formation of citizenship during this period embodies various orientalist assumptions. Often citizenship is taken to mean how modern republican citizenship is defined in Europe. The hegemonic ideal replaces its contested and dissident versions, and it is that ideal that is searched for in the Ottoman Empire, thus further reinforcing its hegemony. A second cluster of problems concerns the formation and treatment of minorities in the Ottoman Empire, especially during the period of its expansion in the sixteenth and seventieth centuries. The debate over the "millet system" has dominated investigations of this question and, as far as I know, the question of minorities has not been interpreted from the perspective of Ottoman citizenship. The question of the status and practices of non-Muslim groups in Ottoman Empire has so far extensively focused on quintessential occidental categories such as autonomy, tolerance, recognition and accommodation (Armağan 2000; Braude and Lewis 1980). Analyses of these practices without relying upon these categories have revealed remarkably rich interpretations, but this work is just beginning to emerge (Ercan 2001; Soykan 2000).

But, more significantly, the question of Ottoman citizenship arises in connection with the Ottoman city. As I mentioned earlier, there has been a debate about the Islamic city that was conducted very much under the shadow of Weberian theorizing about the city. I also mentioned that many of his critics took Weber's description of the occidental city as given and attempted to prove or disprove its applicability to the Islamic city. I would like now to return to this debate briefly to illustrate the ways in which Weberian theses were considered. To return to this debate is important because, as Eldem *et al.* (1999: 1–3) have shown, it was conducted under the shadow of the constitution of the Islamic city. Since Eldem *et al.* provide a succinct summary of this debate, I will avoid repeating their concerns.

From my point of view, this literature raises two points. First, Weber has been uncritically accepted as providing an adequate account of the occidental city. In the entire literature on the Islamic city, I have not encountered an author who questions Weber's theorization of the occidental city. It is simply accepted that the occidental city was a politically and legally unified, autonomous and autocephalous entity with a corresponding spatial form. The subtle and nuanced analyses enabled Albert Hourani and Ira Lapidus, for example, to work through their material assuming that Weberian analysis of the rise of the patricians as a unifying dominant group is essentially an adequate account of the occidental city. Lapidus (1969: 49) argues that merchant or craft guilds in the Islamic city were weak and professional groups never managed to establish hegemony. He assumes that the occidental city was a spatially unified entity with a corresponding unified political organization. He then notes that in the Islamic city there were various fraternities, but these were not urban but rural on account of being located in smaller villages. Similarly, he argues that many political bodies that emerged in the Islamic city were more regional than urban on account of being dispersed throughout the surrounding areas of the city. Of the four groups that Lapidus notes as being dominant in the Islamic city (neighborhood bodies, fraternities, religious groups, and state and imperial authorities), none was an urban group for him except insofar as the city was a natural headquarters for them (Lapidus 1969: 60). For Lapidus, therefore, Muslim cities had no unity. As I have argued against Weber, neither did occidental cities. Had Lapidus been critical of the Weberian occidental city, would his conclusions have been different? Similarly, Hourani argued that Weber's "definition [did] more or less correspond to what Europeans would think of as a city, and if we accept it then we must also accept his conclusion that Near Eastern cities are not cities in the full sense" (Hourani 1970: 13). Yet, Hourani was sympathetic to but critical of Louis Massignon (1931; 1935), who had argued that Islamic cities had developed a corporate organization through their guilds. For Hourani the paradox was how the Islamic city maintained its power of collective action without municipal institutions (Hourani 1970: 14). The critique by Stern (1970), directly on Massignon and implicitly on Lapidus and Hourani, reproduces Weberian theses and elevates them into unassailable truths about the occidental city. The literature on the Islamic city has not, therefore, only been conducted under the shadow of Weber but also took his interpretation of the occidental city, his synoecism, as given.

The second question that this literature raises is that it responds to an idealized and simplified Weber who argues about the differences between the occidental and oriental city on the basis of "common features." Throughout this literature the Weber it is concerned with is the Weber who wrote *The City* and, in fact, its first section that develops a typology of the European city on the basis of five common features. But, as I have argued earlier, Weber advanced his theses on the relationship between cities and citizenship over an extensive body of work that belies the simple typology that has been attributed to him on the basis of five characteristics of the European city. In fact, Weber's argument is not that the occidental city had a corporate organization, a dominant patrician group, and that it was autonomous and autocephalous. In his studies of China, Judaism, India, Islam and Near Eastern civilizations, he repeatedly stressed that some of these elements were present. For Weber what failed to happen in these civilizations was all elements coming together and producing the citizen as a special status. It is worth repeating here that for Weber

> The polis is always the product of such a confraternity or synoecism, not always an actual settlement in proximity but a definite oath of brotherhood which signified that a common ritualistic meal is established and a ritualistic union formed and that only those had a part in this ritualistic group who buried their dead on the acropolis and had their dwellings in the city.
>
> (Weber 1927b: 320)

The emphasis is on brotherhood and the associational character of the city that produced the citizen. His conclusion was that "the associational character of the city and the concept of a burgher (as contrasted to the man from the countryside) never developed [in the Orient] at all and existed only in rudiments" (Weber 1921: 1227). Therefore "a special status of the town dweller as a 'citizen', in the ancient medieval sense, did not exist and a corporate character of the city was unknown" (Weber 1921: 1227). In the literature on the Islamic city, only von Grunebaum, and only tangentially, stressed the importance of this connection made by Weber on cities and citizenship when he argued that "In the ancient town, to become a citizen a recent settler had to obtain admission into the register of the citizenry; in Islam there existed no impediment of this kind to participation in urban life" (1961: 154). Yet, von Grunebaum does not further discuss the potential importance of this.

The debate over the Ottoman city, therefore, runs into these two difficulties: it takes Weber's interpretation of the occidental city as given and responds to an idealized Weber on the common attributes of the city. While Eldem *et al.* note, for example, that Weber's interpretation is akin to Marx's "oriental despotism," they assume that Weber's account of the occidental city was more or less adequate (1999: 9). They argue that studies of different identities in Ottoman cities have just begun and "the resourceful use of kadı court records are beginning to yield portraits of the beliefs, actions, and social roles of men, women, and children, guildsmen, tradesmen, and apprentices, Christians, Jews, and Muslims in Ottoman Anatolian cities" (1999: 11). There arises a possibility here that may well be worth exploring: if we call into question Weber's theses on the relationship between cities and citizenship, should we not ask whether these groups in the Ottoman city were organized around citizens, strangers, outsiders and aliens, producing strategies and technologies of otherness that are specific to certain times and spaces of the Ottoman city? Along these lines, for example, would it not be fruitful to revisit the Weberian thesis on the importance of military organization for citizenship, and compare and contrast the Ottoman janissaries and the Greek hoplites as organizing principles of identity? Similarly, differences between *waqf* and *euergetism* as technologies of citizenship formation could also yield significant insights (Springborg 1986: 190–1; 1987: 400, 413; Veyne 1976). The formation of notables in Ottoman cities as dominant groups, and various arrangements concerning consumption and production, could also yield different interpretations from perspectives mobilized by synoecism and orientalism (Faroqhi 2002a; 2002b; 2002c; Meeker, 2002). In all these investigations, the focus would be on the constellation of groups in a given moment, solidaristic, agonistic and alienating orientations, strategies and technologies in which they were implicated or thrown into, and the forms of citizenship and otherness that each constellation produced. Eldem *et al.* conclude that the

> profound differences in the relationships between aliens and subjects in the three cities of Istanbul, Izmir, and Aleppo suggest something that perhaps should always have been obvious, there simply never has been such a thing as a normative "Ottoman," "Arab," or "Islamic" city, any more than there has ever been a typical "French," "English," or "Christian" metropolis.
>
> (Eldem *et al.* 1999: 213)

Yet, this view is also problematic in that it overlooks the fact that a fundamental purpose of undertaking historical analysis is to develop these typologies. If each city is so irreducibly unique, what is the purpose of historical analysis of *the* city? (Isin 2003).

Conclusion

What these kinds of investigation may provide is a challenge to the hegemony of orientalism and synoecism in interpreting oriental cities in general and Ottoman and Islamic cities in particular. What is at stake is nothing less than rethinking citizenship in both the Occident and the Orient. Avoiding orientalism and synoecism in investigating Ottoman citizenship, and even constituting the Ottoman city as an object of analysis, cannot guarantee productive or effective results at the outset. To my mind, there is no doubt that investigating Ottoman citizenship without orientalism and synoecism has a contemporary significance in the context of the debate over the accession of Turkey to the European Union. Thinking about Turkish citizenship took place under the shadow of the occident for so long that it may well be imperative to articulate certain principles of Turkish citizenship based upon its trajectories and specificities rather than the shadows of European modernities that constantly change. That way, it may also enable European scholars to think critically about "occidental citizenship" itself.

Acknowledgments

I would like to thank Dana Dawson, Erkan Erçel, Bora İsyar, Alexandre Lefebvre, Ebru Üstündağ, Gülay Yarıkkaya, Melanie White and the anonymous referees for their very useful comments on an earlier draft of this chapter.

References

Armağan, M. (ed.) (2000) *Osmanlı'da Hoşgörü: Birlikte Yaşama Sanatı* (Tolerance Amongst Ottomans: The Art of Living Together), Harbiye, Istanbul: Gazeteciler ve Yazarlar Vakfı Yayınları.

Auld, S., Hillenbrand, R., and Natshah, Y. S. (eds) (2000) *Ottoman Jerusalem: The Living City, 1517–1917*, London: The British School of Archaeology In Jerusalem in cooperation with the Administration of Auqaf and Islamic Affairs Jerusalem by Altajir World of Islam Trust.

Aybay, R. (1998) "Teba-i Osmani'den T.C. Yurttasşı'na Geçişin Neresindeyiz?" (Where are we in Transition from Ottoman Subjecthood to Republican Citizenship?), in A. Ünsal (ed.) *75 Yılda Tebaa'dan Yurttaş'a Doğru* (From Subjecthood to Citizenship: 75th Anniversary), Istanbul: Tarih Vakfı.

Braude, B. and Lewis, B. (eds) (1980) *Christians and Jews in the Ottoman Empire: The Functioning of a Plural Society*, vols 1 and 2, New York: Holmes & Meier.

CEC (2002a) *Regular Report on Turkey's Progress Towards Accession*, Brussels: Commission of the European Communities.

——(2002b) *Towards the Enlarged Union: Strategy Paper and Report of the European Commission on the Progress Towards Accession by Each of the Candidate Countries*, Brussels: Commission of the European Communities.

Çelik, Z. (1999) "New Approaches to the 'Non-Western' City," *Journal of the Society of Architectural Historians*, 58 (3): 374–8.

Davison, R. H. (1973) *Reform in the Ottoman Empire, 1856–1876*, New York: Gordian Press.
——(1990) *Essays in Ottoman and Turkish History, 1774–1923: The Impact of the West*, Modern Middle East Series 16, Austin: University of Texas Press.
Deringil, S. (1993) "The Ottoman Origins of Kemalist Nationalism, Kemal, Namık to Kemal, Mustafa," *European History Quarterly*, 23 (2): 165–91.
Eldem, E., Goffman, D. and Masters, B. A. (1999) *The Ottoman City between East and West: Aleppo, Izmir, and Istanbul*, Cambridge Studies in Islamic Civilization, New York: Cambridge University Press.
Ercan, Y. (2001) *Osmanlı Yönetiminde Gayrimüslimler: Kurtuluştan Tanzimata Kadar Sosyal, Ekonomik ve Hukuki Durumları* (Non-Muslims under Ottoman Administration: Their Social, Economic and Legal Status from the Founding of the Empire to the Age of Reform), Ankara: Turhan Kitabevi Yayınları.
Faroqhi, S. (1984) *Towns and Townsmen of Ottoman Anatolia: Trade, Crafts, and Food Production in an Urban Setting, 1520–1650*, Cambridge Studies in Islamic Civilization, Cambridge: Cambridge University Press.
——(1994) "Crisis and Change, 1590–1699," in H. Inalcık and D. Quataert (eds) *An Economic and Social History of the Ottoman Empire, 1300–1914*, Cambridge: Cambridge University Press.
——(2002a) "Between Collective Workshops and Private Homes: Places of Work in Eighteenth Century Bursa," in *Stories of Ottoman Men and Women: Establishing Status, Establishing Control*, Istanbul: Eren.
——(2002b) "Consumption and Elite Status in the Eighteenth and Nineteenth Centuries: Exploring the Ottoman Case," in *Stories of Ottoman Men and Women: Establishing Status, Establishing Control*, Istanbul: Eren.
——(2002c) "Urban Space as Disputed Grounds: Territorial Aspects to Artisan Conflict in Sixteenth to Eighteenth-Century Istanbul," in *Stories of Ottoman Men and Women: Establishing Status, Establishing Control*, Istanbul: Eren.
Goitein, S. D. (1969) "Cairo: An Islamic City in the Light of the Geniza Documents," in I. M. Lapidus (ed.) *Middle Eastern Cities: A Symposium on Ancient, Islamic and Contemporary Middle Eastern Urbanism*, Berkeley: University of California Press.
Goldberg, E. (1991) "Was There an Islamic 'City'?" in R. Kasaba (ed.) *Cities in the World-System*, New York: Greenwood Press.
Holton, R. J. (1986) *Cities, Capitalism and Civilization*, London: Unwin.
Hourani, A. H. (1970) "The Islamic City in the Light of Recent Research," in A. H. Hourani and S. M. Stern (eds) *The Islamic City*, Oxford: B. Cassirer.
İçduygu, A., Çolak, A. and Soyarık, N. (1999) "What Is the Matter with Citizenship? A Turkish Debate," *Middle Eastern Studies*, 35 (4): 187–208.
İnalcık, H. (1990) "Istanbul: An Islamic City," *Journal of Islamic Studies*, 1: 1–23.
Isin, E. F. (1995) "Rethinking the Origins of Canadian Municipal Government," *Canadian Journal of Urban Research*, 4 (1): 73–92.
——(1997) "Who Is the New Citizen? Toward a Genealogy," *Citizenship Studies*, 1 (1): 115–32.
——(2002a) *Being Political: Genealogies of Citizenship*, Minneapolis: University of Minnesota Press.
——(2002b) "Citizenship after Orientalism," in E. F. Isin and B. S. Turner (eds) *Handbook of Citizenship Studies*, London: Sage.

——(2002c) "Ways of Being Political," *Distinktion: Tidsskrift For Samfundsteori*, 4: 7–28.

——(2003) "Historical Sociology of the City," in G. Delanty and E. F. Isin (eds) *Handbook of Historical Sociology*, London: Sage.

Isin, E. F. and Wood, P. K. (1999) *Citizenship and Identity*, London: Sage.

Kadıoğlu, A. (1998) "Milletini Arayan Devlet: Türk Milliyetçiliğinin Açmazları" (A State in Search of a Nation: The Paradoxes of Turkish Nationalism), in A. Ünsal (ed.) *75 Yılda Tebaa'dan Yurttaş'a Doğru* (From Subjecthood to Citizenship: 75th Anniversary), Istanbul: Tarih Vakfı.

Keyman, F. (2000) "Global Modernity, Identity and Democracy: The Case of Turkey," in G. G. Özdoğan and G. Tokay (eds) *Redefining the Nation, State and Citizen*, Istanbul: Eren.

Lapidus, I. M. (1969) "Muslim Cities and Islamic Societies," in I. M. Lapidus (ed.) *Middle Eastern Cities: A Symposium on Ancient, Islamic and Contemporary Middle Eastern Urbanism*, Berkeley: University of California Press.

Lebon, J. H. G. (1970) "The Islamic City in the near East: A Comparative Study of Cairo, Alexandria and Istanbul," *Town Planning Review*, 41 (2): 179–94.

Leeuwen, R. van (1999) *Waqfs and Urban Structures: The Case of Ottoman Damascus*, Studies in Islamic Law and Society 11, Leiden and Boston MA: Brill.

Makdisi, U. S. (2002) "Ottoman Orientalism," *American Historical Review*, 107 (3): 768–96.

Mardin, Ş. (1962) *The Genesis of Young Ottoman Thought: A Study in the Modernization of Turkish Political Ideas*, Princeton NJ: Princeton University Press.

Massignon, L. (1931) "Guilds (Mohammedian)," *Encyclopedia of Social Sciences* (1930–5).

——(1935) "Sinf," *Encyclopedia of Islam*, Leiden: Brill, 4: 436–7.

Meeker, M. E. (2002) *A Nation of Empire: The Ottoman Legacy of Turkish Modernity*, Berkeley: University of California Press.

Montesquieu, C. de S. (1721) *Persian Letters*, trans. J. Davidson, London: Routledge.

Reppetto, T. A. (1970) "Millet System in Ottoman and American Empires," *Public Policy*, 18 (5): 629–48.

Said, E. S. (1978) *Orientalism*, New York: Random House.

Soykan, T. T. (2000) *Osmanlı İmparatorluğu'nda Gayrimüslimler: Klasik Dönem Osmanlı Hukukunda Gayrimüslimlerin Hukuki Statüsü* (Non-Muslims in the Ottoman Empire: The Legal Status of Non-Muslims in Classical Ottoman Law), Tarih Dizisi 1, Kadıköy, Istanbul: Ütopya Kitabevi.

Springborg, P. (1986) "Politics, Primordialism, and Orientalism: Marx, Aristotle, and the Myth of the Gemeinschaft," *The American Political Science Review*, 80: 185–211.

——(1987) "The Contractual State: Reflections on Orientalism and Despotism," *History of Political Thought*, 8 (3): 395–433.

Stefanov, S. (1997) "Millet System in the Ottoman Empire – Example for Oppression or for Tolerance?" *Bulgarian Historical Review – Revue Bulgare D'Histoire*, (2–3): 138–42.

Stern, S. M. (1970) "The Constitution of the Islamic City," in A. H. Hourani and S. M. Stern (eds) *The Islamic City*, Oxford: B. Cassirer.

Timur, T. (1994) *Osmanlı Kimliği* (Ottoman Identity), 2nd edn, Istanbul: Hil Yayın.

——(1998) "Türkiye'de Kimlik, Politika ve Gerçekçilik Tarihi Bir Panorama" (Identity, Politics and Realism in Turkey: A Historical Panorama), in A. Ünsal (ed.) *75*

Yılda Tebaa'dan Yurttaş'a Doğru (From Subjecthood to Citizenship: 75th Anniversary), Istanbul: Tarih Vakfı.
Turner, B. S. (2000) "Outline of a Theory of Orientalism," in B. S. Turner (ed.) *Orientalism: Early Sources*, New York: Routledge.
Ünsal, A. (1998) "Yurttaşlık Zor Zanaat" (Citizenship is a Difficult Art), in A. Ünsal (ed.) *75 Yılda Tebaa'dan Yurttaş'a Doğru* (From Subjecthood to Citizenship: 75th Anniversary), Istanbul: Tarih Vakfı.
Veyne, P. (1976) *Bread and Circuses: Historical Sociology and Political Pluralism*, trans. B. Pearce, London: Penguin.
von Grunebaum, G. E. (1961) "The Structure of the Muslim Town," in *Islam: Essays in the Nature and Growth of a Cultural Tradition*, London: Routledge & Kegan Paul.
Weber, M. (1917) [1994] "Suffrage and Democracy in Germany," in P. Lassman and R. Speirs (eds) *Political Writings*, Cambridge: Cambridge University Press.
——(1918) [1994] "Socialism," in P. Lassman and R. Speirs (eds) *Political Writings*, Cambridge: Cambridge University Press.
——(1921) [1978] *Economy and Society: An Outline of Interpretive Sociology*, eds and trans. G. Roth and C. Wittich, vols 1 and 2, Berkeley: University of California Press.
——(1927a) [1981] "Citizenship." *General Economic History*, London: Transaction Publishers.
——(1927b) [1981] *General Economic History*, trans. F. H. Knight, London: Transaction Publishers.
Wittfogel, K. A. (1957) *Oriental Despotism: A Study of Total Power*, New Haven CT: Yale University Press.
Yeğen, M. (2002) "Yurttaşlık ve Türklük" (Citizenship and Turkism), *Toplum ve Bilim*, 93: 200–17.
Yeğenoğlu, M. (1998) *Colonial Fantasies: Towards a Feminist Reading of Orientalism*, Cambridge Cultural Social Studies, Cambridge: Cambridge University Press.
Young, I. M. (1989) "Polity and Group Difference: A Critique of the Ideal of Universal Citizenship," *Ethics*, 99 (January): 250–74.
Yuval-Davis, N. (1997) *Gender and Nation*, London: Sage.
Ze'evi, D. (1996) *An Ottoman Century: The District of Jerusalem in the 1600s*, SUNY Series in Medieval Middle East History, Albany: State University of New York Press.

2 Community, citizenship and identity in Turkey

Feyzi Baban

Introduction

The nation-state's claim to unite a diverse group of people within the same community rests on the concept of universal citizenship. This provides not only the legal framework for who can be a member of the community but also a social and political framework within which members of the community seek representation. Universal citizenship is the foundation of civic nationalism, where members of the community, irrespective of their backgrounds and identities, are subject to the same legal requirements provided they fulfill the obligations for membership. One of the main promises of universal citizenship of civic republicanism is equal representation before the law, which assumes that despite differences within the private realm, individuals are located in the public sphere as equals in terms of fulfilling their potentials and participating in their own affairs.

There are, of course, variations in modern societies and the way they organize their citizenship regimes. In countries such as Britain or the United States, where the liberal tradition has historically been dominant, the citizenship regime focuses on the primacy of the individual and diversity rather than the communitarian aspect of the republican tradition (Işın and Wood 1999). The republican citizenship regime in Turkey, however, has not been hospitable to the idea of diversity and has usually adopted the position that diversity is detrimental to national unity and social cohesion. An almost obsessive emphasis on unity and cohesion, at the expense of diversity, has not just simply been a republican product. It was also the dominant principle of modernizing the heterodox and autonomous communities of Ottoman society during the nineteenth century. These autonomous communities, with their separate jurisdictions and internal administrations, posed the greatest challenge to the idea of a single political community organized around the same rights and duties. In their subsequent efforts to introduce constitutionalism, the Ottoman modernizing elite aimed to create a single unified community, but failed to recognize that the various communities of the empire desired separation from the empire. It is precisely for this reason that the republican elite identified the heterodox nature of the empire as the principal cause of its disintegration and regarded Ottoman administrators as insufficiently radical to implement the conditions that would be conducive to realizing as unified homogeneous community.

Notwithstanding the historical connections between the Ottoman Empire and France, the French-style, Rousseauian citizenship regime, with its clear distinction between the public and the private, and its assumed role of the state as neutral, became a natural model for the citizenship regime in republican Turkey. The republican regime defined its political project as creating a modern national community and the citizenship regime became the central site through which such a community was to be created. Within the last decade, however, the republican political project has come under scrutiny by groups who claim that their values and aspirations have been excluded from the conditions of membership in the republican project. While Kurdish nationalism has expressed itself in a separatist movement, Islamist groups have addressed the question of citizenship both in terms of political representation and cultural politics. The Islamist challenge to universal citizenship has organized itself in two distinct areas. First, by seeking representation in the political realm, they have utilized the legal framework of citizenship; and second, by raising group-identity demands in the public sphere, they have endeavored to expand the boundaries of universal citizenship. In both areas, Islamist politics question and redraw the boundaries of citizenship in order to gain greater representation in the public sphere. Their demands constitute a radical challenge to republican citizenship, introducing private identities into the public sphere, and seeking representation in the public sphere based on group identities, rather than on the accepted grounds of universal citizenship. Central to Islamist claims is the charge that universal citizenship's promise of equality masks the inherent inequalities of the private realm and fails to address their specific universe or life-world.

This paper argues that these projects – the republican citizenship regime and its critique by Islamists – define themselves in relation to the Ottoman tradition of community. That is to say that the modernizing elite adopted the Rousseauian notion of republican citizenship practices, not only in order to formulate a homogeneous national community united around a single common good, but also as a reaction to the heterodox communal structure of the Ottoman Empire. While trying to overcome the community-based social structure and aiming to separate individuals from their traditional kinship, ethnic and religious ties by making them equal members of modern national society, the republican regime created another communitarian project in which multiplicity and pluralism were limited in order to realize a common good. Although Islamists formulate their challenge as a response to republican citizenship practices, their alternative is another communitarian project, entrenched in the Ottoman definition of community. As a response to the universal citizenship of the republican regime, Islamists' alternative to this date is a community of independent and autonomous communities similar to those that existed in the Ottoman Empire. The paper further argues that both republican citizenship, and the Islamist challenge to it, have at their center a communitarian orientation of citizenship, which refuses to accept the fact that identity positions are always fluid and transferable. In this respect, both the republican and Islamist interpretation of citizenship aim to minimize the role of the democratic political process, through which identities are defined and group boundaries are redrawn.

The following section will look at how republican citizenship excluded private identities from the public realm in order to realize dominant and homogeneous identities. Following this, we shall consider the short-lived "Medina Document" debate to explore the Islamist interpretation of citizenship.

Citizenship and representation of national identity in Turkey

The idea of universal citizenship, that is of individuals having the same rights and responsibilities with respect to representation and participation in public life, is a direct outcome of modern community based on the rights of sovereign individuals. The modern national community struggled hard to establish itself against the persistence of religious, ethnic and various other identities that were the basis of community in the feudal world (Smith 1988); and (Smith 1992) contrary to the feudal notion of community, where membership was based on the hierarchy of groups, the modern notion of civic nationalism saw the sovereign individual as its legitimate agent around which membership in the community was organized (Isin and Wood 1999).

Turkish modernity adopted this republican version of civic nationalism not only as the logical outcome of building a modern nation-state, but as a historically specific response to the heterogeneous Ottoman system which was based on and organized around religious group rights. The modernizing elite in Turkey identified group-based membership as one of the biggest obstacles standing in the way of creating a socially integrated national community. Universal citizenship was important for creating a new self and society because it was the site of all that which was deemed to be new, modern and progressive. The republican elite considered the community defined by ethnic and religious loyalties as one of the biggest obstacles to realizing a modern national gesellschaft. Mardin argues that the Kemalist elite saw the communitarian organization of traditional Ottoman society as a serious obstacle to the creation of this autonomous subject (Mardin 1992).[1] The gemeinschaft nature of the *mahalle*[2] system, with its strict islamic moral value system at its center, did not provide a sphere of independent action for the individual. Putting the community before the individual, the communitarian *mahalle* system not only obstructed the autonomy of the individual but also eliminated any difference that was not in harmony with the values of community. In addition, the *mahalle* system, with its cell-like organization, created islands of communities within the city which were very much in tune with the general organization of Ottoman society as distinct and separate "millets." Generally the millet system and the organization of cities around the *mahalle* system was said to be responsible for the lack of civil society in late Ottoman society. This distinctive character of the Ottoman system kept the traditional societal organization intact and did not allow civil society to emerge as an autonomous social sphere.[3]

The republican modernizing elite knew that in order to create a modern nation-state, they had to break with the gemeinschaft of the *mahalle* system and form an autonomous social space in which the modern subject would be the agent. Mardin argues that Atatürk was aware of the monotonous and uniform nature of the *mahalle* community and the obstacles it posed to the emergence of the modern subject. He was determined to break with the communitarian system by introducing a series of reforms ranging from education to the control of religion (Mardin 1992: 76).[4] Similarly, Sarıbay points out that the modernizing elite, in order to create a sphere of individual autonomy, aimed to replace community with society, gemeinschaft with gesellschaft. For them, it was society, with its diversified division of labor and freedom from religious and communal constraints, and not the community that would provide the basis for individual autonomy (Sarıbay 1994: 146–8). Furthermore, the public sphere of equally situated citizens eliminates the chaotic world of various groups and private identities that may have differing values that do not necessarily conform to those of the common good of the national community.

The relationship between national identity and universal citizenship has another important function in the case of republican Turkey: citizenship facilitates social integration: Individuals are assumed to have one common goal to realize. Particularly in the Turkish republican experience, universal citizenship is the basis for social integration formulated by a Rousseauian General Will. The universal citizenship of the republican tradition replaces the individual wills of private individuals with the Rousseauian General Will of the entire body of citizens (Baker 1992).

In this respect, citizenship in Turkey operated as a societal project through which modern national identity could be created. Because of this the properties of the universal citizenship were rationalism, progress, the modern nation, and secularism, whereas those relegated to the private realm were ethnic identities, religion, and traditional social relations (Sunar 1996). The citizenship regime in Turkey had the specific mission of representing a modern and rational society while the habits of traditional society were left to the private sphere. What is important to emphasize, however, is that the modern project did not seek to eradicate tradition from the minds of the people. Rather, the universal citizenship practices simply worked to confine tradition to the private realm.[5]

As noted earlier, the Turkish Republic based its legal framework on positive law, where all citizens are equal before the law, while establishing a modern bureaucracy to provide services to all citizens. The principle of populism proposed that no differences exist among citizens, refusing "preferential" treatment to any group, class, family or individual. The modern reforms were detailed enough to ensure an impartial public life where the state treats citizens as equals. Toprak defines the neutrality of the citizenship regime in Turkey as follows:

> Turkey is among the few non-Western countries which were not colonized and which inherited a bureaucracy and an intellectual milieu already under the influence of universal legal forms. The reforms of the early republican period laid the foundations for a secular legal system which recognized gender equality, secular education, and a conception of public service, both within the bureaucracy and in the political arena, which did not rest on class differentiation, ethnic background or kinship ties. Thus, the political and the bureaucratic establishment never belonged to a specific ethnic group, family, clan or people of the same class. This is important for state-society relations. A conception of the public sphere which is value neutral in terms of ethnic or kinship ties and which rests on universal criteria does not exist in many parts of the developing world and perhaps explains the unique position of Turkey in the Middle Eastern context.
>
> (Toprak 1996: 87)

Toprak's description of the citizenship regime in Turkey as unique in the Middle Eastern context is a correct assessment. Yet, the implementation of universal citizenship in Turkey is also different from Western experience. Contrary to Western citizenship practices, based on exclusionary practices and a long history of painful political struggle for inclusion by marginalized groups like ethnic minorities or women, Turkish citizenship was inclusionary from the beginning. In order to create a socially integrated national community out of heterogeneous groups of people, Turkish modernization included various ethnic and religious groups under the umbrella of universal citizenship. However accurate Toprak's account of the neutrality of Turkish citizenship, it fails to recognize the double problematic of the citizenship regime. This is that the very principle of universal citizenship is centered around a notion of the common good. This depends on creating a homogeneous national identity, resulting in other forms of exclusionary practices which hinder the representation of particular groups and identities. Like Habermas, Toprak assumes that the neutrality of the public sphere is sufficient to ensure the existence of a democratic and inclusive political system. Like Habermas, Toprak also assumes that the differences and complexities of the private realm can be offset by the public sphere as long as its neutrality can be preserved. Behind this is the assumption that there is a clear separation between the public and private: individuals enter the public sphere without their private identities. The public sphere's neutrality is supposed to ensure inclusion and participation for all, irrespective of background and identity. The Turkish public sphere was probably far more sensitive about the principle of neutrality due to the fact that at the center of the modern reforms was the attempt to create an integrated and homogeneous nation-state.

In stratified societies, as Fraser has argued, the institutional framework produces inequality among citizens and the idea of a single, neutral public does not address these existing inequalities. Furthermore, disadvantaged groups and identities do not have a real chance to participate in the public sphere no matter how neutral citizenship practices may be. Even in a multicultural society, the single, neutral public does not provide justice to all groups and identities within society because the framework of the public is defined by the culturally dominant group (Fraser 1992). In sum, the institutional neutrality of the citizenship regime does not also automatically lead to economic and cultural neutrality. Power imbalances emerging from economic and cultural differences will exclude some groups from full participation, such as the representation of their cultural identities, and limit others from participating in it altogether. The neutrality of the citizenship regime, therefore, does not guarantee equal participation, nor that people may engage in peaceful negotiation of differences.

The cultural, not to mention economic, differences that existed in Turkish society thus rendered meaningless any institutional neutrality in the citizenship regime. The principles of a state-controlled secularism, nationalism and rationalism framed the boundaries of membership in such a way that its citizens could only be equal, and the operation of the citizenship regime could only be value-neutral, within the boundaries of these principles. In the case of state-controlled secularism, where secularism was not only a principle of the regime but also part of the regulative aspect of everyday life, the issue of dress, such as women's dress or male hats, became an important source of exclusion (Göle 1996). Similarly, where national identity constitutes the basis of citizenship, the existence of other particular groups in the public realm could turn into a crisis. Like any other nation-state, Turkey contained, and still contains, different cultural and ethnic groups. By assuming that there was a single public sphere whose authorized identity was the national one, the modern project eliminated the possibility that other groups would participate in the public sphere with their own identity. Citizens could be part of the public only if they left their particular identities in the private realm. This strictly crafted and controlled public sphere, which ensured the unity of the people and the state, not only operated as a strictly communitarian project, but it was also based on the exclusion of those other(s) whose values and aspirations were not in harmony with the general will of the modern project.

Community and citizenship

The key defining characteristic of the post-1980 political landscape in Turkey was the multiplication of identity positions and their struggle for inclusion in the public sphere. Kurdish nationalism and political Islam have presented the most important challenges to the boundaries of universal citizenship, and its homogeneous representation of national identity. By drawing attention to the exclusionary nature of the national identity, Kurdish nationalism poses a serious challenge to its privileged position of Turkish identity. Political Islam represents another challenge to secular citizenship; but unlike Kurdish nationalists, however, Islamists were able to establish themselves in the public sphere as political actors and to question the fundamental aspects of citizenship and national identity (Sakallıoğlu 1996). Islamists have consistently attacked the equating of modernity with secularism and Westernization. The growing urban Islamist population, who have considerable economic power and an intellectual background, demand that a religious life style be included in the public sphere. Islamists have been particularly successful in organizing themselves in civil society (Toprak 1996: 106–22). The Islamic bourgeoisie, with very efficient and active business organizations, and the Islamist intellectuals, with their vibrant publishing community, have been crucial in opening up space in the public sphere.[6]

Central to both Islamist and Kurdish challenges to the Turkish citizenship model is the attempt to question the conditions of membership in the national community. Universal citizenship in Turkey rests on the exclusion of group identities from the public sphere, privileging national identity as the only legitimate identity. It, therefore, functions as a basis for social integration, or as I argued earlier, fulfills the role of realizing the aims of the modernization process. In this way, citizenship is not just simply a set of legal codes, defining the boundaries of membership in the national community, but also a set of cultural practices, representing modern national identity. Ethnic and religious concerns reveal universal citizenship's limits in that having the same legal status does not necessarily satisfy the demands of groups and identities who have specific claims of representation. The tension in the Turkish case runs particularly high, as citizenship has a specific mission of realizing and representing the premises of the modern regime.

However, similar tensions exist in other nation-states where universal citizenship constitutes the basis of membership of the community. In late modern democratic societies there is now a strong demand to extend universal citizenship rights to include groups-rights. Groups who have historically been marginalized, or whose life-world does not conform with that of the dominant national discourse, demand specific rights to protect their own belief system. They, therefore, seek representation in the public sphere, rejecting the idea of a single common good as articulated by national discourse. The communitarian critique highlights the fact that universal citizenship is not sensitive to the value systems of particular groups. Communitarians argue that while citizens may be equal under the law, this does not mean that particular groups will have a chance to create their own space in the public sphere.[7] Furthermore, communitarians criticize the modern belief that the "good life" is an ideal shared by all members of a national community (Benhabib 1992: 78–9). Realizing a multiplicity of "good lives" requires recognizing the autonomy of collective identities in the public sphere.[8] The reasoning behind groups' need for recognition in the public is twofold: (a) skepticism toward the principle of equality; and (b) acknowledging the situatedness of identity. Communitarians are, in general, skeptical of the modern belief that citizens are located equally in the public sphere when in fact they are able to express their particular definition of the "good life" in the public sphere. For this reason, communitarians point to the necessity of acknowledging the autonomy of communities and of recognizing their definition of the good life as legitimate. Rather than promoting a common definition of the good life, communitarians argue that the public sphere should acknowledge a particular definition of the good life and implement the necessary normative and institutional frameworks to protect those particular goods.

The communitarian critique proposes a new mode of societal organization in which the identities of the private realm are not only situated in public life, but their autonomy is granted so that they can protect their own interpretation of what the good life means. To put it differently, by criticizing the equality principle and emphasizing the situatedness of identities in the public sphere, the communitarian critique refuses the primacy of a single common good and aims to restore the condition of plurality not always accommodated within universal citizenship. The communitarian version of citizenship, however, sharply contrasts with the nation-state principle that bases rights and duties of citizens on the individual rather than the group. While attempting to remedy the inequalities in the public sphere, the communitarian critique leads to an equally difficult issue of who decides the boundaries and who defines the common good in each group. More important, universal citizenship and its communitarian critique have a common intersection point as they both inadvertently run the risk of restricting identity negotiation. While universal citizenship attempts to unite society around a single concept of the common good by ignoring the specific conditions and expectations of different groups and identities, the communitarian alternative would box individuals into identity positions and would only represent citizens within the boundaries of their community and not by their individuality. Yet the tension in the universal citizenship regime is a real one, and various groups and identities demand that their specific value systems be recognized and protected. This tension is nothing but a growing contention over how the question of difference and plurality should be addressed in late modern societies, and at its center lies the assertion that those private identities and value systems of different groups are in fact public matters. The demand for the recognition of groups arises from the argument that true equality in the public sphere depends on the protection of their value systems. The argument is that the way to restore equality to the citizenship regime is to protect identities and groups who have historically been marginalized and forbidden to represent themselves in their own right.

The Medina Document: an Islamist alternative to universal citizenship

Islamists in Turkey consistently focus on the fact that their value system and group choices are not always in harmony with the values of the modern regime on which citizenship is based. Apart from the legal framework, they also express disagreement with the representation of modern national identity and their exclusion from it in the public sphere. Islamist demands on citizenship do not simply focus on the legal framework, but also on life style choices and their representation in the public sphere. In other words, Islamists claim that they cannot articulate their group-specific value system in the public sphere and that they are excluded from the representation of national identity. Islamist demands and their critique of universal citizenship usually give rise to suspicion in the secular camp. Secularists claim that Islamist demands are simply an attempt to divert the secular regime and base citizenship on religious practices instead. Furthermore, the Islamist demands are also contentious, as the direct relationship between modernization and universal citizenship leaves religious codes and symbols out of the public domain. The debate therefore is not just simply limited to the Islamist threat to transform citizenship along religious principles, but also about whether it is possible to accommodate the religious life style in the public sphere. It is because of this that the appearance of religious symbols in the public sphere sparks fierce debate. Headscarved women in universities, public buildings and in the parliament; the growing influence of Islamic capital; religious orders; street names and mosques in places that are representative of the republican regime are all areas of political struggle by which the Islamists attempt to broaden the boundaries of the public sphere and exercise their citizenship rights.

As the Islamists' politics gained significant power during the first half of the 1990s, the clash between secular and Islamist life styles became particularly visible in big metropolitan centers where a secular life style is the established norm. The growing Islamist presence in the public sphere, and demands for recognition of associated values, constituted a direct challenge to modern national identity (Toprak and Birtek 1993). In the 1994 municipal elections, the victory of the Islamist Welfare Party further polarized the issue, as it enabled Islamists to gain access to public institutions and to promote an Islamic presence in the public sphere. The growing presence of an Islamist life style in metropolitan centers politicized the debate about the nature of national community, its boundaries, and who is included and excluded, as well as about the rules of membership and the possibility of changing those rules. In a way, the Islamists' demands for recognition in the public sphere, and the debate over whether the modern public sphere should accommodate religious codes and life style choices, is really a debate about the conditions of living together and of membership in the community. The question is one of how to accommodate differences without necessarily imposing them on groups and identities who do not share the specific value systems of groups seeking recognition in the public sphere.

As I mentioned earlier, the secular camp is particularly suspicious about the sincerity of the Islamist position in allowing different value systems to co-exist that are not part of the Islamic one. The widespread argument is that Islamists use the democratic process to further their causes and, at the right moment, they will eliminate the freedom of other groups and identities who do not share their value system. In order to counter this suspicion, Islamist intellectuals proposed a short-lived alternative citizenship project, drawing on the Medina Document as a social contract between various groups of different beliefs. The Islamist proposal of the Medina Document is partly influenced by the Ottoman social organization of the millet system, and was mainly based on the document that defined the rules of relationship between Muslim and non-Muslim communities during the time of the Prophet Muhammad.

A geographical entity that stretched from Africa to Europe, the Ottoman Empire had a heterogeneous, multi-religious and multi-ethnic population which made dealing with difference and particularity an important issue. In terms of the way in which it dealt with particularity, Ottoman universality was radically different from the universalism of the modern nation-state. Rather than creating a unified single community, the Ottoman "millet system" ensured the existence of community rights and organizations of the non-Muslim groups in the empire.[9]

The Ottoman administration divided the population into two major groups or millets: Muslim and non-Muslim. Every non-Muslim group or sect was autonomous millet with its own leader representing it. The leader of each millet was the mediator between his community and the administration. In addition, every millet had complete autonomy in religious matters as well as in the regulation of everyday life from education, marriage, health, communications and social security. The millets of the Ottoman Empire were subjected only to the penal code of the administration. Thereafter, they had complete autonomy guaranteed by declarations. The organizational structure of the millet system not only gave autonomy to the major religious communities, but it also permitted the autonomy of sects and other groups. This system of autonomous communities guaranteed the existence, and relative equality, of different groups, ethnicities and religions within the same administrative unit without subjecting them to a single unitary core.[10] The Ottoman millet system reflected the plurality of the population by recognizing the autonomous organization of different belief systems, and was a clear indication of the fact that Ottomans did not pursue an active assimilation and subjugation policy like other major world empires such as the British Empire (Eryılmaz 1994).

The Ottoman millet system, to a large degree, was influenced by the Islamic Zimmi legal code which could be traced to the Medina Document. The Medina Document was a legal document or a contract acknowledging the autonomy of other religious communities and defining the boundaries between Muslim and non-Muslim communities (Köktaş 1994: 59). After migrating from Mecca to Medina in 622 in order to flee from prosecution, the Prophet Muhammad established a political community in Medina with his followers. In the process of establishing an Islamic community the Prophet signed an agreement with non-Muslims in Medina which was later called the Medina Document. In the Medina Document, non-Muslim communities were given the right to organize a legal system emerging from their own beliefs (Algül 1994: 64). While different groups had autonomy in deciding their legal framework according to their beliefs, in the case of inter-community conflict, they were supposed to seek the arbitration of the Prophet. The historical significance of the Medina Document comes from the fact that it stands as a contractual agreement between the Muslim and non-Muslim communities of Medina, recognizing each community's autonomy. According to Islamists, the fact that the Prophet decided to make a social contract with other communities signifies that it is possible to have a pluralist society in Islam. In other words Islamists read the Medina Document as a societal project, allowing for plurality and tolerance within a society that is governed by Islamic rules.

Islamist intellectuals, particularly Ali Bulaç, introduced the Medina Document in the early 1990s as a Muslim project of "living together." Bulaç criticizes the unitary nation-state model for assimilating differences into a single value system and subjugating them to the power of the majority (Bulaç 1994: 5). He argues that the nation-state with a single executive, the judiciary and legislative system, has a homogenizing function, hindering the manifestation of difference in public and putting minorities at a disadvantage. After pointing to the fragmentation of nation-states within the globalization process, Bulaç indicates the need to propose new forms of "living together" which would enable greater plurality than exists in the arrangements of the nation-state (Bulaç 1994: 8). Unless there are alternatives to the homogenizing forms of nation-states that are crumbling as a result of the globalization process, it would be impossible to stop conflicts from emerging from the coexistence of different religious and ethnic groups. For Bulaç, the only way to enable different belief systems to manifest themselves freely would be to abandon the single judicial system and adopt a system consisting of multiple judicial systems permitting each community to live according to its belief system (Bulaç 1994: 13).

It is argued that a political system based on the Medina Document would not pose any obstacles for organizing different religious, philosophical and ideological positions, as Islam rejects any imposition of a particular religious belief (Bulaç 1994: 13). Pointing to the *Bakara* verse in the Quran, which rejects the imposition of religious belief, Bulaç suggests that different groups, including secular and atheist elements as well as other ideologies, can form their life spaces. As long as they do not wage "war" on Muslims, members of other beliefs should pursue their life style according to their value system.

For Islamist intellectuals, the Medina Document is not simply a utopian ideal but an actual historical experience that created a contractual relationship between the different religious communities of Medina between the years 622 and 632CE (Bulaç 1994: 12). The Ottoman millet system, organized around the autonomy of religious communities, shows similarities with the contractual relationship based on the Medina Document. Yet, the Islamists stress a fundamental difference between the Medina Document and the Ottoman millet system. In the Ottoman millet system a hierarchy existed between religious communities. The Muslim community was the "sovereign nation" (*millet-i hakime*) and non-Muslim communities were "subjected nations" (*millet-i mahkume*), in contrast, in the Medina Document, no such hierarchical division existed, with each community awarded equal status. Islamists point out that, unlike the Ottoman millet system based on the sovereignty of the Muslim community, the Medina Document proposes a project of living together based on equal participation (Canatan 1994: 106). The normative framework of the Medina Document, the Islamists argue, provides a "realistic" alternative, enabling a pluralistic civil-society-based societal project to be realized. The idea of multiple judicial systems in the Medina Document was in fact picked up by the Islamist Welfare Party. Its leader, Necmettin Erbakan, made multiple-judicial systems part of the Welfare Party's election campaign, arguing that unlike the stereotypical image of Islamic parties, the Welfare Party is seeking a pluralistic society in which different communities can live according to their value systems.

The Medina Document as an alternative citizenship contract is, borrowing from Eickelman and Piscatori, an attempt to revoke and reinvent a historical tradition in order to respond to the challenges of the present day (Eickelman and Piscatori 1996: 30). The Islamists' invoking of the Medina Document does not just simply represent an attempt to go back in history, but to reorganize the present by reinventing the past. Given the fact that all nation-states justify their existence by inventing traditions and rewriting the past in order to create "imagined" cohesiveness, the Medina Document constitutes a similar attempt by Islamists to provide an alternative societal project to that proposed by the modern nation-state. The Medina Document, first and foremost, attempts to "transcend modernity and its political forms" to form a new societal contract that would not conflict with Islam (Bulaç 1994: 14). Yet, while attempting to transcend modernity and its political forms, Islamist politics, at least on an intellectual level, addresses an inherently modern concern: plurality and its manifestation in civil society. Islamist intellectuals present the Medina Document as proof that Islam is actually capable of accommodating a pluralist society, since the document clearly states that the relationship between different beliefs is not hierarchical but based on equality (Akçam 1992: 14). Moreover, it is argued that the Medina Document gives priority to civil society over the state because the communities themselves decide what is good and bad for the community

(Çelik 1994: 27). The cultural, judicial and religious autonomy of different communities requires activities like law, culture, science, art, economics, health and education to be left to civil society and that the state not have any say over these areas of societal life (Abdiimamoğlu 1994: 43; Bulaç 1992: 110). In the contractual Medina model proposed, the function of the state is to serve citizens and protect the different values and life styles of communities forming the society (Dilipak 1992: 20).

Similar to the communitarian alternative to universal citizenship, the Medina Document proposes a vision of membership to a community that is radically opposed to the civic republican tradition of the modern nation-state. In the Medina-based project, the agents of the public sphere are autonomous communities, not individual citizens. This is reflected in the advocacy of multiple judicial systems based on the value systems of those communities. The societal project based on the Medina Document, therefore, does not envision a single citizenship regime but multiple citizenships, organized around autonomous communities with their own legal framework. As one of the most distinguishing characteristics of the modern regime is the single public sphere with universal citizenship and unified legal framework, the Islamists' alternative proposes to address the question of plurality outside the framework of the modern regime. Again similar to the communitarian critique, the Islamist demand for multiple citizenship regimes based on the autonomy of communities has two motives. First, since people wishing to live by an Islamic value system do not have the opportunity to fulfill their desires under a single common-good oriented citizenship, they need a special framework that would accommodate their life style choices; and if other communities do not wish to be part of the Islamic framework, then they should be free to organize themselves as they desire. Only in this way, according to the Islamist alternative, can the condition of plurality be realized within the boundaries of the nation-state.

Even though the Medina Document project, by insisting on inclusion of groups-rights into the citizenship regime, exhibits a communitarian orientation, it also differs from it in one important area: the Medina Document does not simply challenge the universal citizenship regime by requiring group-specific rights within it, but goes further and calls for the elimination of the universal citizenship regime and its replacement with segregated, group-based membership. In other words, the Medina Document as a societal project does not call for an accommodation of Islamic values within the existing citizenship regime, but aims to establish separate jurisdictions available to groups who share any given value system.

Conclusion: identity, negotiation and citizenship

Apart from a brief period when the Islamist Welfare Party attempted to use the Medina Document to argue for multiple judicial systems, the whole debate mostly remained an intellectual exercise. Yet, the Medina Document's significance is not so much whether it had a real chance to become a societal alternative, but it is an attempt to discuss how to accommodate the demands and choices of different groups and identities within nation-states. In countries such as France or Turkey, where the civic republican tradition constitutes the basis of the citizenship regime, various groups and identities claim that their specific life style choices are excluded from the public sphere, and, therefore, that they do not have full citizenship rights. The headscarf issue in French public schools and Turkish universities is an example of such claims. In a secular public sphere, Islamists argue that they cannot exercise their rights as citizens since life style choices exclude them from certain places and activities. Their argument points to the fact that the neutral public sphere in which disembedded equal citizens exercise their membership rights is an illusion, not only because citizens take part in the public sphere with their private and group identities, but also because those identities and associated values may be in direct confrontation in the universal citizenship regime.

The issue of a neutral public sphere upon which universal citizenship is based is particularly problematic in Turkey. Here the public sphere, rather than being neutral, reflects a certain interpretation of modernity and functions as an integral part of national discourse. This close relationship between public sphere and national discourse unavoidably influences citizenship in that groups whose values conflict with those of the national discourse are usually excluded from the public sphere. This is why, despite the claim to neutrality, the universal citizenship regime in Turkey has a communitarian orientation: the sites of citizenship practices are reserved for national identity, easily becoming hostile to differences that fall outside of it.

Ironically, the Islamist proposal of the Medina Document, despite its claim to accommodate difference and plurality, results in another communitarian project. The contractual Medina model of citizenship abandons the idea of a single citizenship regime, yet it envisions a society with multiple judicial systems that are separate from one another in a single territory. As the core of society in the Medina Document is based on communities (*umma*), the separation of these communities according to their belief systems begs the question of who defines the boundaries of these communities, who makes the decisions about membership, and more importantly how the relationship between different communities is organized in the absence of a common framework. During the time of the original Medina Document, the Prophet was the arbiter between different communities. It is not clear if the state would take the same kind of role in a society based on the principles of the Medina Document.

As I argued in the earlier sections of this chapter, the debate around citizenship in Turkey only becomes meaningful with reference to Ottoman history. This is particularly visible in the state's response to Kurdish and Islamist claims for greater representation in the public sphere. These demands are usually rejected on two grounds; first, representation of ethnic and religious identities would result in the dismantling of the unity of the nation. Second, the secular establishment usually argues that ethnic and religious identities are entitled to have the same rights and obligations as other citizens, and demands arising from their specific cultural claims belong to the private realm not the public sphere.

When looking at the underlying principles of the civic republican tradition and the Islamist alternative, we see that both approaches deny the dialogical and mobile character of identities and groups. As Taylor argues, one of the fundamental aspects of identity formation is its dialogical character (Taylor and Gutmann 1992: 32). Identity signifies difference, and because of this we do not form our identities in isolation from others but in relation and through dialog with them. This process of individual and group identification is a political one as it sometimes indicates a struggle for identification (Taylor and Gutmann 1992: 33). This political and dialogical aspect of identity formation is also the guarantee that neither single group nor individual has a frozen identity; instead there is constant change and mobility within and between identities.

This is why Habermas' insistence on a disembedded public sphere where universal citizenship operates, is an illusion (Habermas 1989). Instead, the public sphere is a site where claims are constantly made, shaping and redefining identities. While the civic republican tradition may hinder the process of renegotiating identities by insisting on a single common good, around which citizenship practices are defined, the Islamist alternative also denies the interchange and crisscrossing between different identity positions by segregating groups and locking them into separate legal jurisdictions. Since society is based on communities and their value systems, an individual's identity can only be defined in relation to the community of which he/she is a member. The rigid separation of communities rules out the possibility of the shifting of identities, locking identities instead within their respective communities. The priority of the community ignores individual identity, and the separation of communities according to their value systems prevents the possibility of identities being remade through interaction with others.

Citizenship does not constitute an unchanging and static practice but its history in modern times manifests a great deal of struggle by which various groups and identities have sought recognition and inclusion (Isin and Wood 1999). The current debates around citizenship highlight another phase in this process of not only redrawing the boundaries of membership to a national community but also of focusing on how those members use their citizenship rights. Citizenship debates reflect a desire to broaden plurality and accommodate the life-worlds of various groups and identities that exist in nation-states. In this respect, citizenship practices should not simply be seen as legal practices that define the condition of membership, but also as active political struggles that broaden membership boundaries as well as allowing different groups and identities to articulate their differences (Isin and Wood 1999). Citizenship debates in the Turkish context demonstrate that universal citizenship is not flexible enough to enable the representation of different identities in the public sphere. However, any alternative that suggests the reorganization of membership strictly on communitarian principles also contains the danger of not only segregating differences but also potentially freezing the meaning of identities by denying the political negotiation between them. Overcoming this obstacle requires, as suggested by Fuat Keyman, a radical democratization process in which issues of identity/difference cease to be a matter for the private realm but become part of citizenship practices (Keyman 1998: 37). Both universal citizenship and the communitarian alternative of the Medina Document lack a framework within which political struggle and negotiation can take place. Rethinking citizenship practices within the context of radical democracy requires a framework that enables the recognition of contradictions as part of the formation of identities (Keyman 1998: 38). Only here will claims for recognition cease to be a threat to the existing citizenship regime and instead become practices that further democratize it.

Notes

1 The same article was also published in Mardin.

2 Even though *mahalle* in its technical description indicates an administrative system within a city, according to Mardin it is also a social space where the average Ottoman subject used to spend his/her life. *Mahalle* is a self-contained space where residents receive their education and celebrate marriage and birth, as well as where deaths are mourned. The center of the *mahalle* is a mosque where the imam acts not only as a religious leader but also a community organizer. For more see Mardin (1992: 73–4). That the defining characteristic of the *mahalle* system was a strong and strict application of its communal value system ensured individual compliance with these values. It was, for instance, common for *mahalle* residents to break into the houses of single women when there was gossip involving a relationship with a man. In the Ottoman literature and traditional Ottoman theater, themes focusing on the structure of *mahalle* and the relationships in it occupy an important place.

3 For more on the development of civil society in late Ottoman society see Mardin (1987: 7–16) and Sarıbay (1994).

4 Mardin also argues that Atatürk was significantly different from his comrades in the sense that he paid more attention to the concept of "individual autonomy." He argues that, given that during his time fascism and communism were rising as totalitarian systems, he clearly stayed away from populist dictatorship (Mardin 1992: 18).

5 Given the fact that secularism was one of the principles of modern citizenship that received special attention from the modernizing elite, because they firmly believed that society could not be modern if religion played a public role, religion was not banned on a personal level. Comparisons are usually made between the early days of the Turkish Republic's attitude toward religion and those of socialist countries. Unlike the socialist countries, the modernizing elite in Turkey did not ban religious practice altogether but paid special attention to eliminating religion's role in public life. The best example of this attitude is probably the role of the state in religious education. With the 1924 law of unification of all education, religious education

came under strict control of the state. For more on the relationship between the state and religion see Sarıbay (1985) and Tarhanlı(1993).

6 For the case of Islamist intellectuals see Toprak (1993) and Göle (2000).

7 For an outline of the communitarian argument see Mulhall and Swift (1996). For more on the communitarian argument, see MacIntyre (1984). Also Charles Taylor (Taylor and Gutmann 1992).

8 Taylor, for instance, argues that in the case that there is danger to the survival of a particular community, it is justifiable to grant special rights that would allow the community to ensure its survival (Taylor and Gutmann 1992).

9 First it needs to be noted that "millet" (nation) had a different connotation in the Ottoman case. It did not designate nations as we understand them in the modern sense, but religious communities. Eryılmaz points out that "millet" in its Arabic meaning refers to a group of people who accept a certain belief system, and to the Ottoman administration that was based on the communities of belief (Eryılmaz 1994). Only after the emergence of modern nationalism does the word "millet" also designate nations based on culture, language and ethnicity.

10 For more on the Ottoman millet system see Eryılmaz (1992) and Canatan (1994).

References

Abdiimamoğlu, K. (1994) "Modern Anayasa Hukuku Açısıdan Medine Vesikasi" (The Medina Document According to Modern Constitutional Law), *Bilgi Ve Hikmet*, 5 (winter): 38–45.

Akçam, T. (1992) "Türkiye İçin Yeni Bir Toplumsal Projeye Doğru" (Toward a New Societal Project for Turkey), *Birikim*, 42 (October): 10–22.

Algül, H. (1994) "Asr-i Saadette İdari Hayat" (Administrative Life in the Golden Age), *Bilgi Ve Hikmet*, 5 (winter): 61–7.

Baker, K. M. (1992) "Defining the Public Sphere in Eigteenth-Century France," in C. Calhoun (ed.) *Habermas and the Public Sphere*, Cambridge MA: MIT Press.

Benhabib, S. (1992) *Situating the Self: Gender, Community, and Postmodernism in Contemporary Ethics*, New York: Routledge.

Bulaç, A. (1992) "Medine Vesikasi Hakkında Genel Bilgiler" (General Information about the Medina Document), *Birikim*, 42 (October): 22–30.

——(1994) "Birarada Yaşamanın Mümkün Projesi Medine Vesikasi" (The Medina Document as a Project of Living Together), *Bilgi Ve Hikmet*, 5 (winter): 3–15.

Canatan, K. (1994) "Toplum Tasarımları Ve Birlikte Yaşama Felsefesi" (Society Imaginations and Philosophy of Living Together), *Bilgi Ve Hikmet*, 5 (winter): 98–108.

Çelik, O. (1994). "Beraber Yaşama Sorunu, İnsanın Anlam Arayışı ve Siyasal Otorite" (The Question of Living Together, the Quest for Knowledge and Political Power), *Bilgi Ve Hikmet*, 5 (winter): 16–32.

Dilipak, A. (1992) "Farklılıklar İçinde Birarada Yaşama İlkesi ya da Medine Belgesi" (The Principle of Living Together with the Difference or the Medina Document), *Panel*, 41–2, August-September.

Eickelman, D. F. and J. P. Piscatori (1996) *Muslim Politics*, Princeton NJ: Princeton University Press.

Eryılmaz, B. (1992) *Osmanlı Devletinde Millet Sistemi* (The Ottoman Millet System), Istanbul: Ağaç Yayıncılık.

——(1994) "Birlikte Yaşama Düzeni: Osmanlı Millet Sistemi" (System of Living Together: The Ottoman Millet System), *Bilgi Ve Hikmet*, 5 (winter): 60–80.

Fraser, N. (1992) "Rethinking the Public Sphere," in C. Calhoun (ed.) *Habermas and the Public Sphere*, Cambridge MA: MIT Press.

Göle, N. (1996) *Authoritarian Secularism and Islamist Politics: The Case of Turkey*, Leiden: E. J. Brill.

——(1996) *Civil Society in the Middle East*, Leiden: E. J. Brill.

——(2000) "Snapshots of Islamic Modernities," *Daedalus*, 129 (1): 91–117.

Habermas, J. R. (1989) *The Structural Transformation of the Public Sphere: An Inquiry into a Category of Bourgeois Society*, Cambridge MA: MIT Press.

Isin, E. F. and Wood, P. K. (1999) *Citizenship and Identity*, Thousand Oaks: Sage.

Keyman, E. F. (1998) "Globalleşme Ve Türkiye: Radikal Demokrasi Olasılığı" (Globalization and Turkey: Radical Democracy Possibility), in E. F. Keyman and A. Y. Sarıbay (eds) *Küreselleşme, Sivil Toplum Ve İsam* (Globalization, Civil Society and Islam), Istanbul: Vadi Yayınları.

Köktaş, E. (1994) "Medine Vesikasi: İslam'in Çoğulculuk Referansı" (The Medina Document: Islam's Reference of Plurality), *Bilgi Ve Hikmet*, 5 (winter): 55–60.

MacIntyre, A. C. (1984) *After Virtue: A Study in Moral Theory*, Notre Dame IN: University of Notre Dame Press.

Mardin, Ş. (1981) "Türkiye'de Din ve Laiklik" (Religion and Secularism in Turkey), in A. Kazancıgil and E. Özbudun (eds) *Atatürk: Founder of a Modern State*, London: C. Hurst and Co.

——(1987) "Türk Toplumunu İnceleme Araç Olarak Sivil Toplum" (Civil Society as a Tool to Study Turkish Society), *Defter*, 2 (December-January): 52–80.

——(1992) *Türk Modernleşmesi* (Turkish Modernism), Istanbul: İletişim Yayınları.

——(1992) *Türkiye'de Din ve Laiklik* (Religion and Secularism in Turkey), Istanbul: Iletisim Yayınları

Mulhall, S. and Swift, A. (1996) *Liberals and Communitarians*, Oxford: Blackwell.

Sakallıoğlu, Ü. C. (1996). "Islam-State Interaction in Turkey," *International Journal of Middle East Studies*, 28 (2): 102–20.

Sarıbay, A. Y. (1985) *Türkiye'de Modernleşme, Din ve Parti Politikası* (Modernism in Turkey, Religion and Party Policy), Istanbul: İIletişim Yayınları.

——(1992) *Ethnicity and Nationalism*, New York: E. J. Brill.

——(1994) *Postmodernite, Sivil Toplum ve İslam* (Postmodernism, Civil Society and Islam), Istanbul: İletişim Yayınları.

Smith, A. D. (1992) *Ethnicity and Nationalism*, New York: Brill.

——(1988) *The Ethnic Origins of Nations*, Oxford: Blackwell.

Sunar, I. (1996) "State, Society and Democracy in Turkey," in V. Magtny and R. C. Nation (eds) *Turkey Between East and West: New Challenges for a Risinig Regional Power*, Boulder: Westview.

Tarhanlı, I. B. (1993) *Müslüman Toplum, "Laik Devlet:" Türkiye'de Diyanet İşleri Başkanlığı*, (Muslim Society, "Secular State:" Department of Religious Affairs), Istanbul: Afa Yayınları.

Taylor, C. and A. Gutmann (1992)*Multiculturalism and the Politics of Recognition: An Essay*, Princeton: Princeton University Press.

Toprak, B. (1993) "Islamist Intellectuals: Revolt against Industry and Technology," in M. Heper, A. Öncü and H. Kramer (eds) *Turkey and the West: Changing Political and Cultural Identities*, London: I. B. Tauris.

——(1996) "Civil Society in Turkey," in A. R. Norton (ed.) *Civil Society in the Middle East*, Leiden: E. J. Brill.

Toprak, B. and Birtek, F. (1993) "The Conflictual Agendas of Neo-Liberal Reconstruction and the Rise of Islamic Politics in Turkey: The Hazards of Rewriting Turkish Modernity," *Praxis International*, 13: 13–36.

3 The cultural and historical foundation of Turkish citizenship

Modernity as Westernization

Hasan Bülent Kahraman

Introduction

Turkey's relations with Europe have a long and tiresome history. The constitution of a modern nation-state through the discourse of modernity as Westernization is the main outcome of this history. This chapter is an attempt to analyze historically the cultural foundations of Turkish modernity and its state-centric nature. In doing so I will develop and then substantiate the argument that the republican understanding of citizenship has played a crucial role in the process of the state-centric and the "top down" implementation of modernity in Turkish society since the inception of the Republic in Turkey in 1923. Moreover, in playing this crucial role, citizenship has involved not only a legal status, but more importantly a "sociological and cultural practice" by which the nation-state has attempted to transform its society on the basis of such fundamental principles of Western modernity as positivism, rationalism and secularism. Thus, citizenship has constituted a *coup de grâce* forcé for the nation-state in its top-down positivist transformation of society as a way to make it modern, rational and secular.

It should be pointed out, however, that although Westernization has always been a defining element of Turkish modernity, citizenship has never contained in itself the language of individual rights and freedoms. On the contrary, it has always functioned in the service of the *nation-building process* as a cultural and legal code for the historical and discursive construction of the *Turkish national identity*. In what follows, I shall attempt to provide a historical account of the central place that citizenship has acquired in Turkish modernity in its services for nation-building. This account will help us understand the historical fact that neither citizenship nor nationalism in Turkey is immune to modernization. On the other hand, it is mainly the process of modernization as Westernization that constitutes the basic determinant or ground on which Turkish citizenship acts as a crucial cultural code for the construction of the unity between the nation-state and the secular-modern national identity.

In this chapter I will first analyze the cultural background of the Westernization procedure of Turkey as a "civilizing process." Second, I will try to show that in order to understand the shortcomings of Turkish citizenship, one should look into the internal contradictions of Kemalism, which has been the dominant ideology of the state-centric Turkish modernity. As I will elaborate in the following sections, the cultural foundation of Turkish citizenship is over-determined by Kemalism as a self-closing ideology that operates as a combination of liberalism and communitarianism in its modern and state-centric constitution. Finally, in the concluding part of this chapter, I will focus on the present-day crisis of Turkish citizenship, and in doing so I will argue that the further democratization of state-society relations in Turkey requires a liberal and constitutional reconstruction of Turkish citizenship in a way that articulates both individual and group rights, and functions as a civic and democratic identity.

The civilizing process and the sources of Turkish modernity

The notion of citizenship is a child of the nineteenth century and is embedded in the process of modernity. In Turkish modernity, citizenship has played an important role in the process of nation-building which involved both the creation of an independent nation and the modernization of it through Westernization. In this sense, the basic aim of the state was to Westernize the country, but at the same time to make it powerful enough to resist the West. This double-mentality of the Turkish nation-state, which continues even today, started to shape itself by the year 1839, and has evolved in three periods: 1839/1876–1908; 1908/1923–1980; and the 1990s. While the first two of these periods created the implementation and institutionalization of Westernization, the last one was concerned with the deep transformation of the already existing norms and institutions of Turkish modernity to make it compatible with the West, especially with the European Union. In this context the first two periods might be qualified as the formal attempts whereas the third period is more a content-based phenomenon. In these three different time-periods there have emerged drastic social, political, cultural and historical changes that have generated important impacts on state-society relations in Turkey.

This history of Turkish modernity goes all the way back to the Reformation period which began in the year 1839 with the *Gülhane Verdict*. In an empire attached to completely different social and political norms and cultures, the birth of the idea of citizenship in this period demarcated a definitive transition to an entirely new political understanding whose margins can be found in the whole transformative processes of the West. What is epitomized as Westernization in the Gülhane Verdict are the following attempts for (i) the construction of a new political understanding that could be put as the birth of a new political reasoning; (ii) the long process of secularization as the outcome and *raison d'être* of the new political opening and, finally, (iii) the construction of a new identity as the constitutive agent of the new political domain, that is citizenship. Thus,

Westernization is identified as the main process of modernization, functioning as the *legitimizing foundation of the new identity*. However, this new identity of the Gülhane Verdict was not considered within the context of citizenship. In the following section I will try to show how the early notions of Westernization and modernization are interconnected and how they have conveyed to the birth of the political realm as a separate entity geared toward the early conceptualization of the individual as a political agent and a cultural subject, which later gave rise to the emergence of the citizen.

The first period, 1839/1876–1908

As has been verified by Niyazi Berkes, the early attempt to understand Western civilization was made by Sadık Rıfat Paşa, who transferred the word "civilization" into the Ottoman language and left it "untranslated in its French form" (Berkes 1998: 131). Sadık Rıfat Paşa, in his writings, had anticipated the principles of the Reformation period long before its promulgation. In his *Essay*, written before 1837, he mentions "that European civilization was based on the fullest realization of human rights, the freedom and security of life, property and honor" (Berkes 1998: 131). Rıfat approaches European civilization as the foundational ground for modernization. However, insofar as modernization involves fundamental changes taking place both in polity and society, how to maintain the privileged status of polity over society in the process of modernization becomes the crucial question for the state. For this reason, Rıfat's approach to European civilization as modernization also constitutes the beginning of the double-mentality of the Turkish state in that it aims at modernizing its society, but at the same time attempts to maintain its power over societal actors. Thus, modernization in Turkish history also gives rise to a fundamental split between state and society, that is, a split between the societal calls for liberalism and decentralism on the one hand, and the statist and centralized preferences of state elites for order and stability on the other. Hence, the clash between the state and its citizens occurs: "There the governments are for the welfare of the citizens and not the citizens for the sake of the governments. It is because of this that the governments are run according to the rights of the people (*millet*) and according to law" (Berkes 1998: 131).

Şerif Mardin, in his seminal work, analyzing the *Selected Works* of Rıfat, clearly indicates that he advised a new system of law, "the essence of which would determine the limits of the permissible in a way that would preclude the exercise of personal whims" (Mardin 2000: 183). In this framework, Rıfat was proposing a *new system* that would depend on the rule of law. At the time he wrote his *Essay*, as Mardin puts it succinctly, this was a courageous step. What was obvious in his ideal system of law was that the Sultan would still be the source of the legitimacy, but on condition that he obeys the rule of law. Three points could be made regarding Rıfat's ideas in this context: (a) he comes from a Metternichian tradition (Mardin 2000:

178–82), having rather a "reactionary" position according to the European students of political theory; (b) Rıfat, in this conservative approach, is in search of a system that relies on the efficiency of the bureaucracy rather than tackling and developing the "abstract" notion of liberty, as Mardin emphasizes (2000: 179); and (c) no matter how relatively new, his ideas cannot be seen as purely original in the sense that Rıfat stays within the limits of the existing system and continues with constant reference to the Ottoman-Islamic system of law.

The first clash: Mustafa Fazıl, the dead-child of the liberal de-centralist group

The challenge to the suggestions of Rıfat's program comes from the writings of a less prominent figure among the Young Ottomans, Mustafa Fazıl Paşa. Mustafa Fazıl Paşa, in the *Letter* he wrote to Abdülaziz in 1867, eleven years after the proclamation of the Reform Edict, clearly draws attention to the "function" and "position" of religion. In a surprisingly daring way Fazıl writes that

> religion rules over the spirit, and promises other worldly benefits to us. But that *which determines and delimits the laws of the nation is not religion*. If religion does not remain in the position of eternal truths, in other words, *if it descends into interference with worldly affairs, it becomes a destroyer of all as well as of its own self.*
>
> (Berkes 1998: 208–9; emphasis added)

It was an open call for the separation of the sacred and the secular. With this call Fazıl was trying to emancipate the state from the hegemony of religion and place it in the domain of the worldly (Berkes 1998: 277). This approach prepares the fault line and the "famous" crack in the process of "constitutionalism," the dichotomy between state and religion.

Thus, Mustafa Fazıl differs from Rıfat in that he favors de-centralized authority and a less-strong state. Whereas Rıfat argues that

> public opinion and the inclinations of the people are like an overflowing river, and there are two situations which are impossible to overcome, one of them being religious belief and the other public opinion. Since to oppose them is dangerous and difficult, in the case of uprisings and stirrings of public opinion, the state should act accordingly to the currents of nature.
>
> (Mardin 2000: 187)

Fazıl challenges this argument by stating that "efficiency in the state machinery could not be obtained by a mere increase in control ... but, on the contrary, by *decreasing the grip of the state over the citizen*" (Mardin

2000: 279–80, emphasis added). The split between statism and de-centralism which remains always present in the course of Turkish modernity emerges from these two clashing arguments about what constitutes order and progress in society.

The second period, 1908/1923–1980: *plus ça change, plus c'est la même chose*

If one ever looked for the most important and burning question in the history of Turkish politics, it would be whether the period of mass transformations of the post-1923 era has been able to constitute a notion of citizenship. The period is vastly characterized by the idea of modernization as Westernization, and involves the implementation in Turkish society of the basic political and social norms and institutions of the West. In this context the period is considered to be the real basis for the transition to a verified notion of Westernization, enabling the conditions for the birth of civil citizens and the emergence of the autonomous political sphere. This procedure is read by a large group of students of Turkish politics as secularism.

Although it seems that the Kemalist period is radically different from the preceding ones, there is a strong element of continuation. This is quite understandable when the notion of "*derivative discourse*" is recalled. Chatterjee asserts in this context that in transition from one political and historical stage to the other, the discourse developed in the preceding one stays dominant, although it does not appear overt (Chatterjee, 1993). This statement forces us to analyze the Kemalist period and its relation to the *Second Meşrutiyet* (Constitutional) period, i.e. the period of the Young Ottomans. In this section I will attempt to show a remarkable continuity and similarity between the Kemalist period and that of the Young Ottomans. This will enable me to demonstrate convincingly the fact that Kemalism has fallen short in its attempt to create a civil notion of citizenship in the Western sense, although Westernization is the basic characteristic of the Kemalist period.

The man of transition and all seasons: Ziya Gökalp of 1908 and 1923

The main link between Kemalism and the Young Ottomans is nationalism as defined by the main theoretician of the period, namely Ziya Gökalp. He can be taken as the constitutive figure of the basic tenets of 1908 and 1923 in terms of both the way he defined Westernism and the way he handled the notion of Turkism. The basic concern of Gökalp was twofold. He was not only trying to find a mid-way or a synthesis between Westernism and Turkism, but also he was in an unending struggle to make the process of Westernization a cultural project which later was accepted and adapted by Kemal Atatürk. Citizenship, on this ground, once again is pushed back and given secondary importance, even though the cultural project of Westernization provisions a secular, "enlightened" social agent as the bearer of the process. This paradoxical situation can be explained by focusing on Gökalp's understanding of modernity and culture.

According to Gökalp, the notion of Westernism should be handled with care. The idea can be split into two parts: West as ideology and as technology. Between them there should be no hesitation, pertaining to the incorporation of the "Western mind" and significantly the technology it produced, because technology is identical with civilization and should be comprehended likewise and it is universal. Gökalp is extremely confident in his ideas and clearly argues that attaching to Western civilization is the only salvation:

> There is only one road to salvation: to advance in order to reach – that is in order to be equal to – Europeans in the sciences and industry as well as in military and judicial institutions. *And there is only one means to achieve this: to adapt ourselves to Western civilization completely.*
>
> (Gökalp 1959: 276, emphasis added)

At this point, Gökalp starts criticizing the "makers of Tanzimat" by arguing that "however, whatever they wanted to take from Europe, they always took not fully but by half" (Gökalp 1959: 276). This important essay, called "Towards the West", first appeared in the year 1923 then was reprinted in his famous and groundbreaking book *Principals of Turkism*, published in the same year. In it, Gökalp develops his criticism further by stating that the Europeanization of the *Tanzimat* was not a "real" one for it was a sort of Westernism relying on a formal basis. This was a new approach because, as Hanioğlu clearly shows, after World War I there was a group in Turkey calling for Westernization despite Europe (Hanioğlu 1985: 363). However the question turns out to be related to the limits of Westernization. In this context, Gökalp proposes a smart solution to the problem. It is the *differentiation between culture and civilization*. Coming from a Durkheimian origin, Gökalp formulates the relation between culture and nationalism (Parla 1985). According to Gökalp, civilization is universal whereas culture is national (Gökalp 1959: 281). Next, Gökalp tries to bring out the difference between cosmopolitanism and internationality by way of arguing that it is a mistake to believe that "there is only one civilization, common to all men, whose members are not nations but men" (Gökalp 1959: 281). He insists that this is cosmopolitanism and "this view of civilization is irreconcilable with that of the nationalists" (Gökalp 1959: 281).

This framework constitutes a significant attempt aimed at unifying the West and the nationalists. In this context, Kemalist ideology conceives the West as a technological source to be used. Yet Kemalism also considers that Western civilization is the "ideal civilization." This understanding of Gökalp is "repeated" by Atatürk himself. In a speech he delivered in 1924 Atatürk states: "Nations are different. However the civilization is unique and a nation in the course of progress should get united with it" (Atatürk 1954: 66). The crucial point here is that Kemalism, differing from the preceding period, comprehends the social and political norms of the West as part and parcel of "the technology" and civilization, at large. Westernism, under these assumptions appears as merely an "agent of legitimization" of Kemalism's modernization project. Under these assumptions it is clear that even the "social and political" West is not a matter of culture but of civilization.

The nature of the Kemalist model

The "Kemalist reforms" appear to be the implementation of Western social and political norms for the transformation of society. The most important of them is the translation of the Swiss Civil Code into Turkish. This move can be seen as the first step in the construction of a civil society based on the notion of rights which would convey to citizenship. It is also the first move in the implementation of secularism. The Civil Code introduces the idea of contractualism and as a result, on face value, it is a further step in the institutionalization of a positivist-secular understanding. This framework also provides for the birth of the "new citizen." However, in what follows, I will try to show how Kemalism encompasses a set of contradictions and disables the advancement of a civil notion of citizenship as an intended objective.

The key to understanding the constitutive elements of this inadequacy derives to a large extent from the interchangeable character of two concepts, i.e. the sacred/profane and the religious. This is to say that the notion of sacred or profane continues to exist and to be dominant over "the people." Here Kemalism replaces the profane with the state by attributing to it a transcendental connotation. In other words, in the Kemalist period the (secular) state as the supplier of all the rights and the organizer and regulator of the political realm fulfills the role of the transcendental power. In this way a strong *gemeinschaft* is created over the *gesellschaft* by empowering the state over the communal spirit. To understand this further one should compare Kant's and Gökalp's notions of "rights" and "reason."

In Kant, as Seligman points out, and I argued elsewhere, (Kahraman, 2002)

> Right [*Recht*] embraces both personal "rights" and the very notion of justice and is ensured through the autonomous and agentic *individual subject following the dictates of Reason* which in its universality, bridges the distinction between private and public, individual and social.
>
> (Seligman 1993: 149, emphasis added)

This is where the both Scottish idealism of private and public and the French tradition of "natural right" breaks. Instead, Kant begins the differentiation between private and public and he supports the idea that civil society is separate and autonomous from the state. In a synthesis, again according to Seligman, that Kant formulated through the relations between the Right and the Ethical he clearly argues that, quoting Seligman, the "private sphere of morality and ethics is thus divorced from the representative vision of society as juridical community" (Seligman 1993: 150–1). This specific approach contradicts the Kemalist understanding of state and civil society because in the Turkish case the state is set against the citizen with the famous motto by Gökalp: "there is no right but duty" (*hak yok vazife vardır*). This is by all means contradictory to the principals of the Enlightenment (Gökberk 1984: 281–334), even in the sense that it is understood by Atatürk himself. It is Atatürk who declares that the only "guide is science" and calls for society to reject any belief beyond Reason. This is, to put it in another framework, the birth of the hidden communitarianism of the Kemalist state that would hinder the development of a civil society and an emancipated notion of citizenship.

This communitarian spirit develops further in the "single-party era," as both *étatism* as the state-controlled economy and the solidarist-corporatist understanding of the state were chosen under the influence of the totalitarian regimes of 1930s Europe as the main ideologies by which the state was to govern its society. The catchphrase of these ideologies has always been "a united society of no privilege and class." On the other hand, the hegemonic discourse has also confirmed and stressed that there is not and cannot be class differentiation in the society but only a plurality of different professions all running for the good of the society. The remarkable point here is that Gökalp has developed his ideas during the 1908 period on the basis of Turkism as the dominant ideology of the era. The perpetuation of the same ideas in the subsequent years shows the heritage that Kemalism took from Gökalp and also indicates once again the state-centric nature of its citizenship regime. However, to understand this, one needs a relatively advanced understanding of the Kemalist republican model of citizenship.

The anatomy and structure of Kemalist citizenship

In order to provide a deeper understanding of republican citizenship, I will employ Turner's, Tilly's, and Brubaker's approaches to citizenship. As has been argued by Turner, a quick glance at the existing literature on citizenship reveals that there are two systems of citizenship, namely those of citizenship from above and citizenship from below (Turner 1993: 55). As Kadıoğlu has clearly demonstrated in her analysis of Turkish citizenship, the model used in Turkey in the early republic relates to "citizenship from above" (Kadıoğlu 1999: 53–72). The crucial point here is that this model indicates that the construction of Turkish citizenship aims at fortifying the strong position of the state over society. Thus, citizenship is not considered in terms of the language of rights. Instead, it becomes positioned toward the Kemalist will to modernity as civilization, and in this sense citizenship involves duties and services to the state rather than rights and freedoms. Citizens are expected to act as the expressions of modern life in that they give primacy to the national interest over their own rights and freedoms. In this sense, in the process of its construction from above, citizenship serves as an ethical device by which the strong-state legitimizes its dominant position over society. Thus, Turkish citizenship operates both as a way of implementing modernity from above into a traditional society and as an obstacle to the process of the creation of civil society.

On the other hand, in discussing the various different models of citizenship-building procedures in modernity, Tilly uses two different models. Accordingly, Tilly's matrix concludes that there are two categories that have emerged in the process of citizenship-building, namely those of the "exclusive" and "inclusive" models (Tilly 1996a: 10). Furthermore, these models can also be defined as "primordial" and "learned" in their origins. Approaching from this point of view, Kemalist republican citizenship can be classified as a "learned exclusive" model. It should be pointed out in this context that Kemalist citizenship as a learned and exclusive category does not involve ethnic and territorial references. Rather, it is "citizenship as a legal status." If this classification is taken into account as a general framework for an understanding of different models of the process of citizenship building, according to Tilly, we can move toward a more concrete level of analysis. At this level, one can differentiate the two statuses of citizenship as "thick" and "thin:"

> citizenship can then range from thin to thick: thin where it entails few transactions, rights and obligations; thick where it occupies a significant share of all transactions, rights and obligations sustained by state agents and people living under their jurisdiction.
>
> (Tilly 1996a: 8)

The "Turkish citizen" can then be seen as falling into the category of "thick" citizenship with a congregation of rules and obligations.

Third, one could observe that the citizenship-building process in Turkey has been largely part and parcel of the nation-building process. In other words, the dominant mode of understanding of Turkish citizenship has always been over-determined by the discussions about what constitutes an organic linkage between the different segments of a society in a way to make it a nation. Here, one could speak of two models of nation-building which have given rise to two different understandings of citizenship. The preference here is between the French model which acts on the basis of the principle of *jus soli*, to use the term popularized by Brubaker, that is, citizenship embedded in a spatial territoriality, and the German model operating on the basis of the principle of *jus sanguis* that privileges the criterion of noble descendancy (Brubaker 1992). The German model, in this case, is exclusionary and differentialist and *Volk*-oriented, whereas the French model is assimilationist and territorial (Tilly 1996b). Kadıoğlu, taking this distinction, states that the Turkish model of citizenship depends mainly on the French model and takes the principle of territoriality as its basis (Kadıoğlu 1999: 64).

However, it also involves references to ethnicity and in that case it refers to a specific version of the German model. Thus, Turkish citizenship turns out to be partially ethnic-based, exclusionary and once again state-oriented (Yıldız 2001). The combination of these models ends up giving meaning and expression to the peculiar character of Turkish citizenship, which can be seen in the frequently quoted statement of Atatürk, "what happiness to the one who says I am a Turk." The meaning of this sentence is still under debate in Turkey, for it is not clear whether it connotes an ethnic and exclusionary understanding or an inclusionary political one. Certain scholars have different views on this issue. While one group argues that Turkish citizenship does not have a blood and biological foundation and in this sense it has a cultural-assimilationist model, the other group stands for the idea that it, mostly during the 1930s period of single-party rule, has developed an ethnic view of citizenship and become more and more exclusionary. According to İçduygu *et al.*, both arguments are partially correct in their own right, and this has to do with the ambivalence embedded in the Kemalist construction of republican citizenship that "suggests that citizenship is formal, legal membership of a state, *implying loyalty to the state rather than the nation*, and it is also important for both symbolic and practical reasons to put an emphasis on the latter" (İçduygu *et al.* 2000: 191).

As can be seen at every level, Kemalist republican citizenship is definitely state-centric, operating from above, involving a thick notion of loyalty to modernity and combining the elements of the French and German models (Tilly 1996b: 233). Kadıoğlu argues in this sense that the reason for this multi-dimensional character of Turkish citizenship lies in the strong-state tradition and its defining characteristics: modernity as "a state in search of its nation" (Kadıoğlu 1995). On the other hand, we should not forget the fact that in this search the state also employed ethnic references. Yıldız argues that Turkish citizenship has a Germanic character in the sense that "the blood notion" has played an immense and effective role in the formation and institutionalization of citizenship (Yıldız 2001). Both arguments are valid and this condition remarkably shows the eclectic character of citizenship under scrutiny. This peculiarity makes Turkish citizenship itself a significant identity, attaching it to blood ties, giving it a nationalist character rather than being an agent or an element of the identity gaining a transcendental sense. In this context, using Tilly's terminology, Turkish citizenship might be called a "conceptualized citizenship" (Tilly 1996a), insofar as it is constructed by way of symbols, by using certain rhetoric and through the state-based secular education system.

In this sense, the republican model of citizenship with all these procedures and conditions should be comprehended as the constitutive element of

Turkish modernity if not itself an outcome of this "long lasting future." However, in the course of its history, this model has faced serious challenges, as Turkish modernity has begun to undergo serious changes and transformations since the 1980s and especially the 1990s. The state-centric, secular, thick, and inclusionary aspects of citizenship have been challenged by various sources, operating as identity claims, as recognition claims, and as calls for democratization. These challenges have played an important role in Turkey's relations with Europe, in the process of rethinking the idea of modernity as Westernization and with the emergence of the increasing societal will to democratization and the establishment of the language of rights in Turkey. All of these developments together constituted the third period in Turkish modernity as Westernization in the 1990s. In what follows, I shall analyze this period.

The 1990s: the new consciousness of democracy

The new period involves a tension between the strong-state tradition and the language of identity/difference voiced by the peripheral voices and civil society organizations. Thus, the resurgence of Islam, the rise of Kurdish nationalism, the emergence of civil society, the calls for liberal individualism, all emerged in this period (Göle 1994). They all became the internal elements of the changing nature of Turkish modernity, of the emergence of the politics of identity and recognition, and consequently of an increasing antagonism between the state and these forces. The 1990s bear the mark of this antagonism.

Beginning in the early 1990s, the newly founded Islamist party, the Welfare Party (Refah Partisi), with an energetic opposition to the governments of the center-right and left parties, started to reflect the demands of a certain part of the periphery. These demands were related to identity issues. The Islamist wing, for the first time in the history of the republic, voiced strong calls for a change in the notion of laicism, and demanded that the state refrain from intervening in religious affairs. It argued that religious identity could be manifested on the public realm, and it was this condition that would certify the existence of democracy. This argument not only started the identity debates in Turkey, but also put Kemalist tenets under discussion together with the existing norms of modernity.

Another condition which can be analyzed in the context of the widespread effect of identity politics in Turkey is the radical ethno-Turkish nationalist demands backed by the Nationalist Action Party (Milliyefci Hareket Partisi). Organized as a reaction, in the 1970–80 period, to the radical leftist upheaval, this group made another start in the late 1990s in reaction to Kurdish nationalism. The party openly takes a nationalist and introverted position in international affairs. Especially during the coalition government between 1999 and 2002, the bloc formed by the Democratic Left Party and the National Action Party against the Motherland Party (Anavatan Partisi) used Kurdish nationalism also in their indirect and implicit reaction to the EU. The National Action Party argued that it is for Europe as long as it means modernity, but against it if it means democracy, for the European understanding of democracy in its multiculturalist discourse contributes to the emergence of the politics of identity/recognition, the most dangerous of which is ethnic identity (Arıkan 2002).

In this sense, what has defined the new path of relations with Europe in the 1990s has always been the debate over democracy. It first started, as mentioned above, with the arguments concerning secularism in the context of political Islam. Elsewhere I have argued that political Islam stands for, in Turkey, "actual progressive movement" and this clearly denotes the change of roles (Kahraman 1993; 1995). It was no longer the centralist state elites running for a progressive understanding but rather the periphery symbolized in the context of Islam. This situation, taken as a radical challenge to the establishment by the central agents, continued throughout the 1990s with a gradually increasing intensity, and it finally faced the *sui generis* intervention of the army. After the formation of the 1998 coalition government between the (Islamist) Welfare Party and the True Path Party, the army first criticized the government for its anti-secular moves in supporting religious sects and promoting the religious fundamentalist discourse of the Islamic state, and then finally intervened in Turkish politics by asking in a forceful fashion for the resignation of the government. This intervention, known as "28 February coup," was construed as a "postmodern coup" both in public and academic circles. This postmodern coup forced the government to resign, demanded normalization and stability in political affairs that meant the exclusion of political Islam from governing, and ended with the constitutional closure of the Welfare Party.

While the postmodern coup affected negatively the process of democratization, there emerged nevertheless within society new civil calls for the need to transform the state into a more effective, efficient and democratic governing structure capable of creating the language of rights and freedoms in Turkey. Interestingly, these calls were voiced strongly by the Turkish bourgeoisie and its main organization, the Turkish Industrialists' and Businessmen's Association (known as TÜSİAD). The Turkish bourgeoisie, for the first time in its history, and in addition to its main identity as an economic pressure group, started to act as a civil society organization promoting liberal rights and freedoms. Bourgeoisie as a class in Turkey has a significant characteristic. It is not only the urban bourgeoisie which is considered as one of the historical carriers of the social transformations, but also the provincial bourgeoisie, which is usually considered to be the backbone of conservatism. The flow of international finance capital and its search for articulation with the local is the main factor in this development. The urge for unification has forced the Turkish bourgeoisie out of its closet, and required it to put aside its national feelings which have generally committed it to introverted and closed relations with the state. This framework has defined the new targets for the Turkish bourgeoisie, the most important of which is Turkey-EU relations (Müftüler-Baç 2002).

In this long history of Turkey's direct and institutionalized relations with the EU, the last crossroads was the decision of the Helsinki Summit of 10 December 1999 that demarcates the fourth stage of enlargement (Elgün-Kahraman 2000). In that decision, Turkey was accepted as a candidate member. In order to be accepted as a full member, Turkey is expected to fulfill the necessities of the Copenhagen criteria. As a part and parcel of this process, on 8 November 2000 Turkey published the National Participation Document, which declares both the will and the duties of the Turkish Republic. The last step was the National Program that was declared on 21 March 2000. It widely depends on the concretization of the process of democratization, which includes the necessary amendments of various laws and a sort of radical change concerning the state structure. It foresees amendments to fifty-three laws by 2001, and sixty by the end of 2004. In this regard, the Turkish bourgeoisie started to take a sheer pro-EU position, and the end of the 1990s is marked by the tension between it and the various "compartments" of the Turkish Republic, where the army is the central figure (Karabelias 2000).

In the late 1990s, the Turkish bourgeoisie began to be active in pressuring state to initiate political reforms to upgrade the quality of democracy and economic stability. In this regard, as a strong economic pressure group, promoting the globalizing economic interests of the private sector, TÜSİAD prepared two main reports criticizing the "established and valid notion of democracy" and calling for measures to be taken for its enlargement and reinforcement. The democracy reports aimed to modify the 1982 Constitution and called for a restructuring of civil-military relations along democratic lines, criticizing the position of the army in the National Security Council, and demanding a set of political reforms for the promotion of civil rights and freedoms. Thus, for the first time in the history of Turkish modernity, the Turkish bourgeoisie has made serious demands for further democratization and an effective state.

The significant point here is that both democracy and the effective state depend on the transformation of the republican model of citizenship. This transformation has already been demanded by societal forces and the Copenhagen criteria of the EU. The transformation entails a new understanding of citizenship in Turkey as a matter of identity and rights that operates in relation to the values of the post-nationalist order. Identity politics at every level will undoubtedly benefit from this progress. However, it is at this point that the internal clash surfaces. While most of the center parties with a pro-nationalist propensity reacted and, together with other central actors such as the army and the state bureaucracy, opposed the demands of the EU, the societal and peripheral forces attempted to resist this reaction and point out the importance of the EU for the further democratization of Turkey.

The outcome of this clash was twofold. First, in August 2002 the Turkish parliament unexpectedly ratified all laws necessary for the fulfillment of the Copenhagen criteria. Second, the national election was announced. In the November 3rd national election, both the coalition-government parties and the opposition parties lost the election and found themselves no longer in parliament. The winner of the election was the (Islamic) Justice and Development Party. The possibility of a democratic Turkey lies in the success of the Justice and Development Party in governing Turkey effectively and efficiently, as well as in taking Turkey forward to the accession negotiations with the EU.

Conclusion

In this chapter I have argued that Turkey's "experience" and "adventure" in terms of citizenship and European integration consist of a set of historical periods, in each of which Turkish modernity as Westernization has taken different but nevertheless interrelated forms. The other component of this long and tiresome journey is democracy, and this is also interconnected with the political transformation that is usually referred to as modernization. As has been analyzed in a thematic fashion, this history unfolds in three periods. The first period refers to the late Ottoman Empire and the beginning of Turkish modernity; the second period covers the Kemalist construction of the Turkish Republic as a modern nation-state, and the last period concerns the late 1990s and the changing nature of modernity. While in the first two periods of modernity via Westernization the idea of the individual has been neglected, it is in the third period that there have emerged societal calls for democratization of the strong-state tradition. In this last period, modernity as Westernization has become subject to a process of reconstruction in which the main aim was, and still is, to transform the state in such a way that it approaches society on the basis of individualism and the protection of individual rights and freedoms. This is, as I have argued in this chapter, one of the most important outcomes of Turkey's long association with Europe.

In this context, the development of citizenship shows a noteworthy transformation toward democratization and the emergence of the language of rights in the process of modernization as Westernization. Whereas the first period takes the notion of rights as a natural and transcendental entity, in the second period it was comprehended not as a natural entity but as a notion having secondary importance to the state and its interests. It is only in the third period that the notion of rights in terms of the process of democratization constitutes the focal point in the crisis-ridden interactions between the state and the individual. In this period of the 1990s, the notion of rights is considered neither natural nor secondary, but as a secular and political concept involving individual freedoms and directly related to the possibility of the further democratization of Turkey.

This chapter has also demonstrated that the constitutive elements of the process of modernity as Westernization have not remained the same. On the contrary, they have been re-defined, re-described and re-constructed historically in the course of Turkish modernity and its dissemination throughout society. These changes have also been reflected in the processes of modernization and democratization. Accordingly, in the first period the West stands for the constitution of a modern notion of state in the total absence of the notion of democracy. In the second period, the West functioned as a main reference point for the Kemalist will to civilization that understood modernity as modern nation-state building without democracy. It is only in the final and present period that the West is referred to as a source for the process of democratization, which goes hand-in-hand with the critique of the strong-state tradition. Thus the long history of Turkish modernity as Westernization reveals the fact that the state in search of its society has eventually found itself in a situation in which it is negated by its society in search of a democratic state that functions primarily as the institutional guarantor of individual rights and freedoms. In this transformation, which marks the nature of the present time in Turkey, the West, understood as the process of European integration, plays a constitutive role, especially with respect to the possibility of creating a democratic Turkey.

In this chapter, apart from the above-mentioned conditions, I have also made a set of suggestions regarding the question of Turkey's long association with Europe. These suggestions can be summarized as follows:

1 The idea of Europe, as well as Turkey-EU relations, functions as a main point of reference both for the definition of Turkish modernity as Westernization and for the societal critique of the constitutive epistemology of Turkish modernity, namely Kemalism. This is so insofar as the idea of "Europe" involves references to both modernity and democracy. Thus, while it is taken by the state to mean modernity, it also has its place in the recent societal critiques of the strong-state tradition, but this time it is taken to mean democracy. However, whether it means modernity or democracy, the idea of Europe remains the constitutive image of Turkish modernity as Westernization;
2 One of the sites at which we can observe the manifestations of the idea of Europe as modernity and as democracy is Turkish citizenship. In this context, the idea of Europe plays an important role both for the strong-state tradition and for its recent critiques. For the strong-state tradition, Europe as modernity functions as a source of legitimacy for the state in its attempt to view citizenship on the basis of services and duties, to the extent that these services and duties are positioned by the state against civilization and modernization, that is, against the construction of a modern nation aiming at reaching the level of contemporary European civilization. On the other hand, the idea of Europe as democracy is articulated into the recent critique of the strong-state tradition, and in

this sense functions as a source of the language of rights and freedoms. In this context, the idea of Europe becomes an internal element of the liberal and constitutional understanding of Turkish citizenship. In this sense, both nationalism and liberalism make use of reference to the idea of Europe in different ways; and

3 Thus, Europe becomes an agent of legitimization for different agents and actors in Turkey. In this regard, as much as it gives meaning to modernity, civilization, and nation-building, Europe also gives legitimacy to the recent politics of difference, identity and recognition. Both the state-centric attempts to create stability, normality and civility, and the calls for democracy, pluralism and liberalism employ the idea of Europe in constructing their own visions of society.

It can be argued consequently that the history of Turkish modernity cannot be understood without taking into account Turkey's long and tiresome relations with the West and its changing forms and contents. To the extent that the idea of Europe defines Turkish modernity, it also defines the cultural foundation on which the republican model of citizenship was constructed. Likewise, to the extent that the idea of Europe defines the crisis and the changing nature of Turkish modernity, it also defines the cultural foundation on which societal calls are being made for the language of rights and freedoms, carried out by the new, democratic and liberal citizens. It can be suggested, therefore, that Europe constitutes one of the defining elements of a democratic Turkey, the possibility of which lies in the reconstruction of state-society relations on the basis of the language of rights and freedoms.

References

Arıkan, E. B. (2002) "Turkish Ultra-nationalists Under Review: A Study of the Nationalist Action Party," *Nations and Nationalisms*, 8 (3) July: 357–76.

Atatürk, K. (1954) *Atatürk'ün Söylev ve Demeçleri* (The Speeches and Statements of Atatürk), 3, (Şubat 1924), Ankara: Türk İnkılap Tarihi Enstitüsü Yayınları.

Berkes, N. (1998) *The Development of Secularism in Turkey*, London: Hurst & Company.

Brubaker, R. (1992) *Citizenship and Nationhood in France and Germany*, Cambridge: Cambridge University Press.

Chatterjee, P. (1993) *Nationalist Thought and the Colonial World: A Derivative Discourse*, Minneapolis: University of Minnesota Press, reissued edition.

Elgün-Kahraman, S. (2000) "Rethinking Turkey-European Union Relations in the Light of Enlargement," *Turkish Studies*, 1 (1): 1–20.

Gökalp, Z. (1959) *Turkish Nationalism and Western Civilisation: Selected Essays of Ziya Gökalp*, ed. and introduction by N. Berkes, Westport CT: Greenwood Press.

Gökberk, M. (1984) "Aydınlanma Felsefesi, Devrimler ve Atatürk" (The Philosophy of Enlightenment, Reforms and Atatürk), in *Çağdaş Düşüncenin Işığında Atatürk*, Istanbul: Dr Nejat F. Eczacıbaşı Vakfı Yayınları.

Göle, N. (1994) "Toward an Autonomization of Politics and Civil Society," in M. Heper and A. Evin (eds) *Politics in the Third Turkish Republic*, Boulder: Westview.

Hanioğlu, Ş. (1985) *Bir Siyasal Düşünür Olarak Doktor Abdullah Cevdet ve Dönemi* (Doctor Abdullah Cevdet as a Political Thinker and His Time), Istanbul: Üçdal Neşriyat.

İçduygu, A., Çolak, Y. and Soyarık, N. (2000) "What is the Matter with Citizenship? A Turkish Debate," in S. Kedourie (ed.) *Seventy-Five Years of the Turkish Republic*, London and Portland OR: Frank Cass.

Kadıoğlu, A. (1999) "Modern Vatandaşlığın Farklı Boyutları" (Different Dimensions of Modern Citizenship), in *Cumhuriyet İradesi Demokrasi Muhakemesi: Yeni Bir Vatandaşlık Etiğine Doğru* (The Republican Will and the Democratic Reason: Towards a New Ethics of Citizenship), Istanbul: Metis Yayınları.

——(1995) "Milletini Arayan Devlet: Türk Milliyetçiliğinin Açmazları" (A State in Search of Its Nation: The Dilemma of Turkish Nationalism), *Türkiye Günlüğü*, 33 (March-April): 99–101.

Kahraman, H. B.(1993) *Yeni Bir Sosyal Demokrasi İçin* (For a New Social Democracy), Ankara: İmge Yayınevi.

——(1995) *Sağ, Türkiye ve Partileri* (Right, Turkey and its Parties), Ankara: İmge Yayınları.

——(2002) "Modern Türk Siyasetinin Rousseaucu Kısıtlamaları üstüne Rousseau-Kant Bağlamında Bir Değerlendirme" (The Rousseauian Constraints of Modern Turkish Politics: A Kantian Approach), *Toplum ve Bilim*, 93: 55–83.

Karabelias, G. (2000) "The Evolution of Civil-military Relations in Post-war Turkey, 1980–1995," in S. Kedourie (ed.) *Seventy-five Years of the Turkish Republic*, London and Portland OR: Frank Cass.

Mardin, Ş. (2000) *The Genesis of Young Ottoman Thought*, n.p.: Syracuse University Press.

Müftüler-Baç, M. (2002) "Through the Looking Glass: Turkey in Europe," *Turkish Studies*, 1 (1): 21–36.

Parla, T. (1985) *The Social and Political Thought of Ziya Gökalp, 1876–1924*, Leiden: E. J. Brill.

Seligman, A. B. (1993) "The Fragile Ethical Vision of Civil Society," in B. Turner (ed.) *Citizenship and Social Theory*, London: Sage.

Tilly, C. (1996a) "Citizenship, Identity and Social History," in *Citizenship, Identity and Social History*, Cambridge: Cambridge University Press.

——(1996b) "The Emergence of Citizenship in France and Elsewhere," in *Citizenship, Identity and Social History*, Cambridge: Cambridge University Press.

Turner, B. S. (1993) *Citizenship and Social Theory*, London: Sage.

——(1993) "Contemporary Problems in the Theory of Citizenship," in B. S. Turner (ed.) *Citizenship and Social Theory*, London: Sage.

Yıldız, A. (2001) *"Ne Mutlu Türküm Diyebilene:" Türk Ulusal Kimliğinin Etno-Seküler Sınırları* (Happy is the One Who Can Call Himself a Turk: The Ethno-Secular Limits of Turkish National Identity), Istanbul: İletişim Yayınları.

4 European Union-Turkish relations and the question of citizenship

Deniz Vardar

Introduction

The European Union (EU) summit in Copenhagen in December 2002 was a turning point in relations between the EU and Turkey. The EU is preparing to expand from 15 to 25 members in 2004 and, possibly, 27 (with Bulgaria and Romania) in 2007. Turkey lobbied actively before and during the Copenhagen Summit in order to start accession negotiations.[1] It had also initiated a set of almost revolutionary legal, constitutional and institutional changes in the summer of 2002 to make its political system compatible with that of the EU. Although the European Council proposed in its Seville meeting (2002) that a new decision should be taken at the Copenhagen Summit about Turkey's candidacy, Turkey's efforts to obtain a date for joining other candidates on course for integration were not completely successful. Instead, the EU decided to re-examine Turkey's case at the end of 2004. If, by then, Turkey fulfills the EU criteria, accession negotiations will be started "without delay." In these circumstances, the current government and the main political actors are aware that they can no longer postpone the democratization process in Turkey if they want to be included in the next wave of EU enlargement. In this context, the government declared 2003 as the "year of reforms" and 2004 "the year of their application." Turkey responded to the latest Accession Partnership Document of the EU Commission, which recalled Turkey's shortcomings in its attempts to meet the Copenhagen criteria (April 2003), by announcing a renewed National Program (July 2003) and a series of democratic reform packages.

The issues surrounding Turkey's possible accession to the EU stem not only from the country's problems adapting to the criteria set down for all candidate countries, but also from some other implicit issues. They are related, first, to the identity problems inherent in Turkey's "Europeanness" and, second, to the question of Europe's future borders. For this reason, the questions of citizenship and democracy constitute a significant issue in EU-Turkish relations. Moreover, the question of citizenship is also, key to the future of democratization in Turkey. Thus, the relationship between European and Turkish citizenship is at the center of the debate in Turkey concerning the role of the EU in altering the content and scope of the republican understanding of citizenship. (See Keyman, Chapter 12 of this volume, and Kadıoğlu, Chapter 5, on this topic.)

In the first part of this chapter, I will try to assess the scope of EU identity via its political construction and its model of citizenship. In the second part, EU-Turkish relations will be analyzed, with a focus on the structure of Turkish democracy and citizenship. It has become apparent that Turkey's efforts and insistence to join the EU has revealed that Turkey's state-centered version of democracy and citizenship is not compatible with the way these notions are considered in Europe's core democracies.

From "Europeanness" to European Union citizenship through the nation-state

In the debate about European citizenship, the notion of "Europeanness" is taken to refer to a certain intellectual, historical, and political baggage that has contributed to defining Europe, on a cultural level at least. Therefore, in order to understand the impact of the EU on Turkish citizenship we have to look at the emergence of European citizenship on the basis of the idea of "Europeanness." In doing so, we must keep in mind that there has always been tension between two sources of the idea of Europeanness: between the idea of Europe as a socio-political entity on the one hand, and that of Europe as an intellectual and cultural construct on the other. While the former harks back to a notion of citizenship consistent with liberal democracy, the latter promotes a culturally essentialist notion of citizenship. As we will see later, Turkey's integration in the EU depends not only on bolstering democracy at home but also on which of these sources forms the basis of European citizenship.

Europe is a geographical, political, cultural, historical and economic space, with somewhat fuzzy or ill-defined geographical borders. The ambiguous characteristics of European history are reflected in its multiple definitions. As Edgar Morin clearly stated, Europe was constructed on the basis of a set of contradictory processes and ideas, namely those of law and force, democracy and repression, spirituality and materiality, rational calculation and its opposite, the myth of rationality (Morin 1987: 33). Moreover, the definition of "Europeanness" has been largely manipulated by political actors according to their interests, with exclusive or inclusive definitions of the term being used in the debate about political identity. We know that "Euro-centrist Europeans," convinced of Europe's cultural superiority, are opposed by other "Europeans" who argue against such superiority. For the latter, Europe is just one of a number of civilizations of equal inherent value. It should not be forgotten that since its inception there has always been tension within the EU between these two notions.

The EU is today attempting to define itself as an egalitarian and inclusive entity in opposition to the exclusive culturalist discourse associated with certain ideas of "Europe." The Copenhagen criteria owe much to some basic principles associated with inclusive liberal democracy. But one must not forget the existence of influential and culturalist actors and discourses in every EU country. It is important to take into consideration both sides of EU identity: the "European Europe" side and the pluralist one. In other words, the accession of Turkey to full EU membership will involve active negotiation, even quarrels, with these opposing actors and discourses. It will also require that the inclusive and egalitarian notion of Europe remains dominant over cultural essentialism.

Given the fact that cultural essentialism and its exclusivist discourse has, in the past, played a significant role in the outbreak of devastating wars, the problem of racism even in well developed countries and the culturally antagonistic relations between countries throughout the history of Europe, it became apparent after World War II that the European ideal required an egalitarian and inclusive identity for its full realization. The founders of the EU knew this and, as we will see in the following section, they have considered European unification on the basis of the Kantian notion of perpetual peace and the belief that liberal democracies do not fight with each other.

From European Communities to the EU's citizenship and identity

The process of European integration started after World War II through the creation of a number of European organizations. Reacting against the "decadence" and instability of the interwar period, the main declared objective of European integration was to keep the peace in Europe (and to control Germany). Showing some similarities to nation-state building in Europe, the integration process took as its *modus vivendi* the neo-functionalist idea (Haas 1958) that if you establish an economic space, the political construction will follow. Indeed, this aspect of EU's strategy of integration is reflected in the slogan "step by step." However, the integration process has also involved some efforts at identity formation.[2] The "People's Europe" needed some elementary symbols, such as an official Europe day (9 May – introduced in 1985), a European anthem (taken from Beethoven's 9th Symphony, *Ode to Joy* – 1985) and a European flag (a circle of twelve yellow stars on an azure background – adopted by the Community institutions in 1986). "The Single European Act" (1987) was also quite important in European integration. But the turning point in this process was the Maastricht Treaty (1992), which united the economic and political aspects of integration. This treaty provided additional "constitutional" rights to "EU citizens" by creating a new legal category of "European citizenship." The Amsterdam Treaty reinforced the drive to create a European citizenship as part of a move toward political integration. Yet it also sparked a debate within Europe on the nature of political integration, with the question of whether confederation or federation will form the basis for political unification becoming a central concern (Quermonne 1998). The current debate on the EU's draft constitution (presented by the EU Convention in 2003) is very significant in this regard.

The concept of citizenship in modern times has always been associated with the nation-state. The nation has constituted a common link between nationality and citizenship for the European Union. The common space was created by making a distinction between citizenship and nationality, as in the Maastricht Treaty. More precisely, European citizenship is seen as an "additional" citizenship open only to the citizens of EU member states. In other words, EU citizenship is indirectly and automatically obtained via national citizenship status. It gives equal rights to EU citizens in several fields: freedom of circulation, diplomatic protection in third-countries, the right to vote and stand for election in local and EU Parliament elections, the right to petition the EU Parliament and the right to appeal to an ombudsman in case of administrative problems. These are the active and passive rights conferred by EU citizenship, which do not impose any particular direct duties. EU citizens' judicial problems can be dealt with not only nationally but also by the European Court of Justice (Garot 1999: 205–20). All this progress in the construction of EU citizenship was reinforced by the Amsterdam Treaty, which opened the way toward a new form of civic virtue in the sense of Habermas' constitutional citizenship (Habermas 1992: 1–19). The sharing by all EU countries of a market economy, accompanied by notions of general interest, puts "EU citizenship" somewhere in between political union and civil society (Quermonne 2000: 297–309). Protectionary measures aimed at tackling all kinds of discrimination (those founded on sex, race, ethnic origin, religion or other convictions, handicap, age or sexual orientation) are particularly salient features in the common values shared by EU members. Amsterdam's strategy, to get closer to citizens, also underlines EU efforts to tackle labor flexibility and unemployment, as well as environmental, health and consumer protection.

The notion of EU citizenship brings into focus the "new citizenship" debate. The disconnection between citizenship and nationality favors the settlement, local participation and search for minimum common values that will enable Europeans to live together irrespective of ethnic origin (Roux 1992: 233). Research aimed at discovering "European values," shows that in European countries, individual identity is already based more around professional activities (*Futuribles* 1995) than on ethnic or religious values. But we observe also that in EU countries existing communities (whether determined by birth or by other, more recent criteria) provoke a need for a new political project that connects individual citizenship with the collective one, the legal citizen with the political one. Made up of pluralist nation-states, the EU finds itself at the center of this debate. Just as the EU represents an unfinished political project, the notion of EU citizenship is still at an early stage. We are currently in the process of moving from a notion of citizenship based exclusively on the nation-state to one that also takes into account transnational identities.

This brief account of European citizenship and its development constitutes the necessary background for an adequate understanding of the historically somewhat ambiguous relationship between the EU and Turkey. Turkey's accession to full membership of the EU requires both democratization of state-society relations and the transformation of the republican model of citizenship into a liberal one based on the protection of individual rights and freedoms. Turkey's accession remains achievable as long as Europe maintains its egalitarian and inclusive stand on unification and citizenship. Next, I will attempt to provide a brief historical account of EU-Turkish relations in the context of such issues.

EU-Turkish relations: does Turkish citizenship fit into the EU's model?

In the second part of this chapter I will attempt to answer the following questions: Why does Turkey want to join the EU? What impact is membership likely to have on Turkish politics? What criteria must Turkey's democracy fulfill to join the EU? Do Turkish notions of democracy and citizenship fit the EU's model?

In order to understand why Turkey insists on membership of the EU, I will first present some key stages in the history of the partnership between Turkey and the EU. I will then try to place these relations in their political and strategic context. Second, I will focus on the impact of European integration on the Turkish political scene so as to provide some insight into the ongoing changes in the behavior of different actors. This will then bring us to the problem of Turkish democracy with respect to EU membership. Finally I will emphasize the need for rethinking the republican model of Turkish citizenship by placing it in the EU context.

Historical background

Integration into the EU would be the last step in Turkey's century and a half-long march toward modernity via "Westernization." This march was inaugurated by the Ottoman Empire and then accelerated by the Turkish Republic after World War I. Integration with Europe has progressively become an official policy goal since the inception of the Republic of Turkey in 1923 (Vardar 1993: 147–57), with Turkey's application for associate membership to the EC (the forerunner of the EU) on 31 July 1959 (just after Greece's application). The Association Agreement (Ankara Agreement), signed between Turkey and the EC/EU in 1963 defined the terms of Turkey's admission as well as its timetable.[3]

Since the Ankara Agreement, EC/EU-Turkish relations have been highly politicized. In the Turkish political arena, pro-systemic actors (center-left or right-wingers) have almost automatically placed themselves in an openly pro-EC/EU position, while newly emerged and anti-systemic actors have adopted an overtly anti-EC/EU stance. For far-left actors the EC/EU is a capitalist organization wishing to colonize Turkey, while for far-rightists (in accordance with their search for an imagined "organic community") as well as for ultra-nationalists Turkey should return to its Turkish origins and fight to reunify the Turks of the world rather than become a part of Europe. In a similar vein, Islamists believe the country should return to its Islamic origins and should attempt to reunify Muslims of the world. Such polarization reached fever pitch after the signing of an additional protocol with the EC/EU in 1970 (which entered into force in 1973). One should constantly remember that in Turkish society's "imaginaire" one could find easily pro- or counter-feelings and arguments on Europe.

The decision in 1978 by Prime Minister Bülent Ecevit (center-left) to suspend Turkey's relations with the EC/EU was without doubt determined by the radicalization of the political scene. Nevertheless, the most negative factor from the point of view of European integration was the military coup of 1980 that completely halted the functioning of parliamentary democracy in Turkey. For the first time, the EC/EU authorities decided to suspend their relations with Turkey in 1983, arguing that the transition to democracy in Turkey was far behind from European standards.[4] In other words, the return to democracy in Turkey was not fulfilling minimum EC/EU norms for a liberal democracy. Similarly, after the center-right Motherland Party (ANAP) government had applied for full membership of the EC/EU in 1987 (article 237 of the Treaty of Rome), the European Commission's report two years later declared that Turkey was not ready for full membership because of its lack of democracy and economic development. Yet the report did not stop Turkey's attempts to ease and overhaul its relations with the EU. These attempts resulted in the revitalization of the Ankara Agreement, the outcome of which was the Customs Union (1995) between the EU and Turkey.

We should note that the revitalization of Turkey's long association with the EU occurred as a result of the changing attitudes and discourses of different political forces. After the military regime came to an end, all pro-establishment actors sustained their positions in favor of European integration. More importantly, the Turkish left (and even the new left) changed its anti-EU stance and progressively became pro-EU (except for some small radical groups). Thus the EU's criticism regarding Turkish democracy was instrumental in causing a transformation in political discourse. The international context also played an important role in the emergence of this new pro-EU consensus. Indeed, during the 1980s, the EU was considered, especially by the Turkish left, as an alternative to Turkey's dependency on the USA. EU surveillance of Turkish democracy was also welcomed as a guarantee of human rights and freedom of thought.

However, this new pro-EU environment did not go unchallenged. In the 1990s, the "rediscovery" of Turkic-speaking ex-Soviet countries and Turkish

Muslim minorities in the Balkans motivated a sort of tribal solidarity feeling in Islamist and ultra-nationalist circles. The involvement of these circles in communitarian projects (the "periphery" against the "center") drew support for their commitment to all kinds of Turkic-speaking populations (in the case of the ultra-nationalists) and/or Muslims of the world (in the case of the Islamists). They thus positioned themselves against official Turkish policy regarding the EU (Vardar 1996: 405–11).

As it was excluded from the official list of candidate countries in the Luxembourg Summit of 1997, Turkey suspended its "political dialogue" with the EU. This tension continued until the Helsinki Summit of December 1999, which decided to include Turkey (and Malta) as a candidate for future enlargement.[5] This decision was of utmost importance for Turkey's integration into Europe in two crucial respects: First, it created a sense of certainty in EU-Turkish relations by giving Turkey an institutionally-recognized status of candidate for accession to the EU. Second, it triggered important changes in the positions adopted by different Turkish political formations with regard to Europe. This new sense of certainty in EU-Turkish relations and the increasing support in Turkish society for European integration began to determine the terms of political discourse, and it became increasingly difficult for political actors to take a clear anti-EU position. For instance, Islamic political actors changed their critical stance on Europe and began to express their support for Turkey's accession to the EU, for they realized that European integration served their own long-term interests by providing a pluralist and democratic ground for the protection of individual rights and freedoms, which necessarily include religious beliefs. As Keyman and İçduygu underlined in their introductory chapter in this volume, this change in Islamic discourse has become very apparent in the Justice and Development Party (JDP), which became a kind of conservative party (called by some analysts a "Muslim democrat party") even before its victory in the national elections of 3 November 2002. Similarly, nationalist and ultra-nationalist parties have found themselves unable to voice clearly and directly their opposition to the EU. The National Action Party (ultra-nationalist), which was a member of the coalition government that lost power in the November 2002 elections, could not openly express its opposition to the EU because of its fear of losing popular support. Thus, the EU has become one of the most powerful determinants of Turkish politics.

In this sense, it can be argued that in spite of some periods of crisis, there has been continuity in EU-Turkish relations. Indeed, the association of full EU membership with modernization, democratization, Westernization and economic growth has produced a growing consensus in Turkish society around this topic. As we have already noted, entry into the EU has been traditionally presented by the political center as representing convergence with a "richer and better world," and EU-Turkish relations have been used as a "complementary source of legitimacy for the political system" (Apter

1988; Badie 1992) in Turkey. However, the decision taken at the EU's Copenhagen Summit of December 2002 to open the possibility of full-membership status for Turkey on condition that it satisfies fully the requirements of the Copenhagen criteria has forced the political center to take serious decisions regarding democracy, human rights and individual freedoms. The Copenhagen Summit also indicated that if Turkey did not work toward full democracy in its state-society relations, it could find itself outside the new and enlarged Europe. It is here that the question of citizenship becomes extremely important, insofar as it constitutes the main area in which the application of the Copenhagen criteria to Turkish society can be clearly observed. In what follows, I will focus on the impact of EU-Turkish relations on Turkish citizenship and democracy.

The EU and its impact on democratization and citizenship in Turkey

Historically, Turkish citizenship is a combination of both "contractual political citizenship," in the sense of French nationalism's (republicanism's) political inclusive model, and "ethnic citizenship," whose exclusive features can be traced back to the German nationalist tradition. Thus, Turkish republican history has in a certain sense swung between these two notions of citizenship. The roots of the modern Turkish state in Western modernity and, consequently, its synthetic nature was the main reason for such a complex and ambivalent form of citizenship. In the long history of Turkish modernization and Westernization, one of the most difficult problems was how to transform the subjects of the Ottoman Empire into citizens of the Turkish Republic. The invention of the notion of "Turkish citizen" was indeed the product of a very determined and authoritarian one-party regime. In its efforts to forge a republican model of citizenship, the Kemalist elite subordinated the individual to ethnic and religious considerations. As Kadıoğlu points out, this model excludes the liberal individualist dimension; thus, "the citizen precedes the individual" (Kadıoğlu 1998: 24). Moreover, the dimension of legal equality between citizens was not entirely fulfilled. Thus, although revised and adapted again and again (largely to take into account "national security" considerations), Turkish citizenship – like Turkish democracy – has always been considered as of secondary importance *vis-à-vis* the republic and the need for a strong state.

However, as has been pointed out elsewhere in this book, the necessity of a strong state has been challenged (especially since the 1980s) by different groups claiming that the exclusionary nature of the republican model of citizenship is unable to deal effectively with their problems and demands. The dynamism of radical Islamist groups and of openly ethnic movements illustrates this inability further. Thus, Kurds and Islamists, and also Turkish ultra-nationalists, have considered themselves as being excluded by Turkish citizenship, which is perceived by these groups as either being respectively too ethnically focused, too secular or too republican and not Turkish enough.

To understand the reason why the challenges to republican citizenship could have taken such different forms, it is useful to look at the Turkish education ministry's "textbooks" on "civic education" studied by F. Üstel (2002: 275–83). Üstel's study reveals that in the decades following the foundation of the Turkish Republic, textbooks aimed to form a "new civilized citizen" capable of taking on board modernity and a certain idea of "citizenship" (militant-ethnic) that was rooted in particularist and culturalist notions of ethnicity. From the 1950s to the 1980s, efforts were made to emphasize "political" citizenship, but this process was not coupled with the introduction of any new language of rights for Turks because of the strong-state tradition. In 1980 came the military intervention, after which "Turkish citizenship" regained its militant and communitarian character. But this time the military also used religious identity to construct what has come to be known as the "Turkish-Islam synthesis" as a way of counteracting the left's definition of identity and an emerging Kurdish ethnic identity. This change in the content and the perception of Turkish citizenship occurred, paradoxically, at a time when Turkey was beginning to make serious efforts to meet the criteria set down for entry to the EU. In the 1990s, however, aspirations to join the EU became an argument in favor of importing and adapting the individualist liberal form of citizenship for Turkey. This was the beginning of the period in which the EU began to have a considerable impact on the strong-state tradition and its republican model of citizenship, to the extent that it has created a strong civil movement in Turkish society in favor of liberalism, individualism and democracy.

As noted, the EU's notion of citizenship has come from above, in a rather "passive" way (Turner 1994: 199–226) and as an addendum to liberal democracy. EU citizenship is based on a civic conception of citizenship as opposed to an ethnic one, and argues for the need for responsible individuals to make liberal democracies work. It should be pointed out here that EU citizenship and its emphasis on the importance of responsible and active individuals for democracy to function, was compatible with the dominant civil society-based regimes of its current member countries. This was not the case in Turkey, where the strong-state requires passive and obedient citizens who are supposed to recognize the primacy of the national interest over individual rights and freedom. Thus, EU citizenship has played an important role in the emergence of a series of clashes between the state and society, as well as between Turkey and the EU. The ground for these clashes has been the shallowness of Turkish democracy, the boundaries of which have always been defined by the strong-state tradition. We can see why this strong-state tradition has become a real obstacle in the way of Turkey's full accession to the EU. We can also understand why Turkey had to implement a set of legal, constitutional and institutional changes at the end of the 1990s to join the enlargement process. For the EU authorities, democracy is technically measurable, and they indicate that Turkey still had a lot to do to protect human and minority rights if it was to fulfill the criteria for EU membership candidates. Like other candidate countries, Turkey would have to introduce major reforms in its political and economic systems in order to achieve democracy and economic stability. Moreover, these reforms would have to be in line with the Copenhagen criteria, which set out the EU's understanding of liberal democracy and citizenship.

The Copenhagen criteria were accepted as the objective accession criteria in June 1993 by the European Council Summit. These were enshrined in the Amsterdam Treaty of May 1999, which established its essential principles in the following fields:

Political principles Stable institutions guaranteeing democracy, the rule of the law, human rights enforcement, protection of minorities. All these principles were reiterated in the Charter of the European Union signed in Nice in 2000 included now to the EU Constitution draft.

Economic criteria A functioning market economy and the capacity to cope with competitive pressures and market forces within the Union.

Incorporation of the Community acquis Implementation of the Union's legislation and adherence to the various political, economic and monetary aims of the European Union. European Councils (especially that of Madrid in 1995) have continuously stressed the importance of incorporating the acquis into national legislations to assure convergence at the European level.[6]

The pre-accession strategy of the EU that guides the preparation of candidates for membership also applies to Turkey. In doing so, the EU aimed to help candidates to adopt the Community acquis step by step.[7] Thus, every year, the European Commission's Regular Report on Turkey evaluates progress toward accession.[8] These annual reports on Turkish democracy have been an important element in the ongoing transformations of Turkish democracy, especially since the Helsinki Summit of 1999. The Accession Partnership Document (APD) and the National Program, issued respectively by the Commission services in December 2000 and by the Turkish coalition government in April 2001, established a list of issues to be addressed in preparation for Turkey's accession negotiations.

However, although all Commission reports recognized Turkey's status as an applicant country, they also stressed that negotiations could not start until the political criteria had been met. Turkey's main problem seems to be the process of democratization in accordance with EU norms, even if the European Commission does recognize the huge efforts undertaken by Turkey. The JDP government's updated National Program of July 2003 was principally conceived to overcome the shortcomings of Turkey mentioned in the Accession Partnership Document issued on April 2003 and in "Regular Reports" of the Commission.

The Commission Reports of 2002 and 2003 compare the state of Turkish democracy with EU criteria.[9] One notes that the reports' main reference is a post-national notion of human rights, affecting the republican model of citizenship.[10] Both reports point out Turkey's shortcomings in meeting the political criteria, such as the persistence of a "number of significant limitations" on the full enjoyment of fundamental rights and freedoms, as well as limitations on the principles of freedom of peaceful assembly, freedom of association, freedom of religion, and rights to legal redress. However, Report 2002 notices also that the candidate status obtained in Helsinki (1999) has encouraged Turkey to introduce a series of reforms. Thus major constitutional reforms, introduced in October 2001 and aimed at strengthening guarantees in the field of human rights and fundamental freedoms, were welcomed by the EU. So is the new Civil Code adopted in November 2001 and the lifting of the death penalty in time of peace. The end of the state of emergency in provinces in the southeast of Turkey has also been well received. The three reform packages adopted successively in February, March and August 2002, then the four further sets of reforms following them, adopted in January-February 2003 and July-August 2003, seek to deepen the process of democratization and its main defining element, the protection of individual rights and freedoms. The Regular Report of 2003 points, in particular, to improvement in the areas of freedom of expression, freedom of demonstration, cultural rights and civilian control of the military over the past year.

This 2003 report notes also that Turkey has achieved a certain level of success in eliminating torture and ill-treatment (a "zero tolerance" policy toward torture had been declared by the government). According to the 2002 report, the Turkish prison system continues to represent a real problem in this regard, especially the inhuman conditions in the F-type prisons where prisoners can be subjected to long isolation periods. However, conditions in the prison system had "improved considerably," but reforms still had to be carried through in their entirety (as mentioned in 2003's Regular Report).

Writers, journalists and publishers continue to be prosecuted despite some legislative changes. According to the 2003 Regular Report, the lack of civilian control over the military also remains a problem even if some improvements are underway.[11] By contrast, while the EU recognizes positive developments in the area of human rights, the question of minority rights is one of the key points in Turkey's "democratic deficit." Turkey has not yet signed the Council of Europe Framework Convention for the Protection of National Minorities. Moreover, minorities other than those mentioned in the 1923 Treaty of Lausanne (Greeks, Armenians and Jews) are not recognized in Turkey as minorities. Nevertheless, in August 2002, the Turkish state authorized "broadcasting and educating in languages other than Turkish." Although the Regular Report of 2002 welcomed this development, it also raised some reservations regarding the "limited improvement in practice in the ability of members of ethnic groups with a cultural identity and common traditions to express their linguistic and cultural identity." The 2003 report, which underlines the progress made by the latest wave of reforms, also states that sufficient progress has still not been made in this field. Indeed, although the Law on Foundations has been amended, religious minorities continue to face limitations regarding legal status, property rights, training of clergy, and education matters. Finally, the Commission report states clearly that the Human Rights Conventions should be ratified fully by all candidate countries. So far, Turkey has achieved only partial ratification.[12]

All these problems inherent to Turkish democracy and underlined by the European Commission reports manifest themselves in Turkish citizenship and indicate the insufficiency of the republican model of citizenship in enlarging individual and group rights. Thus, Turkey has been declared unfit to join the "fourth wave of democracy"[13] (McFaul 2002: 213–14) of countries joining the EU in 2004 (most of the ten countries set to join are eastern-European). The Copenhagen Summit decided that Turkey's situation would be reconsidered in December 2004. The focus is to be on a series of legal, constitutional and institutional measures taken recently by the state that are designed to improve citizens' rights, and to conform with EU criteria for Turkey's application for membership. Being one of the oldest democracies in the Middle East and in the Third World at large, Turkey (considered by some as a "démocratie d'ailleurs," Jaffrelot 2000) has now an exceptional opportunity to join the group of "central democracies." However, the possibility of transforming this opportunity into reality requires a radical transformation of the republican mode of citizenship to better match the language of individual rights and freedoms. In other words, the relations between state and society in Turkey will need to be overhauled in conformity with the Copenhagen criteria.

Conclusion

Growing EU pressure for the introduction of a democratic, constitutional, and even post-national form of citizenship in Turkey should be welcomed. However, this pressure creates something of a paradox in the strong-state tradition in Turkey. This is because the Turkish political elite perceives EU membership as a badge of modernity and civilization but does not necessarily see membership as entailing the construction of a fully democratic and liberal society. The nuance established between modernity and liberal democracy by the political elite has laid the ground for ambivalent relations between the EU and Turkey. This ambivalence can only be dispelled if Turkey becomes a full member of a newly enlarged Europe. However, the EU's position on Turkey has become as important as the will of the strong-state to transform itself into a liberal democracy. If the EU avoids cultural essentialism and employs an inclusive and liberal understanding of citizenship (with a notion of constitutional citizenship widening the basis of the new Europe), it will prepare the ground for Turkey's full membership. Thus, an inclusive and constitutional understanding of the new Europe would be a real incentive for the Turkish state to act in accordance with the discourse of modernity and democracy as it agrees to transfer a measure of national sovereignty to a supranational center. Indeed, constitutional citizenship, capable in principle of articulating universalism and particularism at the same time, may constitute a real opening in the closed space created by the combination of "the blindness of universalism and the short-sightedness of culturalism" (Badie and Perrineau 2000: 32).

In this sense, the fact that the EU has required each candidate state to start the accession process by deepening their own democracies (by "democratizing their own democracies") should apply to the EU itself in its own identity as a liberal democratic and inclusive space in which postnational values go hand-in-hand with constitutional citizenship in creating "unity in diversity." It is also in this context that the impact of the EU constitutes a positive force for the creation of a diverse, democratic and strong Turkey within the EU. In the world in which we live, the principle of unity in diversity has a very important role to play in resisting the idea of a "clash of civilizations" that seems to underpin world affairs at the present time. A democratic Turkey could make a crucial contribution to the new Europe's efforts to play an essential role in world peace.

Notes

1 At the 1999 Helsinki Summit, thirteen countries were officially designated as candidates for membership of the EU: Bulgaria, Cyprus, Czech Republic, Estonia, Hungary, Latvia, Lithuania, Malta, Poland, Romania, Slovakia, Slovenia and Turkey.

2 In the 1970s, the original nine member states of the European Community (joined by Great Britain, Denmark and Ireland in 1973), worked further on the creation of a European identity. The "Report on European Identity" presented at the Copenhagen Summit (1973) was followed by other steps in this direction, such as the organization of direct elections to the European Parliament. In the 1980s, efforts were made to create a "European consciousness" through the "Spinelli Project," the "Declaration of Europe" (1983) and the Fontainebleau Summit (1984). The latter referred symbolically to a "Europe of citizens" and undertook practical measures to remove border controls on EU citizens and harmonize European passports, driving licenses, etc.

3 The formation of a customs union and financial cooperation with Turkey aimed to help the country to align its economic and social policies with that of the European Community. This originally included the free movement of labor, but actual progress on this front has not been to schedule.

4 This was not the case either after the first military coup in 1960 (which simply slowed down negotiations) or after the second military coup of 1971 (during which the political parties – but not the parliament – were dismissed).

5 The Helsinki conclusion stated that

> Turkey is a candidate state destined to join the Union on the basis of the same criteria as those applied to the other candidates. This has enabled the country to benefit from a pre-accession strategy that includes enhanced political dialogue. The emphasis of this dialogue has been the fulfillment of political criteria with particular reference to human rights border disputes and Cyprus. Turkey is to participate in all Community programs and agencies and meetings between candidate States and the Union as part of the accession process. An Accession Partnership (AP) will be drawn up, combined with a National Program for the Adoption of the Acquis (NPAA). Appropriate monitoring mechanisms will be established. The Commission will prepare a process of analytical examination of the acquis. A single framework for coordinating all sources of EU financial assistance for pre-accession will be presented by the Commission. The proposal establishes the legal base to draw up an Accession partnership for Turkey and define a single framework for coordinating all sources of EU financial assistance to Turkey for pre-accession.
>
> (Proposal for a Council Regulation, 2000/2005 – CNS)

6 The entire list of principles to be respected is long. They include: confirmation of the democratic functioning of government; consolidation and modernization of the public administration needs in conformity with EU norms; reformation and strengthening of the juridical system; intensification of efforts to fight against corruption, fraud and economic crime; reinforcement of the legislative and institutional framework for gender equality; adoption of the EU anti-discrimination acquis; and the guarantee of protection for minorities.

7 In the case of Turkey the document "A Strategy for Developing Relations between Turkey and the European Union" describes the rules in depth.

8 The evaluation of each applicant/candidate country is summarized annually since 1998 in the European Commission's Progress Reports.

9 Commission of the European Communities, Brussels, 9.10.2002, SEC (2002) 1412 – COM (2002) 700 final, "Towards the Enlarged Union – Strategy Paper and Report of the European Commission on Progress towards Accession by each of the Candidate Countries"; 5.10.2003 "2003 Regular Report on Turkey's Progress Towards Accession," europa.eu.int/comm./enlargement Report 2003.

10 It may be seen as an advancement of postnational membership, as noted by Y. Soysal (1994).

11 On this topic, the 2002 report notes: "The constitutional amendment introducing changes to the composition and role of the National Security Council has been put into practice. Nonetheless, these changes do not appear to have modified the way in which the National Security Council operates in practice." The 2003 report confirms this appreciation regarding the reforms carried out last year.

12 By October 2003, Turkey had ratified the European convention on Human Rights-Protocol 1 (rights of property) and Protocol 6 (death penalty – ratified in June 2003). The international covenant on civil and political rights (ICCPR) and the International covenant on economic, social and cultural rights (ICESCR) were both ratified in June 2003 (but with reservations in relation to the right to education and to minorities' rights). Also ratified were the European Convention for the Prevention of Torture, the European Social Charter (but not the revised one), the Convention Against Torture (CAT), the CERD (Convention on the Elimination of all Forms of Racial Discrimination), the Convention on the Elimination of all Forms of Discrimination against Women (CEDAW) and its Optional Protocol, and the Convention on the Rights of the Child (CRC). (In 1969, Turkey also ratified the United Nations Convention on the Elimination of all Forms of Racial Discrimination, and has since signed the European

Agreement Relating to Persons Participating in Proceedings of the European Court of Human Rights). But other conventions are still waiting for ratification. These include the European Convention on Human Rights (Protocol 4 – freedom of movement *et al.*; Protocol 7 – *ne bis in idem*), the revised European Social Charter, the Framework Convention for National Minorities, the Optional Protocol to the ICCPR (right of individual communication), the Second Protocol to the ICCPR (death penalty), and the Optional Protocol to the CEDAW.

13 The "fourth wave" of democracy designates the transition from the Soviet model of communism to democracy (or in some cases to dictatorship). "The unequal distribution of power that produced the quickest and most stable transition from communism ... to democracy emerged therefore in countries where democrats enjoyed a decisive power advantage."

References

Anderson, B. (1987) *Imagined Communities*, London: Verso.

Apter, D. E. (1988) *Pour l'Etat contre l'Etat*. Paris: Economica, Collection Politique Comparée.

Badie, B. (1992) *L'Etat importé*. Paris: Fayard, Coll. L'espace du politique.

Badie, B. and Perrineau, P. (eds) (2000) *Le citoyen*. Paris: Presses des Sciences PO.

Documents on Europe : europa.eu.int

Futuribles (1995) no. 200, July-August.

Garot, M. J. (1999) *La citoyenneté de l'Union européenne*, in l'Harmattan, Logiques, Juridiques, Paris and Montreal.

Haas, E. B. (1958) *The Uniting of Europe's Political, Social and Economical Forces – 1950–1957*, Stervens & Sons Ltd, The London Institute of World Affairs.

Habermas, J. (1992) "Citizenship and National Identity: Some Reflexions on the Future of Europe," *Praxis International*, 12: 1–19.

Jaffrelot, C. (2000) *Démocraties d'ailleurs – démocraties et démocratisations hors d'Occident* Paris: CERI, Karthala.

Kadıoğlu, A. (1998) "Citizenship and Individuation in Turkey: The Triumph of Will over Reason", *CEMOTI*, 26: 23–42.

McFaul, M. (2002) "The Fourth Wave of Democracy and Dictatorship – Non-cooperative Transition in the Postcommunist World," *World Politics*, 54: 212–44.

Morin, E. (1987) *Penser l'Europe* , Paris: Gallimard/Au Vif du Sujet.

(Le) Parlement Européen – Information (1950) "Déclaration de Robert Schuman", Discours du 9 Mai.

Quermonne, J. L. (3rd edn 1998) *Le système politique de l'Union européenne* translated by A-R Maisonneuve Arcouz, Paris: Montchrestien.

——(2000) "L'impact du Traité d'Amsterdam sur la citoyenneté européenne: paradoxes ou Révolution?", in B. Badie and P. Perrineau (eds) *Le citoyen*, Paris: Presses des Sciences PO.

Roux, M. (1992) *"Le paradoxe des identities", La citoyenneté dans tous ses états – De l'immigration à la nouvelle citoyenneté*, Paris: CIEMI, l'Harmattan.

Soysal, Y. (1994) *Limits of Citizenship – Migrants and Postnational Membership in Europe*, Chicago and London: University of Chicago Press.

Turner, B. S. (1994), "Outline of a Theory of Citizenship," in B. S. Turner and P. Hamilton (eds) *Citizenship – Critical Concepts*, London and New York: Routledge.

Üstel, F. (2002) "Türkiye Cumhuriyeti'nde Resmî Yurttaş Profilinin Evrimi" (The Evolution of the Profile of Citizenship in the Republic of Turkey), *Modern Türkiye'de Siyasi Düsünce – Milliyetçilik*, Istanbul: İletisim.

Vardar, D. (1993) "L'intégration de la Turquie en Europe et son impact", *Toplum ve Ekonomi*, 5 (September): 147–76.

——(1996) "Les enjeux européen et régional de la Turquie dans la construction des légitimités", in *Enjeux économiques et rapports de force en Turquie et en Méditerranée orientale*, eds J. Thobie, R. Perez and S. Kançal, Montreal and Paris: L'Harmattan, Coll. Varia Turcica, 399–415.

Part II

Citizenship, state and democracy

5 Can we envision Turkish citizenship as non-membership?

Ayşe Kadıoğlu

> The politics of citizenship today is first and foremost a politics of nationhood. As such, it is a *politics of identity*, not a *politics of interest* (in the restricted, materialist sense). It pivots more on self-understanding than on self-interest. The "interests" informing the politics of citizenship are "ideal" rather than material. The central question is not "who gets what?" but rather "who is what?"
>
> (Brubaker 1992: 182)

Modern allegiances and senses of loyalty are determined by nation-states. The modern notion of citizenship involves membership of the nation-state. In the course of the past few years, there has been an increase in academic efforts in the West to critically examine and perhaps redefine the notion of modern citizenship. Today, the notion of modern citizenship is in the process of being divorced from its inherent attachment to the nation-state. In other words, we live in an era in which increasing demands are being expressed in order to widen the public realm to accomodate differences that were previously relegated to the private realm. These demands for opening up the public realm to differences involve women, immigrants and blacks, as well as ethnic and religious groups. Since the modern notion of citizenship that involves membership of a nation-state is inadequate in representing the demands of such groups, it has become an obstacle to the democratization efforts of modern nation-states.

At the close of the twentieth century, political theorists who have focused on the question of democratization began to discuss social and political allegiances and senses of belonging. Such debates went hand-in-hand with social movements that either advocated egoism/atomist individualism or altruism. Hence, there emerged individualist anarchism on the one hand and communitarian tendencies on the other. The common denominator of these trends is that they both question and put under scrutiny modern notions of identity, albeit from different angles, i.e. while one glorifies the atomized individual, the other glorifies the community. What seems certain is that modern notions of identity and belonging that mainly revolve around allegiances to the nation-state are declining. With the increasing public expression of identities other than the national one, many of the categories of modern politics have proved themselves inadequate.

I have earlier argued that the limitations of the feminist arguments in Turkey basically stem from an assumption of women as citizens prior to being individuals (Kadıoğlu 1996a; 1998a; 1993a). Feminist demands in Turkey are usually posed by way of attachment to grand social and political projects such as Kemalism or Socialism, as well as Islamic identities. Kemalist feminists emphasize women's public visibility in modern attire, especially in the political arena, such as their presence and visibility in the parliament and within political party structures. Socialist women, in the course of the 1970s, emphasized a view of equality of women which came to mean "similarity with men." Hence, they denounced their sexuality and femininity and posed as "sisters" of socialist men (Berktay 1990). Islamic women, on the other hand, have been staging a fight of the costumes since the early 1980s. With the advent of political Islam, the covered bodies of the Moslem women are perpetuated in stark contrast with the bodies of modern women. These women resort to veiling in order to emphasize their personality rather than their sexuality (Göle 1991: 125; Kadıoğlu 1994). Veiling, then, has become a way of denouncing sexuality outside of the confines of a marital arrangement. Thus Turkish women, in the course of serving such grand social and political projects, denounced their individual identities. The trajectory of Turkish men is not too different from that of Turkish women in terms of the denouncement of individuality. Hence, Turkish men and women first and foremost perceive themselves as Turkish citizens who are responsible for performing certain duties.

In this chapter, the Turkish notion of citizenship will be examined by referring to existing categorizations in the literature on citizenship. Accordingly, first of all, the structural and historical factors that shape the notion of citizenship will be portrayed by focusing on the respective sequence of the state-formation and nation-building processes in Turkey. Second, the Turkish notion of citizenship will be examined from the angle of the liberal versus civic-republican traditions in political philosophy. Third, whether the Turkish notion of citizenship can be characterized as active or passive will be discussed, while at the same time assessing the extent of interference into the private realm of Turkish citizens. The evaluation of the Turkish conception of citizenship along these lines will involve references to statements of some of the founding elite of the Republic as well as certain institutional arrangements that were undertaken especially in the early years of the Republic. The main thesis of this chapter is that "the citizen precedes the individual" in Turkey (Kadıoğlu 1999). A critical evaluation of the literature on citizenship will pave the way to the inadequacy of a view of *citizenship as membership* (either of a nation or a state). Hence, at the end of this chapter, a view of *citizenship as a position* will be suggested.

The citizenship problematique

The roots of the modern concept of citizenship can be located in the French Revolution and its immediate aftermath. Citizenship is a modern concept. It evolved along with the evolution of various nationalisms in Europe in the aftermath of the French Revolution. In fact, the beginning of immigration control in Europe was an outcome of the French Revolution. In England, for instance, the 1792 Aliens Bill was a direct response to the flight of French refugees (about 8,000) from the French Revolution (Plender 1972: 43). In America and Switzerland too, immigration control began as a reaction to the French Revolution and fears that Jacobin emissaries had infiltrated immigrant groups.

The modern concept of "citizen" is closely associated with the notion of civilization which entails a movement from rural to urban centers. A citizen is someone from the *cité* (city). In the course of the eighteenth century, the *cité* was a place where individual freedoms were pushed to the forefront and feudal hierarchical structures were destroyed. Accordingly, the *citoyen* (citizen) was the motor of these changes away from feudal bondage relations toward capitalist contractual relations. The nineteenth century, on the contrary, was characterized by many Romantic views of the *cité* as the center of decadence and deterioration. The most important reaction to the French Revolution and Napoleon's conquests in the German states was felt not in the political, legal and institutional realms but in literature. Accordingly, nineteenth-century German Romanticism was characterized by a yearning for the provinces and rural life away from the *cité*.

Today, with the increasing scrutiny of the basic categories of modernity, the modern notion of citizenship has begun to be viewed outside of its inherent attachment to the nation-state. The need to revise the modern category of citizenship is an implication of the process of globalization. Globalization and the transfer of images and populations across countries has prompted the opening up of the public realm to differences that were earlier relegated to the private realm. Such differences are usually expressed in terms of languages pertaining to gender, race, religion, and ethnicity.

In the Turkish context, the urge to revise and redefine the notion of citizenship has stemmed from a visible accentuation of the expression of women's as well as Islamic and Kurdish identities during the political climate of the late 1980s and 1990s. The presence of such differences that were earlier part of the private realm began to make their debut in the public realm. The absolute, homogeneous, all-encompassing category of Turkish citizenship was demystified and began to crumble due to the predominance of an "identity politics" in Turkey based on gender-related, religious and ethnic identities.

While the issue garnered increasing attention in academic circles,[1] a new notion called "constitutional citizenship" began to be discussed in political circles and the expression was even used by the then president, Süleyman Demirel (Vergin 1996; Üstel, 1996a). In the midst of these debates on

Turkish citizenship, some people began to refer to themselves as "I am from Turkey" (*Türkiye'liyim*) rather than "I am a Turk" (*Türküm*). This event symbolized the demystification of the official view of Turkish citizenship declared in Mustafa Kemal Atatürk's famous expression "How happy is the one who calls himself a Turk!" (*Ne mutlu Türküm diyene!*). I believe the issue of citizenship poses the question of democratization in Turkey from the angle of modernity rather than focusing on the specific features and problems of the Turkish modernization project. Scrutiny of the modern notion of citizenship has not been peculiar to Turkey. It is a process that has been unleashed all over the world as a result of the dynamics of globalization.

Almost all the new analyses of the modern notion of citizenship in the literature refer to T. H. Marshall's classic works (Marshall 1950; 1977). Marshall refers to three dimensions of citizenship: civil and legal, political, and social. First of all, the civil and legal rights of citizens evolved in the course of the seventeenth century *vis-à-vis* the absolutist states. Accordingly, courts and individual legal rights began to appear. Second, political rights evolved in the course of the eighteenth and nineteenth centuries alongside the evolution of modern parliamentary systems. Third, the social dimension of citizenship is a phenomenon of the twentieth century and is related to the welfare state. This dimension paved the way to certain social rights of individuals such as employment, health, and education. Marshall then pointed to a uniform, evolutionary and teleological history of the notion of citizenship. As a result, his citizenship theory was criticized extensively in the recent literature for failing to account for various types of modern citizenship (Turner 1992; 1993; van Steenbergen 1994).

Still, the sequence in the emergence of the three dimensions of citizenship can be utilized in accounting for different trajectories toward modern citizenship. In cases where democratization preceded bureaucratization, civil and legal rights acquire predominance to the detriment of social rights. In the United States, for instance, the notion of "social citizenship" is an oxymoron (Fraser and Gordon 1994). Citizens relate to the state either via contractual arrangements or they receive aid from the state in the form of charity. Hence, the recipients of welfare state benefits are usually viewed as lazy parasites who are unworthy of the honor of citizenship. Quite contrarily, in Germany, where bureaucratization preceded democratization, citizens (members of the *Volk*) benefit from welfare state provisions as "rights." In Turkey, the distinguishing feature of civil and legal, political and social rights is the fact that they were given from above rather than acquired as rights in the aftermath of demands and struggles from below. Hence, citizenship was bestowed from above prior to the birth of a bourgeoisie that posed demands and ignited the fire that culminated in constitutionalism.[2]

Anatomy of Turkish citizenship[3]

In what follows, the evolution of Turkish citizenship in the early republican era will be portrayed by situating it within the existing literature on citizenship. Accordingly, first of all, the evolution of the concept will be connected to the evolution of nationalism in Turkey. Second, the impact of the civic-republican tradition in shaping the contours of Turkish citizenship will be addressed. Third, the evolution of Turkish citizenship from above will be portrayed while pointing to the invaded nature of the private realm of Turkish citizens.

A state seeking its nation: the evolution of Turkish nationalism and citizenship

The years between 1789 and 1815 signaled the emergence of both French and German nationalisms (Kohn 1967). German nationalism emerged alongside a literary tradition called Romanticism. One of the most distinguishing features of this tradition was its critical attitude toward French cosmopolitanism. German Romantics thought that the rationalism of the eighteenth century was artificial. They relied on intuitions and emotions rather than reason and intellect. The German Romantic tradition reveals the dark and anti-rational aspects of German nationalism. The notion of a German nation that evolved in the course of the nineteenth century stemmed from a *Völkisch* ideology which later formed the basis of the National Socialist worldview. German Romantic literature became the medium for the expression of German nationalism in the course of the nineteenth century, prior to the formation of a German nation-state. Since German nationalism preceded the nation-state, it was expressed in ethnic and cultural terms. Accordingly, Rogers Brubaker refers to an "ethnocultural conception of nationhood" in Germany (Brubaker 1989; 1990; 1992). In comparing the German and French conceptions of nationhood and citizenship, Brubaker says:

> It is one thing to want to make all citizens of Utopia speak Utopian, and quite another to want to make all Utopiphones citizens of Utopia. Crudely put, the former represents the French, the latter the German model of nationhood. Whether juridical (as in naturalization) or cultural, assimilation presupposes a political conception of membership and the belief, which France took over from the Roman tradition, that the state can turn strangers into citizens, peasants – or immigrant workers – into Frenchmen.
>
> (Brubaker 1992: 8)

Hence, while the French conception of citizenship evolved in an assimilationist and state-centered manner, the German conception acquired an organic, differentialist, dissimilationist and Volk-centered character. French nationhood evolved in a predominantly political way while German nationhood became predominantly ethnocultural. As Brubaker puts it:

> In fact, traditions of nationhood have political and cultural components in both countries. These components have been closely integrated in France, where political unity has been understood as constitutive, cultural unity as expressive of nationhood. In the German tradition, in contrast, political and ethnocultural aspects of nationhood have stood in tension with one another, serving as the basis for competing conceptions of nationhood. One such conception is sharply opposed to the French conception: according to this view, ethnocultural unity is constitutive, political unity expressive, of nationhood.
>
> (Brubaker 1992: 10)

Hence, the temporal distance between the state-formation and nation-building processes, as well as their sequence, gave shape to the conceptions of nationhood and citizenship in France and Germany (Kadıoğlu 1991; 1992; 1993b; 1993c; 1996c). Since French nationalism appeared at about the same time as the French nation-state, political and social unity was the work of statesmen. German nationalism preceded by half a century the formation of the German nation-state. The German Romantic tradition was laden with motifs of yearning for a national state. Such a temporal distance made ethnic and cultural unity constitutive of German nationalism. This paved the way to the significance laid on blood ties and/or descent as the basis of modern German citizenship.

The distinction between French and German nationalisms and conceptualizations of citizenship are significant in understanding Turkish nationalism at two points: First of all, Turkish nationalism displays the characteristics of both French and German nationalisms. It embraces both Civilization and Culture; hence it has a paradoxical nature (Kadıoğlu 1996d). The paradox between Civilization and Culture is nowhere better expressed than in the writings of Ziya Gökalp. The type of nationalism that Ziya Gökalp mentioned in his writings was individualist and cosmopolitan, yet it also espoused the retainment of a local, pristine identity. Hence, the concepts of Civilization and Culture were not antithetical, mutually exclusive entities in Ziya Gökalp's thought. Rather he tried to synthesize them. Niyazi Berkes, in his analysis of Ziya Gökalp's thought, maintains that:

> If his analyses are taken as a whole, however, these two concepts (Culture and Civilization) do not represent antithetical and mutually exclusive entities, but rather two closely related and complementary traits of social reality. ... Civilizational elements assume meaning and function in the life of men only when they enter into the service of culture. Without a cultural basis, civilization becomes merely a matter of mechanical imitation; it never penetrates into the inner life of a people and never gives fruit of any kind.
>
> (Berkes 1959: 23)

It is possible to argue that if nationalism is a modern Janus, the Turkish version had two faces as well. While in most instances Turkish nationalism looked similar to the civic French nationalism, there were certain periods in the founding years of the Republic when the organic, ethnic face that is akin to German nationalism became more pronounced. In a study that attempts a periodization of Turkish nationalism, and accordingly the formation of citizenship practices, Ahmet Yıldız (2001) brings out into the open the pronounced ethno-cultural dimension of Turkish citizenship, especially in the period between 1929 and 1938. His book is aptly titled *Ne mutlu Türküm Diyebilene* (How happy is the one who *can* call himself a Turk) in pointing to a subtle distinction between "calling oneself a Turk" and "*can* call oneself a Turk." The latter expression, i.e. the ability to call oneself a Turk, makes references to ethnic, ascriptive qualifications and it was an expression used by one of the ideologues of the Turkish revolution, Bozkurt Mahmut Esat in 1934 (Yıldız 2001: 212). In unraveling the mostly neglected "evil" face of Turkish nationalism, Yıldız refers to legal, political arrangements, the records of parliamentary proceedings and the proceedings of the Republican People's Party, as well as memoirs and texts of the leading ideologues of the early republican years. According to Yıldız's periodization of the early republican years, the fundamental references of Turkish nationalism evolved from religious (1919–23) to secular (1924–29) themes and then became suffused by ethnocultural (1929–38) motifs. The citizenship practices evolved in accordance with these core elements in their respective periods.[4]

Second, it is important to point to the sequence of the emergence of state and nation in Turkey. Whereas in the German case, it is possible to refer to a nation preceding a state, i.e. "a nation in search of its state," in the Turkish scenario the historical order of things is reversed. In the case of modern republican Turkey, one can refer to a state preceding a nation, i.e. "a state in search of its nation" (Kadıoğlu 1995). The Turkish nation was constructed by means of certain measures that were undertaken by the republican elite. In the words of Şerif Mardin (1981: 196): "Mustafa Kemal took upon a hypothetical entity, the Turkish nation, and breathed life in it." In this construction, political unity appears as the constitutive unit of the Turkish nation-state. In short, the indivisibility of the Turkish state with its nation, and the irreversibility of the holy borders – contrary to the case in Germany – constitute the cornerstone of Turkish national identity.

Hence, Turkish citizenship appears as a notion defined from above by the leading figures in the People's Republican Party at the time of the founding years of the Republic that was based on a one-party regime. The distinguishing features of this notion of citizenship were delineated in the 1931 Congress of the Republican People's Party and were formulated as the "six arrows" that became the insignia of the party. These were: nationalism, secularism, populism, republicanism, etatism, and revolutionism. These founding principles constitute the core of the Turkish Republic.

On 19 February 1932, the People's Houses (*Halkevleri*) were founded in fourteen cities in order to promote these core principles of the Republic. They aimed at creating the ideal republican citizen who had embraced these core principles that were represented in the insignia of the People's Republican Party. It was through the activities of the People's Houses that the republican elite aimed at breathing life into the citizens of the Turkish nation (Soyarık 2000). The main aim of the journal of the People's Houses (*Ülkü*) was to provide the six arrows with a theoretical framework as well as teaching them to the people. The function of the People's Houses was further supported by the formation of two other institutions, namely the Turkish History Society (Türk Tarih Kurumu) and Turkish Linguistic Society (Türk Dil Kurumu) in 1931 and 1932 respectively. The Turkish History Society researched the history of Turks in the pre-Islamic period and aimed at spreading the view that all the civilizations of the world stemmed from the Turkish civilization that was rooted in Central Asia. The Turkish Linguistic Society, on the other hand, tried to bring out the beauty and richness of the Turkish language as the mother of all languages.

The People's Houses, as well as the Turkish History Society and Turkish Linguistic Society, aimed at creating a Turkish citizen prior to the emergence of an individualist ethic in Turkey. Hence, they were instrumental in forming a notion of citizenship that emphasized obligations instead of rights.

Militant Turkish citizen burdened with duties

Another classification of the modern notion of citizenship in the literature stems from a philosophical distinction between the liberal or liberal-individualist traditions and the classical or civic-republican tradition. Adrian Oldfield (1990; 1994), who classifies modern citizenship on the basis of these philosophical traditions, refers to the differences between citizenship as "status" and citizenship as "practice." Liberal-individualism has been the dominant strain of thought in Anglo-American political thinking since the seventeenth century, roughly from Hobbes onward. According to Oldfield (1990: 1), liberal individualism accords the individual an ontological, epistemological and a moral priority. Liberal individualism defines citizenship as a status on the basis of "rights," and hence gives rise to a language of citizenship in terms of needs and entitlements. "The status of citizenship" imposes no "duties" on the individuals beyond the minimally civic ones. Individuals relate to each other on a contractual basis. Any other form of public involvement and political activity is their "choice." Hence, in the liberal-individualist tradition, the conception of citizenship generates no social bond other than contract. It does not prompt any type of social solidarity, cohesion, and any sense of common purpose (Oldfield 1994: 190). It produces an individual who is deficient and impoverished as a social being.

The classical or the civic-republican tradition has its origins in the ethical and political thought of Aristotle. It was reinforced and modified by a succession of political thinkers from Macchiavelli to Rousseau and beyond. In the words of Oldfield (1990: 5), "it addresses much more cogently the twin themes of citizenship and community." In the classical tradition, citizenship appears as an activity or a practice so that not to engage in the practice is, in important senses, not to be a citizen (Oldfield 1994: 192). Citizenship, in this tradition, is expressed in terms of a language of "duties," and/or obligations to the community. Practices empower individuals to act like citizens. It is the shared commitment to these practices which makes individuals citizens. It is action in such spheres as military service which is both constitutive of citizenship and sustaining of the community of which the citizen is a member. In this view, individuals are not thought of as logically prior to society (Oldfield 1994: 191). Moreover, they have no moral priority. As a result, claims may be made on their time, resources, and lives for the morally superior entity which is the community. Oldfield's (1994: 193) major endeavor is to instigate an articulation between these two traditions and redefine the notion of modern citizenship by benefiting from the good aspects of each:

> In the Western world, the ideal of citizenship as status is one which it is not difficult to think of as achievable, even if vigilance is required to ensure that the achievement is sustained. Our confidence here is in large part a product of the sheer amount of thought and struggle which have been invested in the ideal. The same cannot be said of the ideal of citizenship as practice, and in large part this reflects the very success of the liberal-individualist achievement, which was to liberate the individual from the constricting influences of society and the state. The thinking has been there, but the struggle has not. The question, therefore, is whether the struggle is worthwhile. [*We must not expect to displace the idea of citizenship as status, but we can use elements of this conception to further the project of citizenship as practice.*]
>
> (Oldfield's 1994: 193)

The Turkish notion of citizenship in the aftermath of the proclamation of the Republic evolved in a manner that is more akin to the civic-republican tradition. Accordingly, Turkish citizenship is based more on "duties" than on "rights." Citizenship education started in the education system of the Turkish Republic in 1924 with the course on Information About the Motherland (*Malumat-ı Vataniye*) for the primary and secondary school curriculum. This was replaced in 1927 with another course called *Yurt Bilgisi* and later on *Yurttaşlık Bilgisi*. After 1985 a new course on Information on Citizenship (*Vatandaşlık Bilgileri*) appeared, and in the 1990s a course on Citizenship and Human Rights (*Vatandaşlık ve İnsan Hakları*) was introduced. In a study surveying the books utilized in citizenship education courses in primary and secondary schools in Turkey in the republican era, Füsun Üstel (2002) underlines the evolution of a notion of citizenship based on duties. Accordingly, the most outstanding aim of citizenship education appears as the achievement of civilization and the inculcation of patriotism. Üstel refers to a "militant" citizen who evolved until the end of the 1940s and who was "burdened with duties." The obligations of the militant citizen were strengthened by referring to a perceived threat to the Republic. The "Other" that is portrayed as a threat or an enemy was a leitmotif in citizenship education. What is implied by the Other is sometimes the sultanate and the *ancien régime*. In units that describe the War of Independence, the Other becomes the Greeks. The duties of citizenship were also outlined in a book that was prepared by Mustafa Kemal's adopted daughter Afet İnan (1969). Mustafa Kemal contributed to the preparation of the book that was called Civic Information for the Citizen (*Vatandaş İçin Medeni Bilgiler*). This book was first published in 1930. The book mainly describes the duties of citizens toward the family, society, and the state. Accordingly, citizens were required to pay taxes and obey rules pertaining to public order, as well as participate in elections. Men were expected to serve in the military, which was regarded as an enlightening institution.

Fuat Keyman (1997) presents a notion of republican citizenship that is constituted by means of duties in order to promote a "common good" to the detriment of individual rights. He interprets the concept of citizenship in Turkey within the framework of the Platonic nature of the Kemalist project of modernity. Accordingly, "common good" is defined by reference to a "will to civilization" on the part of the state elites. Hence, politics in this context does not entail an articulation of different demands into the decision-making process, and therefore their representation, but rather the steering of society toward a common good defined by the state elite in accordance with their will to civilization. This common good has ontological priority over demands coming from society. As a result, the citizen appears both as the object of the Kemalist modernization project and its carrier. She or he is not only expected to internalize this project but also reproduces the sovereign position of the state.

Passive Turkish citizenship with an invaded private realm

Bryan Turner (1992; 1993) puts forward a classification of the modern notion of citizenship based on the two axes of active versus passive and the extent of its definition within the public realm. Accordingly, there exist four types of modern citizenship that evolved in four different contexts: first of all, in revolutionary contexts, citizenship involves a struggle from below (active citizenship) with an emphasis on the public arena (citizenship evolved in the public realm). As a result, the private world of the individual is regarded with suspicion. Second, in the liberal pluralist context, citizenship, once again involves a struggle for rights from below (active citizenship), yet there also exists a continuous emphasis on the rights of the individual for privatized dissent (citizenship evolved in the private realm). Third, in passive democratic mediums, citizenship rights are given from above without or prior to a struggle from below (passive citizenship or citizen as subject) combined with a legitimacy of representative institutions, courts and the welfare state system (citizenship evolved in the public realm). Fourth, in plebiscitary authoritarian mediums, citizenship rights are once again given from above (passive citizenship). Yet, although the state invites the citizens to periodically elect a leader, the latter is no longer responsible to the electorate on a daily basis, and therefore, private life emerges as a "sanctuary from state regulation" (citizenship evolved in the private realm) (Turner 1992: 46).

Turner refers to the French conception of citizenship within the revolutionary tradition, where there existed an attack on the private space of the family, and religion. The American conception of citizenship contained motifs of the liberal pluralist solution, since participation was emphasized yet contained by a continuous emphasis on the privacy and the sanctity of individual opinion. The English case under the seventeenth-century settlement, in Turner's opinion, was an example of the passive democratic solution, since citizens appeared as mere subjects combined with a legitimacy of the representative institutions. German fascism constitutes a degeneration of plebiscitary democracy where "the individual citizen is submerged in the sacredness of the state which permits minimal participation in terms of election of leaders, while family life is given priority in the arena of personal ethical development" (Turner 1992: 55–6). The failure of a radical bourgeois revolution in Germany in the 1840s and the realization of unification from above in 1870 by means of Bismarckian legislation, paved the way to passive citizenship which became the main carrier of social rights. The absence of a successful liberal revolution produced an underdeveloped public realm in Germany (Turner 1993: 10).

The Turkish conception of modern citizenship, when viewed from the angle of Turner's classification, seems akin both to the French Revolutionary tradition, since there exists an attack on the private space of the family and religion, and the German passive tradition. In Turner's (1992: 56) formulation, the former tradition may collapse into totalitarianism when the "state in pushing egalitarianism to the extreme closes off the private sphere from influencing the course of political affairs." The Turkish conception differs from the French one, since it was defined from above and therefore is passive. It is similar to the German conception because the absence of a successful liberal revolution and hence participation produced an underdeveloped public realm. Turkish citizenship is defined from above (passive) within an exaggerated public space which smothers the individual and invades the private space of the family and religion. Üstel (1996b; 2002) observes an effort to supervise and regulate the private realm in citizenship education, such as the listing of appropriate fun and recreational activities, the regulation of health and hygiene, as well as dress codes, until the end of the 1940s. She, for instance, highlights the sections in books on citizenship education dealing with "appropriate" forms of entertainment and physical education that are suggested by virtue of being "hygienic and moral" (Üstel, 2002: 281). As Minister of the Interior Şükrü Kaya argued (cited in Soyarık 2000: 113–14) in reference to the enactment of a law on the necessity of physical education in 1938:

> Every regime seeks an appropriate type of citizen and finds it. We know the citizen of the absolutist regime. The man of the regime of Atatürk, the Kemalist revolution, is well shaped, clever, brave, dignified, merry and serious, and defends his rights and ideas in every circumstance. We are looking for this. The aim of this physical education is intellectual, moral, and ethical training. This is the type our regime entails. ... Being well behaved, polite, dignified and serious are Turks' most obvious features in confrontation with the world. ... We would like to see our citizens dignified, in their public life as well as in their private life.
>
> (Soyarık 2000: 113–14)

Perhaps what distinguishes the Turkish notion of citizenship from the French tradition is the absence of an Enlightenment prior to the establishment of citizenship. If, following Immanuel Kant (cited in Reiss 1970), Enlightenment is defined as "man's emergence from his self-incurred immaturity," the Turkish notion of citizenship presumes an unenlightened, immature individual. Hence, the notion of Turkish citizenship was constructed prior to an enlightened, "free" individual capable of producing demands. Such a notion purports to steer the common lives of immature beings by means of duties. The citizens are not expected to reason. Rather, they are expected to follow. In elaborating on national morals, Mustafa Kemal says:

> In a nation which is developed and has reached a perfect level, the requirements of national morals are undertaken by the individuals in that nation [*– without resorting to reason – by means of the voice of their conscience and emotional instinct*].
>
> (Tezcan 1996: 17; my translation)

Writing in 1929–30, Mustafa Kemal acknowledged the immature state of the Republic and argued that what is usually relegated to individual initiative in developed countries should be considered as vital state undertakings in our country. As he put it:

> Our Republic is very young; it is not yet capable of contemporary undertakings and all the grand tasks that it has inherited from the past. As in political and intellectual life, in economic undertakings too, it would not be correct to wait for the results of individual initiatives. The

> significant and grand tasks should be realized in a successful way only by a government that relies on national wealth and organizes the dispensing and bearing of national sovereignty by relying on all the institutions and power of the state.
>
> (Tezcan 1996: 54; my translation)

The concept of modern citizenship evolved in such a way as to exclude a liberal individualist dimension in Turkey. Whereas in Western Europe the notion of the individual appeared in philosophical writings prior to the emergence of modern citizenship, in Turkey, the citizen precedes the individual. Hence, Turkish citizens found themselves in a position to be absorbed in grand social projects such as Kemalism, Socialism, and political Islam. Trapped in the missions of such projects, they were unable to recognize the significance of becoming an individual prior to becoming a Kemalist, Socialist, or political Islamist.

In Turkey, the civil and legal, political and social rights associated with citizenship were given from above. They were not acquired as a result of struggles from below. The notion of Turkish citizenship evolved within the civic-republican tradition by emphasizing practices that were viewed as duties. In the early years of the Republic, Turkish citizens were geared toward embracing the fundamental tenets of the Turkish revolution, namely nationalism, secularism, populism, republicanism, etatism, and revolutionism. The association of such aspects of the Republican ideology with citizenship paved the way to its definition by disregarding a distinction between the public and the private realm. The republican elite defined not only the public duties of the citizens but also their private roles, dress codes, and their recreational activities. It is, then, possible to argue that the notion of Turkish citizenship was defined from above by the republican elite by disregarding the privacy of individuals. In sum, it is possible to argue that in the founding years of the Turkish Republic, Turkish citizenship was defined from above by a state elite within the civic-republican tradition, by emphasizing duties over rights and by disregarding the privacy of the individual.

In sum, the republican citizen was expected to "follow" rather than reach certain decisions via his or her own reflection. She or he was the subject of another will. According to Hans Reiss, who interpreted Kant's definitive study on the Enlightenment:

> He [Kant] does not consider it to be the purpose of politics to make people happy. Happiness is subjective. …
>
> This argument, of course, does not mean that he does not wish people to be happy. It only means that *political arrangements should not be organized in such a way as to aim at promoting happiness, but that they should permit men to attain happiness in their own way.*
>
> (Reiss 1970: 25; my italics)

Accordingly, Turkish citizens were discouraged from pursuing their own happiness. Rather, they were integrated into a grand civilizational design which was believed to promote happiness. The individual that was defined in some liberal texts was quite delimited. She or he was not that different from the citizen envisioned by the state elite. Hence, a political culture that prompted the will to follow rather than the courage to reason began to evolve in the Turkish Republic. Will triumphed over reason. Perhaps the most revealing metaphor pertaining to the triumph of will over reason in Turkey is the place deemed appropriate for the replica of Auguste Rodin's famous sculpture *The Thinker*, which represents a naked, reflecting man. The most distinguished Turkish replica of *The Thinker* resides in the yard of a mental hospital in Istanbul, as if signifying a tribute to the discouragement of a naked moment of reflection (read Enlightenment tradition) in Turkey.

Citizenship and membership

When the issue of citizenship was being discussed publicly in Turkey in the course of the 1990s, the notion of "constitutional citizenship" attracted some attention. When the then president, Süleyman Demirel, used it in one of his speeches, he referred to an umbrella concept that bestowed on citizenship an identity without regard to ethnic, religious, gender differences. The concept was appropriated from the German context, where the difference between citizenship as membership of a nation (*Volk*) and citizenship as membership of a state had paved the way to a critical debate. The notion of "constitutional patriotism" was initially suggested by Jürgen Habermas (1992). By this notion, Habermas referred to a post-traditional citizenship that involved membership of the state. In the midst of the *Historikerstreit* (historians' debate) in Germany that gained momentum with the move toward unification in the late 1980s, Habermas challenged traditional versions of identity and argued for state-citizens in place of nation-citizens (Kadıoğlu 1997). Since citizenship entailed membership of a nation (*Volk*), in a Germany on the eve of reunification, Habermas' argument for citizenship as membership of a state was pertinent. Nevertheless, while Habermas has emptied the ethnic content of the notion of citizenship, he still views it as a "membership" of a post-traditional entity. He is basically arguing that the German notion of citizenship should be more like the French one. But what about the French notion of citizenship?

Rogers Brubaker (1992) argues that in France nationhood was understood in political rather than ethnocultural terms. Yet, he also argues that: "The politics of citizenship is first and foremost a politics of nationhood." It makes references to questions of identity rather than self-interest. Hence, although nationhood has secular political references, it still has a cultural basis. In evaluating Brubaker's position relating nationhood and identity, James Donald (1996: 173) argues that in this view *civic identity* cannot be extricated from *national identity*. Donald (1996: 174) declares that "the position of citizen must not have a substance." This is the starting point of Donald's attempt to envision citizenship as non-membership and as a position. As Donald puts it:

> Any claim to identify citizenship in terms of cultural identity – even, I would say, the identity of post-traditional constitutional patriotism – undermines democratic popular sovereignty and the rights of citizenship by drawing a line separating those who are members of this political community from those who are not. My argument is therefore that "the citizen" should be understood in the first instance not as a type of person (whether German nationalist or constitutional patriot) but as a position in the set of formal relations defined by democratic sovereignty. Just as "I" denotes a position in a set of linguistic relations, an empty position which makes my unique utterances possible but which can equally be occupied by anyone, so too "the citizen" denotes an empty place. It too can be occupied by anyone – occupied in the sense of being spoken from, not in the sense of being given a substantial identity.
>
> (Donald 1996: 174)

This view of citizenship as "an empty space" or pure Cartesian cogito, is quite significant in envisioning citizenship as non-membership, as detached from notions of identity. Hence, while Habermas gives a post-traditional content to membership that signifies citizenship, Donald suggests the "substancelessness of citizenship" by drawing from Slavoj Zizek (1991). He elaborates on the unmasking of the "person" from the attire of the modern masquerade. "Modern" means the creation of an unreadable surface. The seclusion of the individual, his or her invisibility, stands in the way of a notion of citizenship as an empty space.

In the Turkish context, the development of the individual was curbed to a great extent. In the words of Ahmet Ağaoğlu (1933: 27) who was one of the well-known liberals who fell in opposition to the Republican People's Party at the time of the founding of the Turkish Republic:

> In the Orient, the individual was drowned, in the Occident he had liberated himself; on the one side the individual was squeezed, weakened, and made into a meager being under an increasingly ferocious despotism, and put into his own narrow and constricted sheath. In the Occident, on the other hand, the individual gradually took a hold of his freedoms and, by constantly opening up, felt the pleasure of living and working as a result of the weakening of despotism. As a result, the Oriental societies composed of constricted individuals placed into their own sheath also became constricted and weakened.
>
> (Ağaoğlu 1933: 27; my translation)

Citizenship preceded and had prevalence over the notion of the individual in Turkey. The notions of citizenship, will and republic ended up taking precedence over the notions of individual, reason and democracy. Citizenship was embedded in national identity as well as defined in accordance with duties in a rather weak public space. Hence, it is rather difficult to envision citizenship as an empty space, as non-membership.

Notes

1 Many international and national conferences held in Turkey began to be organized around the themes of citizenship, identity, multiculturalism, etc., especially in the latter half of the 1990s. There was a pioneering international symposium organized by Marmara University's International Relations Center in Istanbul on 28–9 March 1996 entitled "Redefinition of Nation, State and Citizenship." A subsequent national conference was organized by Ege University in Izmir on 10–12 April 1996 entitled "Republic, Democracy and Identity." The papers were collected in a book, *Cumhuriyet, Demokrasi ve Kimlik* (Republic, Democracy and Identity), edited by Nuri Bilgin, 1997. A similar international conference was organized by Mersin University and Deutsch-Türkische Vereingung zum Sozial- und Geisteswissenschaftliche Austausch in Mersin on 28 October–1 November 1997 entitled "Multiculturalism, Immigration and Globalization."

2 Hasan Bülent Kahraman refers to the construction of all the Marshallian aspects of citizenship in Turkey "in a dash," rather than its gradual "completion" as a process (Kahraman, 1996: 6). See also the papers and discussions in *Türkiye'de İnsan Hakları Semineri* (Seminar on Human Rights in Turkey), 1970: 65.

3 In this part, I have drawn on a similar classification that I have made in an earlier article. See Kadıoğlu (1998b). The present version has been reinforced by enriching the information regarding the institutional developments in Turkey.

4 For a review of such practices pertaining to Turkification, such as those regarding the necessity to speak Turkish (1931), utilization of Turkish family names (1934), the law on the settlement of minorities (1934) and the tax on the property of Muslims, non-Muslims, foreigners and converts (1942), see Aktar (2000); Soyarık (2000); Yıldız (2001).

References

Ağaoğlu, A. (1933) *Devlet ve Fert* (State and the Individual), Istanbul: Sanayii Nefise Matbaası.

Aktar, A. (2000) *Varlık Vergisi ve "Türkleştirme" Politikaları* (The Wealth Tax and the Policies of Turkification), Istanbul: İletişim Yayınları.

Berkes, N. (1959) "Translator's Introduction", in Z. Gökalp, *Turkish Nationalism and Western Civilization: Selected Essays*, Westport CT: Greenwood Press.

Berktay, F. (1990) "Türkiye Solu'nun Kadına Bakışı: Değişen Bir Şey Var mı?" (The Turkish Left's View of Women: Has There Been a Change?), in S. Tekeli (ed.) *Kadın Bakış Açısından 1980'ler Türkiye'sinde Kadınlar* (An Account of Women by Women in Turkey in the 1980s), Istanbul: İletişim Yayınları.

Bilgin, N. (ed.) (1997) *Cumhuriyet, Demokrasi ve Kimlik* (Republic, Democracy and Identity), Istanbul: Bağlam Yayınları.

Brubaker, R. (1989) *Immigration and the Politics of Citizenship in Europe and North America*, Lanham MD: German Marshall Fund of the United States and University Press of America.

——(1990) "Immigration, Citizenship, and the Nation-state in France and Germany: A Comparative Historical Analysis", *International Sociology*, 5 (4): 379–407.

——(1992) *Citizenship and Nationhood in France and Germany*, London: Harvard University Press.

Donald, J. (1996) "The Citizen and the Man About Town", in S. Hall and P. du Gay (eds) *Questions of Cultural Identity*, London: Sage.

Fraser, N. and Gordon, L. (1994) "Civil Citizenship Against Social Citizenship? On the Ideology of Contract-versus-Charity," in B. van Steenbergen (ed.) *The Condition of Citizenship*, London: Sage.

Göle, N. (1991) *Modern Mahrem: Medeniyet ve Örtünme* (Modern Privacy: Civilization and the Veil), Istanbul: Metis Publications.

Habermas, J. (1992) "Yet again: German identity – a unified nation of angry DM-burghers?" *New German Critique*, 91: 84–102.

İnan, A. (1969) *Medeni Bilgiler ve Atatürk'ün El Yazıları* (Civic Information and Atatürk's Hand Writings), Istanbul: Çağdaş Yayınları.

Kahraman, H. B. (1996) "Kemalist Cumhuriyetçilik, Yurttaşlık ve Demokrasi İlişkisi" (Kemalist Republicanism, Citizenship and Democracy), *Varlık*, 1069, October 1996: 2–8.

Kadıoğlu, A. (1991) "Tarihsel Açıdan Alman Milliyetçiliği, Vatandaşlık Kavramı ve Göç Politikaları" (German Nationalism From a Historical Perspective: the Concept of Citizenship and Immigration Policies), *Türkiye Günlügü*, 17: 104–9.

——(1992) "Citizenship, Immigration and Racism in a Unified Germany with Special Reference to the Turkish Guestworkers", *Journal of Economics and Administrative Studies*, 6/1–2: 199–211.

——(1993a) "Alaturkalık ile İffetsizlik Arasında Birey Olarak Kadın" (Women as Individuals: Between Being Traditional and Unchaste), *Görüş*, 9 May: 58–62.

——(1993b) "Devletini Arayan Millet: Almanya Örneği" (A Nation in Search of its State: The German Case), *Toplum ve Bilim*, 62 (fall): 95–111.

——(1993c) "The Human Tie: International Labor Migration," in C. Balkır and A. M. Williams (eds) *Turkey and Europe*, London: Pinter Publishers/St Martin's Press.

——(1994) "Women's Subordination in Turkey: Is Islam Really the Villain?," *Middle East Journal*, 48/4 (autumn): 645–61.

——(1995) "Milletini Arayan Devlet: Türk Milliyetçiliğinin Açmazları" (A State in Search of Its Nation: The Dilemmas of Turkish Nationalism), *Türkiye Günlüğü*, March-April: 91–101.

——(1996a) "Cumhuriyet Kadını: Vatandaş mı, Birey mi?" (Republican Woman: A Citizen or an Individual), *Varlık*, 1069, October: 12–15.

——(1996b) "Kamusal Alan ile Özel Alanın Yeniden Eklemlenmesi: Demokratik Vatandaşlık" (Rearticulation of the Public and the Private Realms: Democratic Citizenship), *Diyalog*, 1: 119–34.

——(1996c) "Is Racism Being Combated Effectively in Germany: The New Immigration Legislation?" in G. Rystad (ed.) *Encountering Strangers: Responses and Consequences*, Sweden: Lund University Press.

——(1996d) "The Paradox of Turkish Nationalism and the Construction of Official Identity", *Middle Eastern Studies*, 32/2, April: 177–94.

——(1997) "Alman Yeni Sağı: Bir Başka Tarihbilim Tartışması" (The New Right in Germany: Another Debate on Historiography), *Toplum Bilim*, 7, October: 63–9.

——(1998a) "Cinselliğin İnkarı: Büyük Toplumsal Projelerin Nesnesi Olarak Türk Kadınları" (Denouncing Sexuality: Turkish Women as Objects of Grand Social Projects), *Bilanço 98, 75 Yılda Kadınlar ve Erkekler*, Istanbul: Türkiye Ekonomik ve Toplumsal Tarih Vakfı.

——(1998b) "Citizenship and Individuation in Turkey: The Triumph of Will Over Reason," *CEMOTI*, 26, July-December: 23–42.

——(1998c) "Republican Epistemology and Islamic Discourses in Turkey in the 1990s," *Muslim World*, LXXXVIII/1, January: 1–21.

——(1999) *Cumhuriyet İradesi, Demokrasi Muhakemesi* (Republican Will, Democratic Reason), Istanbul: Metis.

Keyman, F. (1997) "Kemalizm, Modernite, Gelenek" (Kemalizm, Modernity, Tradition), *Toplum ve Bilim*, 72, spring: 84–99.

Kohn, H. (1967) *Prelude to Nation-states: The French and the German Experience, 1789–1815*, New Jersey: D. Van Nostrand.

Marshall, T. H. (1950) *Citizenship and Social Class and Other Essays*, Cambridge: Cambridge University Press.

——(1977) *Class, Citizenship and Social Development*, Chicago and London: University of Chicago Press.

Mardin, S. (1981) "Religion and Secularism in Turkey," in A. Kazancıgil and E. Özbudun (eds) *Atatürk: Founder of a Modern State*, London: C. Hurst.

Oldfield, A. (1990) *Citizenship and Community: Civic Republicanism and the Modern World*, London and New York: Routledge.

——(1994) "Citizenship: An Unnatural Practice," in B. Turner and P. Hamilton (eds) *Citizenship: Critical Concepts*, vol. 1, London and New York: Routledge.

Plender, R. (1972) *International Migration Law*, Leiden: A. W. Sijthoff.

Reiss, H. (ed) (1970) *Kant's Political Writings*, Cambridge: Cambridge University Press.

Soyarık, N. (2000) "The Citizen and the State and the State of the Citizen: An Analysis of the Citizenization Process in Turkey," unpublished Ph.D. thesis, Bilkent University, Department of Political Science and Public Administration.

Tezcan, N. (1996) *Atatürk'ün Yazdığı Yurttaşlık Bilgileri* (Citizenship Information Written by Atatürk), Istanbul: Çağdaş Yayıları.

Turner, B. (1992) "Outline of a Theory of Citizenship," in C. Mouffe (ed.) *Dimensions of Radical Democracy: Pluralism, Citizenship, Community*, London and New York: Verso.

——(ed.) (1993) *Citizenship and Social Theory*, London: Sage.

Türkiye'de İnsan Hakları Semineri (Seminar on Human Rights in Turkey), 9–11 Aralik 1968, *Tebliğler, Tartışmalar* (Papers, Discussions), 1970, Ankara Üniversitesi, Hukuk Fakültesi Yayıları, 256, Kamu Hukuku ve Siyasal Bilim Enstitüsü Yayıları 1, Ankara.

Üstel, F. (1996a) "Anayasal Vatandaşlık Hangi Anayasaya Vatandaşlık?" (Constitutional Citizenship According to Which Constitution?), *Radikal* (daily), 17 December.

——(1996b) "Cumhuriyet'ten Bu Yana Yurttaş Profili" (The Citizen Profile Since the Republic), *Yeni Yüzyıl* (daily), 24 April.

——(2002) "Türkiye Cumhuriyeti'nde Resmi Yurttaş Profilinin Evrimi" (The Evolution of the Profile of the Official Citizen in the Turkish Republic), *Modern Türkiye'de Siyasi Düşünce Tarihi: Milliyetçilik* (History of Political Thought in Modern Turkey: Nationalism), vol. 4, Istanbul: İletişim Yayıları.

Van Steenbergen, B. (ed.) (1994) *The Condition of Citizenship*, London: Sage.
Vergin, N. (1996) "Anayasal Vatandaşlık Ne Demektir?" (What is the Meaning of Constitutional Citizenship?), *Milliyet* (daily), 28 December.
Yıldız, A. (2001) *"Ne Mutlu Türküm Diyebilene:" Türk Ulusal Kimliğinin Etno-Seküler Sınırları* ("How Happy is the One Who Can Say He is Turkish:" The Ethno-Cultural Limits of Turkish National Identity, 1919–1938), Istanbul: İletişim Yayıları.
Zizek, Slavoj (1991) *Looking Awry*, Cambridge MA: MIT Press.

6 Legal and constitutional foundations of Turkish citizenship

Changes and continuities

Nalan Soyarık-Şentürk

Introduction

Recent years have witnessed ongoing debates and negotiations between the European Union and Turkey concerning legal and constitutional reforms. The Copenhagen criteria set forth requirements to be met by candidate countries, and are concerned with the existence and stability of institutions guaranteeing democracy, the rule of law, human rights and respect for and protection of minorities. Therefore in the process of candidacy for the European Union not only are the legal and constitutional features gaining more significance, but also they can no longer be regarded as distinct from the political sphere. Thus, within a year, major legal and constitutional amendments have been carried out, which would in turn affect the mainstream understanding of citizenship in Turkey. Especially after the Copenhagen Summit held in December 2002, these legal and constitutional aspects seem to loom larger on the agenda. In the conclusion of the Summit, the European Union stated that:

> It strongly welcomes the important steps taken by Turkey towards meeting the Copenhagen criteria, in particular through the recent legislative packages and the subsequent implementation measures which cover a large number of key priorities specified in the Accession Partnership. The Union acknowledges the determination of the new Turkish government to take further steps on the path of reform and urges in particular the government to address swiftly all remaining shortcomings in the field of the political criteria, not only with regard to legislation but also in particular with regard to implementation.[1]
>
> (Copenhagen Summit Conclusion)

Therefore, the legal and constitutional aspects of Turkish citizenship stand out as one of the significant and debated issues both in the domestic politics of Turkey and in its relations with the European Union.

Among the various aspects of citizenship, such as identity, civic virtue and legal status, the legal aspect stands out as one of the core aspects. In other words, citizenship-as-legal-status provides the basis of citizenship. This chapter aims at providing the legal and constitutional basis of Turkish citizenship throughout republican history. This basis is significant because legal and constitutional arrangements stand out as political phenomena within the modernity project. The legal side of citizenship is usually interrelated with the political history of a country. In analyzing the development and evolution of Turkish citizenship, the legal developments and the three constitutions are reflective of the developments and changes experienced in the history of the Turkish Republic. Therefore, the constitutions of 1924, 1961 and 1982 will be evaluated subsequently, in addition to the citizenship laws enacted throughout the history of the republic. However, it can be argued that the legal and constitutional developments cannot by and of themselves reflect the whole process of citizenization. Even though the social and political conditions of the country are usually reflected in the constitutions, the actual processes sometimes diverge from the path delineated by the constitution and the related laws. In other words, while a constitution stands out as an abstract document, the practices might be quite different or deviate from the basic principles of the constitution. Or the constitution and those laws cannot be satisfactory for the conditions of the society. This is one of the reasons for this study. The elaboration of the constitutions in republican history and current developments will highlight both the issue of Turkish citizenship and the ongoing debates between the European Union and Turkey concerning legal reforms.

The legal and constitutional foundations are one of the core elements of citizenship in any country. As Bendix (1964: 74) argues,

> In the nation-state each citizen stands in a direct relation to the sovereign authority of the country in contrast with the medieval polity in which, that direct relation is enjoyed only by the great men of the realm. Therefore, a core element of nation building is the codification of the rights and duties of all adults who are classified as citizens.
>
> (Bendix 1964: 74)

Those foundations sometimes go in parallel with the process of nation-building and construction of citizenship identity, or diverge from this process in certain aspects.

One of the major tasks of the new Turkish Republic that was promulgated in 1923 was to determine who would be defined as a Turkish citizen in terms of the Constitution and the laws. The following section will analyze the Constitution of 1924, the Citizenship Law of 1928, and the Law on Settlement enacted in 1934, which is still in use for the admission to citizenship. Then the 1961 Constitution and the Citizenship Law of 1964 will be elaborated. The last constitution of Turkey, namely the 1982 Constitution will be the concern of the final section.

The 1924 constitution

When the Turkish Republic was proclaimed on 29 October 1923, the first and major task was the formation of a nation-state. Regarding the Ottoman dynasty and the regulation of the state as the real cause for collapse, the new republic aimed at a complete renewal. Therefore, the republic went through widespread reforms in every aspect of life. The Gregorian calendar and twenty-four hour clock were adopted. On 4 October 1926 the Swiss Code was adopted as the Turkish Civil Law. The previously used Arabic alphabet was changed to the Latin alphabet on 3 November 1928, and public usage of the Arabic alphabet was prohibited (Lewis 1961: 278). This was a real break from the Ottoman heritage, and it was also designed for the formation of the Turkish nation. These reforms were the main steps taken for the creation of a nation that was composed of "civilized" citizens who were educated in modern methods, and whose modernity was reflected in their appearance. It was believed that the survival of the new republic was dependent on the adoption of nationalism and secularism, and the construction of a Turkish citizenship that would be parallel to both nationalism and secularism.

The 1924 Constitution was in fact preceded by a constitution devised after the Turkish Grand National Assembly was formed in 1920. Even though the concern is the republican period, for the purpose of this chapter, the way the 1921 Constitution defined the "Turkish people" is also significant. Accordingly, the "Turkish people" were "the masses who were living within the boundaries of the armistice, regardless of their ethnic origin, that got together on the basis of political unity and independence" (Tanör 1988: 250). In other words, the "Turkish people" was defined on the basis of political and geographical parameters (*ibid.*: 249). However, this was the period of struggle for independence, and the definition had to be inclusive. Even though the formation of the Parliament was a fundamental break from the Sultanate, at that time the intentions for the proclamation of the republic were not explicit; therefore this constitution had to appeal to all the people living within the boundaries of the National Oath. We can assume that the people were still considered as the citizens of the Ottoman Empire, subject to the Ottoman Citizenship Law of 1868, as there were no clear statements about the citizenship status of the people in the Constitution of 1921.

When we return to the 1924 Constitution, Article 88 of the Constitution stated that "the people of Turkey regardless of their religion and race are Turkish in terms of citizenship" (Gözübüyük 1995: 76). Yıldız (1998: 302–3) points to the novelty in the law about mentioning Turkishness,[2] and stresses the debates over who will be defined as a Turk. After long debates, as Tanör (1988: 309) notes, the Constitution stressed that Turkishness was defined in terms of geographical and political parameters rather than racial parameters, despite the existence of racial and religious differences. During the same period Mustafa Kemal stated that "The people of Turkey who promulgated the Turkish Republic are called the Turkish Nation." In other words "the core of nationality is not race, but political loyalty" (Turan 1969: 73). I also suggest that in that early phase of the period in question, there was an inclination toward the French or the Western type of citizenship based on territory. Besides, the usage of "Turk" can also be seen as the reflection of the aspiration for the formation of a new nation.

The 1924 Constitution seemed to be a liberal constitution with regard to individual rights. The basic rights and freedoms were listed in the fifth section, *Türklerin Hukuku Ammesi* (The Public Rights of the Turks). Those were, briefly, security of life, liberty, honor, and property; freedom of conscience; freedom of press and communication; and freedom to form associations (Gözübüyük 1995: 71–6). It is noted by both Gözübüyük and Tanör that the 1924 Constitution was inspired by the French Revolution. Tanör argues that the constitution had a liberal and individualistic approach; and that the limits of the liberties were not drawn by the benefits of the state, public or the society, as had been the case in the following constitutions. However, Gözübüyük (1995: 54), on the other hand, argues that the constitution merely listed basic rights and liberties with short definitions, but that there was not a regulation that safeguarded those rights and liberties, and that the regulation and boundaries of those rights was left to the executive. In line with Gözübüyük's point, it can be argued that the Public Rights of the Turks section of the Constitution looks like a mere delineation of rights and liberties, which was not guaranteed by any body or institution. On the other hand, when the citizenization process in the early republican period is analyzed, it is seen that there was no emphasis on the rights of the citizen. Rather, the process repeatedly emphasized the duties of the citizen toward the state, therefore it was civic republican. For instance, İnan, whose *Medeni Bilgiler* (1988) can be viewed as the manifesto for Turkish citizenship, stated that citizens could only gain rights through completing their duties toward the state. The 1924 Constitution is an example of the differences and contradictions between the discourse of the legal documents and actual practices. The early Republican understanding of citizenship can be regarded as civic republican. The emphasis on duties toward the state and the community as part of the identity of the citizen, and the notions of common good and general will were reflected in the discourse of the period. It is also argued that those notions were reflected in the 1924 Constitution (Tanör 1988). However, the 1924 Constitution in and of itself is not sufficient for understanding the conceptualization of citizenship in the period concerned; therefore certain laws like the Citizenship Law and the Law on Settlement should also be utilized in order to reach a more comprehensive legal understanding of Turkish citizenship.

The 1928 Turkish Citizenship Law

As mentioned above, citizenship had been a crucial element in the nation building process and the republic. However, the first citizenship law of the Turkish Republic had not greatly occupied the agenda of the Parliament. The

1312 numbered and 23 May 1928 dated Turkish Citizenship Law was decided to be enacted by 1 January 1929 (*TBMM Zabıt Ceridesi*, 23.5.1928). No debates or questions were raised at the parliamentary meeting concerning this law. All the articles were read and voted upon without any objections.

The law adopted both descent and territory principles. According to Article 1, "children born from a Turkish father or mother, either in Turkey or in a foreign country, are considered as Turkish citizens." Also, according to article 2/c, determination of the child's citizenship was not based on the official marriage of the parents. Those articles reflect the principle of *jus sanguinis* by granting citizenship to the children of the Turkish citizens, even if they were abroad, or born out of wedlock. Articles 2/a, 2/b and 3, clarifying the circumstances for the admission of the children of foreigners or stateless people settled in Turkey, were designed for the exercise of the *jus soli* principle. Nomer (1989: 45) argues that those articles were designed in a complementary manner.

The first Citizenship Law of the republic provided merely a definition of the Turkish citizen. It was probably enacted as part of the nation building process, and it is evident from the parliamentary records that it was not regarded as a crucial issue by its legal definition. The legal status of Turkish citizenship can be regarded as the abstract definition of citizenship. But, the actual practices in a sense deviate from that abstract definition. The nation was defined as a political and social group with a unity of language, culture, and ideals. This was an inclusive definition in the first instance. However, the degree of inclusion varied by the religious or ethnic differences in actual practice.

According to the Lausanne Treaty, signed on 24 July 1923, the non-Muslim population of Turkey, namely Greeks, Armenians, and Jews, were granted minority status. The articles of the treaty relating to minority status are numbered between 37 and 45. Those articles granted minorities the freedoms of worship, travel and migration, the right to speak their own languages, and form their own religious, educational and social service associations (Levi 1996: 19). According to Article 42, the minorities had the right to regulate their own traditions and customs and their own laws in family and personal matters (Aktar 1996).

However, the republic intended to grasp all of its population under one law, namely the Civil Law. During the preparation of this law in 1925, the minorities gave up their rights granted by Article 42, either willingly or unwillingly (Aktar 1996; Levi 1996: 68–9; Bali 1999: 90–102). But this did not better their situation, or help them to be accepted as full citizens of the Turkish Republic.

The Law on Settlement

The 2510 numbered Law on Settlement is significant for the issue of citizenship, as it is still used for admitting people to Turkish citizenship. Besides, as will be elaborated below, this law points to the transformation in the understanding of citizenship from a territorial notion toward a more common culture and descent-oriented one.

The 2510 numbered Law on Settlement was enacted on 14 June 1934. According to the Minister of Interior Affairs, Şükrü Kaya, thanks to this law, the country "would be transformed into a country where a single language is spoken, and the same thoughts and sentiments are shared by the people" (*TBMM Zabıt Ceridesi*, 14.6.1934: 141). In the introductory speech, the Kütahya deputy, Naşit Hakkı Bey, noted that this law was one of the fundamental laws of the revolution (*TBMM Zabıt Ceridesi*, 7.6.1934: 67). In his long speech, he mentioned the importance of unity in language, culture and ideals, and added that this law would help the assimilation of those who regard themselves as non-Turkish, or who had lost Turkish identity. By taking measures for people to speak Turkish, and abolishing tribal organizations, those who were from other cultures or who spoke other languages would be absorbed, and assimilated, into the Turkish culture (*ibid.*: 70).

The first article of the Law on Settlement stated that the dispersion and the settlement of the population would be regulated according to the degree of adherence to Turkish culture. Thus, the Turkish territory was divided into three regions: the first region was the territory where the population with Turkish culture desired to concentrate. The second region was the territory spared for the settlement of those who were to be assimilated into Turkish culture. The third region would be evacuated for health, political, military and security purposes; settlement in that region would be prohibited (Article 2).

Article 3 stated that those people of Turkish descent, or those close to Turkish culture who migrated with the desire of settling in Turkey, would be accepted by the decision of the Ministry of Interior and be called *muhacir* (émigré). Those émigrés and refugees would resettle in the places shown and would not be permitted to leave those places (Article 7). Besides, the émigrés would be helped in their resettlement, and naturalization would be made easier for them (Article 6). On the other hand, those who did not adhere to Turkish culture, anarchists, spies, nomadic gypsies, and those who were deported, would not be admitted as émigrés (Article 4).

The nomadic gypsies of Turkish nationality would be dispersed to villages of Turkish culture; foreign nomadic gypsies and nomads who did not adhere to Turkish culture would be deported (Article 9). In addition, Article 10 abolished leadership of the nomadic tribes (*aşiret reisliği*). Those two articles were designed especially for the dispersion of the Kurdish tribes. More specifically, Bali (1999: 256) noted that the law was designed in order to disperse the Kurds after their rebellions.

Article 11 is significant for the situation of the non-Turkish minorities. The spread and assimilation of those people were safeguarded by this article. It stated that those people whose mother tongue was other than Turkish would not be permitted to form separate wards or associations. Also the number of foreigners permitted to settle in towns and villages was limited to 10 percent. The Law on Settlement aimed at mass resettlement and dispersion of the population, and those resettled people could not move to other places even after ten years of settlement (Article 29).

The Law on Settlement was a major development in the process of Turkification. For the sake of assimilating non-Turkish elements, major rights of freedom of movement were violated. Besides, pressure on people to speak Turkish intensified. The non-Turkish population was spread over the country so as to be absorbed by the Turkish culture. The Law on Settlement was a perfect reflection of the motto of the republic: "one language, one culture, one ideal."

The legal definition of citizenship in the early republican period was egalitarian, and sought to benefit from both *jus sanguinis* and *jus soli*. In the first instance, Turkish citizenship was close to the French model that was based on territory with the premise that "those who are affiliated to the Turkish State by citizenship are known as Turks." However, later a shift can be depicted in the attitude toward minorities, the emphasis on adoption of Turkish culture, and the admittance of those people who were regarded as close to Turkish culture as émigrés and to citizenship. This shift reflects the German type of citizenship based on descent and unity of culture.

The 1961 Constitution and its aftermath

This section will dwell upon the period after the military intervention of May 1960 and the Constitution devised afterward. This period is significant, because it can be regarded as the period when there was a liberal atmosphere to a considerable extent. A shift in the understanding of citizenship was experienced during this period. The citizen of the period was active and there was a primacy of rights as compared with the duty-laden citizenship of the early republican period.

As the Democrat Party (DP) was reaching ten years in office, social unrest, especially among university students and the military, was increasing. The military had already lost its dominant status in state affairs. Together with the bureaucracy they had been regarded as the key actors of the state during the early republican period. In fact, the tension between the political elites and the state elites had always been, and would continue to be prevalent in Turkish politics. Combined with the DP's movement toward an authoritarian regime, and the sympathy felt to the Republican People's Party and its leader İsmet İnönü, who had served in the War of National Independence, the unrest of the military increased. To make matters worse, the DP tried to use the military against demonstrations opposing its rule. Thus the first military intervention in republican history took place (Tachau and Heper 1983; Harris 1988). The military claimed that "they were safeguarding democracy and the state, and the legacy of Atatürk," which would also be a justification for future interventions (Karpat 1988: 141).

The 1961 Constitution that was devised after the military takeover is significant for the transformation of the society and the understanding of citizenship. The Constitution was written in a rather detailed format, in order to eliminate the misuse of power. During preparation of the Constitution, the Commission for the Constitution benefited from the two drafts prepared by the Faculty of Law of Istanbul University and the Faculty of Political Science of Ankara University. Also, the French, Italian, and German constitutions were utilized, in addition to Universal Declaration of Human Rights, The European Human Rights Agreement and the French Declaration of Human and Citizenship Rights (Tanör 1988: 74). The Constitution was promulgated after a referendum held on 9 July 1961.

The new Constitution was based on the supremacy of the rule of law. It was stated repeatedly that every issue would be carried out in accordance with the law, and in certain cases in accordance with international law. The Constitution had a preface where the main characteristics of the Turkish nation were defined, stating that:

> The Turkish nation ... inspired by Turkish nationalism that gathers all the individuals sharing the joy and grief as an indivisible whole around the national consciousness and ideals, and that aims at raising our nation with a spirit of national unity as an honorable and equal member of the world family ... in order to consolidate a democratic rule of law with all its legal and social basis, that would safeguard the realization of human rights and freedoms, national solidarity, social justice, welfare of the individual and the society. ... approves and proclaims this Constitution prepared by the Constitutive Assembly of the Turkish Republic, and entrusts this Constitution to the guardianship of its sons devoted to freedom, justice, and virtue.
>
> (Kili and Gözübüyük 1985: 171–2)

It was evident from its preface that this Constitution relied on universal norms like human rights, social justice, and welfare, and that the individual was given more importance and an active role, especially with the mention of the right to resist.

Whereas the 1924 Constitution defined the Turkish Republic in Article 2 in accordance with the Kemalist principles defined by the "six arrows" as "the Turkish Republic is republican, nationalist, populist, etatist, secular, and revolutionary," the 1961 Constitution declared in its definition that "the Turkish Republic is a national, democratic, secular and social rule of law, that relies on human rights and principles" (Gözübüyük 1995: 56, 115). This article and the Constitution as a whole reflects the desire for the introduction and implementation of universal standards and human rights, and for a social state that seeks the welfare of its citizens.

When we dwell upon the novelties introduced by the 1961 Constitution with respect to citizenship, we see that this detailed Constitution placed importance on individual rights and liberties and aspired to a more active citizenship. Article 54 of the 1961 Constitution (*ibid.*: 131) defined the Turkish citizen by stating "everyone who is tied to the Turkish State through citizenship ties is a Turk" and continued:

> The child of a Turkish father or a Turkish mother is a Turk. The citizenship status of child born from a foreign father and a Turkish mother will be arranged by law. Citizenship is acquired and lost under the circumstances defined by law. No Turk can be expelled from citizenship, unless he/she engages in activities contrary to their loyalty to the country. The decisions and implementations of expulsion can be subject to appeal.[3]
>
> (Article 54, 1961 Constitution)

The 1961 Constitution differed from the previous constitution in many respects. First, the 1961 Constitution was designed in a more inclusive, humanitarian and universal manner. In contrast to the 1924 Constitution that used "Turk" as its operative term, the 1961 Constitution used "everyone," and included foreigners as well, but designed their status and the limitations of their freedoms in accordance with international law (Article 13).

The Constitution limited the interference of the state into the affairs of the individual and defined the duties of the state toward the individual, which was a significant departure from the primacy of the obligations of the citizen toward the state in the early republican period. In this respect, this Constitution was a liberal constitution and aspired to a more liberal kind of citizenship.

The exposition of basic rights and liberties took up almost two thirds of the Constitution, and was very detailed. In Article 10 it was stated that everyone had inviolable basic rights and liberties. Article 11 safeguarded these liberties thus:

> The basic rights and liberties can only be limited through law that is in accordance with the spirit and statement of the Constitution. However, this law cannot restrain the core of the rights or liberties even for reasons of morality, public order, social justice or national security.
>
> (Article 11, 1961 Constitution)

The basic rights and liberties of the individual were mainly the immunity of private life (Article 15) and residence (Article 16), the freedoms of communication (Article 17), travel and settlement (Article 18), faith and conscience (Article 19), thought (Article 20), education (Article 21), and right to property (Article 36). Under this section the freedom of the press was expressed. The rights and freedoms of meetings and demonstrations, and to form associations without seeking permission, were safeguarded

(Articles 28 and 29). The only limitations on these rights would be drawn by law for the protection of public order.

The emphasis on the social welfare state is evident in the section on "Social and Economic Rights and Duties." Here, the right to work (Article 42), to rest (Article 44), to a just wage (Article 45), to form trade unions (Article 46), to go on strike (Article 47), to social security (Article 48) and to medical treatment (Article 49) were listed. Those articles reflect an evolution toward the social phase of citizenship in Marshall's (1965) analysis. However, the social rights were again granted from above, as had been the case for both civil and political rights. The atmosphere of the social welfare state would be curbed later, after the 1980 military coup and with the 1982 Constitution, which limited most of the rights and liberties granted by the 1961 Constitution with the reason that the 1961 Constitution was too liberal for Turkish society.[4] Therefore, the period between 1961 and 1980 can be viewed as the transitory social welfare state with an active and liberal understanding of citizenship.

Those articles mentioned above also reflect the importance given to social justice. In addition, equal educational opportunities for every citizen, male or female, and sufficient nutrition were safeguarded by the Constitution. Tanör (1988: 392) states that this social aspect was a novelty of the 1961 Constitution, the elements of which were "the object of social justice, social rights granted to the individuals and groups, the social duties bestowed upon the state, the developmental plans and the establishment of the State Planning Organization."

The 1961 Constitution points to the divergence from a republican understanding of citizenship that focused on the duties of the citizen toward the state, which was implemented during the early republican period. By this Constitution, the individual was given a higher value and the reconciliation of the individual's and the society's rights and liberties was the major target (Tanör 1988: 378). By an extension of the rights and liberties of the citizen and a limitation on the state's interference, a more liberal and active understanding of citizenship was introduced. During this period, a new citizenship law that is still in use today was also amended.

The 1964 Turkish Citizenship Law

The 403 numbered Turkish Citizenship Law was put into effect on 11 February 1964.[5] The reason for the new law was to reform Turkish citizenship law in line with conventional citizenship law. The new Citizenship Law was another step on the move toward the rule of law. The aim was to base the law on universal principles of citizenship and citizenship rights. In line with this principle of the rule of law, the right to appeal was included in the 403 numbered and 11 February 1964 dated Turkish Citizenship Law. The proposal was based on three universal principles of citizenship law. The first was the principle that everyone should have citizenship and the situation of statelessness should be eliminated. The second was the principle that everyone should have only one citizenship. And third, everyone should be free to choose his or her own citizenship and no one should be forced to hold a citizenship he or she does not want.

The other feature of the 403 numbered Turkish Citizenship Law was to distinguish between expulsion from citizenship and loss of citizenship. The former 1312 numbered Citizenship Law did not distinguish between those two, and all citizens had been subject to expulsion under this law. Under the 403 numbered law, those people who ascribed to Turkish citizenship would not be subject to expulsion, with the exception stated in Article 26. However, those who acquired Turkish citizenship could be subject to expulsion under the circumstances stated in the same article. Those persons who acquired Turkish citizenship and were expelled from citizenship due to the article mentioned above could not by any means be re-admitted to Turkish citizenship (Turkish Citizenship Law Proposal: 3).

Loss of citizenship was designed to deal with activities that are not in line with loyalty to the state. Therefore, those persons who were living abroad and had not applied to the Turkish embassy in the last five years,[6] or those persons who published criticisms of the Turkish government abroad, would lose their Turkish citizenship (Turkish Citizenship Law Proposal: 3). In addition, loss of citizenship was defined by Article 25.[7]

The 403 numbered and 11 February 1964 dated Turkish Citizenship Law explicitly stated that the principle of *jus sanguinis* was exercised in Turkey. It might be suggested that this principle was exercised to an almost extreme level, by barring Turkish women married to a foreigner from citizenship on the grounds that the father's citizenship was the determinant. This would, however, be changed in 1981, perhaps due to changing international dynamics and attempts to eliminate discrimination against women.[8]

The 1982 Constitution

In 1980 Turkey experienced another military intervention. There was extreme ideological polarization and turmoil within the country. The reasons given by the military for the takeover were the safeguarding of the integrity of the country, preventing civil war and re-establishing the authority of the state (Tachau and Heper 1983: 26). In 1982 a new constitution was devised. As mentioned previously, the rights and liberties of the 1961 Constitution were curbed to a great extent, and we can depict a return to the civic republican understanding of citizenship.

In the 1982 Constitution, the fourth section is related to political rights and obligations. Article 66 of this section states that:

> Everyone who is annexed to the Turkish State with citizenship ties is a Turk. The child of a Turkish father or a mother is a Turk. Citizenship is acquired and lost for the reasons clarified by law. No Turk can be

> expelled from citizenship unless behaving in a manner disloyal to the country. The judicial process cannot be closed to the decisions and proceedings of expulsion from citizenship.
>
> (Article 66, 1982 Constitution)

But before the enactment of the Constitution, citizenship had been the issue on the state level. The debates around citizenship started in February 1981, right after the military coup. At that time the National Security Council was in charge of state affairs, and it made an amendment in the Turkish Citizenship Law together with the Consultative Assembly. Even though the Turkish Citizenship Law was enacted in 1964, there were considerable changes and annexations made during this interregnum period, therefore most of the data used in this section is limited to this period of 1981–3. The changes were to three significant aspects. First was the improvement concerning dual or multiple citizenship. With the amendment on 13 February 1981,

> withdrawal from Turkish citizenship is subject to permission of the Council of Ministers when … citizenship of a foreign country has been acquired in any manner or when there is convincing evidence that someone is going to acquire a foreign country's citizenship.
>
> (Turkish Citizenship Law)

This amendment was particularly significant for Turkish people who had gone to, for instance, Germany as guest workers but who had eventually settled there. Previously, holding dual or multiple citizenship had not been permitted; however, because of the problems arising from the situation of Turkish emigrants settled in other countries, this new law was designed as a solution (Abadan-Unat and Kemiksiz 1986; İçduygu 1996a; 1996b; İçduygu *et al.* 1999). According to this law, people wanting to acquire citizenship of another country would first apply to the authorities and obtain the permission documents for withdrawal from Turkish citizenship. However, after they acquire another country's citizenship, there is still an opportunity to retain Turkish citizenship by returning the required documents to the Turkish authorities within three years of obtaining the permission documents. According to İçduygu *et al.* (1999), Turkey decided to permit dual citizenship for its citizens living abroad because of the practical national interests of "the wish to keep close contacts with its citizens abroad, and therefore encouraging emigrants to retain their citizenship and transfer it to their children." Even though the implementation of dual citizenship is a challenge to the general definition of citizenship which holds that "citizenship should be unique" (Brubaker 1989), Turkey took an adoptive attitude in this dual citizenship debate. Although Turkish emigrants had some uncertainties about dual citizenship (İçduygu 1996a; 1996b) they responded quickly to the new developments. Starting from the amendment of the law, until the transition to multi-party politics in November 1983, a total of 1,171 people applied for permission to renounce their Turkish citizenship.[9]

Another significant development was related to the circumstances the country went through after the military coup. The military leaders of the period viewed the ideological polarization in the country as the real cause of the situation, especially as represented by the left. Therefore many leftist intellectuals and people were arrested and imprisoned. Some fled the country; however, a new law was put into effect which would leave them without Turkish citizenship. The meeting on these changes to the citizenship law was held in camera and thus the debates were not made public.

According to the law numbered 2383 and dated 13 February 1981 (*Resmi Gazete*, 21.3.1981, no. 17,286), which was annexed to Article 25 of the Turkish Citizenship Law dated 11 February 1964 and numbered 403,

> a person who has been engaged in activities violating the internal and external security of the Turkish Republic or the economic and financial security of the country in the form of an offense described by the law or a person who, after being engaged in such activities at home, has in any manner gone abroad such that it is not possible to file a public action against him or to initiate penal proceedings or to enforce a ruling and who has failed to return despite notification within three months, or in the case of a Martial Law or Emergency Situation within one month, shall lose his citizenship.
>
> (Turkish Citizenship Law)

In line with this law, people who had fled the country for fear of being arrested because of ideological affiliations or offenses, lost their Turkish citizenship (*Resmi Gazete*, 1981–3). This law and its enactment are significant in the sense that many people were left without citizenship for the first time, and this would lead to problems after the transition to civilian rule. Another significant aspect related to this law is that it determined "who would deserve membership of the state and who would not"; besides, the law was used as a kind of punishment for those who did not act in accordance with the principles of the regime.

Starting from 1981 there is a large-scale loss of citizenship on the part of the non-Muslim elements of the republic for the reasons expressed in Article 25 of the Citizenship Law, paragraphs (a),[10] (ç), (d) and (e). The amendment of these paragraphs indicates the increasing concern for those who have left the country and have not returned. However, the two articles of the Citizenship Law – Article 20 for withdrawal permission and Article 25(a) – seem contradictory. While one states that "a person who has acquired the citizenship of a foreign country in any manner can have withdrawal permission," Article 25(a) refers to, as mentioned above, "those who have acquired foreign citizenship without obtaining permission." As the former does not mention any form of permission before the acquisition of foreign citizenship, it becomes problematic to decide who would lose his/her Turkish citizenship and who would get withdrawal permission. Rather it seems to be a kind of method used to eliminate those non-Muslim citizens who were living abroad, even though this argument may seem rather tough.[11] On the other hand, there was the naturalization of large numbers of people of "Turkic origins" in a significant manner. When decisions of the Council of Ministers are issued in *Resmi Gazete* (Official Gazette) it is quite easy to find pages of lists of people of Bulgarian, Yugoslav or Afghan nationality who have been admitted to Turkish citizenship. The legal reason for this admission is found in the Law on Settlement mentioned above. By analyzing those two developments we can draw some significant conclusions. Even though it seems to be merely a legal process, while forcing non-Muslim citizens to give up their citizenship, admitting others to citizenship reflects more than that. It resembles the process of Turkification of the population in the early republican period, especially when the increasing emphasis on the Turkish-Islamic synthesis in the 1980s is taken into consideration.

During the period of 1981–3 many people were admitted or re-admitted to Turkish citizenship in line with the laws mentioned above. During this three-year period there was an ongoing process of both withdrawing citizenship from some people and admitting others to citizenship. Compared to the previous periods there is an increasing concern with the issue. It seems as if by taking hold of the state, the military regarded itself as responsible for issues related to citizenship and started to put forward new solutions to these problems. However, the changes made during this period led to other problems after the transition to civilian rule.

Issues of citizenship did not appear on the agenda of the Parliament again until 1989. Starting from January 1989, some aspects and articles of the Citizenship Law began to be debated in the Parliament. For instance, it was proposed to annul Article 25(g). Even though the proposal was rejected, it paved the way for discussions on the practices of the military regime on citizenship. During this period we witness an increasing concern with citizenship, which was viewed as a basic human right from which no one should be expelled arbitrarily. Also, those implementations were seen as an obstacle to Turkey's relations with the EC, and the military regime was criticized for its implementations on citizenship (Speech of Ali Haydar Erdoğan, *TBMM Tutanak Dergisi*, 20.4.1989: 309–12). It was a period when Turkey's citizenship issues were starting to be discussed with reference to the Universal Declaration of Human Rights, international law, and Europe.

The annulment of Article 25 paragraph (g) came eleven years later, on 27 May 1992. The proposal was discussed in Parliament on 13 February 1992. In the proposal it was stated that a total of 227 people had lost their citizenship in accordance with paragraph (g). The reason behind this proposal was declared as in order to make this law and practices of human rights in Turkey compatible with universal traditions, international treaties, Turkey's political regime and with the society's aspirations for integration with the modern world (*TBMM Tutanak Dergisi*, 17.2.1992). Thus, the annulment of paragraph (g) of Article 25 was accepted and the documents and records of the people concerned were updated; furthermore, all their property, which had been confiscated by the government, was returned.

During the 1990s, Parliament was concerned mostly with the dual citizenship problem and legal procedures. On many occasions questions were raised about the process of withdrawal from citizenship and the problems and shortcomings of the system. In order to solve this problem and find a solution to the status of those living in other countries, withdrawal from Turkish citizenship was made easier. The requirement of completing military service before withdrawal was annulled (*TBMM Tutanak Dergisi*, 7.6.1995, pp. 98–101). Besides, Article 29 of the Citizenship Law stating that a person who has lost Turkish citizenship will be treated as a foreigner, was changed by adding a statement that they may have the rights of a Turkish citizen in matters such as residence, acquiring and transferring real estate, inheritance and labor (*ibid.*).

The underlying goal of this change was to encourage dual citizenship among Turkish migrants living in other countries. This encouragement however, was based on the promotion of the interests of Turkey in those countries by placing those people in key positions in, for example, political life. When the proposal was being debated in the Parliament, all party representatives emphasized the importance of the Turkish people's votes, if they were to be naturalized in the countries concerned, for the formation of coalition governments. In other words, those people were regarded as the representatives of Turkish interests in the countries where they lived. It was not an attempt to solve the problems of those people's status in their country of residence and help them enjoy equal rights with the natives of those countries.

Hammar (1989: 81) notes that debate over dual citizenship involves the question of the meaning of citizenship. In the dual citizenship debates in Turkey, citizenship in this sense was limited to a legal definition, that of acquiring legal membership of the host country. However, the social and cultural aspect was perceived to be reserved for Turkish citizenship. In other words, it was believed that those people who acquired another country's citizenship would still serve the interests of Turkey in the host country.

Starting from the early 1980s, citizenship became a significant issue in Parliament. At first it was used as a kind of control mechanism and as a form of punishment for those who were "against the regime." After the transition to the democratic multi-party system, it was again an issue, but this time to meet the requirements of democracy. As had always been the case, parliamentary and legal concerns on citizenship were limited to the European or Western point of view. The legal codes and implementations were criticized and annulled because they were seen as obstacles to the modernization and development of Turkey. The changes regarding dual citizenship, as mentioned above, were made with secondary concern for Turkish people seeking the benefits of Turkey in the countries where they lived and had become citizens. As is clear from the changes made, dual citizenship was encouraged. It was stated that citizenship laws stem from the internal and special needs and features of each individual country. However, the internal problems of citizenship were not even debated in Parliament. But as identity problems increased, and new problems related to Turkish citizenship as defined by the state emerged, new discussions and debates came onto the agenda.

Conclusion

When we examine the history of the Turkish Republic, we witness certain shifts in the conception of citizenship. During the formation of the Republic the legal conceptualization was more in line with the French version. However, starting from the 1930s it became closer to the German version. On the other hand, there was and is a close affiliation to the civic republican understanding, which emphasizes the primacy of the state and the duties of the citizen. The citizenization process in the early republican period had the major objective of constructing a citizen who was devoted to the sustenance of the Kemalist revolution. This was carried out not only through legalistic developments, but in almost all aspects of life as well (Soyarık 2000). The 1961 Constitution represents a transitory period when the emphasis shifted toward the rights of the citizen and a more liberal understanding. However, after 1980 there was a revival of the early republican conception, one which the state still tries to adhere to. When increasing identity claims and social unrest are taken into consideration, we can argue that there is a deep need in Turkey for a change in the Constitution, which was one of the major requirements for candidacy to the EU. The recent constitutional amendments of 2001 and 2002, regarding basic rights and liberties, the abolition of capital punishment, the extension of opportunities for broadcasting in mother tongues, and the new package of reforms of the new government of the Justice and Development Party for the extension of freedoms and adoption of the standards of the European Union, hold out some hopes for a more rights-oriented and liberal understanding of citizenship. However, in my view, there is still a need for a new constitution. This new constitution should be devised not from above, but by taking the people's desires, opinions and needs into account. In order to accomplish this, "an interplay between institutionalized processes of opinion and will formation and the informal networks of public communication should occur" (Habermas 1994: 351). Then we might see the possibility of democratic state-society relations in Turkey, which would be based on a new constitution, recognizing the importance of the language of the rights of individuals as citizen-subjects.

Notes

1 http://www.eu2002.dk/news/upload/ conclusions_DER_CPH2002121323534.doc The concern over implementation of the legal reforms is expressed also in the EU's 2003 Regular Report on Turkey's progress towards accession. http://europa.eu.int/comm/enlargement/report_2003/index/htm

2 Here Yıldız (1998) quotes the statement of reasons for Article 88 as:

> Since the Ottoman Empire had been obliterated and perished, the members of the nation could no longer be called "Ottoman." National self-honor cannot accept belonging to a dynasty. Our state is a national state, not an international or supra-national one. The state can recognize no nation other than the *Turk*. It is not proper to consider racial differences as an obstacle to nationality since there are peoples of different origins in the country who possess equal rights. Likewise, since freedom of conscience is certified, religion also has not been considered as a hindrance to nationality. The Turkish nation too, like all the new nationalities, could embody people of different races. But it is the community of the Turks (*Türklük camiasi*) that has the capability of bringing together all the races.
>
> (see *TBMM Zabıt Ceridesi*, 2nd period, meeting 2, 7: 216, 9.3.1340 (1924))

3 This article is different from Article 88 of the 1924 Constitution that stated that everyone who is admitted to citizenship through the Citizenship Law is considered as a Turk. The 1312 numbered Citizenship Law stated that every child born of a Turkish father or a Turkish mother would acquire Turkish citizenship. The 1961 Constitution granted citizenship status only to those children born of Turkish fathers, and leaves the status of children born of Turkish mothers ambiguous by stating that their status would be arranged by law. The citizenship law will be analyzed below.

4 In fact, the limitation on the rights mentioned in the Constitution of 1961 started with the 1971 coup by memorandum and many of the related articles were re-amended.

5 The Law Proposal was dated 28 May 1962. See *TBMM Tutanak Dergisi*, 20/1: 477–97, 507–11, 29.8.1963. Also see *TBMM Tutanak Dergisi*, 26/1: 504–8, 11.2.1964.

6 This provision was laid down in Article 11 of the 1312 numbered Turkish Citizenship Law.

7 The Council of Ministers may rule that the following persons have lost their Turkish citizenship:

(a) those who have acquired foreign citizenship without obtaining permission,
(b) those who were in any service of a foreign country not in line with the interests of Turkey and were notified in the name of the government by embassies or consulates abroad or by local administrative officials at home to give up such services but declined to do so voluntarily during the given period which may not be less than three months,
(c) those who continue to work without the permission of the government in any service of a country which is at war with Turkey,
(ç) those persons abroad who are called by the competent authorities to do their military service or, in time of war, to join home defense but have not done so within three months without excuse,
(d) those who abscond to foreign countries while being forwarded for military service or after joining their units and do not return within the legally prescribed period,

(e) those members of the armed forces or military incumbents who are abroad on duty, on leave, for changing climate or for medical treatment and fail to return home within three months without excuse after the expiry of their terms,
(f) those persons who after acquiring Turkish citizenship by the competent authority, live outside Turkey for at least seven years without a break and do not undertake any formal contacts and transactions to indicate that they have not cut off their interest in and ties with Turkey and that they have maintained their Turkish citizenship.

But the formerly excercised requirement for them to leave Turkey and clarify their properties was annulled, and they were given the possibility of re-admittance to Turkish citizenship. But before or during the re-admittance process, they would be considered as foreigners.

8 However, Nomer (1988: 46–7)) argued that those articles were not discriminatory or contrary to the provisions of the International Convention on the Elimination of All Kinds of Discrimination of Women, which was enacted on 3 September 1981 and signed by Turkey in 1985. (Here it should be noted that this is a later development, and during the 1960s the international debates on the status of women were not very strong). Nomer stated that the articles concerned granted a more "privileged" status to women than men, rather than discriminating or subordinating them. Nevertheless, it seems a bit naive to suggest that an article that excludes children born of Turkish mothers and foreign fathers from Turkish citizenship, or in a way urges the Turkish woman concerned to admit her husband's citizenship is a privilege.

9 Those resolutions can be found in *Resmi Gazete* (Official Gazette) of 1981–3.

10 This paragraph is amended per law no. 2383/6 on 13 February 1981, like paragraph (g) of Article 25 of the Citizenship Law. However, as mentioned in the text, the original draft of the law cannot be scrutinized as the meeting was held in camera. The Turkish Citizenship Law and the Official Gazette are used in this text as references.

11 It is not possible to list all the names here, but they are available in the relevant issues of *Resmi Gazete* (Official Gazette).

References

Abadan-Unat and Kemiksiz, N. (1986) *Türk Dış Göçü: 1960–1984* (Turkish External Migration: 1960–1984), Ankara: Siyasal Bilgiler Fakültesi.

Aktar, A. (1996) "Cumhuriyetin İlk Yıllarında Uygulanan Türkleştirme Politikaları" (Turkification Policies Implemented in the First Years of Republic), *Tarih ve Toplum*, 156 (December): 324–38.

Bali, R. N. (1999) *Cumhuriyet Yıllarında Türkiye Yahudileri: Bir Türkleştirme Serüveni (1923–1945) (The Jews of Turkey During the Republican Years: An Adventure of Turkification)*, Istanbul: İletişim Yayınları.

Bendix, R. (1964) *Nation-building and Citizenship: Studies of Our Changing Social Order*, New York: Wiley.

Brubaker, W. R. (1989) "Introduction" in W. R. Brubaker (ed.) *Immigration and the Politics of Citizenship in Europe and North America*, Lanham MD, New York and London: The German Marshall Fund of the US University Press of America.

Ekinci, T. Z. (1997) *Vatandaşlık Açısından Kürt Sorunu ve Bir Çözüm önerisi* (The Kurdish Problem regarding Citizenship and a Proposal for its Solution), Istanbul: Küyerel Yayınları.

General Secretariat of the National Security Council (1982) *12 September in Turkey: Before and After*, Ankara: Ongun Kardeşler Printing House, 229, cited in Tachau and Heper, "The State, Politics and Military in Turkey," 26.

Gözübüyük, A. Ş. (1995) *Açıklamalı Türk Anayasaları (Explanatory Turkish Constitutions)*, Ankara: Turhan Kitabevi Yayınları.

Habermas, J. (1992) "Citizenship and National Identity: Some Reflections on the Future of Europe," *Praxis International* 12, reprinted in B. S. Turner and P. Hamilton (eds) (1994) *Citizenship: Critical Concepts*, London and New York: Routledge.

Hammar, T. (1989) "State, Nation and Dual Citizenship," in W. R. Brubaker (ed.) *Immigration and the Politics of Citizenship in Europe and North America*, Lanham MD, New York and London: The German Marshall Fund of the US University Press of America.

Harris, G. S. (1988) "The Role of the Military in Turkey in the 1980s: Guardians or Decision-Makers?," in M. Heper and A. Evin (eds) *State, Democracy and the Military: Turkey in the 1980s*, Berlin: Walter de Gruyter.

İçduygu, A. (1996a) "Becoming a Citizen in an Immigration Country: The Case of Turks in Australia and Sweden and Some Comparative Implications," *International Migration*, 2.

——(1996b) "Citizenship at the Crossroads: Immigration and the Nation-State," in E. Kofman and G. Youngs (eds) *Globalization: Theory and Practice*, London: Pinter.

İçduygu, A., Çolak, Y. and Soyarık N. (1999) "What is the Matter with Citizenship? – A Turkish Debate," *Middle Eastern Studies*, 35 (4) October: 187–208.

İnan, A. (1988) *Vatandaş İçin Medeni Bilgiler ve M. Kemal Atatürk'ün El Yazmaları* (Information for the Citizen and the Manuscripts of M. Kemel Atatürk), Ankara: Türk Tarih Kurumu Basımevi.

Karpat, K. H. (1988) "Military Interventions: Army-Civilian Relations in Turkey Before and After 1980," in M. Heper. and A. Evin (eds) *State, Democracy and the Military: Turkey in the 1980s*, Berlin: Walter de Gruyter.

Kili, S. and Gözübüyük, A. Ş. (1985) *Türk Anayasa Metinleri: Sened-i İttifaktan Günümüze* (Turkish Constitutional Texts: From Sened-i İttifak until Today), Ankara: Türkiye İş Bankası Kültür Yayınları.

Levi, A. (1996) *Türkiye Cumhuriyeti'nde Yahudiler* (*Jews in the Turkish Republic)*, Istanbul: İletişim Yayınları.

Lewis, B. (1961) *Emergence of Modern Turkey*, London: Oxford University Press.

Marshall, T. H. (1965) *Class, Citizenship and Social Development*, Garden City NY: Anchor Books, Doubleday and Company.

Nomer, E. (1989) *Vatandaşlık Hukuku* (Citizenship Law), 8th edn, Istanbul: Filiz Kitabevi.

Resmi Gazete (Official Gazette), 21 March 1981, 17286.

Soyarık, N. (2000) "The Citizen of the State and the State of the Citizen: An Analysis of the Citizenization Process in Turkey," unpublished Ph.D. thesis, Bilkent University, Ankara.

Speech of Ali Haydar Erdoğan (SDPP – Istanbul Deputy) (1989), *TBMM Tutanak Dergisi*, 25 (18): 309–12, April 20.

Speech of Naşit Hakkı Bey (1934), *TBMM Zabıt Ceridesi*, 23 (4): 67, 7 June 1934.

Speech of Şükrü Kaya (1934), *TBMM Zabıt Ceridesi*, 23 (4): 141, 14 June 1934.

Tabiiyet Kilavuzu [The Guide to Nationality] (1939) Istanbul: Cumhuriyet Matbaası.

Tachau, F. and Heper, M. (1983) "The State, Politics, and the Military in Turkey," *Comparative Politics*, 16: 17–33.
Tanör, B. (1988) *Osmanlı-Türk Anayasal Gelişmeleri (1789–1980) (OTAG)* (Ottoman–Turkish Consitutional Developments (1789–1980)), 2nd edn, Istanbul: Yapı Kredi Yayınları.
TBMM Zabıt Ceridesi(1924), 7 (2): meeting 2, 9.03.1340 (1924).
——(1928) 4 (3): 1st meeting, session 80, 23.5.
TBMM Tutanak Dergisi (1963), 20 (1): 477–97, 507–11, 29.8.
——(1964), 26 (1): 504–08, 11.2.
——(1995), 38 (19): 98–101, 7.06.
——(1995), 38 (19): 88–109, 7.06.
Turan, İ. (1969) *Cumhuriyet Tarihimiz* (Our Repulican History), Istanbul: Çağlayan Ktb.
"Türk Vatandaşlığı Kanununun 25inci Maddesinde Değişiklik Yapılmasına İlişkin Kanun Tasarısı ve İçişleri Komisyonu Raporu (1/345)," (Proposal for the amendment of article 25 of the Turkish Citizenship law and the report of the Ministry of Interior), *TBMM Tutanak Dergisi* (1992), 12 (19), 12.02.
Yıldız, A. (1998) "Search for an Ethno-Secular Delimitation of Turkish National Identity in the Kemalist Era (1924–1938) with Particular Reference to the Ethnicist Conception of Kemalist Nationalism," unpublished Ph.D. thesis, Bilkent University, Ankara.

Part III

Challenges to Turkish citizenship

7 The making of familial citizenship in Turkey[1]

Nükhet Sirman[2]

The aim of this chapter is to put forward an account that provides a gendered perspective to issues of citizenship and sovereignty in the Turkish postcolonial context. The chapter starts from the premise that a rights discourse, as is common in most of the studies on citizenship, is not adequate to grasp the real operation of gendered citizenship, and this especially so in postcolonial conditions. The classic discussions on citizenship starting from Marshall usually provide a classification of the nature of the rights that have been accorded to the individual citizen using a universalistic discourse (e.g. Turner 1990). This universalism is premised on a particular reading of liberal democracies that does not pose the issue of belonging to a polity in terms of identity and the constitution of the subject as citizen, nor of the constitution of the polity itself.

The two important debates that have taken place over citizenship in recent decades have problematized the issues of individual versus group rights on the one hand, and issues of recognition versus redistribution on the other (Yuval-Davis 1997). These debates were largely concerned with accommodating difference and extending participation within the polity and the extent to which citizenship as a politico-legal tool could be redefined to allow for such revisions. Discussions regarding the constitution of the citizen showed how race, class, and gender cut across discourses that constituted the subject as a proper citizen. More recently, the extension of the politics of neoliberalism over most of the globe has prompted another revision of the concept, this time with a view to accommodate diasporic and indigenous rights (e.g. Ong 1999; Povinelli 2002). Concern with the new global order meant that the nature of the polity to which the citizen belonged was thrown into question for the first time. Discourses that produced identity and citizenship both as a status and a practice were taken up in the context in which the boundaries of the nation-state were assailed by transnational flows of capital, labor and culture (Isin and Wood 2002).

The issue that this chapter addresses is the constitution of the nation-state under postcolonial conditions in order to show that questions regarding the nature of identity and polity cannot be assumed to operate in a universal manner even before neoliberalism. What is often ignored in this scholarship are the cultural codes that make it possible to maintain the exclusionary effects of class, gender and race without naming them as such in the discourses constitutive of citizenship. Most of these theories deploy these categories of difference as analytic categories drawn from academic practices and show how discourses of citizenship position them within their discursive narratives. What this chapter aims to do is to show that these categories of difference are effects of the discourses themselves. In order to be able to do this, it is necessary to look at the production of the master discourse constitutive of the polity itself, and see how exclusion becomes an effect of the production of a holistic and therefore sovereign community, that is, the nation-state. The aim is to be able to isolate the discursive moves through which the discrepancy between rule (for example, egalitarian constitutions) and practice are made understandable and acceptable to the subjects of the nation without resorting to an analytic of interest or deceit. This, I hope, will allow us to understand the resilience of these exclusions in the face of discourses of human rights deployed to counter them and provide the possibility of alternative discourses of opposition.

I shall argue that the building of a national sovereign state is always the product of discourses of the identity of the nation in the process of constituting the nation-state as a specific kind of polity. These discourses simultaneously construct the identity of the proper citizen. Consequently the citizen is endowed with a particular package of rights and duties, made the subject of specific operations of power and of a particular moral subjectivity that differs according to these constitutive discourses. Looking at these discourses in the case of Turkey, I argue that the particular form of citizenship that was produced can best be described as familial citizenship. This, as I shall show, indicates a gendered discourse in which the ideal citizen is inscribed as a sovereign husband and his dependent wife/mother rather than an individual, with the result that position within a familial discourse provides the person with status within the polity. Public identities are made sense of primarily through familial identities that are also peculiar to the discourses that produce them and should not be understood as another universal. The use of categories that are supposed to have universal meanings, such as family and citizen, thus renders the resulting discourse of the nation and its relation to its subject seemingly universal, turning the analysis of citizenship on the basis of this universal discourse largely into a list of lacks: of human rights, of individual freedoms, of women's rights and so on.

Thus, rather than start from the universal discourse of the citizen, this chapter will attempt to delineate the discourses and practices under which the Turkish nation-state was first produced. It will argue that the production of an imaginary of the nuclear family took place in tandem with the creation of the nation-state as modern. This preoccupation with modernity is what I would identify as the postcolonial condition, which as Hall argues, means that we have to read the discourses and practices of a particular locality in relation to the "Euro-imperial adventure" (1996: 252). The general outline of the process of imagining the nation as modern in Turkey follows *grosso modo* the trajectory depicted in many theoretical narratives. What this chapter tries to do is to articulate this narrative first to the nature of the polity and to the way the modern was imagined in this polity. The precise identification of the agents of change with regard to their position in the polity will serve to explain how they linked change in the nature of the polity to change in intimate relationships. I will show that the main preoccupation was the creation of a proper national subject, the ideal citizen, and that this preoccupation prompted a revision of the ties of dependency that characterized the political order in which the agents of nationalism found themselves. As the Ottoman Empire, "the sick man of Europe," found itself the object of various imperial desires, its elites began to think of the polity as a whole in relation to Europe and with a view to resist these imperial designs. The invention of new forms of intimate relationships, that is, the patriarchal "nuclear" family, produced a new regulation of desire, constituting sovereignty, national community and the modern individual all at once. In this process, the will to create a national community, be it Ottoman or Turkish, will be shown to be the decisive step that would ensure the sovereignty of the polity.[3] It was through the forms of intimacy pertaining to the nuclear family that the morality of the proper citizen was to be produced and citizens turned into the subjects of the modern nation-state. Finally, to the extent that this family is a gendered construction, it will be possible to analyze the gendered nature of citizenship itself.

Gender, nationalism and the postcolonial condition

Approaches to nationalism as a form of discursive practice have largely taken their cue from Anderson's *Imagined Communities* (1983). That nationalism was the work of the imagination was also proposed by Gellner (1983) and Hobsbawm (1990). While the former saw nationalism as the attempt to align the boundaries of polity and culture, the latter defined it as the bourgeoisie's call of the masses into history. These approaches spelt a going away from purely political accounts of nationalism and initial attempts to theorize the subjects and objects of nationalism. Anderson's was a first foray into the content rather than the function of nationalism. His emphasis on print capitalism and homogeneous empty time indicated a structural relation between discourse and practice and the role of cultural content in the production of the nation as a community.

But it was Chatterjee who underlined the specificity of postcolonial nationalisms. For Chatterjee, nationalism was primarily a matter of difference from the colonial metropolis under conditions where the very discursive structures that allowed such difference to be articulated were provided by the metropolitan discourse based on the epistemology of rationalism (1986). At stake was the issue of the sovereignty of the postcolonial subject, who, in taking over the discourse of rationality was placing this subjectivity within the ambit of power/knowledge discourses that constituted European domination. As argued by Hall, the identity of the sovereign postcolonial subject could henceforth be thought only in a painful relation of identity/difference with the colonizer.

Feminist interventions in the debates on nationalism followed on from the impasse reached by approaches that searched for the explanation of the universal subordination of women in the sphere of production and reproduction. Under the impact of these approaches, the articulation between capitalism and the family had been investigated in detail. What prompted feminists to look into nationalism was the realization of the role of the nation-state in structuring these relations and producing the ideological discourses that reproduced them. The 1989 volume edited by Floya Anthias and Nira Yuval-Davis was focused around the question of the role of the nation-state in producing and reproducing women as second-class citizens. Arguing that the category of the citizen was not as inclusive as purported, Anthias and Yuval-Davis argued that exclusions and limitations were inherent to the relation of different categories of people to the state. Women were made part of the nation through the control of their bodies, and through cultural elaborations of femininity came the definition and control of the cultural boundaries of the nation. By contrast, another scholarship had already started to problematize the gender-blind categories of liberal theories of citizenship. Feminist political theorists started to call for the gendering of concepts such as democracy and citizenship (Pateman 1988; Phillips 1991). The different and secondary status of women in liberal democracy, according to these theorists, could be explained neither through its theory nor its practice. New concepts, such as the private/public distinction (Phillips) or patriarchy (Pateman) needed to be included in the theory and practice of citizenship.

Reference to nationalism was strangely absent from these discussions. Feminist theory directed its criticisms at liberal tenets such as contract theory or the assumption of universal equality. Concern with nationalism was only articulated by those theorists who dealt with postcolonial states. This was in general due to the realization that analyzing women's status in such states through the categories developed in so-called liberal democracies ended up simply by listing what the former lacked in comparison to the latter. Kandiyoti (1989; 1991) conceptualized nationalism as an ideology and, as such, was perhaps the first analyst to take the content of nationalism seriously. She argued that nationalism had to provide a solution to the "woman question," that is, develop an answer to the issue of what the position of women in a "modern" society should be. Different political projects competed with one another on the basis of the answer they provided to this question. What she called "Islamic society" was one such answer and it served to signal the constitution of a polity that was different from the West. In any case, women were used as mere pawns in the delineation of a modern national identity in these "other" societies.

These theoretical steps went a long way towards raising the issue of gender identity as constituted in (nationalist) discourse and, conversely, how nationalist discourse itself was itself gendered. And yet, they assumed that gender identity could be constituted by discourse alone. It is only this assumption that can explain their inability to look for the institutions that could reproduce this identity in everyday life. Gender identity has to do with subjectivity, and subjectivity has to be constituted both at the level of the everyday and with the appropriate technologies that can sustain it (albeit with changes and variations) over time. Finally, one also has to look for the conditions in which subjects desire to appropriate this identity. If, as Kandiyoti argues, one can talk of competing nationalist projects, then one should also be able to see how men and women are addressed by these competing projects, how each of them differently invite subjects to take part in public, to form families that they will think of as belonging to something called the private, and to even fight to uphold these projects. The approaches discussed above ultimately see identity as an already constituted product rather than as a constantly shifting process that involves the subject in myriad ways. In the end, an analysis of the practice of gendered citizenship and the institutions such as the law or the family that buttress a particular gendered definition of citizenship are strangely absent from these approaches.[4]

In spite of the central role played by the concept of patriarchy (and therefore of power) in informing feminist approaches to gendered citizenship, one has to turn to Fanon for an analysis of the power dynamics of gender and colonialism in the making of nationalism. The neglect of Fanon in feminist writing is striking. In his analysis of the gendered desires informing colonialism, Fanon argued that the French desire for uncovering the veiled Algerian woman, seen as the essence of the colony, was only matched by the Algerian man's desire to have the French woman as a useless antidote to his impotence as the colonized (1965; 1967). This analysis clearly linked national impulses to sexual desires, and subjectivity to power. However, as argued by Anne McClintock, this theory rendered the subject strangely genderless and therefore implicitly male (1996). Nevertheless, by situating the relation between nationalism and gender in its historical context and relating it to the issue of the subject, Fanon was able to draw attention to the gendered nature of all power relations in (post-) colonial society.

From the woman question to gender: the new family

To see how nationalism constitutes gender, it is necessary to look at the polity as a whole and see how gender relations are articulated to other power relations, especially in postcolonial conditions. Studies on nationalism usually single out the family as the site of intervention in most nationalist discourse. Most of these approaches see the use of the family in these discourses as a metaphor for the polity. Fanon, for example, talks about the colonial desire to domesticate the colony, to govern it as one governs a family (McClintock 1996: 265). But confusingly, he also talks about the new familial regulations of colonial rule. In effect, most nationalisms have attempted to re-fashion families according to new principles. However, very little has been said about the reasons why the family becomes such a major site of nationalist intervention, especially in postcolonial conditions. It is striking that under these conditions this re-fashioning has often been imagined in relation to some notion of modernity, that is, to discourses of society developed by the colonizer. This relation between the family and nationalism needs to be scrutinized more carefully.

If, as argued by Anderson, imagining the nation means imagining a new model for the community, then it is possible to argue that the new models of the family function to provide content to this national community. Theoretically, the relations between the imagined community (the nation) and the family can be constituted in numerous ways. Many analysts see this relation primarily as a metaphorical one (e.g. Sommer 1991; McClintock 1996). According to this view, the family is used to represent the bonds that are presumed to exist between the persons making up the nation because it provides a natural model for such bonds. The invention of the new family and of the nation as natural serves to render invisible and legitimize the power relations that are constitutive of both types of community. However, the new family is not imagined as natural in many postcolonial contexts, but as modern.

Other writers have sought to provide sociological, structural accounts of the relation between nation and family. Kandiyoti, for example, argues that the new family serves to dissolve social structures that hinder drives toward centralization, especially in Islamic societies such as the Ottoman Empire (1991). Jayawardena, on the other hand, sees both the new family and the new woman as better fitting the local bourgeoisie's yearning for modernity. For her, the new family is also able to provide an educated labor force in modernizing societies (1988).

These approaches, although alerting us to the importance of women and the family for nationalist projects, do not pay enough attention to the relation between power and gender. At best they conceive of power as somehow external to gender, imposed upon it through political means. To see how the nation and power are inscribed in the subject, one would need to look at the process of the production of subjectivities that are gendered and national at the same time. The new woman and the new family are not simply categories produced by the state; they are themselves productive of new configurations of power and desire. These configurations require that power and sovereignty be imagined in completely novel ways. As Kandiyoti (1998) states in a more recent article, these configurations also involve the production of new masculinities, and indeed new citizens. However, Kandiyoti continues to situate these new masculinities within the problematic of modernism. With modernity, she argues, the authoritarian man is associated with the peasant and thereby turned into the symbol of backwardness. What is not mentioned here is the modern man's sources of power, which are closely related to the new familial order.

The new man, the enlightened father who carefully plans his children's (especially his daughters') education, is, as Chatterjee shows, himself the product of the new techniques of subjectification, and is as such deeply implicated in modern forms of power. Chatterjee asserts that in colonial societies such as India, women and the family become critical categories for nationalist discourse because the colonizer dominates the public arena (1993). The cultural problem in such situations, according to Chatterjee, is that they have to imagine their national identities as both modern and as different from the Western colonizer. Chatterjee describes those who are the main actors of this imaginary activity as the middle class, rather than the bourgeoisie. He uses this term to indicate that he is referring to a class of people who are, in a sense, caught in the middle and who engage in a process of cultural production from this rather new position within society. They are caught in the middle in the sense that they feel impotent under the British colonial apparatus whose mode of exercising sovereignty they cannot help but admire. They thus desire modernity for themselves because they see it as an efficient means of establishing their own sovereignty. It is this section of society that is involved in imagining a new community, a process that leads them to re-invent existing discourses and practices ranging from religion to literature, the family to science in relation to modernity. What this process amounts to is a new realignment of the fragments of old cultural discourses and desires under the sign of Hindu nationality under colonial conditions. It is under these conditions that the Hindu family, and especially the Hindu woman, is cast as the representative of Hindu Eastern morality that has been able to be preserved unsullied by alien domination. Thus, it is the desire for power and sovereignty that prompts the Indian middle class to produce a Hindu middle-class culture around their notions of family, femininity and masculinity, a desire that in the process also produces the new Hindu family, and the new masculine and feminine citizens of the new Indian nation.

This approach is especially useful for attempts to theorize the sovereignty of the nation-state and the processes of subject formation under postcolonial conditions. It becomes possible for the first time to see the attempts of nationalist discourse and practice to restructure the family and the identity of national subjects as something more than a metaphor to think the new nation through (as in the nation as a family writ-large), or the means through which the social capital (as in patriotic citizens or an educated labor force) necessary for the new polity can be produced. The family, the nation and gender can now be linked to the manner in which power is constituted, understood and exercised in the post-colony. Nationalism thus becomes the constitutive force of the family, of the relations that should obtain between the members of the family, and of the relations that should obtain between families and institutions of the state. It also becomes possible to see beyond the public/private dichotomy, in fact to see it not just as the naturalization of power, but its constitution at the level of the polity. Gender and the family are thus placed at the center of what Foucault has called governmentality. Nationalism, too, becomes more than a political ideology, but a discursive practice that is constitutive of institutions, subjectivity and everyday life. Above all, this perspective allows us to link the operations of micro-power to the macro issues of state formation and citizenship. Issues such as family practices, gender, culture and even emotions like love can be made to talk to each other as Chatterjee has done with regard to India in his analysis of life stories and social positions. Studying the autobiographies of people who have somehow fallen foul of the new gender identities, he is able to describe the violence involved in assuming the identities of the new gender order, as well as the violence reserved for those who cannot (1993). Postcolonial gendered identities are in this way linked to both the desire for power and the processes through which the individual becomes constituted through the new technologies of power.

This new scholarship on modernity, nationalism and power has produced numerous studies of postcolonial states ranging from South Asia to Latin America and South Africa. The volume edited by Lila Abu-Lughod (1998) on Middle Eastern states focuses on the technologies that produce the new mother, the new femininity and especially the new housewife. It is the theoretical perspective described above that allows cultural practices such as prescriptions to raise children, novels, fashion, education, policies of employment and sexuality to become the new objects of analyses of nationalism. Looking at these cultural practices as effects of technologies of power has allowed subjectivity and sovereignty, gender and the nation to be studied together. Rather than an identity imposed from outside, it is now possible to see national masculinity and femininity as forms of subjectivity desired by those aspiring to the power positions offered by these forms of identity.

To be a man:[5] gender construction in Turkey

There have been a number of studies looking into the actors of nationalism in Turkey. Kandiyoti, for example, in an article on the novels written in the Ottoman Empire after the reform movements of 1839[6], shows that these novels are about the discomfort the (male) novelists felt with regard to the femininity they observed in their society. By arguing that this discomfort is a product of male views of what reform and modernity should constitute, Kandiyoti situates femininity once more within a problematic of modernity. To situate the problem of femininity within its proper context, one has to turn to Şerif Mardin's analysis of the Young Ottoman movement. In this classic study, Mardin argues that these first nationalists of the Ottoman Empire were made up of aspiring bureaucrats and intellectuals whose expected upward mobility was blocked by the changes made to the bureaucracy after 1839 (Mardin 1966). I think it is possible to see these young men as occupying the same middle position identified by Chatterjee as the agents of nationalism. In view of the dearth of studies on everyday life and the family in the late Ottoman period, I will propose a model informed by anthropological studies of Turkish society of the gender order of this society that produced what would later turn into a class of writers and thinkers who demanded social change on the basis of their own impotence. I hope that in this way, it will be possible to pose new questions regarding the changing power relations of late Ottoman society in relation to gender, family and nationalism, and thus to identify the proper citizen in his and her gendered specificity.

To define the sociological nature of the late Ottoman Empire, it is necessary to imagine a social order composed of what I call "big houses" or what others have called "house societies" (Joyce and Gillespie 2000). Topkapı Palace as the biggest house of the land provides a good model for conceiving the nature of the relation between power and social order. A careful analysis of the operation of the palace as an institution shows that the relation between family and political power is much more intertwined than a simple model of a metaphor would allow. In this model, the social and familial order, politics and kinship are mutually constitutive and the head of the house is at once the father and the sovereign. In order to rule over its territories, this big house constantly spawns smaller replicas of itself that it sends as administrators to centers all over the surface of the empire. Bureaucrats of Christian origin, converted not only to Islam, but in fact transformed into members of the Ottoman house (including the Grand Vizier)[7] were married to women from the harem, also converts or daughters of such converts (including the daughters or sisters of the sultan) and posted to different parts of the empire to establish and represent the Ottoman order (Peirce 1993). In time, the young men transformed into members of the big house began to be drawn from among the Muslim population as well. The smaller houses spawned from the big house produced their own spawns, attracting bright young men from their district to the house and transforming them into members of the house. This system produced the houses as satellites of each other, with the palace at the apex of a social order where kinship and power were intimately linked.

The most important personal virtue in this system is for someone to know their place, to be able to accurately gauge who to respect and be subordinate to and who to dominate. Brides, grooms, cooks and gardeners are the dependents of the household head. To know one's place is to answer the question "who are you?" by providing the name of the head of the house one belongs to. This question is usually followed by another one which serves to place the person even more accurately: "and what are you?" The proper answer to that question is to name the bond that links the respondent to the position of power represented by the household head. The answer to this question may be the naming of a kinship relation, as in "I am the younger bride," or a relation that pertains to the division of labor, as in "I am the coffee maker." In the western village of Tuz in the 1980s these questions were routinely asked to people like me who could not immediately be placed (Sirman 1988). In this village, where subsistence depended on cotton-producing family farms, relations of identity and power operated as they did in the Ottoman palace, a form of operation which in the 1980s was depicted as traditional. Economic exchange within the house followed the pattern anthropologists call redistribution. All the material and symbolic resources of the house would be collected at the center and redistributed to members of the house according to their status. All the dependents of the house, from the young daughter collecting cotton in the fields to the son working in the nearby fishing cooperative, would give their wages to the household head, usually the father, and he would allocate this collected income according to his view of need and justice. The household head was often referred to as "owner of the house." In the Ottoman model too, the owner of the house would justly allocate to his retinue the resources that accrued to him as a function of his relation of dependence to a more powerful suzerain. This hierarchy among houses had the palace at its apex, and produced what Mardin has called a personalized society in which morality was structured around the reality that power was a more important resource than wealth (1991).

One cannot speak of a private/public distinction in this kind of social order. Social order and the possibility of sovereignty is the product of the control of relations of kinship and sexuality. The big houses are contiguous and there is no physical or metaphoric space outside them that could structure social relations. This space began to open up only with the *Tanzimat* when the locus of sovereignty was transferred beyond the walls of the palace. How this space was to be structured became an object of anxiety both for the Ottomans and the republicans that followed them, since the code of conduct and the topics of conversation appropriate to this space retained their ambiguity for a long time. The problem was nothing less than the restructuring of power and sovereignty. Ottomans began to worry about conduct in public, and a literature on manners and conduct began to appear, offering an educated public (translated) codes that would regulate relations between strangers, that is, people whose place *vis-à-vis* one another was ambiguous. This lack of manners has always been understood as an inability to adapt to modernity, a lack of the Turkish modern, and continues to this day to plague the national imaginary. What this anxiety indicates, is the continuation of the operation of the old imaginary of state and sovereignty in conditions where they have lost their legitimacy to another mode called modern, a mode which is devised and understood by looking somewhere else, by looking at the imperial West.

Mardin describes the most important changes that came with the *Tanzimat* as the new bureaucratic obstacles that began to be raised in the channels of social mobility that had been available to the lower echelons of the administrative apparatus (1966). With power and sovereignty spilling out of the confines of the house, social mobility was increasingly determined by factors other than the personal attachment of young men to big houses. As social position began to be transferred from father to son on the basis of the new European styles of upbringing adopted by a now emancipated bureaucracy, men of modest backgrounds were increasingly rendered homeless in the sense that they could not readily find a patron and a big house to belong to. It is these men who were caught in the middle of a process of transformation they could not control who formed the middle class in Chatterjee's sense of the word. They were positioned between a bureaucracy that was beginning to close itself off from the rest of the population and the uneducated lower classes of the traditional Istanbul quarter. The first nationalists were drawn from the ranks of this discontented middle class. Unable to enjoy the fruits of the redistributive mechanisms, this middle class translated their malaise into a dissatisfaction with the social order, a malaise which they began to express in the newly developing print technology and the new literary genres that this technology made possible. Newspapers, novels, plays and the essay began to fill the spaces that appeared in the interstices of the big houses, carrying new ideas and a completely novel form of political opposition. This opposition started by questioning what to it seemed interlinked processes: the manner in which big houses were formed and the lack of consultation (*meşveret*) with what began to be called "the people" about decisions regarding the governing of the domain. Mardin tells us that through these developments, ideas of the French Revolution were brought to Ottoman society and that the first Constitution (1876) was a result of these changes. Reading Mardin's work through the lenses provided by Chatterjee's perspective, one can see these incipient nationalists as men feeling the impotence of being caught in the middle and who thus became the agents of a new discourse that hybridized the forms and the content of local Ottoman and European politico-cultural discourse. New categories of discourse such as the people, society, and Ottoman culture began to appear with the critique of the *Tanzimat* and went as far as transforming the forms of subject formation, cultural categories and the social order itself.

To see the precise meanings of these new categories and the functions that were attributed to them in discourses that advocated change, it is necessary to take a closer look at some of these literary texts. The novels and plays of what is called the *Tanzimat* era express deep anxiety about the polity and about the proper conduct of both everyday life and government (Mardin 1966; 1974; Kandiyoti 1988; Parla 1990; Sirman 2000a). In effect this new writing addresses this uncertainty and attempts to fill with various diagnoses and solutions the gap left by the retreat of the big house away from the community. This retreat is felt mostly by educated men who would have, in the old order, been able to form attachments to the big house and move upward along the echelons of the bureaucracy. The *Tanzimat*, by instituting the autonomy of the bureaucrats *vis-à-vis* the palace, had allowed the powerful men of the realm autonomy of action *vis-à-vis* both the community and the palace (Mardin 1966).[8] This had resulted in a withdrawal of the big house from the community and the creation of a hereditary class with its own restricted definition of kinship. The central question posed in these texts is the issue of how one becomes a proper man in a new order in which the big house as it was known no longer structured social and political relations. The trope of romantic love thwarted by power-hungry fathers of the *Tanzimat* novel turns out to be the way the authors attempt to de-legitimize this new bureaucratic class. In the process, they end up by de-legitimizing the big house itself and creating a need to find alternative bonds that will serve to define and legitimize social relations. Love, as an expression of the divine, becomes one of these alternative bonds grounded in the person rather than the house because it can impart legitimacy to new arrangements (Sirman 2000a).[9] But not all kinds of love get sanctioned: some are sacred but others are to be rejected as mere lust. The issue at stake is individual desire and how to domesticate it. A double operation is involved in this attempt to make the desire of the individual as the ground on which the new order should be built. On the one hand desire needs to be defined, but at the same time its boundaries must be set. Love is thus defined as a powerful force that needs to be monitored since it can both make and break order. Novelists taking on the task of defining the proper limits of love thus are involved in setting out the morality of the new order by claiming to represent "common sense" through what Parla calls absolute texts that refuse the possibility of any alternative point of view (Parla 1990).

In the *Tanzimat* novel, love is the foundation of the subject, of relations between subjects and the new basis for the operations of power. The gender identities defined and developed in these novels did indeed become the norm after the establishment of the Turkish Republic in 1923. The Civil Code that was promulgated in 1926 rules that the husband is the head of the family and is the breadwinner, while the wife is defined as the husband's helper and advisor. Thus women in the family were made subordinate to the husband and the married woman's relation to the state was mediated through her husband, the representative of the family in the public sphere. At the same time that women were thus subordinated to a male representative, the Constitution, adopted in 1924, made all citizens equal, regardless of class, gender, creed and ethnicity. As a result of this legislation, gendered citizenship in Turkey was brought into line with practices that prevailed in Europe at the time. However, the different path followed to reach a comparable end point proved to be crucial with regard to women's position in Turkish society. While numerous reforms in Europe and the United States altered women's legal status *vis-à-vis* the husband, such revisions proved to be very painful in Turkey. In effect, it was not until 2002 with Turkey's bid to accession to the European Union that husband and wife were legally made equal in marriage.[10] Thus, the operation of citizenship in Turkey was based on discourses that were different to those that constituted the citizen in the West. These discourses were informed by a nationalism that, as argued by Chatterjee and Hall, saw the national self in relation to that of the sovereign West.

The nation functioned in these discourses as the fund of legitimacy that drew the boundaries of change and defined its main goal. The problem these discourses attempted to address was nothing less than the constitutions of the subjects of the new order: what the identity of the new rulers would be, who would help them and provide them with legitimacy, who they were going to rule over and how relations between rulers and ruled would be imagined. The search for answers began at the seat of power of the old order, the house, and the solution found was to transform this house into a family. This solution meant that a wedge was driven between the identity of those with a bid to sovereignty and the nature of government, the domain of the house and the domain of the state. With nationalism, this separation of the private from the public started to function as a new source of anxiety regarding the wholesomeness of society, an anxiety which today expresses itself in the fascination for corruption and nepotism.[11] For the critics of the old order, however, thinking the personal and thinking the nation was simply a matter of hierarchies rather than a set of separate and unrelated issues.

Thus, the transition from the house to the family is nothing less than the transition to a new polity where the processes for the production of the subject who can engage in the political process of consultation have to be remade. This transition would affect all the subjects in such a way as to make the phrase "sovereignty belongs to the people"[12] a reality, a transition that amounts to nothing else than a change in the political regime from monarchy to republic. In the process, the nation composed of suitable gendered subjects, and the form of the state would mutually constitute one another. Nationalism plays a pivotal role in this transformation since it is love for the nation that allows legitimate criticism of the old order, provides justification for the creation of new hierarchies and legitimizes the domination that men now made equals as husbands/heads of household can exercise over women as wives. The family thus emerges as the central unit that makes the new system of government possible.

The new family is the result of shedding many of the appendages of the old house, such as the retainers and the aspiring young men, and places the married couple and the children rather than the father at its center. It is no surprise that this unit is called the nuclear family.[13] The nucleus of the house, now stripped of its protective dependencies emerges into the full view of the public, an unstructured and empty space in need of definition. In the absence of the old hierarchy, the patterns of dependency and the code of kinship that regulated these dependencies, the problem is how to imagine and structure the relations of equality that are supposed to obtain between the heads of these new (small) houses. In spite of these difficulties, the model of the nuclear family is today hegemonic at the level of social and cultural practice. Unlike the case described for India by Chatterjee, the nuclear family in Turkey has been hailed as European and therefore modern and reasonable. Any other form of householding or sexuality is neither accepted nor understood. Celibacy, for example is not a desirable social status and the proper citizen is a husband or a wife. This is not simply so for society at large but is also inscribed as such into the coercive apparatus of the state. An unmarried person is much more likely to be suspected of a political or other felony than a person who is married and has children. The proportion of ever married persons in the population was over 95 percent in 1990.

With the emergence of competing models for the national, the new rulers have clung to this model of the family even more forcefully. These other models as well as the old have served as the disparaged other of the hegemonic discourse in this struggle for the proper national order and culture. This has allowed the ruling classes to cast any counter-discourse proposed on the basis of Islamic or regional/ethnic identity and difference as the eternal struggle of the new with the old. Through this juxtaposition, a cultural politics emerged that could disavow being political altogether and that posed all political problems in terms of this dichotomy (as in modern/traditional or progressive/obscurantist). Women were once more called upon to invent the singular traditional that this dichotomy required. The Ottoman woman was hereafter cast as totally subordinate to the whims of the extended family and compared to the emancipated woman of the republic. This myth of the Ottoman woman can remain a myth because of the virtual lack of research into Ottoman everyday life compared to the proliferation of treatises penned by republicans in support of their cause. This discourse could also serve as a regulatory practice, since different practices within the polity could be rendered meaningful according to the terms of this dichotomy. Some family and gender practices could thereby be lauded while others excluded as traditional. The totality we call the nation is thus the product of the cultural efforts exerted by those subjects who find it imperative to sustain these myths and who thereby become the proper citizens of the Turkish nation-state.

The resulting configuration that I have called familial citizenship is one whose terms can seemingly very well be understood through the classical liberal model. With exceptions that tell the real story, individual rights are seemingly upheld in law, a private sphere is demarcated outside the realm of the public which is seen to be competitive in economic terms but corporatist in the political sense, and a universalistic definition of the citizen appears to govern state-subject relations. Exceptions to this kind of rule are not set out by defining certain categories of persons, whether defined through religious community or ethnicity. As argued by Joseph for Lebanon, the private defines a sub-national boundary within which patriarchal controls operate (Joseph 1997). But this is not a domain in which kinship is allowed to establish connections between a large set of persons. On the contrary, laws in Turkey put into place a specific imaginary of the modern patriarchal family that recognizes no ties outside its boundaries. Nevertheless, in Turkey, as in many postcolonial states, it is the morality of kinship rather than the law that regulates conduct between persons in the public sphere. This might seem to contradict the previous statement, and therefore needs further explanation. Relations between strangers in the public sphere are converted into fictive kinship through the use of kinship terms or other communal forms of belonging such as localism (Duben 1982; Erder 1999). The transformation of the public into the communal is effected through a discourse of intimacy, described below, that is produced by nationalism as a way of regulating relations between strangers, or the fraternity described by Pateman. Rather than a weak state, as Joseph argues, it is the strength of the state in Turkey and especially of its discourses on the nature of society and polity that reintroduces kinship into the public sphere. And yet this form of citizenship is regarded as somehow inferior by the educated elites, with the result that these everyday forms of citizenship are placed in the domain of the excluded in the guise of the as-yet not modernized. Thus, the rights of the citizen in Turkey can be curtailed in the name of producing a strong modern state with its constituting unit, the strong nuclear family. What remains to be done now is to show the means through which the subjectivity required of the modern citizen was made hegemonic, to identify the kind of subject that this hegemony excluded and to see how these exclusions are rendered invisible to the imaginary of modernity in Turkey.

The happy family in Turkey and its secrets

If, as shown by Roland Barthes (1970), myths hide the socially (semiotically) constituted nature of reality, they must perforce carry in their bosom the traces of their process of production. If I were to be allowed to see these traces as secrets, then the greatest secret is that both the nation and the modern are themselves fragile constructions. The nation is indeed quite a fragile unity, a unity traversed by major fissures. Secondary myths are often produced to patch up these cracks and crevices. One way of doing this patching-up, is to forget other identities, other desires and other histories, as Renan reminds us so appositely with his phrase "to remember to forget" (1990). To forget that the national nuclear family composed of father, mother and children was constituted as a new form of governing the nation by a certain section of the population, big houses, extended families and tribal forms of kinship had to be turned into signs of the past, of backwardness that thereafter were to function as the other of this hegemonic construction. The old order had first to be dismembered and forgotten and then re-membered only under defined disciplines, theories and discourses. The key term under which this reorganization took place was love (*sevgi*).[14]

Love remained the main theme of cultural production until the middle of the twentieth century. This preoccupation with love is nothing but the refining of the nature of the relationship that was to obtain between the citizens constitutive of the nation as well as the family, and was meant to take the place of the complex set of dependencies that had been delegitimized. This love was established as a personal quality that kept reason and emotions in balance and that produced dependency as the product of individual desire rather than coercion. It is through an analysis of the concept of love that desire can best be investigated as a socially constituted desire (Abu-Lughod 1986). To the extent that love defines a relationship between ego and alter, it can be seen as a potent emotion constitutive of the subject. Through love, the subject can conceive of the other as that which will fill the hole that will allow him/her to become a whole. This desire for the other to finally achieve completion has, at the same time, to be kept under surveillance, since only the right kind of love can fulfill this task. Thus, to define love turns out to be the means through which gender relations, sexuality and subjectivity are constituted simultaneously as the constitution of the communities that make this completion possible: the family and the nation.

It is necessary to turn to novels once more to trace the path through which this kind of love is produced. The first novels written in the Ottoman Empire are concerned with balancing the liberating aspects of passionate love (*aşk*) with the dangers that it can pose to any social order. The novels, often set in big houses, depict the chaos that the family falls into when a legitimate order cannot be established. The absence of the absolute father creates the conditions in which different actors vie with each other for power, deploying different discourses. But over time, it is the nature of femininity rather than masculinity that becomes the critical node on which hangs the well-being of the family and the nation. The subjectivity of men is no longer questioned, but accepted as natural. Women are the ones who have to slowly and painfully transform themselves into modern subjects for the sake of stability and order. Thus male subjectivity is naturalized and stabilized, while women's subjectivity is constituted as problematic and therefore in need of vigilance. As Barthes says of the bourgeoisie, the modern man finally becomes sovereign by establishing himself as "the social (category) that refuses to be named" (Barthes 1986: 163, quoted in Gürbilek 1992: 44). Leaving aside the mustachioed – in other words the backward – peasant, the only social anxiety that remains is passionate love (*aşk*). The only solution to the issue of how this volatile emotion is to be kept in check lies in the subjectivity of women. They will have to be turned into educated subjects, conscious of the nation and of scientific methods so that they can undertake the responsibility for establishing and running the new family.

The problematizing of women in the Turkish novel created a problem for women of the middle classes who found themselves in the position of bearing the brunt of these transformative processes. As the novels of Halide Edip Adıvar, Turkey's first woman novelist, show, women found it very difficult to identify with this woman who effortlessly knew her place in society, and to transform themselves into heroines who could sacrifice everything, including their own lives, for their nation. Most of the romances published in the first two decades of the republic attempted to provide different narratives depicting the ways in which women's desires were to be transformed into love (*sevgi*) for nation, husband, children and social order. These narratives produce a femininity which is rather different than the one depicted by Chatterjee for India. Although this model also posits women as the essence of the national, this is not due to a purity inherent in femininity but to women's ability to reason. Love and sacrifice for the nation are in these narratives portrayed as feminine qualities that nonetheless are not natural, but learned through education and self-discipline. The plot typical to these romances is centered on the heroine's choice of a spouse. Wrong choices, and misrecognition of the suitable partner, produce a series of trials the heroine must struggle through until she finally realizes that knowing one's place in society is the greatest virtue, and only emotions moderated through reason can achieve this outcome. The correct femininity is to be the merciful and virtuous mother of the nation. It is now this status that defines the new woman, and any woman, no matter how suspect her past is, can achieve this ideal. And it is this new woman who will be the maker of the new family (Sirman 2000b).

This invitation to women to remake themselves in the image of republican femininity was disseminated throughout the first half of the twentieth century through numerous mass media such as cheap romances, weekly women's magazines, films and even more literary journals. Women who aspired to a middle-class life were thereby guided along the steps of the same narrative structure. Various weekly magazines in the 1940s and 1950s used the same formulaic statement to address women: "we reveal the secrets of a happy family life". The secret was usually the same; only the wording changed. These magazines told women that if they wanted to be happy, they had to make others happy, that the problem was that women looked for happiness where it would not be found. Happiness could only be found if women respected their spouse's personality. A popular series entitled "Happy Families Reveal the Secrets of Their Happiness" ran for years and featured very structured interviews with the wives of prominent politicians, doctors and university professors, and were published under large photographs picturing nuclear families in formal dress and seated according to familial hierarchy, with the father towering over the children and the helper and the advisor. The secret of happiness was always the same: love (*sevgi*) and respect. Passionate love (*aşk*) was finally driven away, everything settled into place and the order best fitting reason established both in private (family) life and in public. The new sovereigns could now proudly stand for the discourse that brought them to power, displaying in their very bearing its constitutive parts.

In order to make the conjugal family hegemonic both at the institutional and the subjective level, a series of measures was adopted in a wide range of domains. School books defining the family as composed of father, mother and the children pictured through very Western-looking drawings of this imaginary family were made part of the mandatory curriculum.[15] The Civil Code itself enshrines a particular form of the conjugal family with relations of power clearly demarcated according to gender. In 1934, the Surname Law was passed according to which people over eighteen were bound to take on a last name within three months of the premulgation of the law. This measure was directed against the big house, where belonging was marked by a number of intricate appellations regulated by the hierarchical code of kinship. In this one stroke, a person's identity was fixed and singularized, and any trace of dependence between men was erased. Identity cards were made mandatory and population registers began to be kept. Marriages were also to be registered with the municipality, and only couples married in this fashion were allowed to enjoy the inheritance rights provided by the new Civil Code.[16] It is this code which still symbolizes the secular republican order, because it is made to stand for gender equality. Marriage and personal life are deemed to be henceforth ruled by reason, which in itself is seen as ensuring gender equality, the equality to end all inequalities. The nuclear family, the linchpin of this order, is charged with structural as well as cultural functions. Structurally, it is the means by which equality among men is established and the hierarchies of the Empire toppled at what can be called revolutionary speed. From now on new hierarchies with other legitimating discourses will be established, and any similarity that may exist between these and the old versions will be carefully covered up. Above all, power will be linked at the level of discourse to reason and to education rather than to relations of dependence with the already powerful. Most important of all, men as husbands rather than as fathers become legally the sovereign power within the family and the polity. They are the ones who are defined as independent subjects able to enter into a formal relation with the state. Women, exalted as mothers, are citizens only to the extent that they fulfill their role as helpers and advisors.[17]

In cultural terms, the relation between the family and the state is cast as an analogy. The nation is understood as the family writ large, and the relation among citizens as well as between citizens and the state is cast in familial terms. This analogy also allows the creation of a boundary between what is deemed public and what henceforth will be seen as private. The private is understood as the secret, the sacred, the forbidden, as well as the deprived.[18] By making the family a public secret, relations of hierarchy within the family are rendered natural and invisible and real sovereignty is positioned outside family boundaries and in the state, thereby discursively turning the former into a site deprived of any power. Thus, the private makes the structural relations between the family and the state invisible. It is only an analysis of the genealogy of the constitution of the subject that is able to uncover this relation and show that these two imagined communities, the family and the nation, are mutually constitutive.

The public/private distinction as defined through classical liberal theory posits that the private is ruled by relations of amity and altruism, or what I have been calling *sevgi*, while relations of interest dominate the public sphere. And yet in Turkey *sevgi* is also supposed to characterize relations within the public domain. As Nurdan Gürbilek writes of Yakup Kadri Karaosmanoğlu's novel *Ankara*, "soul will be added to private life, love (*aşk*), friendship and marriage" only if the sensibility of the new subject can infuse the public domain (Gürbilek 1992: 62). Ankara, the capital, will transform itself from "a makeshift prop" into a model of the nation only when it prioritizes intimacy in the public sphere. Privacy will then make no sense in Ankara since it is home, since there will be no aliens in this city (Gürbilek 1992: 63). This public described by Karaosmanoğlu in terms reserved for the subject is nothing but the nation itself. That is why Herzfeld (1996) coins the term "cultural intimacy" when describing the cultural construction of the proper way of behaving as a national subject, a term which indicates that certain things can only be shared among those who really belong.[19] The subject who acts according to this dictum in both the public and private spheres can only be a subject who understands what *sevgi* means and who desires the satisfaction that this emotion will provide. Only *sevgi* makes it possible for a subject to keep a secret, and only such a subject will in turn remove the boundary between the private and the public.

The practice of keeping secrets is developed first and foremost within the family. All social researchers who try to conduct some form of family research in Turkey are immediately confronted with a question: "why are you interested in our family secrets?" These secrets can be various. The lack of love, respect, and frankness is perhaps the major secret interviewees have in mind when posing this question. The 1980s feminist movement in Turkey revealed domestic violence to be another well-guarded secret of the family. Feminists had and continue to spend considerable energy to turn domestic violence into an issue that could be publicly addressed. From a developmentalist, liberal perspective, it could very well be argued that this is another example of a lag in political awareness. But feminists come from the ranks of those women whom nationalist discourse has empowered, and found it difficult themselves to uncover this secret of the family, especially when violence could not only be associated with the "traditional" world of the peasantry.[20]

There is another category of secret which feminists have not yet uncovered: the secret of the "traditional." Many practices, such as arranged marriages and marriages to close relatives labeled as traditional, continue to inform familial relations even in urban and middle-class sections of society. These are of course familial practices that are associated with the big house and with kinship as the regulator of social order. Labeling these practices as traditional indicates that they are evaluated in relation to modernity, and expresses the hope that some day in the future they will be eradicated.[21] Thus the biggest secret of the nation is the shaky hegemony enjoyed by the nuclear family. Anthropologist Emelie Olson has discovered to her surprise that in Ankara, the seat of modernity, the majority of middle-class women with careers prefer to spend their leisure time with other women, and that homosociality is dominant among both genders of the modern middle classes. In other words, the very class that produced conjugality as an ideal is unable to put into practice the communion of minds and souls that this imaginary entails (Olson 1982: 54–5). Relations within the house do not follow the pattern of conjugality either. As Duben and Behar discovered for Istanbul in the early 1900s (1991), aunts and uncles, brothers-in-law and sisters-in-law are not kept outside the walls of the house, but are significant categories of people with whom cooperative and competitive social relations are carried out in everyday life.

In his 1982 article, anthropologist Alan Duben argues that these kinship categories regulate not only relations between kinsmen, but are also effective in regulating relations among total strangers. Duben explains the salience of kinship imaginaries in terms of the absence of any code of moral conduct apart from kinship that can regulate civil society. In effect, it is the use of kinship terms between strangers in urban space that produces the intimacy described by Gürbilek. In so doing, this usage also helps to establish the hierarchies based on gender and age that these terms connote. In Duben's terms then, the code of morality still depends on people knowing their place in relation to the (absent) sovereign. The insistence on seeking this spilling out of the use of kinship terms among the (now urban) backward and therefore traditional shantytowns only serves to make invisible the importance of the kinship imaginary in regulating the social relations of the modern. The big house is indeed alive and well in all aspects of social life, ranging from politics to institutional relations, to labor and capital markets. Fathers, dependent young men and relations of hierarchy between heads of households have not been eradicated. They have simply been recast in the terms of modernity, and the two exist side-by-side without causing much complication. The simultaneous operation of the big house and the nuclear family is made possible by a developmentalist discourse through which familial practices can be (mis)read through terms provided by modernity and produce what I have called familial citizenship. Thus the greatest national secret is that the nuclear family ideal can be sustained alongside the ubiquity of the big house in organizing the discourse and practice of national sovereignty.

The last category of secret to consider is located at the level of the subject. The dependent subject of the big house is reproduced alongside the independent subject of modernity, the citizen of liberal discourse. In middle-class subjects who strive to identify with this ideal subject of the modern all their lives, the coexistence of these two subjectivities causes serious problems, evidenced in the difficulties experienced by women interviewees over the age of sixty-five in using the first person pronoun when asked to recount their life story (Sirman 2000c; Çetinoğlu and Koğacıoğlu 2000). The middle-class man's life story turns out to be a story of the republic and a list of all the wrong decisions taken by successive governments – in other words, the story of a frustrated sovereign whose domain has not encompassed the whole polity. It is at the level of subjectivity that the confusion caused by familial citizenship and the burden of carrying too many secrets is experienced as pain.

Conclusion

This chapter has tried to trace the discursive constitution of citizenship in Turkey as a way of understanding the particular form in which it is exercised by focusing on the way it produces gendered subjects. The problem that the chapter tackles is how to explain what has been identified as the discrepancy between the practice and the rule. Turkish citizenship categories purport to be universal, and yet many of the rights associated with citizenship cannot be enjoyed by the majority of the population. The nature of the state, its inability to provide equal access to all its citizens to the rights defined by law, has often been ascribed to structural weaknesses such as economic instability or various obstacles in effecting an equitable distribution of resources. Given that this indeed might be the case, it still does not explain how the fiction is maintained. To answer this question, this chapter has attempted to trace the conditions and discourses through which citizenship was instituted in Turkey around the problem of realizing national sovereignty.

Nationalist discourses in Turkey were produced around the very real fear of being the object of imperialist aggression, thus making sovereignty the nodal point of the way the new community was imagined. Concerns regarding the sovereignty of the polity produced discourses that identified the position of the enlightened male subject within this polity as the source of the problem, hence making citizenship the ground upon which the new polity would be constructed. Rather than dependency on a powerful overlord, love was identified in nationalist discourses as the new, rational and therefore modern relationship that would bind the citizen to the nation-state, with the nuclear family as the locus where this emotion would be produced and fostered. This configuration produced the model of the citizen, placing him (and by extension, her) within an imagined lifestyle that was meant to cover all aspects of social interaction. As Lomnitz argues for the case of Mexican citizenship, those sections of the population that did not fit this lifestyle, the peasant, the tribals, the uneducated and the overly religious (in the sense that reason is overshadowed by belief) were excluded as the "abject" (Lomnitz 1999). In Turkey, this "abject" took on the name of the traditional and was associated with Ottoman practices of government that had to be superseded if national sovereignty was to be maintained. It is this discursive construction of the traditional that constitutes the secret of Turkish citizenship.

The problem that this formulation intends to address is that rather than the categories named above, all citizens can turn into the abject at any moment. This is because the "traditional" is part and parcel of their normal everyday lives as a matter of routine. It is this fear that the magazines described above address, that denials of extended kin networks attempt to cover up and, more generally, that the legal subordination of modern, middle-class women reveals. What is called the traditional in fact informs the very way in which the modern is understood and practiced. Middle-class life styles are only made possible as a result of the creation of extended networks that are regulated through kinship norms. Love does not suffice to foster the bonds of equality envisaged by nationalist discourse, but ends up by creating ties of dependency not only between husband and wife within the patriarchal nuclear family, but also among heads of household. In the name of love for the nation and the creation of a conflict-free public, relations of intimacy are made to infuse the domain where interest was meant to rule. Thus it is the meanings of the old order, the traditional, that provides content to how love is supposed to regulate relations among citizens and between the citizen and the state. The constitution of the modern Turkish subject as citizen is therefore premised on the operation of bonds that are modeled on the old order, an operation that is concealed at the very moment in which those bonds are made effective. The traditional is located at the heart of the constitution of the modern, and becomes the secret that has to be denied at all cost if the fiction of the rule is to be maintained.

Notes

1 A different version of this chapter was originally written in Turkish and published as Sirman, N. (2002) "Kadınların Milliyeti," (Nationality of Women) in T. Bora (ed.) *Milliyetçilik Modern Türkiye'de Siyasi Düşünce* (Nationalism Political Thought in Modern Turkey), vol. 4, Istanbul: İletişim. I would like to thank Meltem Ahıska, Nazan Üstündağ and Abbas Vali for a very helpful discussion of some of the ideas in this chapter.

2 Boğaziçi University, Department of Sociology.

3 The first nationalists in Turkey imagined an Ottoman polity, meaning a multi-ethnic state where religion and ethnicity were secondary to the acceptance of the just Ottoman order represented by the sultan. By the 1890s, and in view of the secessionist movements of different ethnicities within the Empire, this project began to be replaced with a Turkish nationalism that finally became articulated in its present form in the process of the Turkish War of Liberation fought in the aftermath of World War I.

4 Ironically, so is the politico-legal view of citizenship that dominated studies of liberal democracies. Thus, it seems two different approaches were needed to study the status of the person within a polity, depending on what that polity was: politico-legal practice for the West and discourse analysis for the rest.

5 *Adam Olmak* in Turkish. The term "man" in Turkish is *adam*, as in Adam and Eve, and refers primarily to the wisdom and power associated with this status. One can be a man but not an *adam*. The titles used in this section of the chapter were developed by the author for an exhibition entitled "Three Generations of the Republic" (*Üç Kuşak Cumhuriyet*) that was organized by the Turkish History Foundation in 1998 for the 75th anniversary of the establishment of the Turkish Republic.

6 These reform movements, called the *Tanzimat* in Turkish historiography, were initiated by the central bureaucracy. The effects of the social change these reforms led to began to appear in Turkish literature after the 1870s.

7 These semi-indentured bureaucrats were called *devşirme*, a term which means "transformed."

8 The major change instituted in 1839 was the emancipation of the ruling class which had hitherto been an indentured bureaucracy. The members of this class, as the slaves of the palace, could not pass wealth and power to their own sons since this wealth could be revoked by the palace at any moment. The *Tanzimat* gave these bureaucrats security of wealth which they used to train members of their families for government office.

9 For the relationship between love and the divine in classical Ottoman literature, see Holbrook (1994).

10 The effects of this change in the code are still not clear at the moment. Many clauses of the penal code that regulate gendered crimes such as adultery and honor killings are now under revision.

11 Corruption and nepotism in the bureaucracy and in government has been singled out in recent years as a disease that needs to be combated. The term is used to denote a failure in keeping the private separate from the public, kinship and family from affairs of the state.

12 This slogan is today inscribed on the wall of the Turkish Grand National Assembly, the parliament.

13 Sociologically, it would be appropriate to designate this family as the conjugal family, since it is the links with the previous generation that are devalued. See Duben (1982) for a discussion of these terms.

14 There are two terms for "love" in Turkish. *Aşk*, which refers to passionate love, and *sevgi* which refers to brotherly or motherly love. I shall use the term love to designate *sevgi*, and use the term passionate love to indicate the first reference and indicate the Turkish term in parentheses. Another term, *muhabbet*, used until the 1920s, also refers to love as in *sevgi*.

15 These drawings were also used in the hand-drawn advertisements for home appliances and products that began to appear in newspapers and magazines. One magazine in 1935 gave a list of easily available medicinal treatments (soda, vinegar and the like) next to a serialization of Jean-Jacques Rousseau's *Emile*, all capped by a drawing of this ideal family.

16 These marriages are called state (*resmi*) marriages, while the traditional ceremony is called a religious ceremony since it is effected according to the laws of the Kur'an. Many marriages continued to be effected through this religious/communal ceremony alone, and the state had to pass amnesty laws every ten years to recognize the children of such marriages who were by law illegitimate.

17 The narratives of the War of Independence (1920–3), as foundation myths, represent this relation in terms of men fighting for the nation while women carry ammunition to the front.

18 These are the different meanings of *mahrem*, the term used in Turkey to depict the private. I am indebted to Meltem Ahiska for pointing out that the term also connotes deprivation. See Göle (1996) for an analysis of the private in terms of the forbidden.

19 An oft-quoted Turkish adage communicates the same attitude: the broken arm must remain within the sleeve.

20 The secret of familial violence in Turkey is not that it is so widespread, as was the case for feminists in Europe, but that it was also prevalent in educated homes.

21 A distinction with regard to modernity has to be introduced here. While arranged marriages contravene the expectation of the individual endowed with reason, marriage to close relatives is defined as a medical risk and linked to the traditional in the sense that it shows ignorance, another term, which through its reference to science, comes back to speak to the modern.

References

Abu-Lughod, L. (1986) *Veiled Sentiments: Honor and Poetry in a Bedouin Society*, Los Angeles: University of California Press.

Abu-Lughod, L. (ed.) (1998) *Remaking Women: Feminism and Modernity in the Middle East*, Princeton: Princeton University Press.

Anderson, B. (1983) *Imagined Communities: Reflections on the Origins and Spread of Nationalism*, London: Verso.

Anthias, F. and Yuval-Davis, N. (1989) *Woman-Nation-State*, Londra: Macmillan.

Barthes, R. (1986) *Günümüzde Söylem, Yazı Nedir?*, trans. R. Ege, Istanbul: Hil.

——(1970) *Mythologies*, Paris: Seuil.

Bhabha, H. K. (1990) "Dissemination: Time, Narrative and the Margins of the Modern Nation," in H. K. Bhabha (ed.) *Nation and Narration*, London and New York: Routledge.

Çetinoğlu, D. and Koğacıoğlu, D. (2000) "Reading Together: Two Life Stories of the Republican Era," in *Crossroads of History: Experience, Memory, Orality*, proceedings of the 11th International Oral History Association Conference, vol. 2, Istanbul: Boğaziçi Üniversitesi.

Chatterjee, P. (1986) *Nationalist Thought and the Colonial World: A Derivative Discourse?*, London: Zed Books.

——(1993) *The Nation and Its Fragments: Colonial and Postcolonial Histories*, Princeton: Princeton University Press.

Duben, A. (1982) "The Significance of Family and Kinship in Urban Turkey," in Ç. Kağıtçıbaşı (ed.) *Sex Roles, Family and Community in Turkey*, Indiana: Indiana University Press.

Duben, A. and Behar, C. (1991) *Istanbul Households: Marriage, Family and Fertility, 1880–1940*, Cambridge: Cambridge University Press.

Erder, S. (1999) "'Where Do You Hail From?': Localism and Networks in Istanbul," in Ç. Keyder (ed.) *Istanbul Between the Global and the Local*, New York: Rowman and Littlefield.

Fanon, F. (1965) *A Dying Colonialism*, New York: Grove Press.

——(1967) *Black Skin, White Masks*, New York: Grove Press.

Gellner, E. (1983) *Nations and Nationalism*, Oxford: Blackwell.

Göle, N. (1996) *The Forbidden Modern: Civilization and Veiling*, Ann Arbor: University of Michigan Press.

Gürbilek, N. (1992) *Vitrinde Yaşamak 1980'lerin Kültürel İklimi* (Living in the Showcase: The Cultural Climate of the 1980s), Istanbul: Metis.

Hall, S. (1996) "When Was the Post-Colonial? Thinking at the Limit," in I. Chambers and L. Curti (eds) *The Post-Colonial Question: Common Skies, Divided Horizons*, London and New York: Routledge.

Herzfeld, M. (1996) *Cultural Intimacy: Poetics in the Nation-State*, London: Routledge.

Hobsbawm, E. (1990) *Nations and Nationalism Since 1780: Programme, Myth, Reality*, Cambridge: Cambridge University Press.

Holbrook, V. R. (1994) *The Unreadable Shores of Love: Turkish Modernity and Mystic Romance*, Austin: University of Texas Press.

Isin, E. F. and Wood, P. K. (eds) (2002) *Citizenship and Identity*, London: Sage.

Jayawardena, K. (1988) *Feminism and Nationalism in the Third World*, London: Zed Books.

Joseph, S. (1997) "The Public/Private: The Imagined Boundary in the Imagined Nation/State/Community – The Lebanese Case," *Feminist Review*, 57 (autumn): 73–92.
Joyce, R. A. and Gillespie, S. D. (eds) (2000) *Beyond Kinship: Social and Marital Reproduction in House Societies*, Philadelphia: University of Pennsylvania Press.
Kandiyoti, D. (1988) "Slave Girls, Temptresses and Comrades: Images of Women in The Turkish Novel," *Feminist Issues*, 8 (1): 33–50.
——(1989) "Women and the Turkish State: Political Actors or Symbolic Pawns?" in F. Anthias and N. Yuval-Davis (eds) *Woman-Nation-State*, London: Macmillan.
——(1998) "Some Awkward Questions on Women and Modernity in Turkey," in L. Abu-Lughod (ed.) *Remaking Women: Feminism and Modernity in the Middle East*, Princeton: Princeton University Press.
Kandiyoti, D. (ed.) (1991) *Women, Islam and the State*, Philadelphia: Temple University Press.
Karaosmanoğlu, Y. K. (1994) [1934] *Ankara*, Istanbul: İletişim.
Lomnitz, C. (1999) "Modes of Citizenship in Mexico," *Public Culture*, 11 (1): 269–93.
Mardin, Ş. (1966) *The Genesis of Young Ottoman Thought*, Princeton: Princeton University Press.
——(1974) "Superwesternization in Urban Life in the Ottoman Empire in the Last Quarter of the 19th Century," in P. Benedict and E. Tümertekin (eds) *Turkey: Geographical and Social Perspectives*, Leiden: Brill.
——(1991) "Türkiye: Bir Ekonomik Kodun Dönüşümü" (Turkey: The Transformation of an Economic Code), in *Türk Modernleşmesi* (Turkish Modernization), vol. 4, Istanbul: İletişim.
McClintock , A. (1996) " 'No Longer in a Future Heaven': Women and Nationalism in South Africa," in G. Eley and R. G. Suny (eds) *Becoming National*, Oxford: Oxford University Press.
Olson, E. A. (1982) "Duofocal Family Structure and an Alternative Model of Husband-Wife Relationship," in Ç. Kağıtçıbaşı (ed.) *Sex Roles, Family and Community in Turkey*, Indiana: Indiana University Press.
Ong, A. (1999) *Flexible Citizenship The Cultural Logics of Transnationality*, Durham NC and London: Duke University Press.
Parla, J. (1990) *Babalar ve Oğullar* (Fathers and Sons), Istanbul: İletişim.
Pateman, C. (1988) *The Sexual Contract*, Stanford: Stanford University Press.
Phillips, A. (1991) *Engendering Democracy*, Cambridge: Polity Press.
Peirce, L. P. (1993) *The Imperial Harem, Women and Sovereignty in the Ottoman Empire*, Oxford: Oxford University Press.
Povinelli, E. (2002) *The Cunning of Recognition*, Durham NC and London: Duke University Press.
Renan, E. (1990) "What is a Nation?" in H. Bhabha (ed.) *Nation and Narration*, London: Routledge.
Sirman, N. (1988) "Peasants and Family Farms: The Position of Households in Cotton Production in a Village of Western Turkey," unpublished Ph.D. dissertation, University of London.
——(2000a) "Gender Construction and and Nationalist Discourse: Dethroning the Father in the Early Turkish Novel," in F. Acar and A. Güneş-Ayata (eds) *Gender and Identity Construction: Women of Central Asia, the Caucasus and Turkey*, Leiden: Brill.

——(2000b) "Writing the Usual Love Story: The Fashioning of Conjugal and National Subjects in Turkey," in V. A. Goddard (ed.) *Gender, Agency and Change*, London: Routledge.

——(2000c) "Who Can Have a Life Story?: Cultural Contexts and the Gendered Narration of Lives," *Crossroads of History: Experience, Memory, Orality*, Proceedings of the 11th International Oral History Association Conference, vol. 2, Istanbul: Bogaziçi Üniversitesi.

Sommer, D. (1991) *Foundational Fictions: The National Romances of Latin America*, Los Angeles: University of California Press.

Turner, B. (1990) "Outline of a Theory of Citizenship," *Sociology*, 24 (2): 189–218.

Yuval-Davis, N. (1997) "Women, Citizenship and Difference," *Feminist Review*, 57 (autumn): 4–27.

8 Entrepreneurs, citizenship and the European Union

The changing nature of state-business relations in Turkey

Ziya Öniş

Introduction

Business leaders and business associations have increasingly assumed key political roles within their nation-states in terms of determining the course of democratization and condition of citizenship, especially in second or third wave democracies in late industrialization settings. While this role may not necessarily be always positive, recent literature on the relationship between business and democracy has drawn attention to the increasingly progressive or favorable role that "business" or entrepreneurial groups can play in the process of democratic transition and consolidation.[1] This is in sharp contrast with the traditional accounts of business-democracy relationship, which have so long argued that businessmen are typically interested in stability, and whenever considerations relating to stability come into conflict with political pluralism and democratic opening they tend to swing in the direction of authoritarian solutions. Hence, the transformation of business, and especially big business, into an active pro-democratization force, and the paradoxes involved in this process, are issues that deserve serious investigation.

Today, two broadly different conceptions of democracy or democratization appear to have gained increasing currency worldwide, in the context of neo-liberal globalization, albeit with differing speeds. The first dimension, which is narrower in its scope, emphasizes that democratization is a process aimed at attaining "good governance" in the economic, political, social and legal affairs of a country, which would in turn bring about transparency and accountability into the system. Heavily influenced by the rhetoric of neo-liberalism and the new right, this understanding of democratization and the consequent citizenship regime it entails appears to be significantly technocratic in its approach to social phenomena. Furthermore, primary emphasis seems to be placed on individual rights such as the right to own private property, as opposed to an extension of social rights. Indeed, rights and freedoms in general in this schema seem to be defined in close relation to entitlements through the "market." The second dimension of democratization highlights the necessity of improving civil or human rights, such as the right to assert one's ethnic identity, in addition to the market-centered rights and freedoms. Whilst the two approaches intersect at certain points, such as demands for greater transparency, accountability and better governance, the latter approach is clearly more ambitious and far-reaching in its understanding of democracy and the extension of citizenship rights.

In spite of the difficulties involved in drawing a firm dividing line between the two routes of democratization and two understandings of democracy, it is still possible to argue that the business community will be more supportive of a democratization agenda, which at least predominantly, follows the first (narrower) path. An interesting question to pose in this regard is how the business associations, leaders or community in general, situate themselves in relation to the second and broader understanding of democracy and democratization. If "self-interest (on the part of the political elites) is the proper starting point" in analyzing the process of democratization, what is the interest of the business community in supporting this kind of a democratization agenda?

Motivated by these broader considerations, in this chapter I shall analyze the role of business actors, who have a significant weight in Turkey's economy and society. These actors have played a crucial role in the democratization of Turkey during the recent era by bringing to the forefront a liberal notion of citizenship. They have acted as powerful interest associations as well as civil society actors in pushing for democratization in Turkey, with the European Union as their primary point of reference. The most influential among these business actors is the Turkish Industrialists' and Businessmen's Association, or TÜSİAD. TÜSİAD, established in 1971, has emerged as the most vocal element of the pro-EU coalition in Turkey in recent years.

I shall inquire into how TÜSİAD, a voluntary interest association representing the big business or large conglomerates in Turkey, approaches the broader understanding of democracy and citizenship, particularly in the light of Turkey's potential membership of the European Union. Turkey, itself, is an interesting case to examine from a comparative standpoint. It is an example of a second wave democracy, where a broadly open polity has existed, albeit with certain interruptions, over a period of five decades. Yet the democratic order falls considerably short of being fully consolidated, judged by the norms of Western-style liberal democracies (Özbudun 2000).[2] What is noteworthy in the Turkish context is that the Turkish business community, notably the big business represented by TÜSİAD, has become quite vocal in its pleas for democracy during the last decade. Even more striking is the relatively strong emphasis placed by big business on the broader understanding of democratization, which calls for a deepening of cultural and social rights in addition to individual and property rights. Hence, an organization like TÜSİAD has increasingly assumed the character of a broad-based civil society organization as opposed to a narrowly based interest association, although considerable tension continues to exist between the two distinct roles of the organization, as will be highlighted later on in this chapter.

It is fair to say that big business, as represented by TÜSİAD, has been questioning the fundamental principles associated with the republican model of top-down citizenship in Turkey. The increasing role performed by business associations in general, and by TÜSİAD in particular, is important in challenging and presenting an alternative to the republican notions of citizenship by emphasizing citizenship claims based on extension of individual rights as opposed to duties that individuals have to perform for the state. Hence, the growing role of civil society organizations like TÜSİAD has been important in the modernization and liberalization of the Turkish state, helping to transform it into a political organization whose power and activities are "accountable" to society.[3]

Especially considering the relatively undemocratic nature of TÜSİAD throughout the 1970s and its relatively disinterested stand toward political issues during the 1980s, the transformation just mentioned presents an interesting set of questions. How do we explain the striking shift in the preferences of the business community in the direction of participating or even actively leading the pro-democratization coalition? What does big business understand by the term "democracy" in the first place and how does the second dimension of democracy fit their understanding of democracy? How does the first dimension of democratization interact and possibly conflict with the second dimension in the discourse of the business actors and associations? How sensitive is the business community to the issue of "social rights" as opposed to "individual" and "civil" rights, and how do they approach the issue of citizenship in this context?

A related issue concerns the extent to which the business community is genuinely interested in democracy *per se*, or does it conceive of democracy in purely instrumental terms, as a means to an end? Does the idea of capitalizing upon the economic benefits associated with full membership of the European Union influence the business community in the direction of giving a warm reception to the second route of democratization, and is this reception sincere? Finally, how significant is the EU factor in relation to other domestic and external forces that have also tended to push the business community toward adopting a more vocal democratization agenda.

Closer relations with the "New Europe" and desire to become a full member of the new EU has played an instrumental role and contributed a powerful external anchor in the efforts of the Turkish business community (and notably big business) to consolidate and deepen democratic norms during the 1990s. Yet, one should also acknowledge the presence of other powerful forces at work, notably the increasing maturity of private capital reflected in its desire to free itself from a structure of perpetual dependence on the state and achieve a radical re-ordering of state-business and state-society relations. Indeed, major emphasis is placed on the interaction of external and domestic dynamics in explaining both the emergence of business as a powerful pro-democracy actor, as well some of the inherent constraints or tensions concerning its ability to pursue its democratization agenda in a consistent and single-minded fashion.

Business and democracy in the context of neo-liberal globalization and the New Europe: a conceptual framework

Neo-liberal globalization, as a late twentieth-century phenomenon, constitutes the principal context in which business actors have come to adopt a pro-democratization stance in the 1990s. Casual observation would suggest that its impact, in terms of both economic growth and prospects for democracy, is unambiguously favorable. Market-driven globalization facilitates economic expansion through rapid development of technology, as well as growth in international trade and capital flows. In the cultural and political arena, authoritarian regimes can no longer isolate themselves and shield their citizens from the unifying influence of global norms and the devastating impact of the information revolution, which, at an unprecedented pace, tears down the national walls and brings the "better" home. Increasingly, democracy is recognized as the norm and as a necessary counterpart of market-oriented reforms in a wide variety of national settings, previously dominated by authoritarian or semi-authoritarian governments.

In the more relaxed environment of the post-Cold War order, with the triumph of capitalism as an economic system, powerful actors such as the United States and the European Union have become much more sensitive to the issues of democratization and human rights in different parts of the world. Moving beyond the realm of powerful nation-states or supranational actors, human rights activism has also been encouraged via the proliferation of non-governmental organizations forming the beginnings of a genuinely transnational civil society. Because of these developments, it becomes increasingly difficult to disentangle domestic politics from transnational influences. For the political and business elites in emerging democracies, the costs involved in failure to conform to global norms are considerable. Failure to conform means isolation, insecurity and inability to capitalize on economic benefits, such as large-scale investment on the part of transnational capital and membership of supra-national organizations such as the European Union.[4]

A closer inspection, nevertheless, reveals the need to be extremely careful in handling the concept of democracy in relation to neo-liberal globalization. The nexus between neo-liberal globalization and democracy does not appear to be as linear and precise as we have indicated so far. In fact, a two-dimensional understanding of democracy, which has been mentioned in the previous section, becomes a meaningful analytical tool to understand this nexus. While not rejecting the positive links associated with neo-liberal globalization and democracy, those involving "better governance" or extension of individual freedoms, it would be fair to argue that the understanding of democracy which has a strong affinity with the rise of neo-liberal globalization, is indeed rather limited.

The "narrow" understanding of democracy, as we have called it so far, involves an expansion of certain types of rights, notably "individual" or "civil" rights. Indeed, in this environment, citizenship rights are increasingly defined in relation to the norms of the "free market." Consequently, a disproportionate degree of emphasis in the realm of individual rights is placed on the extension and consolidation of "property rights" and "consumer rights." At the same time, however, neo-liberal globalization tends to produce a certain type of illiberal democracy by leading to a contraction of other kinds of rights, notably "social rights," in spite of the increasing demands on the part of different social groups or identities for greater recognition and representation.

Arguably, as a consequence, the concept of citizenship loses its true meaning in an environment where social rights are increasingly undermined and "rights," in general, are interpreted in rather narrow fashion as entitlements dictated through the logic of the market. Such limited understanding of rights, as well as the absence of choice among genuine alternatives in the type of democracies which emerge in the context of neo-liberal globalization, have led certain commentators to characterize emerging polities as "illiberal democracies," "low-intensity democracies," "the limits of politics" or the "politics of anti-politics." These terms point to an inherently weak or superficial democratic order, in which recognition or representation does not necessarily imply the presence of a significant capacity to transform the existing set of power relations.[5] Similarly, certain authors have also attracted attention to the "decline of citizenship in an era of globalization," because of the rise of global market forces and worldwide spread of the version of democracy affiliated with this rise (Falk 2000).[6] Whilst the European-style welfare state and the associated notion of social citizenship is confronted with some kind of a crisis, the crisis manifests itself in a much more profound form in societies lower down the income scale with only rudimentary forms of welfare provision. It is also fair to say that the process of financial globalization places severe limits on the range of available alternatives and permissible politics at the level of the individual nation-state.

A central conclusion which emerges from this set of observations, is that we need to analyze the relationship between business and democracy within the parameters of the broad and at the same time contradictory structure or environment, which is emerging in the current era of global neo-liberalism. Nonetheless, if we are to accept the premise Przeworski has put forward that "self-interest" is the essential motive guiding the political elites during the transformations toward democracy, it would be more realistic to expect that "business" will support the narrow definition of democracy. Such a version of democracy, in the final count, provides a mechanism to increase stability and predictability, and to prevent the search for alternatives beyond neo-liberal ideology, as well as invalidating the risk of being isolated from the global economic and political system. Global market forces tend to put greater emphasis on the narrow dimension of democracy and democratization, and stress the second dimension rarely if ever.

The significance of the European Union appears vividly right at this particular point. As a key supra-national entity and as one of the major global powers, the EU seems to promote the broader understanding of democracy in addition to the emerging dominance of the narrow understanding. While the EU does not exclude totally, and indeed does adopt to a great extent, the basic items of the narrow agenda, it also embraces and effectively promotes democratic credentials such as cultural rights or social rights, which are definitely part of the broader definition. Whilst the EU (or previously the EC) has always required "democracy" as a pre-condition for full membership, a stringent set of conditions associated with the "quality of democracy" have become the hallmark of the New Europe in the context of the 1980s and the 1990s.[7]

Such an emphasis on the second dimension of democracy and democratization inevitably causes certain changes in the incentives of the business groups within the EU countries, as well as those of countries seeking to join the EU, including Turkey. While this is not to say that the norms of the European Union are the sole forces in shaping the stance of business communities toward democracy in the mentioned countries, the importance of such norms should not be taken for granted. The benefits associated with full membership of the EU are quite considerable for the business communities of all the candidate countries.

Hence, what the EU, notably in its present form, presents is yet another powerful external incentive for the business community to favor democracy and democratization. The boundaries of the version of democracy portrayed by the European Union are rather broad, however. This probably puts business groups in the Eastern European countries, or Turkey, for that matter, in a rather different position than their counterparts in Mexico or Brazil. In the former case, there exists effectively a double external anchor attaching the countries concerned to the idea of democracy, one of which clearly corresponds to the broader conception of democracy.

The emergence of TÜSİAD as a pro-democratization actor, and the European Union

The 1990s have witnessed the emergence of TÜSİAD as a significantly vocal political actor in articulating the demands of big business for democratization. Although TÜSİAD has been one of the pivotal actors and agenda-setters in Turkish politics from its very inception in 1971, the 1990s have displayed a considerable discontinuity with the previous decades, particularly due to the significant shift of focus toward political issues with a strong economic orientation.

In fact, it is possible to deconstruct the evolution of TÜSİAD since its inception into three distinct phases (Öniş and Türem 2002).[8] The initial period, from 1971 to 1980, can be regarded as one during which the dominant import-substitution model of industrialization (ISI) reached a crisis point, a process aggravated further by a series of severe external shocks. Leading industrialists who had benefited from the ISI model based on protectionism and a large internal market in the past, became increasingly concerned with the negative side of ISI manifested by chronic shortages of foreign exchange and pronounced macroeconomic instability. The late 1970s constituted a period of severe economic and political crisis in Turkey. TÜSİAD made its presence felt on the public scene as a key political actor during this period. A vivid illustration of this was the toppling of the Ecevit government after TÜSİAD's widely advertised criticisms of the coalition government and its policies during the course of 1979 (Arat 1991).[9] Clearly, it would be a rather simplistic pro-authoritarian entity in the pre-1980 era. Certainly, the organization right from the start displayed a commitment to the principles of secularism, Westernization and liberal democracy. Nonetheless, what is significant for our purposes is that when a trade-off appeared to manifest itself between stability and democracy, they opted for the former. Indeed, TÜSİAD failed to challenge the collapse of democracy and its subsequent replacement by a temporary military government.

The 1980s marked the second distinct phase in the evolution of the organization. The 1980s in Turkey represented a radical departure from the inward-oriented industrialization model of the 1970s, toward a more open, export-oriented model of accumulation. The early phase of this transformation occurred under a military government during the 1980–3 era and subsequently under a regime of restricted parliamentary democracy following the general elections of November 1983. TÜSİAD's primary concern during this period was to contribute to the successful implementation of economic reforms and to criticize inconsistencies in the government's economic policies, notably the growing fiscal deficits and rising inflation, which became increasingly endemic toward the end of the decade.

In retrospect it is clear that TÜSİAD's approach during these two early phases was primarily motivated and dictated by economic considerations. This was closely evident in the organization's publications, which concentrated almost exclusively on identifying major economic problems and providing appropriate solutions to such problems which would be beneficial not only to big business but also to society at large. Certainly, this does not mean that TÜSİAD was not interested in politics during these periods. Quite the contrary; it was very much interested. Nonetheless, the essential axis around which TÜSİAD has formulated its political agenda was very much driven by purely economic concerns. A technocratic and economically oriented vision of society, which is in striking parallel especially with the rising neo-right and neo-liberal understanding of the post-1980 period, which found its ultimate expression in the policies of Reagan, Thatcher and Özal in Turkey, was dominant in TÜSİAD's reports in the periods concerned.

The 1990s, the third distinct phase in TÜSİAD's evolution, represented a marked departure from the previous two decades in the sense that an explicit agenda for democratization, involving a series of legal and constitutional reform proposals, became the focal point of the association's activities. This is evident from the organization's publications as well as in the public pronouncements of its leaders.[10] This is not to suggest that TÜSİAD's interest in economic issues faded into the background. This is clearly not the case. The organization continued to display considerable interest in issues pertaining to the reform of state finances, the implementation of the Customs Union Agreement and other major economic indicators of the day. What is crucial for our purposes is that an explicit democratization agenda occupied center stage during the course of the 1990s that, in turn, made a sharp contrast with the single-minded interest in economic issues that had characterized the association's approach in the previous periods.

The European Union, and Turkey's potential membership of it, has been significantly instrumental in the evolution of TÜSİAD's shift to a democracy-and-politics-oriented outlook in the 1990s. Although the European dimension does not constitute the sole motive for TÜSİAD to turn its attention to political issues and democratization, the weight of this dimension should be taken for granted. Indeed, the EU, its norms and priorities, have been instrumental in conditioning TÜSİAD's approach to domestic politics and the course of democratization right from the early days of the association's inception. In fact, it is widely known that the ultimate objective of TÜSİAD at its very foundation was to press for a model which closely resembles that of Western European countries.[11] Similarly, although the association has been predominantly interested in economic issues in the pre-1980 period, it appeared to be quite apprehensive about the possibility of a military government, which had been established in the immediate aftermath of the coup of 12 September, for longer-term reasons. One of the most important reasons for this apprehension was the threat of isolation from the European Community, with whom Turkey was trying to restore its relations at that time. Influential members of the business community were also rather apprehensive about the possibility of arbitrary government that an extended military government might entail (Arat 1991).[12] The 1990s, nevertheless, appear to be much more illustrative in demonstrating the strength of European influence in moving TÜSİAD toward a highly vocal stance in its democratization efforts. Relations between the EU and Turkey have been restored, and the desire on the part of the Turkish political elites for full membership of the Union has re-emerged during the 1990s. Consequently, the influence of the European Union has become more profound in pushing Turkey toward greater democratization and political opening-up.[13]

Certainly, closer relations with the European Union alone do not present a sufficient explanation for the mounting EU pressure on Turkey in terms of its democratic agenda. Turkey's potential membership of the Union is, in fact, what constitutes the "anchor," "pulling" Turkey toward a democratic opening. Democracy and democratization, as a vital prerequisite of eventual EU membership, have been assumed to be among the most important goals that Turkey should aspire to.

Having been required to take certain democratic measures, particularly in the second half of the 1990s, in the post-customs union period since 1995 Turkey has faced a challenging environment in terms of its relations with the EU. Such an environment has naturally created certain conflicts as well as opposing points of view between those who want to be part of the Union and those who do not. TÜSİAD has been a vocal supporter, almost the leader, of the pro-European coalition in this context. If self-interest, as we have suggested earlier, is the proper starting place for understanding the elites' support for democratization, TÜSİAD, representing business increasingly integrated into the international economy at large and the EU market in particular, would be a clear beneficiary from eventual membership of the EU. As an organization claiming to represent the interests of the public at large and not the narrowly defined, sectional interests of the business community *per se*, TÜSİAD's view is that EU membership is beneficial to Turkish society as a whole. From an economic point of view, TÜSİAD frequently points to the importance of joining the EU club and reaping its benefits.[14]

It would be misleading in this context to identify the European Union as the sole factor in positively influencing TÜSİAD's stand in respect to democracy and democratization in Turkey, however. In fact, a number of other factors do exist, both in the internal and external environment, which have been instrumental in leading TÜSİAD to actively support and voice demands for democratization. The external environment already provides a strong stimulus for democratization. Willing and eager to capitalize on the benefits of the emerging new economic system, and trying to attract as much foreign capital as possible to the country, TÜSİAD members believe that it is vital to democratize the system so that it embraces and honors the principles of the market economy, principles such as transparency and accountability.[15] Similar aspects of democratization are also necessary to create a predictable and stable domestic environment where capital can acquire itself a safe environment. A rather technocratic, and hence narrow, understanding of democracy is promoted by TÜSİAD in order to accomplish these aims, an understanding which is very much in line with the pronouncements of key institutions of neo-liberal globalization such as the World Bank.[16] However, the broader agenda of democratization is supported by the organization primarily because it is a requisite of full EU membership.[17]

Whilst the EU factor is of paramount importance, one should take into account one of the central lessons of the comparative democratization literature, namely that external factors can be influential but only up to a certain point. Clearly, if the domestic ingredients of democratization are missing, then a favorable external environment *per se* cannot be sufficient for significant transformation in the direction of democratic deepening.[18] Favorable developments in the domestic sphere are, therefore, extremely relevant, and the "maturity of capital thesis" assumes particular significance in this context.[19] A central tenet of the maturity of capital thesis is that the bourgeoisie or private business that develops under the strong guidance and influence of the state in the early stages of industrialization will demand increasing independence from the state as it reaches a certain threshold of development. Hence, democratization becomes an instrument whereby the business community itself can relieve itself from tutelage of the state and achieve a radical reordering of state-business relations. Clearly, external and domestic dynamics are inter-related. For example, greater liberalization of the economy allows the private sector to achieve easy access to external forms of finance, which, in turn, renders it correspondingly less dependent on state finances. As a logical corollary of this, the private sector can push for further democratization, which at the same time means a more autonomous domain of action *vis-à-vis* the state. Another dimension of the maturity capital thesis that is worth highlighting is that once private capital reaches a certain threshold of maturity it is increasingly concerned with its public image, and tends to assume a civilizing mission in the process. This, in turn, becomes another motive for democratization both in the narrower and broader sense of the term. Indeed, it is this very mix of domestic transformation and externally induced influences which have increasingly converted TÜSİAD at large and the younger generation of businessmen in particular, to an active pro-democratization agenda in the context of the 1990s.[20]

The principal points and contrasting aspects of TÜSİAD's democratization agenda

A close inspection of the periodic reports published by TÜSİAD and the messages conveyed by its leadership to the public points toward two separate lines of thinking in the association's democratization agenda. The first line of thinking, which closely conforms to the narrow vision of "neo-liberal democracy," represents an attempt to redesign political institutions with a view to injecting a certain degree of political stability into the system, which, in turn, is considered to be a necessary condition for sustained economic growth. Hence, in a sense, a certain degree of continuity can be detected between this particular approach and TÜSİAD's single-minded emphasis on economic issues during the previous two decades. The dominant notion of democracy in this line of thinking is primarily motivated by a desire to depoliticize the economy and contain "populist" pressures for redistribution by redesigning key political institutions or arrangements, such as the electoral system or the laws governing the operation of political parties.[21] Heavily influenced by ideas originating from Buchanan-style constitutional political economy, significant attention is paid to the issue of reducing the size of the state and limiting the scope of its activities whilst at the same time improving the functioning of the smaller state through greater transparency and accountability. Clearly, far more emphasis is placed in this framework on attaining stability as a pre-condition for economic efficiency, as opposed to extending the boundaries of representation or the frontiers of representative democracy.

At the same time, however, TÜSİAD toward the end of the decade embarked upon a more ambitious democratization agenda, which proved far more extensive in its demands as compared with the narrowly technocratic or economistic vision based on institutional engineering and "good governance." The report published in 1997 entitled "Perspectives on Democratization" marked a major turning point in TÜSİAD's democratization agenda, and clearly represented a departure in a more radical direction (TÜSİAD 1997).[22] The report, written by an academic constitutional lawyer, Bülent Tanör, touched on a number of sensitive political issues and challenged established state ideology in a number of critical respects, and has put forward concrete proposals for constitutional reform to advance the very frontiers of democratic politics. Among the wide range of issues discussed and the recommendations for reform, particularly striking was the need to eliminate restrictions on freedom of expression, to improve the state of prisons and the treatment of prisoners, to provide cultural and language rights for the "Kurdish minority," and to radically reorder civil-military relations. Among the proposals for reform, probably the most radical step concerned the status of the National Security Council (NSC). The NSC, as an institution heavily dominated by the military, emerged as a critical organ of executive power and decision making in the highly unstable political environment marked by the rise of political Islam, on the one hand, and the on-going civil war with the Kurdish separatists, on the other. The report made a specific representation that the NSC should cease to be a constitutional organization and, hence should be disbanded, as a pre-condition for transition from a semi-authoritarian to a truly democratic regime. This recommendation was crucial in the sense that the realization of many other recommendations outlined in the report was conditional to a large degree on a radical realignment of civil-military relations in the Turkish context.

The report published in 1997 was unique in the sense that it appeared to have the full endorsement of TÜSİAD's leadership. The usual disclaimer that a report reflects solely the views of the author and not the organization itself did not apply in this instance. Indeed, the "democratization report" attracted far more public attention than any other TÜSİAD report published over the years. The report generated widespread public debate and controversy, and elicited major criticism from the military and state elites as well as from important segments of TÜSİAD's own membership.

TÜSİAD's democratization drive that fits into our second and broader definition of democracy continued in the post-1997 era, but arguably in a more subdued form. The organization published yet another report, in 1999, that tried to deal with the reactions to the original report of 1997 and counteract some specific criticisms leveled against that pioneering report (TÜSİAD 1999).[23] Its tone was more defensive and qualified compared with the original report. More recently, in the context of 2001, yet another report was published by the association, which specifically examined the extent of progress made in terms of satisfying the EU's basic Copenhagen criteria, absolutely crucial for the eventual transition from candidate country status to full membership. One of TÜSİAD's more recent reports, very much in line with its own radical democratization agenda set out in the two previous reports, presents a highly critical account of the "National Program" prepared by the government to meet EU requirements following the promotion of Turkey to candidate country status in the European Council's Helsinki Summit of December 1999 (TÜSİAD 2001a).[24] A more recent TÜSİAD report argues quite vigorously that a number of the explicit political criteria specified by the EU before any negotiation for possible full-membership could ever take place, have been effectively omitted or treated in a rather cursory fashion in the "National Report."[25] The extremely limited steps taken in the direction of satisfying the political component of the Copenhagen criteria, in turn, imply a significant delay in Turkey's attempts to accomplish the transition to full EU membership.

A certain degree of continuity may be detected involving the three reports aimed at tackling the broader democratization agenda in the light of potential EU membership. One area of significant retreat from earlier positions in the context of the latest report, however, concerns the status of the National Security Council. This is important because it is critically tied to quite fundamental and far-reaching issues concerning the nature of civil-military relations and the accountability of key state institutions such as the military. The latest report once again raises the thorny issue of the status of the NSC, and clearly suggests that this is likely to constitute a serious barrier in terms of satisfying the basic Copenhagen criteria. The report also clearly emphasizes that this is an issue that the EU is very sensitive to. Yet, at the same time, the report clearly states that it would be inappropriate, given the special circumstances in which Turkey finds itself, to discuss the constitutional status of NSC. The recommendation, instead, is to render the Council more compatible with the EU norms and the Copenhagen criteria.[26] Clearly, this is quite a conservative position to adopt, especially judged by the standards set in earlier reports. Furthermore, it represents a significant retreat in TÜSİAD's position considering the fact that all other aspects of the democratization agenda are so critically tied up with this particular issue.

Inherent ambiguities and limits in TÜSİAD's pursuit of its democratization agenda

From a certain perspective, TÜSİAD has clearly played a positive role in terms of promoting both its narrow and broad democratization agenda in the context of the post-1990 era. In retrospect, it is fair to say that the organization has been more active and vocal than any other major political party or civil society association in this respect during the period concerned. Indeed, TÜSİAD's lead has been followed by other business associations in

Turkey. Many other business associations also developed their agendas for democratization and pursued them with varying degrees of commitment and intensity during the course of the decade (Öniş and Türem 2001).[27]

Yet, at the same time, a more critical perspective would suggest that TÜSİAD's push for democratization has not been sufficiently vigorous and consistent to be able to present a major challenge to the existing order. Indeed, relative to the significant structural power that big business enjoys in Turkish society, the ability of TÜSİAD to achieve its goal of a more transparent and accountable state has hitherto been quite limited. Furthermore, its plea for a genuine extension of civil rights and a corresponding reordering of state-society and civil-military relations appear to have generated little concrete success. This immediately raises the question of why this has been the case. A number of hypotheses may be advanced to account for this apparent paradox.

First, one ought to acknowledge that TÜSİAD itself is not a homogeneous entity, and hence should not be conceived of as a unitary actor articulating demands for some kind of democracy which is genuinely acceptable to all its members. Significant cleavages exists within the organization, centering around the axis of younger-generation versus older-generation businessmen, those with stronger links to the state establishment versus those with loose links to the state, an inward versus outward orientation (Aydın 2001).[28] The external versus domestic orientation dichotomy that used to be far more pronounced in the context of the 1980s seems to be progressively more blurred. Increasingly more and more businesses are assuming a profoundly more outward-oriented character following two decades of trade liberalization and notably Turkey's entry into a customs union with the EU at the beginning of 1996. The first two cleavages, however, are very much alive and create certain conflicts within the organization. The nature of such cleavages suggests that younger-generation businessmen with more limited linkage to the state establishment are far more likely to favor the democratization agenda, particularly its broader version, compared with older generation, whose enterprises continue to enjoy significant linkage to and dependence on state resources. Indeed, such cleavages were clearly manifested following the publication of the pioneering democratization report in 1997, which was heavily criticized by the more conservative factions beneath the TÜSİAD umbrella.

This, in turn, highlights the fundamental point that the dependence of big business on the state may have been reduced during the past two decades, but it has certainly not ended. Although it is hard to document in a precise manner, significant elements within the business community continue to enjoy and benefit from preferential access to state resources and favors. Furthermore, the military, as a key component of the established state, is a major economic actor in its own right and significant components of the business community depend on military contracts for their livelihood (Parla 1998).[29] Hence, this situation of continued dependence on the state (albeit in a more limited and modified form, at least for large segments of TÜSİAD membership) restricts the ability of the organization to mount a sustained challenge to the existing set of economic arrangements involving individualized access based on clientelistic ties. This also naturally limits its ability to challenge official state ideology in conjunction with the broader issues of civil and human rights.[30] This set of observations points to an inherent paradox. The long-term interests of the business community as a whole depend on the realization of the neo-liberal agenda of a more accountable and transparent state. In the short term, however, significant individual elements within the big business community continue to derive substantial benefits from the existing system of economic relations based on clientelistic ties to the state.[31]

A second line of explanation shifts our attention to the external plane and focuses specifically on the influence of the EU. It is undoubtedly the case that TÜSİAD has been the most powerful and vocal pro-EU actor in the Turkish context. Indeed, the organization has played an active role in lobbying for Turkey's promotion to the full-candidate status leading up to the EU's Helsinki Summit of December 1999 (Öniş 2000).[32] TÜSİAD's broad democratization agenda reflects heavily the influence of the EU and conforms closely to the political aspects of the Copenhagen criteria as applied to the Turkish case. It may be argued, however, that the kinds of signals provided by the EU have not been powerful enough to really activate the pro-democratization or the pro-EU coalitions in Turkish society. Consequently, such coalitions, of which TÜSİAD is a major component, have not been able to challenge the established state apparatus with any kind of consistency or vigor. Admittedly, Turkey has been named as a candidate country at Helsinki, a decision that has helped to reverse the disappointments of the earlier Luxembourg Summit of December 1997, when Turkey faced the humiliation of being excluded from full-candidate status.

In spite of this favorable development, however, the attitude toward Turkey's eventual membership within the Western European core has been lukewarm to say the least. Furthermore, the mix of conditions and incentives facing Turkey on the path to full membership has arguably been rather unbalanced, particularly when compared with some of the candidate states of Central and Eastern Europe. Such states appear to have received substantial financial support on the path to a relatively smooth and unproblematic transition to full membership that is likely to be realized over a short space of time. It is also not an exaggeration to say that Turkey faced particularly stringent conditions in such key areas as the Cyprus issue or the "Kurdish problem," conditions which touch upon highly sensitive domains concerning sovereignty in Turkish society. It would be misleading to blame the EU for failure to resolve long-standing problems. Any kind of resolution to such issues is confronted with severe political constraints in the domestic sphere. Nonetheless, it is fair to argue that the relatively insensitive attitude displayed by the EU toward the resolution of such problems has helped to strengthen the "anti-globalization" or the "anti-EU" coalition in Turkey. The most vocal components of this coalition are the military and radical nationalist parties such as the "National Action Party" (MHP).[33] Moreover, frequent references to the "Armenian genocide" in key countries such as France have helped to raise nationalistic sentiments within Turkey's business community. Such influences once again facilitated the empowerment of the anti-democratization lobbies, inducing a drift away from the EU anchor in the process. Finally, the limited role played by the EU in the context of the most recent financial crises in Turkey has also brought in other key external actors, such as the IMF and the World Bank, whilst at the same time relegating others to the background.

The central point to emphasize is that the EU constitutes a powerful external anchor in the Turkish context, and its role is quite crucial to the progress of the broad democratization agenda. Ambiguous signals provided by the EU, however, tend to strengthen the position of those groups in Turkish society who resist change. Ambiguous signals also limit the power and influence of organizations such as TÜSİAD who are in favor of change, even if it is partly molded by instrumental considerations relating to the potential economic benefits of full membership.

Certainly, the rise of political Islam in Turkey during the course of the 1990s, and the threats which this presented to the business community as well as secular Turkish society at large, also increased the leverage of the military and the state elites. This, in turn, has limited the ability of civil society associations to challenge the state apparatus and the military establishment in other respects. The turning point here was clearly the so-called "28 February Process" of 1997, a process in which the military-led National Security Council played an instrumental role in the collapse of the coalition government of which the Islamist Welfare Party (RP) was the dominant partner. The process culminated with the closure of the party by the Constitutional Court in January 1998. What is striking for our purposes is the following. Increased state protection against the threat of political Islam, in general, and the rise of Islamic capital, in particular, meant a correspondingly reduced domain of autonomous action for the secular business elites in terms of challenging the basic precepts of the established state and advancing its claims for democratization (Öniş 1997).[34]

Finally, the recent wave of economic crises in Turkey, in November 2000 and February 2001 respectively, deep crises by any standards, generating heavy losses in output and employment, have been quite instrumental in shifting attention to narrow economic issues. Consequently, issues concerning the deeper democratization agenda have been very much relegated to the background. Although TÜSİAD has published its third major democratization report, as referred to earlier, in the midst of the economic crisis in 2001, considerations relating to economic crises and recovery from the crises certainly helped to downplay issues relating to the criticisms of the "National Report." The rather slow progress made by the state in terms of fulfilling the political component of the Copenhagen criteria (which TÜSİAD has tried to highlight in its third report on democratization) has largely escaped public scrutiny in a year marked by a full-blown economic crisis.

TÜSİAD and the problem of representation: some broader questions

Probing more deeply into TÜSİAD's conception of democracy and citizenship, an interesting question to problematize concerns the organization's representational character. In other words, how representative is TÜSİAD of its own membership, the collective interests of the business community and the society as a whole? We have already drawn attention to the fact that certain cleavages which seem to exist within big business itself have prevented TÜSİAD from acting as a unified actor and in a coherent fashion on key issues such as the promotion of its deeper democratization agenda.

Turning to the business community as a whole, TÜSİAD's claim to be the key representative of the business community has been challenged by a number of organizations claiming to represent other segments of the business community. Among these, one can single out the voluntary Islamist business association, MÜSİAD, as being the most vocal. MÜSİAD, as a key representative of small- and medium-scale firms originating from the rising Anatolian centers of power, reached the peak of its influence during the mid-1990s parallel to the rise of the Islamist Welfare Party.[35] TÜSİAD can claim to be the major representative of business interests in Turkey in terms of its overall weight in the economy. Yet its membership size is small and tends to be heavily concentrated geographically in Istanbul and the adjacent Marmara region.[36] Hence, one of the central criticisms leveled by other business associations, notably but not exclusively by MÜSİAD, is that the organization is not representative of the country as a whole.[37] TÜSİAD, in recent years, has been trying to respond to such criticisms, largely by extending its activities beyond its natural frontiers to cover major Anatolian towns. This, however, has not been synonymous with the addition of new members from the Anatolian regions, given the limitations concerning the size of the establishments originating from the region.[38]

TÜSİAD's leadership has consistently denied allegations concerning the presence of intra-capital conflict in Turkey, and argued that the only type of intra-capital conflict which could possibly be present in the Turkish context is between "legitimate" versus "illegitimate" business practices, or stated somewhat differently, legitimate versus "illicit" wealth creation.[39] A logical corollary of this proposition, clearly put forward in TÜSİAD's "optimal state" document, concerns the need to discipline the large informal, or unrecorded, economy in Turkey (TÜSİAD 1995a).[40] The distinction made by the TÜSİAD leadership concerning legitimate versus illegitimate business practices constituted a major challenge to MÜSİAD in the sense that a number of members of the latter organization have been involved in illegal fundraising operations.

MÜSİAD's response in this context has centered on the inherent asymmetry between big and small business in Turkey and the lack of access to financial or state resources, which prevented small or medium size capital from growing on an adequate scale.[41] This is clearly an issue which seems to have been downplayed in TÜSİAD's publications. Another question raised in this context is, to what extent is TÜSİAD's membership totally free from allegations concerning illicit wealth creation practices?

Turning to yet another issue, how representative is TÜSİAD of Turkish society as a whole? This is a legitimate question to raise in the sense that right from its very inception, TÜSİAD has tried to project itself as a voluntary organization acting in the broader public interest. It never visualized itself as a narrow, sectional interest group representing or promoting the interests of large-scale business establishments *per se*. It is interesting to highlight a certain dichotomy in this context. An organization, which claimed to represent the interests of society as a whole, nonetheless adopted a highly elitist approach and tried to distance itself from other business associations or organized interest groups within civil society.[42] In retrospect, its failure to be part of a broader and coherent civil initiative might also have prevented TÜSİAD from a playing a more effective role in terms of promoting its pro-democratization and pro-EU platforms.

Finally, another significant missing link in TÜSİAD's claim to be an institution representing the broader public interest involves a certain lack of concern with the issue of pervasive relative income inequality and the question of social rights. Admittedly, a report has been published very recently highlighting the fact that pervasive income inequality is a major problem in Turkish society (TÜSİAD 2000).[43] To be fair also, it is generally accepted that inequality in Turkey is a deep-seated problem that cannot be handled by a series of short-term measures. Yet, at the same time, TÜSİAD's conception of democracy holds a rather restricted view of social rights, very much in line with neo-liberal conceptions of democracy. The underlying logic here is that with greater economic efficiency and more rapid economic growth, poverty can be largely eliminated, with the implication that in such a context persistence of relative income inequality will be a secondary issue. Nonetheless, this particular conception of democracy, which tends to push issues of justice and inequality into the background, is open to serious criticism, particularly if the organization is claiming to represent the broader public interest as opposed to the narrow interests of big business itself.

Conclusions

Business actors have played a central role in the democratization of Turkey by bringing to the forefront of debate the liberal notion of citizenship. These actors have a significant weight and influence in Turkish society and the economy. They have acted as both as powerful interest associations and civil society actors in pushing for democratization in Turkey, with eventual membership of the European Union as their primary reference. Among them, the most significant is TÜSİAD. Indeed, TÜSİAD has been the most powerful and vocal element of the pro-EU coalition in Turkey. Whilst TÜSİAD has challenged the state on a number of key issues, there have also been definitive limits to its challenge.

The deep economic crisis that Turkey experienced during November 2000 and February 2001 caused a major dislocation in the Turkish economy, resulting in a substantial loss of output and massive unemployment. In contrast to its profound costs in the short run, the crisis had one positive consequence from a longer-term perspective. It contributed to the acceleration of economic and political reforms. Indeed, the process gathered momentum, resulting in a series of path-breaking reforms, including the removal of the death penalty altogether and a major extension of cultural rights for the Kurdish segments of the Turkish society during the summer of 2002. Clearly, the material benefits of EU membership had become all the more attractive to society at large during a period of acute economic crisis.

TÜSİAD revitalized its challenge as a key element of the pro-EU coalition during the course of 2002. What was striking in this respect was that TÜSİAD, in contrast to its earlier stand, increasingly found itself in close alliance with other business and civil society organizations. Particularly important in this context was the emergence of a broad-based civil initiative called The Movement for Europe (in Turkish, *Avrupa* 2002). TÜSİAD established itself as a key component of this civil society alliance during the critical summer of 2002 and clearly favors its role in pushing for a series of EU-related reforms.

Looking to the post-Helsinki era from a more critical perspective, TÜSİAD could have done more to accelerate the reform process, especially in the early stages. It could have utilized its significant power and influence to challenge the state in a more vigorous and consistent manner, particularly on such critical issues as the Cyprus dispute. This, in turn, would have helped facilitate a more favorable conditional date for initiating accession negotiations with the EU, compared with the more distant date of December 2004 offered by the EU at its Copenhagen Summit of December 2002 (Öniş 2003).[44]

Notes

1 For evidence on and explanation of the underlying reasons for the conversion of big business into a pro-democratization force in the recent period, particularly in the context of Latin America and East Asia, see Bartell and Leigh (1995) and Whitehead (2000).

2 For a comprehensive examination of the challenges facing Turkish democracy, see Özbudun (2000).

3 On the nature of the republican model of "top-down citizenship," based on duties to be performed toward the state as opposed to rights to be claimed from the state, see Keyman and Özbudun (2002). Keyman and Özbudun also highlight the growing challenges posed by civil society organizations, in general, and busi-

ness associations, in particular, in challenging the centralized state tradition and pushing for a new model of liberal citizenship.

4 On the relationship between globalization and democracy, and concerning the positive linkages between the two phenomena, see Diamond and Plattner (1993).

5 For a pessimistic evaluation and emphasis on negative linkages between neo-liberal globalization and democracy from a radical democracy perspective, see Barber (2000). On the "illiberal" or "low intensity" democracy and "the politics of anti-politics" or "limits of politics" theses, see Zakaria (1997).

6 Particularly relevant in this context is Falk (2000).

7 On the "New Europe" and its single-minded insistence on the quality of democracy as a precondition for full membership, see Alston (1999).

8 For a more elaborate account of these three distinct phases, see Öniş and Türem (2002).

9 For an assessment of TÜSİAD-Ecevit controversy in the late 1970s, see Arat (1991).

10 During the 1971–90 period TÜSİAD has published a total of ninety-three reports, all of which were almost exclusively on economic issues. In the post-1990 period, however, a distinct shift toward a democratization agenda would be discerned in TÜSİAD's publications. Out of 111 reports in the post-1990 era, twenty-two are closely related to the Association's democratization agenda.

11 See the interview with Nejat Eczacıbaşı, a key businessman in Turkey and an influential figure in TÜSİAD's early leadership. The details of the interview are reported in Buğra (1994).

12 On the reasons for TÜSİAD's reluctance to see a military government in office on a longer-term basis, see Arat (1991).

13 See the regular reports of the European Commission on the deficiencies of the democratic system in Turkey.

14 See in this regard an article reflecting the views of Feyyaz Berker, one of 'the founding fathers of TÜSİAD', *Liberal Bakış* (1998) and the article reflecting the views of a former president of TÜSİAD, Muharrem Kayhan, *Hürses Daily* (1998).

15 For evidence on the proposition that democracy is a pre-condition for capitalizing on the material benefits of economic globalization, see *Milliyet Daily*(1998) and *Dünya Daily*(1998).

16 Indeed a significant share of TÜSİAD reports are, directly or indirectly, devoted to the issue of establishing a competitive market system and the necessary conditions for accomplish this project through a smaller, transparent and accountable government. One of the most important efforts of the association towards this direction was the report on the "optimal state." See TÜSİAD (1995a). Leaders and key figures of the association have also placed great emphasis on the market system and the urge to render the state more accountable and smaller. See, for example G*lobus* (2001).

17 For evidence supporting this proposition see, *Sabah Online,*(2000) *Sabah Online*(2001a), *Sabah Online* (2001b).

18 On the importance and limits of a favorable international context for democratization, see Whitehead (ed) (1996).

19 On the "maturity of capital" or "maturity of the 'bourgeoisie'," see Harris (1989). Also relevant in this context is Aydın (2001).

20 An interesting development in this context concerns the emergence of an explicit political movement, "The New Democracy Movement" (YDH), during the mid-1990s under the leadership of the younger generation businessman and a former TÜSİAD Chairman, Cem Boyner. The movement clearly portrayed the liberal aspirations of some of the younger generation business figures. After an initial wave of popularity, however, the movement lost its early momentum and was

dissolved following its failure to generate electoral success. For an elaboration of this phenomenon see, Ertebey (1996).

21 A good example of such a technocratic approach focusing on the "quality of governance" see TÜSİAD, (1993), (1995b). On the reform of the electoral system see TÜSİAD (1996).

22 See TÜSİAD (1997).

23 See TÜSİAD (1999).

24 See TÜSİAD (2001a).

25 On the details of the "national report" see The Ministry of Foreign Affairs website.

26 For evidence on this issue see TÜSİAD (2001a: 26).

27 See in this context Öniş and Türem (2001).

28 For a detailed exploration of the nature of cleavages within TÜSİAD see Aydin (2001).

29 For elaboration of the role of the military as a key economic actor in Turkey and its linkages to private business interests see Parla (1998).

30 Indeed the severe criticisms levelled against the initial democratization report from the military and other components of the state elites as well as certain sections of TÜSİAD membership itself has led to a significant loss of momentum in the degree of vigor whereby the association has pursued its more ambitious democratization agenda in the subsequent periods.

31 For evidence on divisions within TÜSİAD which came into the surface following the initial report on democratization see Finansal Forum (1997), Milliyet Daily (1997), Sabah Daily (1997) and Ekonomist (1997). For a good example of a conservative reaction to the report by an Ex-Chairman of TÜSİAD, Halis Komili, see Global (1997). More recently, the conservative resurgence within TÜSİAD seems to have reached a peak following the new initiative on the part of some influential members of TÜSİAD to distance them from the organization on the grounds that the association is too preoccupied with political as opposed to explicitly economic issues. This new informal initiative popularized in the media as "the club of the super bosses" should not be over-exaggerated, however, since it does not involve a complete break with the association. See Milliyet Daily (2001).

32 See in this context, Öniş (2000).

33 Terms such as "anti-globalization" or "anti-EU" coalitions are inherently problematic in the sense that none of the actors concerned are openly against globalization or the EU per se. Yet, their opposition clearly manifests itself when it comes to the question of "transfer of sovereignty" which globalization or deeper integration with the EU entails. Perhaps it is not an exaggeration to argue that groups such as the military are quite receptive to the idea of full EU membership as long this does not involve thorny questions involving loss of sovereignty over key policy areas. We should also be careful and avoid presenting the Turkish state as a monolithic entity. A detailed analysis would reveal an increasing divergence between different components of the state particularly in relation to the sovereignty issue.

34 For a detailed analysis of the rise of political Islam in Turkey during the course of the 1990s and its consequences, see Öniş (1997).

35 On the "Independent Association of Industrialists and Businessmen" (MÜSİAD), see Öniş (1997) and Buğra (1998).

36 TÜSİAD enjoyed a membership of 458 establishments as of February 2001, accounting for 40.9 percent of total value added to the Turkish economy. For an elaboration of the details see the organization's website: http://www.tusiad.org.tr

37 Indeed, the term "the Duchy of Istanbul" has been employed by other business associations such as MÜSİAD to caricature the heavily geographically concentrated nature of TÜSİAD membership.

38 In order to break down the image of not being representative of large parts of the country, TÜSİAD has intensified its efforts to forge closer and more lasting links with SİADs (Local Industrialists' and Businessmen's Associations, which are NGOs set up in various parts of the country). Indeed, this became a priority issue during the chairmanship of Muharrem Kayhan, the first chairman to be elected from Anatolia. TÜSİAD's efforts to build closer relations with the local SİADs reached a peak with the organization of the first SİAD Summit organized in Istanbul in 1997.

39 On this distinction between legitimate versus illegitimate business practices as opposed to different types (and colors) of capital, one may refer to the interview with a recent chairman of TÜSİAD, Aykut Yucaoğlu, on CNN Turk.

40 See TÜSİAD (1995a).

41 MÜSİAD's position on the need to channel significantly more resources to small- and medium scale firms are elaborated in detail in its annual reports on the Turkish economy. See MÜSİAD (2000).

42 A clear manifestation of this claim can be found in the "mission statement" of the association. For the statement, see TÜSİAD (2001b: 7). Similarly, leaders and key figures of the association have portrayed the association as a "civil societal organization" aiming to contribute to the well-being of the society as a whole. See for instance the interview with the then chairman of TÜSİAD, *Radikal Daily* (1998).

43 See TÜSİAD (2000).

44 For an elaboration of the role of civil society organizations in challenging the state and pushing for EU-related reforms, see Öniş (2003).

References

Alston, P. (ed.) (1999) *The EU and Human Rights*, New York: Oxford University Press.

Arat, Y. (1991) "Politics and Big Business: Janus Faced Link to the State," in M. Heper (ed.) *Strong State and Economic Interest Groups: The Post-1980 Turkish Experience*, Berlin and New York: de Gruyter.

Aydın, T. İ. (2001) "TÜSİAD in the 1990s: A Transformation," unpublished M.A. thesis, Department of Sociology, Boğaziçi University.

Barber, B. (2000) "Can Democracy Survive Globalization?," *Government and Opposition*, 35 (3): 275–301.

Bartell, E. and Leigh, A. P. (eds) (1995) *Business and Democracy in Latin America*, Pittsburgh and London: University of Pittsburgh Press.

Buğra, A. (1994) *State and Business in Modern Turkey: A Comparative Study*, Albany: State University of New York Press.

——(1998) "Class, Culture and the State: An Analysis of Interest Representation by Two Turkish Business Associations," *International Journal of Middle East Studies*, 30 (4) November: 521–39.

Diamond, L. and Plattner M. F. (eds) (1993) *The Global Resurgence of Democracy*, Baltimore and London: Johns Hopkins University Press.

Dünya Daily (1998) "Demokrasi Ekonomiyi Etkiliyor" (Democracy is Affecting the Economy), 25 February.

Ekonomist (1997) "TÜSİAD Raporu Ayrılık Getirecek" (TÜSİAD Report Creates Divisions), 16 March.

Ertebey, N. Ö. (1996) "Türkiye'de İşadamları ve İşverenler" (Businessmen and Employers in Turkey), *Cumhuriyet Dönemi Türkiye Ansiklopedisi,* 13: 736–44.

Falk, R. (2000) "The Decline of Citizenship in an Era of Globalization," *Citizenship Studies*, 4 (1): 5–17.

Finansal Forum (1997) "Paket TÜSİAD Genel Kurulu'nu İkiye Böldü" (Reform Package Causes Split in TÜSİAD's Governing Board), 24 January.

Global (1997) "MGK Rejimin Sigortasıdır" (National Security Council is Insurance for the Regime), 24 January.

Globus (2001) "Bülent Eczacıbaşı ile Söyleşi" (Interview with Bülent Eczacıbaşı), 1 January: 102–7.

Harris, N. (1989) "New Bourgeoisies?" *Journal of Development Studies*, 24: 2.

Hürses Daily (1998) "Türkiye Demokrasi ile Gelişir" (Turkey Develops with Democracy), 25 February.

Keyman, E. F. and Özbudun, E. (2002) "Cultural Globalization in Turkey: Actors, Discourses, Strategies," in P. L. Berger and S. P. Huntington (eds) *Many Globalizations: Cultural Diversity in the Contemporary World*, New York: Oxford University Press.

Liberal Bakış (1998) "Globalleşen Dünyanın Yolu Avrupa'dan Geçer" (The Path to Globalization Depends on Europe), 15 February.

Milliyet Daily (1997) "Demokrasi TÜSİAD'ı Salladı" (Democracy Has Shaken TÜSİAD), 24 January.

——(1998) "İnsan Hakları ve Demokrasi Ekonominin Önünde Engel" (Weak Performance with Respect to Human Rights and Democracy Constitutes an Obstacle for the Economy), 25 February.

——(2001) "İşadamları Yeni Çatı Kuruyor" (Businessmen Are Forming a New Umbrella Organization), 28 February.

Müstakil Sanayici ve İşadamları Derneği (MÜSİAD) (2000) *Türkiye Ekonomisi, 2000 (Turkish Economy in the Year 2000)*, Istanbul: MÜSİAD.

Öniş, Z. (1997) "The Political Economy of Islamic Resurgence in Turkey: The Rise of the Welfare party in Perspective," *Third World Quarterly*, 18 (4): 743–66.

——(2000) "Luxembourg, Helsinki and Beyond: Towards an interpretation of Recent Turkey-EU Relations," *Government and Opposition,* 35 (4) Autumn: 463–83.

——(2003) "Domestic Politics, International Norms and Challenges to the State: Turkey-EU Relations in the post-Helsinki Era," *Turkish Studies*, 4 (1): forthcoming.

Öniş, Z. and Türem, U. (2001) "Business, Globalization and Democracy: A Comparative Analysis of Turkish Business Associations," *Turkish Studies*, 2 (2) Autumn: 94–120.

——(2002) "Entrepreneurs, Democracy and Citizenship in Turkey," *Comparative Politics*, 34 (4) July: 439–56.

Özbudun, E. (2000) *Contemporary Turkish Politics: Challenges to Democratic Consolidation*, Boulder and London: Lynne Rienner.

Parla, T. (1998) "Mercantile Militarism in Turkey," *New Perspectives on Turkey*, 19 (fall): 29–52.

Radikal Daily (1998) "Muharrem Kayhan'la Söyleşi" (Interview with Muharrem Kayhan), 29 June.

Sabah Daily (1997) "Rapor TÜSİAD'ı Böldü" (The Report Divides TÜSİAD), 24 January.

Sabah Online (2000) "Patronların Siyasi Reform Beklentisi" (Bosses Hope for Political Reforms), 17 May.

——(2001a) "TÜSİAD: Krizin İlacı Siyasi Reformlar" (TÜSİAD: Political Reforms Constitute the Medicine for the Crisis), 22 May.

——(2001b) "Rapor Bombardımanı" (The Agenda Overwhelmed by Successive Reports), 13 April.

Turkish Ministry of Foreign Affairs website: http://www.mfa.gov.tr

Türk Sanayicileri ve İşadamları Derneği (TÜSİAD) (1993) *Toplam Kalite Yönetimi* (Total Quality Management), Istanbul: TÜSİAD.

——(1995a) *Optimal State: Toward a New State Model for the 21st Century*, Istanbul: TÜSİAD.

——(1995b) *Dünya Çapında Bir Performansa Doğru* (Toward World Class Performance), Istanbul: TÜSİAD.

——(1996) *Seçim Sistemi Tartışması ve İki Turlu Sistem* (Debate on the Electoral Law), Istanbul: TÜSİAD.

——(1997) *Türkiye'de Demokratikleşme Perspektifleri* (Perspectives on Democratization in Turkey), Istanbul: TÜSİAD.

——(1999) *Türkiye'de Demokratik Standartların Yükseltilmesi: Tartışmalar ve Son Gelişmeler* (Upgrading Democratic Standards in Turkey: Debates and Recent Developments), Istanbul: TÜSİAD.

——(2000) *Türkiye'de Bireysel Gelir Dağılımı ve Yoksulluk: Avrupa Birliği ile Karşılaştırma* (Household Distribution of Income and Poverty in Turkey: A Comparison with Europe), Istanbul: TÜSİAD, Aralik.

——(2001a) *Türkiye'de Demokratikleşme Perspektifleri ve AB Kopenhag Siyasal Kriterleri* (Perspectives on Democratization in Turkey and the Political Component of the Copenhagen Criteria), Istanbul: TÜSİAD.

——(2001b) *TÜSİAD 2000 Yılı Çalışmaları* (TÜSİAD's Agenda for the Year 2000), Istanbul: TÜSİAD, 7.

Whitehead, L. (2000) "Comparing East Asia and Latin America: Stirrings of Mutual Recognition," *Journal of Democracy*, 11 (4): 65–79.

Whitehead, L. (ed.) (1996) *The International Dimensions of Democratization: Europe and the Americas*, London and New York: Oxford University Press.

Zakaria, F. (1997) "The Rise of Illiberal Democracy," *Foreign Affairs*, November/December: 22–43.

9 The international migration and citizenship debate in Turkey

The individual level of analysis

Ahmet İçduygu

Introduction

In the domain of citizenship there are two main actors: the nation-state and its citizens. Until recently, the position of the individual in this domain has not been a central focus of inquiry in political science and sociology. Mainly due to the overemphasis in recent social and political theories on structures and institutions (Kymlicka and Norman 1994: 353), the nation-state or its societal context has been the primary core subject of the debate on citizenship. The centrality of citizens to the whole citizenship concept is often neglected. More importantly, the reciprocal relationship between these two main actors in the arena of citizenship has been even more neglected. I will argue that we are now more than ever in need of rethinking both the theoretical and empirical interrelatedness of the nation-state and its citizens, and of doing so in full consciousness of taking the dynamic link between these two into consideration. The position of citizens has become more, not less, in need of central attention in citizenship debates, and this position is more, not less, important in the related political and social theories. Hence I will also argue that what is crucial for our debate is something like Durkheim's concept of modern conscience collective, combining a cult of the individual with a core notion of citizenship, that attempts to outline a politically inclusive social theory which is sensitive to the position of individual as citizen (Dodd 1999: 12).

This chapter takes international migration as one of the significant sites at which the continuing interplay of a nation-state and its citizens can be elaborated more analytically and critically. In fact, apart from the various forms of minority-majority questions which have direct implications for citizens, international migration is the only social phenomenon which directly refers to the citizenship positions of individuals. In other words, it is international migration that makes citizens feel challenged by the conventional notion of citizenship and often puzzled by accounts of their legal status, identities, and civic virtues on the one hand and those of their membership status, sense of belonging, and attachment on the other hand. As I have noted elsewhere (İçduygu 1996: 150) what happens to citizens when they are faced with the phenomenon of international migration is that they lose their "comfortable certainties concerning the nation-state" (Young 1993: 3). What follows this stage, using Giddens's terms,[1] is that an "ontological uncertainty or insecurity" becomes a constitutive element of life in citizens' life strategies. International migration creates new challenges for citizenship, and consequently citizens question the basis for being a citizen in a nation-state. It is within this context that international migrants, and their own perceptions and experiences of citizenship, are the central themes of this chapter. The focus is on a person's citizenship in an environment of uncertainty, which has been created by the phenomenon of international migration. In so doing this chapter fulfills two ancillary aims: it allows the meaning of citizenship for individual citizens to be explored, and it enables some aspects of the reciprocal relationship between the individual citizen and the nation-state to be elaborated.

Turkey, in this respect, provides an illustrative case, in which the nation-state and its citizens encounter citizenship issues as they become subject to international migration. Here I will attempt to demonstrate the mechanisms of the interrelationships between the nation-state, its citizens, and international migration by focusing on the case of Turkish migrants and by showing empirically the ways in which these migrants perceive their own citizenship position in the process of international migration and their citizenship status in their sending-state and receiving-state. Arguing that the citizenship domain can no longer be conceived as being restricted to the state-dominated political and social theory debate, I will also attempt to relate this citizen-level empirical discussion to state-level theoretical debates. This will be done by considering: (1) an overview of the international migration and citizenship debate in Turkey; (2) an elaboration of the notion of citizenship with reference to the concepts of membership, belonging and attachment; (3) at the individual-level understanding of a person's citizenship with reference to three categories: status, identity, and civic virtue; (4) the question of what is the meaning of citizenship for international migrants; and (5) the specific implications of the position of individual citizens for the broader citizenship debate.

An overview of the international migration-citizenship debate in Turkey

The first major challenge to the established notion of citizenship in Turkey was a consequence of international migration. Since the early 1960s, millions of Turkish citizens in search of work and a better life, and sometimes of political freedom, have left their homes and been admitted as legal residents of Western countries.[2] Many Turkish immigrants have lived in these states for several decades, have paid taxes and have been affected by political decisions, but have never had full political rights, since they do not, or cannot, become the citizens of the country they now live in. In fact, before 1981 it was extremely rare to see Turkish emigrants anywhere in the world being given citizenship by the receiving country. Even if it was the case, it was not possible for a Turkish emigrant to take out citizenship in another country without surrendering his or her original Turkish citizenship. In short, before 1981 Turkish citizens could not hold multiple (dual) citizenship. In April 1981 the regulations were changed, allowing dual citizenship for the first time.[3] The effect of this has now become apparent in the figures for Turkish emigrants gaining citizenship status in the countries where they live.[4] For instance, official statistics indicate that 126,000 Turkish citizens were granted German citizenship in 1996, while up to the year 2000 another 220,000 Turks became naturalized, bringing the total number of naturalized Turkish citizens in Germany to almost 400,000. During the second half the 1990s, the annual number of naturalizations for Turkish emigrants ranged from 60,000 to more than 80,000.[5]

It is obvious, as is the case in most migrant-sending states, that Turkey today prefers the blood principle of citizenship. Based on national practical interests, the country wishes to keep close contacts with its citizens abroad, and therefore tends to encourage emigrants to retain their citizenship and transfer it to their children. Of course, concerning naturalization policies and practices in migrant-receiving countries, no one can expect the Turkish state to have any sympathy for a process in which several hundred thousands of its citizens abroad will be definitely lost. Acknowledging the reality of the permanent presence of its emigrants abroad, and considering the ongoing process of access to citizenship rights in the receiving states, the Turkish state today tends to stress the importance of legal regulations which permit the emigrants to qualify for naturalization without giving up their original citizenship.[6] Accordingly, from the viewpoint of the state in Turkey, dual citizenship is increasingly seen as an important and practical tool for the integration process of its emigrants in the receiving societies.[7]

It seems that dual citizenship provides an opportunity for the Turkish state to overcome several negative consequences of the permanent settlement of its citizens abroad, while at the same time offering some practical solutions to the naturalization difficulties experienced by the migrant-receiving states and the emigrants themselves. Since the renunciation of native citizenship is often considered to be an enormous psychological and practical barrier to naturalization, it is widely held that acceptance of dual nationality by the receiving and sending states increases the proclivity of immigrants to naturalize.[8] Although a basic consensus is achieved on the main advantage of dual citizenship, which is to facilitate an easy and quick solution to the anomalous situation of immigrants' status in the migratory process, the inconveniences of dual citizenship have received much more attention than its positive aspect. For instance, it is argued that dual citizenship will create some complicated situations, which cannot be squared with egalitarian democratic norms, such as dual military obligations, dual loyalties, and dual political rights. As pointed out by many proponents of dual citizenship, however, it is apparent that these inconveniences can be limited by bilateral and international agreement. The content of dual citizenship in itself reveals that the process of acquiring the citizenship of another country without giving up the original citizenship involves consequences for governments of both sending and receiving states, as well as for international migrants. For instance, emphasizing the idea that "everyone should be the citizen of one country and no one should be a citizen of more than one,"[9] means many Turkish emigrants living abroad have worried about the application and some consequences of dual citizenship. From this perspective, closely related to the debates about citizenship in Turkey are the emigrants' perceptions and attitudes concerning their own position in the processes of access to citizenship and citizenship rights. What it means to Turkish emigrants to take out the citizenship of a host country; why some of them change their membership status while others do not: these are the questions that require some solid answers. In the final part of this chapter, some research findings will give us an opportunity to comment on the question of what kinds of meanings, costs and benefits are involved in Turkish emigrants' naturalization decisions.

Citizenship: membership, belonging, and/or attachment

As indicated repeatedly in the related literature, the growing international mobility of people challenges the basis of citizenship.[10] Millions of people do not live in their country of citizenship. Millions have multiple citizenship and live in more than one country. Millions are disenfranchised because they cannot become citizens in their country of residence. More significantly, millions have the formal status of citizenship in a nation-state yet lack many of the rights that are meant to go with it. In short, millions have been faced with a crisis of their citizenship. The anomalous status of citizens indicates that new approaches to citizenship are needed, which take account of new understandings of citizenship: with growing international mobility, for instance, one should think the position of individual citizens beyond notions of membership and/or belonging in a nation-state.

In its common usage, citizenship essentially refers to either *a membership status*[11] in a particular nation-state recognized in international law, or to *a sense of belonging*[12] to the national community represented by that nation-state. In fact, these two perceptions of citizenship totally dominate the scholarly literature on citizenship. Partly derived from the notion of nation-state and partly derived from the concept of sovereignty, is the freedom of each state to decide whether a person is its member, in other words whether someone is a citizen. Hence, formal state membership is called citizenship. On the other hand, it could be argued that every nation-state needs the participation of all its members, so that everybody is meant to belong. As noted by Brubaker (1990: 380), debates about citizenship often turn into debates about nationhood: this is what it means and what it ought to mean to belong to a nation-state.

If one defines the state as a legal and political organization with the power to require the obedience and loyalty of its citizens, and nation as a community whose members are bound together by a sense of solidarity, a common culture and a national consciousness, then it is possible to formulate citizenship in the range of possible definitions of membership. Citizenship has a formal aspect as a legally acknowledged membership status between the individual and the state. Citizenship also involves a real or an imagined community membership of a nation. A central theme in debates on the membership notion of citizenship has been the duality of membership, as seen in the concept of citizenship as membership both of a nation and a state. For instance, Hammar argues that:

> Even if citizenship in a legal sense implies membership of the state, it is often viewed to be just as much membership of a nation, especially in states where nation and state largely coincide. As we have already seen, the two forms of membership are often mixed up and it seems to be very hard to clearly distinguish them from each other. As the claim of most nation states is that there is congruence between state and nation, membership in one is taken to mean membership in the other as well.
>
> (Hammar 1990: 37)

What is noteworthy about much of the debate around taking citizenship to be membership of a nation is that this model of membership mostly implies a sense of belonging. This sense assumes the presence of a shared national identity, or it requires necessities for fostering a national identity. It is assumed that an individual has a sense of belonging to a nation if and only if he or she identifies with the rest of the people forming the nation. In other words, citizenship seems to be referring to national belonging in the sense of membership of a cultural community. It has been argued that belonging to a shared national identity is required in order for the citizens of a state to avoid alienation from their social and political institutions. The main argument is that the citizens of a state identify with their major institutions and practices if they think that there is a deep reason why they should associate with them – that is a sense of belonging provided by the belief that citizens share a history, ethnicity, mother tongue, religion, culture or conception of the good.[13]

Looking at citizenship as formal membership of a state is to see the legal aspect of its status. Considering citizenship as membership of a nation or belonging to a shared identity is to emphasize its identity aspect. The former involves the formal dimension of rights and duties, and the latter refers to the substantive dimension of participation and identity. It is supposed that these two aspects are necessary conditions in practice for the realization of the liberal understanding of citizenship. Both aspects of citizenship take the nation-state as the normative reference point. However, the way in which I believe we should evaluate the contemporary notion of citizenship should go beyond this reference point. There are at least four claims which are relevant here. First, today the context for citizenship based on both membership in and belonging to a single nation-state is being eroded. For instance, due to the increasing intensity of international migration, and as a consequence of considerably rising cultural diversity in nation-states, neither a well functioning formal membership status of citizenship nor the presence of a shared national identity remains unquestionable. Second, within the given hegemonic character of the relationship between the nation-state and individual citizens, a state-oriented and membership-based understanding of citizenship mostly ignores the citizen's struggle for secure attachment to universal rights and sees it from a very mechanical point of view. In fact, this view, which implies in part an exclusive link between nation-state and its citizens, is very contrary to contemporary discourses and practices of citizenship: today such a citizenship should not be territorially specific but based on the universal rights of personhood. Third, despite the hegemonic feature of the citizen-state relationship, the belonging-based conception of citizenship suggests a transcendental relationship in which the two main actors, nation-state and citizens, are organically and inclusively linked to each other. This is a necessary consequence of the fact that citizenship in this discourse is primarily about nationality and has reflected the tradition of nation-building. Fourth, both the membership and belonging arguments seem to assume a notion of citizenship that is an either/or situation. Such a citizenship would be unique, in other words, exhaustive and mutually exclusive. However, today there are blurred boundaries of citizenship status: the construction of in-between categories, such as "denizens,"[14] is a reflection of this ambiguous picture.

The four arguments above are variously related and mutually reinforcing: one can conclude that basing citizenship on membership and belonging in a nation-state is no longer adequate, since the traditional notion of nation-state itself is being partly collapsed. One can also conclude that the new global system and the dilemmas it creates for the nation-state and citizenship, such as the new politics of international migratory regimes and transnational communities, undermines the two established conceptions of citizenship, membership and belonging, and creates a vacuum where both nation-states and citizens have difficulties in entering fully functioning reciprocal relationships in terms of rights, duties, participation and identity (Delanty 1997: 285). Obviously, new approaches to citizenship are needed, which might reformulate the reciprocal relationship between the nation-state and citizens. Accordingly, these approaches should see citizenship beyond the notions of membership and belonging.

Here I will use the term *attachment* for the new conception of citizenship. This may cause problems for some, but as already elaborated, the alternatives already in use, membership and belonging, are not much better. Considering citizenship as an attachment rather than membership or belonging will, I believe, enable us to look at how each of us, as a citizen, perceives and creates a world of predictable relationships out of our unique experiences with the state. I would argue that citizenship provides us, citizens, with an environment of certainties and securities – a world of predictable relationships. This context is our attachment to our state. I would also argue that a citizen's attachment to his or her state is the crucial bond from which understandings of citizenship develop. The quality of this attachment experience affects our social and political perceptions, but that experience is itself conditioned by the pressures of state actions and ideologies. Here we should note that the attachment between citizens and the state is an asymmetric relationship where by definition the state has excess power over its citizens. Therefore, at this stage we should look at how states sustain or undermine the sense of certainty or security that we, citizens, struggle to attain. Competition for autonomy and control, at various level of state-society relationship, displaces the burdens of uncertainty, with the heaviest falling on the weakest (that is, citizens) with the fewest social and economic resources. And at this point one should think about the possibilities of control of uncertainty with cooperative and reciprocal strategies, and explore the conditions which could encourage a politics of reciprocity. It is within this context that I wish to propose that an adequate model of citizenship must be based on the attachment-type of reciprocal relationship between citizen and state.

Here let me continue by simply stipulating what I mean by a sense of attachment to a nation-state: the primary relationship on which we depend in citizenship is our relationship to the state figure which takes care of us and with which we seek a secure bond of attachment. The conception of attachment is concerned with the way this bond between state and citizen grows out of their unique interaction, to create or frustrate a sense of security and certainty in the citizen. This experience influences how we approach all different aspects of citizenship, and our perception of the citizenry at large. But it will be influenced in turn both by the conceptions of citizenship, which the state holds, and the security and certainty of circumstances between the state and its citizens. The development of citizenship understanding within each individual is also a social inheritance. We develop our citizenry, not only creating meanings, but learning how to use meanings which the state and other citizens have evolved, through them grasping the world of experience open to them. We use this universe of citizenship to predict and control, but we are also controlled by it, because to use it we must conform to its complex, specific rules. The importance of a well functioning reciprocal relationship between state and us brings us to the whole picture of citizenship at this point. Among other things it is international migration that creates an environment in which citizens openly question the quality of this reciprocal relationship, seriously try to reconsider it, and consciously reestablish it in terms of an attachment relationship. This newly emerging attachment-based relationship is compact enough to accommodate the dimensions of rights, duties, participation and identity that are the dislocated elements of the classical membership and/or belonging-based conception of citizenship.

Taking the notion of attachment-based citizenship into consideration, if one pays attention to the cases of international migrants, it is possible to make the following successive arguments: first, international migration creates a considerable level of uncertainty and insecurity for citizens who move from one country to another; second, one way of overcoming the problems of these uncertainties and insecurities is naturalization; third, the process of becoming and/or being a citizen in a migration context (dual or multiple citizenship) creates an environment in which citizenship appears as an attachment tie between state and citizen. These arguments were indirectly illustrated in the words of three interviewed Turkish immigrants living in three different countries, Australia, Sweden, and the United Kingdom:[15]

> There are big differences between our homeland and this land ... this foreign land. ... Probably I should not say "foreign land," because I am now a citizen of this country. ... Some of these differences are good, the others are bad ... some of them are even bitter. ... So feeling this contrast, and living with it, our lives now are full of contrast ... this contrast is like the contrast of summer and winter ... but when I became an Australian citizen, and a dual citizen, I started feeling this is like being in between summer and winter, maybe like spring or autumn ... you feel better ... I mean dual citizenship gives me a kind of security. ... No longer I am forced to think that either I'm Australian or Turkish ... first I was thinking how might a Turk become an Aussie ... but now after becoming an Australian citizen I feel comfortable, I feel that I have many choices ... I really think that I am both Turkish and Australian ... I have obvious attachments to both Turkey and Australia.
>
> (R. no. 0802042 – a forty-three-year-old immigrant woman in Melbourne, 1987)

> I have been here since I was three years old. ... I always thought "I am a Swede" ... although neither my Swedish friends nor Turkish ones looked at me in that way ... I used to hate being a Turk ... when I became a Swedish citizen I felt better and even I started enjoying my Turkishness ... I feel that I belong to these two places ... On the one hand I feel that I am attached to Sweden, and on the other hand I feel that I am attached to Turkey.
>
> (R. no. 0201037 – a twenty-six-year-old [second-generation] immigrant man in Stockholm, 1991)

> Why should I became a British citizen, what is the use of it ... I am a Turk, I feel that ... I do not feel anything else ... I do not feel that I am a part of this culture ... I have been here for the last sixteen years and I will go back to Turkey when I retire. ... The future of my children is here, and they will stay here, they feel they belong to this country ... that is fine ... they are citizens here. ... They are also Turkish citizens. ... The

> dual citizenship provides comfort for them … they do not think that they are in between – they think that they are both … I have became deeply attached to Britain … but I am also attached to Turkey.
>
> (R. no. 49 – a fifty-four-year-old immigrant man in London, 1999)

Citizenship: status, identity and/or civic virtue

In their recent study of citizenship issues in diverse societies, Kymlicka and Norman (2000: 30) remark that the concept of citizenship could be used in three differing ways. It could, first, be used to refer to a person's *status*, defined largely by a discourse of the legal rights and duties that actually operate between citizens and the state. A second aspect of citizenship would be a person's *identity*, represented by membership in one or more political communities which is often compared with other more particular identities based on race, ethnicity, religion, class, gender, etc. A third aspect of the concept of citizenship would be concerned with person's *civic virtue* (activity), seen as being essential for a responsible citizenship which requires some "social capital," such as the ability to trust, willingness to participate, or a sense of justice. Kymlicka and Norman add a fourth aspect of citizenship: the ideal of *social cohesion*, which includes concerns about social stability, political unity, and civil peace.[16] Each of these four aspects is conceptually and empirically linked to the other. Thus citizenship constitutes a dynamic site of various elements at which, when citizenship in itself is confused by various situations (reflected in such examples as the Turkish case below), its constituting elements are spontaneously confused too.

Turkey, in this respect, provides an illustrative case, of where the state is no longer able to operate and maintain its citizenship policies and practices as a result of external factors such as international migrations. In this section, I will analyze the way in which these external elements affect the changing nature of the citizenship regime in Turkey in a global context. I will argue that when various factors challenge the notion of citizenship, attention should be paid to defining the four aspects of citizenship and to exploring various ways in which the links among these four are constructed historically and discursively.

Since its inception, the Turkish Republic has been guided by a series of rationales that view citizenship as serving goals and practices of a universal kind reflected in Western political and philosophical traditions (İçduygu *et. al.* 1999: 187). Defining the rights, obligations and identity of individuals in the country, and considering the virtues of individuals and social cohesion, citizenship concerns the relations that individual members of the state have with each other and with the governing body. A *civic-republican* understanding has been prevalent in the formation of Turkish citizenship (Soyarık 2000). The emphasis has been on duties rather than rights, and citizenship is considered to be a social practice rather than status. In the last decade, because we are living in a time of apparently profound changes, Turkey's citizenship regime has been challenged on two fronts: first, being subject to a mass emigration movement, thousands of Turkish citizens have been faced with the question of acquiring the citizenship of other countries; and second, experiencing the revival of Kurdish nationalism and political Islam, the Turkish state is having to deal with some radical identity and status demands from its own citizens. Although these two issues, international migration and ethnic and religious revivals, are utterly dissimilar in nature, the challenge that they pose to the notion of citizenship has a similar source, which requires rethinking of the politics of citizenship. Both issues *spontaneously* contribute to the two basic debates: the rights and status of ethnocultural minorities in diverse societies, and the virtues, practices and responsibilities of liberal-democratic citizenship.

International migration constitutes a crucial site at which one can see how the process of globalization dismantles the conventional understanding of citizenship and relates it to the politics of identity/difference. However, in the Turkish case it seems quite practical for us to devote considerable attention specifically to the international migration-citizenship debate, but relatively less to the ethnic and religious revival-citizenship debate. I argue that debating the international migration and citizenship issues not only often directly refers to the core debates of the politics of identity/difference under the concept of citizenship, but also often practically relates the migration-based debate to the identity revival debate. As I discuss in the following pages, for instance, there is clear evidence that the emigration of Turkish citizens itself has contributed to the revival of Kurdish nationalism and political Islam in the context of a diaspora formation.[17]

As argued in the related literature, international migration-citizenship issues are debated at three levels: that of the migrants themselves, that of the country they enter, and that of the country they leave. Among these three, the third level has received relatively little attention. The discussion here, with its focus on the case of Turkey, is an attempt to fill this gap at the third level. By doing so, I elaborate the changing citizenship policies and practices in a migrant-sending country, and consequently from the perspective of sending countries I relate these changes to the wider context of the globalization, migration and citizenship triangle.

As noted earlier, the international migration-citizenship debate in Turkey begins with the 13 February 1981 amendment of the Turkish Citizenship Law.[18] Prior to this there was no existing statutory regulation of multiple citizenship. The amendment was added at a time of mounting concern over the citizenship positions of millions of Turkish citizens living abroad. Since the early 1960s Turkey had experienced mass emigrations, which posed the first major challenge to the established notion of citizenship in the country. Millions of Turkish citizens had left their homes and had been admitted as legal residents of Western countries.[19] Many Turkish immigrants had lived in these states for several decades, paid taxes and had been affected by political decisions, but had never had full political rights, since they did not, or could not, become citizens of the country in which they lived. In other words, the status of these Turkish emigrants had become socially and politically anomalous: *they were registered citizens of one state and were denizens living in another.*[20] In the receiving states they were foreign citizens who, for all intents and purposes, were permanent residents but could not benefit from the various civil, political and social rights granted to citizens of the state; in the sending state they were the lost citizens who only visited their own country from time to time and only partly exercised their legal rights and duties. As noted earlier, in April 1981, Turkey's citizenship regulations were changed, allowing dual (multiple) citizenship for the first time.[21] Within the context of this change, Turkish citizens who wished to acquire the citizenship of another country would first apply to the authorities and get permission for withdrawal from Turkish citizenship. After acquiring another country's citizenship, there was still an opportunity to keep Turkish citizenship by returning the required documents to the Turkish authorities within three years of receiving the permission papers. Of course, this dual citizenship application could work only if the receiving nation-states also applied the dual citizenship principles.

However, as some migrant-receiving nation-states do not allow dual citizenship, Turkish citizens living in those countries have faced the dilemma of either withdrawing from Turkish citizenship or remaining as aliens in the countries in which they live. This dilemma becomes even more complex as Article 29 of the Citizenship Law[22] indicates that a person who has lost Turkish citizenship will be treated as a foreigner and such a person may only benefit from the rights of foreigners as recognized by Turkish law in matters such as residencc, acquiring and transferring real estate, inheritance and labor. Accordingly, many emigrants have been reluctant to give up their Turkish citizenship for fear of losing some of their legal rights in Turkey (İçduygu 1996: 50). Repeatedly hearing the complaints of emigrants on such inconveniences, in 1995 the Turkish state made a change in the law, allowing those who held Turkish citizenship by birth and yet had acquired another country's citizenship, and their inheritors, to benefit from the rights of Turkish citizenship.[23] Based on this legal change, the application of the so-called "pink card" regime[24] protected some of the original citizenship rights of those who held Turkish citizenship by birth but had acquired another country's citizenship. This has been an *ad hoc* arrangement, which legitimates a new membership status implying something more than a foreigner but less than a citizen. This has actually been a move from a dual citizenship understanding to a sort of dual nationality principle. As indicated by Faist (2000: 271), dual nationality is different from dual citizenship in that rights under the former are more restricted than under the latter in which a person holds the passports of two nation-states and has full rights and duties in both. For instance, holders of the Turkish "pink card" would not able to vote or hold political office in Turkey or to serve in the Turkish armed forces.

Hammar (1989: 81) argues that the debate over dual citizenship involves a debate over the meaning of citizenship. The peculiarities of the meaning attributed to the term "citizenship" in Turkey and the changing nature of this meaning may be elaborated in the context of the emigration-citizenship debate. As mentioned earlier, dual citizenship was obviously seen as an important and practical tool for the integration process of Turkish emigrants in the receiving societies. However, when the migrant-receiving states did not operate a dual or multiple citizenship, the one-way application of this regulation by the sending-state was not at all practical, and often caused inconveniences for the three main actors of the migration scenario, namely the migrant, the sending nation-state and the receiving nation-state. Practically, this one-way application appeared to be an acceptance of dual nationality, but a rejection of the notion of dual citizenship (Faist 2000: 272).

As I noted earlier, when we think of citizenship in terms of its four dimensions – status, identity, activity, and cohesion – it is necessary to distinguish various changes observed in the citizenship regime (in its meaning, policies, and practices) in terms of these four dimensions that are supposedly transformed by the ongoing changes. If one takes the case of Turkish citizenship as it begins to face several dilemmas through international migration, then as a first step one should focus on the changing position of the four elements of citizenship. Obviously, the major change has occurred in *citizenship status*: this aspect has been first enriched by the articulation of dual citizenship, but then eroded by the shift to dual nationality. At the heart of both changes, it seems to me that citizenship was reduced to a legal definition, that of acquiring the receiving countries' legal membership.

Among these four aspects, that of status has been considered as the major one that might be subject to deliberate change. In other words, the status aspect is an element of Turkish citizenship which could be given up. On the other hand, *citizenship identity* has been seen as something unchangeable; or more correctly, as something which should not be changed. Turkish expatriates with dual citizenship or dual nationality were regarded as the representatives of Turkish interests in the country in which they lived. Having perceived the general notion of citizenship as being a common belonging to the Turkish state – or nation or both – and keeping and living with the national (citizenship) identity seem to be the basic enforceable duties for expatriates. One aspect of this is directly related to the notion of *patriotism* that is very elementary in Turkish citizenship. As far as *civic virtue* and *social cohesion* are concerned, citizenship plays the role of a strategic tool in the double existence of individuals both in the receiving states and the sending state. What is expected by the Turkish state is that citizenship worries about civic virtues and social cohesion should be taken into consideration without undermining the interests of both receiving and sending state, but in the last instance the Turkish state's national interests regarding these elements appears more important than the similar interests of the receiving states.

What is most striking is that although in the republican notion of membership to the Turkish state, individual-self-interest-based citizenship activity has not been an important point of concern, in the case of the Turkish expatriates it begins to be inserted into Turkish citizenship. As far as the view of the Turkish state is concerned, with the ideals of creating and preserving the defined profiles of *civilized* and *patriotic* citizens of the Turkish Republic, citizenship virtues and cohesion seem to be main elements which should be carefully protected in parallel to the protection of national interests. These are the elements which should be actively and mainly kept in the realm of the sending state, as they are functioning before emigration and even when dual citizenship or nationality becomes operative. But they should also be extended to the realm of the receiving state, as they are seen as quite functional for the integration process of Turkish emigrants in the countries they live. Overall, in the eyes of a Turkish state challenged by international migration, citizenship became less a continuing series of formal transactions between the state and its citizens, and more a public perception of attachments to Turkey's national interests. The underlying factor behind this understanding is a strategy to become more pragmatic and less normative.

Generally speaking, in the Turkish state's understanding of citizenship, what is mainly underestimated, if not ignored, is the fact that each of the four dimensions of citizenship is conceptually and empirically linked to the other. The above discussion indicates that when we talk about changes in a citizenship regime, we should not only consider the changes themselves in each dimension, but should also pay attention to the intrinsic interconnectedness of these dimensions, and consequently to the question of how these links between citizenship elements are affected as well. For instance, the type of citizenship status and identity of Turkish emigrants will have an impact on their motivations to participate virtuously in civic and political activities and on their contribution to social stability, political unity, and civil peace. Any change on the citizenship cohesion side may affect both the types of citizenship status and identity.

In order to have a better understanding of this interconnectedness of the dimensions of citizenship, one must look at the example of the Turkish state's position *vis-à-vis* the emergence of cultural-revivalist trends among Turkish emigrants that are directly associated with the growth of identity politics based on ethnic and religious elements. Once abroad, many Turkish emigrants adopt a discernibly more Islamic orientation, and many Turkish citizens of Kurdish origin reinforce their ethnic allegiance. This phenomenon is mainly based on two factors: the defense mechanisms of emigrants in a foreign environment, and the social, political, and cultural climates of the host countries, which allow these religious and ethnic revivals. In such cases, emigration as a process leads to the emergence of worries about the erosion of citizenship in terms of its various aspects that should supposedly be compatible with the general understanding of citizenship. It is within this context that, for instance, the ethnic and religious challenges to Turkish citizenship are not only directed at the citizenship identity itself but also to the citizenship activity and citizenship cohesion. The Turkish state considers that the danger starts when Turkish expatriates begin to lose their sense of citizenship identity, activities and cohesion. Meanwhile, losing the status aspect of citizenship appears to be something certainly affordable. This understanding is founded upon a pragmatic logic that not only directly manifests the challenges of globalization and transnationalization to the notion of citizenship, but also indirectly recognizes the multiple definitions of citizenship.

An analysis: the meaning of citizenship for international migrants

As noted earlier in this study, closely related to the debates about citizenship and nationhood in the migrant-receiving societies are the immigrants' perceptions and attitudes concerning their own position in the process of access to citizenship and citizenship rights. What does it mean to immigrants to take out citizenship of the host country? Why do some of them change their citizenship? Why are some of them reluctant to take out citizenship of another country? These questions need to be answered. The term "life strategies" is relevant to finding some of these answers and to explaining and interpreting the meaning of the process of becoming a citizen for immigrants. Indeed, each major event in an immigrant's life, like access to citizenship, involves a process of adaptation, alone or with others, that is related to various factors including economic and social conditions and expected outcomes of events. The successive steps of significant events can be seen as plans and actions made sequentially, constituting a life strategy. From this perspective, the main question guiding our analysis here is: what are the strategic implications of changing citizenship for immigrants within the larger context of the migration and settlement process?

Of course, these strategic implications would depend on the nature and type of the migration process, on whether the receiving society is permanent-settlement oriented or temporary-settlement inclined, the documented or undocumented status of the migrants, the qualifications and positions of the migrants in the labor market, the duration of their stay, and the kinship or other informal ties the immigrants maintain in their host and origin countries. The discussion in this section of the chapter, focusing on the particular cases of the naturalization process of Turkish immigrants living in Australia, Sweden and the United Kingdom, does not take into consideration the variation of factors within the context of different types of migration and groups of migrants. Therefore, the generalizability of findings here is limited. Nevertheless, the comparative empirical evidence which was collected in the three different settings gives us an opportunity to comment on the question of what kinds of meanings, costs and benefits are involved in immigrants' naturalization decisions.

The information about changing citizenship strategies put into plan and action by immigrants was obtained as part of three extensive surveys concerning the migration, settlement and integration experiences of Turkish migrants in Melbourne, Australia; in Stockholm, Sweden; and in London, UK.[25] The surveys indicated that although Australian immigration policy emphasizes permanent settlement and the soil principle of naturalization, and Swedish immigration policy accepts the likelihood of both permanent and temporary settlement and grants citizenship mainly according to the blood principle, the majority of Turkish migrants to both of these countries had, on arrival, no intention of permanent settlement. In the United Kingdom, the situation is more complex, where again the likelihood of both permanent and temporary settlement is perceived and the soil principle is usually the main rule of naturalization. Although most Turkish migrants have tended to regard their stay in Australia, Sweden or the United Kingdom as temporary, it appears that only a few actually to return to Turkey. This process reveals that while migrants' willingness to go back to Turkey still remains alive in their minds, the Turkish settlement in both countries has been characterized by a transition from temporary sojourn to unintended settlement (İçduygu 1994: 82). There is no doubt that the issue of becoming a citizen in the host country plays a very important strategic role in this transition.

The Melbourne survey indicates that among the interviewed Turkish immigrants who were eligible to become Australian citizens, 63 percent had taken out Australian citizenship at the time of interview in 1987. According to the Stockholm survey, the proportion of Turkish-born persons with Swedish citizenship was 39 percent in 1991. The London survey shows that among the interviewed Turkish immigrants who were eligible to become British citizens, 45 percent had taken out British citizenship at the time of interview in 1999. Despite the time gap among these three surveys, the fact that the Melbourne survey figure was higher than the Stockholm and London figures was mainly due to the differences between the immigration, settlement and consequent citizenship policies in Australia and those in Sweden and the United Kingdom. Considering the residential history of the Turkish immigrants in these three countries, one might expect that those who were exposed to the pronouncedly permanent characteristics of Australian immigration would adopt the idea of permanent settlement and naturalization far more readily than those who were subject to Swedish and British immigration and settlement policies, with the latter two countries' lack of any clear objectives about whether or not immigration should be permanent, and whether or not immigrants should take out citizenship.

The surveys show that when immigrants were asked why they had become the citizens of the receiving states or whether they intended to become citizens, mostly pragmatic considerations were given as important factors affecting their decisions. For instance, apart from only 3 percent of the respondents in Stockholm, 7 percent of the respondents in London, and 10 percent of those in Melbourne who mentioned the advantages of traveling with the passports of the receiving states, more than one third of the sampled immigrants in Stockholm and London and nearly a quarter of those in Melbourne said that becoming a citizen of the receiving state gave them a chance to live both in host and home countries without having visa and residence-permit problems. Having citizenship rights and the right to seek permanent positions in the public and government services, many immigrants believed that job opportunities would be more abundant not only for themselves, but, most importantly, for their children. While 25 percent in Stockholm, 17 percent in London, and 13 percent in Melbourne gave "making the future for their children more easy and comfortable in the receiving societies" as their reason for choosing to be an Australian or Swedish citizen, among them were many who said that because of their decision they expected their children, who had become citizens of the receiving states, to be able to find permanent jobs in government offices.

For a quarter of respondents in London, a fifth of respondents in Stockholm and over two fifths of those in Melbourne, the reasons for becoming a citizen covered some normative and moral motivations, together with pragmatic considerations. For instance, in the Australian environment, while 21 percent felt that it was a proper step which should be taken after their decision on permanent residency in Australia, another 21 percent indicated that they would be able to use various rights of citizenship, such as voting, in the country where they live. In the Swedish case, the corresponding figures were 5 percent and 15 percent respectively. In the British case, these figures are 12 percent and 14 percent. Meanwhile, respondents often pointed out that the legal arrangement on dual citizenship in Turkey was a stimulus for their decision.

While those who had become citizens of the receiving states, or intended to become so, emphasized the pragmatic aspects of their decision, among those who indicated that they did not have any intention of becoming citizens in these receiving states, a large proportion also give pragmatic reasons to explain their attitude. A third in Melbourne, a quarter in Stockholm, and a fifth in London believed that they would not get any benefit from naturalization in the host country; and 23 percent in Melbourne, 21 percent in Stockholm, and 18 percent in London felt that they might lose some of their rights in Turkey, such as owning property there. In this context, some complained that the dual citizenship regulations in Turkey were unclear and mentioned the rumor about confiscation of properties in the homeland by the Turkish government if they took another citizenship. More than a fifth of respondents in Australia, nearly a third of those in Sweden, and almost a quarter of those in London said that they were not willing to become citizens, because they intended to go back home, to Turkey, for good. For a fifth, both in Melbourne and Stockholm, and for a quarter in London, the main reason for refusing citizenship rights was based on a basic psychological and moral considerations: they said that becoming citizens in these countries was inappropriate because they considered themselves Turkish rather than Australian, Swedish or British.

Whether the level of distinction shown by the figures from the three surveys which reflect some differences among the Australian, Swedish and British cases is a result of the historical, social, and economic contexts of the migratory processes to the three countries, or of the different characteristics of Turkish immigrant populations, or some combination of these factors, is a complex issue. Any attempt to understand this complexity is beyond the purpose of this chapter. Although distinctions among the three cases are apparent, there exists a similar pattern among immigrants in Melbourne, Stockholm, and London: with respect to immigrants' perception and attitudes toward their own position in the processes of settlement and access to citizenship, a feeling of temporariness is more notable among the Turks in Sweden and the United Kingdom than among those in Australia, but for the vast majority in both countries, the issue of access to citizenship is mostly a matter of pragmatic choice rather than a matter of normative and moral commitment.

Concluding remarks

This chapter is a part of my ongoing effort to explore the theorizing of individual citizenship practices in the context of international migration. The main purpose has been to examine the citizenship attitudes and experiences of Turkish emigrants, specifically as these attitudes and experiences were affected by their movements to other countries. It has been argued that a theory of citizenship that extends beyond the classical nation-state centered theory of citizenship is important for several reasons. First, as far as the individual citizens are concerned, international migration has a strong impact and leads to reassessment and questioning of the meaning of citizenship. The new context of citizenship that appears with the dynamics of international migration and transnational communities requires a personhood (individual citizen)-based understanding of citizenship rather than a state-based one. Second, to better understand the personhood-based conception of citizenship we must consider not only the notions of membership and belonging, but also the concept of attachment. Again, the new context of citizenship, as transformed by the international geographical mobility of citizens, is grounded in the experience of attachment, which indicates a bond between the state and its citizens that grows out of their unique interaction, to create or frustrate a sense of security or certainty in the citizens. Often, naturalization seems to minimize uncertainty or insecurity for international migrants by strengthening the reciprocity essential to successful social, economic and political incorporation of immigrants into the transnational settings of international migration. Third, it appears that while we are seeking a secure bond of attachment in the context of the migration-citizenship puzzle, it makes sense to consider citizenship in terms of these three categories: status, identity, and civic virtue. Each of these categories is conceptually and empirically linked to each other and is affected by the experiences of international migration. Hence, it is possible to argue that if international migration has the potential to make the interrelatedness of these three aspects of citizenship more complicated and multi-dimensional, whose dynamic nature cannot be captured within the conventional limits of established theories and practices of citizenship, then attention should be paid to an adequate model of citizenship. What this chapter demonstrates more than anything else is that this comprehensive model of citizenship involves not only all three dimensions – status, identity, and civic virtue – but also their interrelated nature, and reconsidering citizenship as a bond of attachment is especially relevant to how we, citizens, experience uncertainties or insecurities in our relationship with our states and try to deal with them. If we want to further elaborate the politics of citizenship in the context of international migration, we should devote much more attention to the questions of how a bond of attachment operates through the three dimensions of citizenship, or what links this attachment to these three dimensions theoretically and empirically

Notes

1 See Giddens (1996), for elaboration.
2 For a voluminous annotated bibliography of studies on Turkish migration to Western European countries, see Abadan-Unat and Kemiksiz (1986). For a recent study of Turkish emigration to Europe, see also Abadan-Unat (2002).
3 Some articles of the Turkish Citizenship Law, originally dated 22 February 1964 and numbered 403, were changed on 13 February 1981, with the Law no. 2383.
4 Of course this was not solely the result of changes in Turkish legislation, but it was also something to do with the legislation changes in some of the receiving countries.
5 For some detailed statistics on the naturalization of Turkish emigrants, see OECD (2001).
6 For an example of the increasing Turkish official interest in the dual citizenship issue, see Akın (1988) (interview with the Deputy Director of the Office of Population and Citizenship, Ministry of Interior).
7 For instance, the dual citizenship debate was intensified when in May 1993 five Turkish women and children were killed in an arson attack in Solingen, Germany. After the incident, Turkish officials often argued that Turkey wanted easier naturalization and dual citizenship for Turkish nationals in Europe, which is seen as a tool to discourage violence against Turks abroad.
8 For an account of the naturalization issues, see Brubaker (1989) and Miller (1989).
9 See, for example, for a related debate, Council of Europe (1991: 3).
10 See, for a recent study on the relationship between citizenship and international migration, Castles and Davidson (2000).
11 For further discussion on membership-based citizenship, see Hammar (1990: 26), Safran (1995: 105), and Brubaker (1990: 380).
12 For a related discussion, see Mason (1999) and Castles and Davidson (2000).

13 For some aspects of the belonging-based conception of citizenship, see Mason (1999).
14 "Denizens" are a group of alien residents. They are not citizens of the country; they may have lived such a long period in the country, their family ties may be so strong (the parents or children may be citizens) or they may hold such an honored position that they in fact constitute a new category of foreign citizen whose residence status is fully guaranteed or almost so. For a detailed discussion of denizens, see e.g. Hammar (1990: 12–18).
15 The Australian data were collected by the author in 1987 from interviews with 276 Turkish immigrants in Melbourne. The Swedish data were obtained in 1991 from interviews with 297 Turkish immigrants in Stockholm. The British data were collected in 1999 from interviews with 257 Turkish immigrants in London.
16 The first three aspects of citizenship – status, identity, and activity – are at the individual level of a person's citizenship, while the fourth aspect is at the level of the political community as a whole.
17 For an analytical discussion on the related diaspora issues of Turkish emigration see Sayarı (1986: 96), Abadan-Unat (1997: 240).
18 See, İçduygu (1996) and İçduygu *et al.* (1999), for elaboration.
19 For instance, there were nearly three million Turkish citizens living abroad by the early 1980s. Within a comparative perspective, this figure was less than one million in the mid-1970s and almost four million in the late 1990s. For a historical review of Turkish emigration, see Abadan-Unat and Kemiksiz (1986) and Abadan-Unat (2002).
20 The term "denizen" is used here to refer to persons who are foreign citizens with a legal and permanent residential status in the host society. For a detailed discussion on the notion of denizen, see Hammar (1990: 12–18).
21 According to the new arrangement, for instance, "withdrawal from Turkish citizenship is subject to permission by the Council of Ministers when … citizenship of a foreign country has been acquired in any manner or when there is convincing evidence that someone is going to acquire a foreign country's citizenship." Article 20(c) of the Turkish Citizenship Law.

> "If the person who wants to withdraw from citizenship is at the same time a citizen of another country, the withdrawal documents are immediately issued to him. If the person who wants to withdraw from citizenship is not a citizen of another country, the Ministry of Interior Affairs issues him a document of permission. When the person in question brings the document showing that he has acquired foreign citizenship, the same ministry gives him a withdrawal certificate. In accordance with the rationale set by the Council of Ministers, the Ministry of Interior Affairs may issue permission document to a person who wants to acquire another country's citizenship. The permission document is valid for three years. Those who receive the permission documents have to hand over to the competent Turkish authorities the required information and documents within this period" (Article 22 of the Turkish Citizenship Law).

22 "A person who has lost Turkish citizenship as per this law is to be treated as a foreigner as from the date of such loss. Such a person may only benefit from the rights of foreigners as recognized by Turkish law in matters such as residence, acquiring and transferring real estate, inheritance and labor" (Article 29 of the Turkish Citizenship Law).
23 Changes made to Article 29 of the Turkish Citizenship Law have brought the following statement into the new legal arrangement: "However, those, who held Turkish citizenship by birth and acquired another country's citizenship after

getting the withdrawal permission by the decision of the Council of Ministers may, as well as their inheritors, benefit from the rights of Turkish citizens in matters such as residence, acquiring and transferring real estate, inheritance and labor, while the provisions for the national security and public order of the Turkish Republic are reserved."

24 For a critical discussion of the issue of the "pink card," see Çağlar (2000).

25 See note 15 above.

References

Abadan-Unat, N. (1997) "Ethnic Business, Ethnic Communities, and Ethno-Politics among Turks in Europe," in E. M. Ucarer and D. J. Puchala (eds) *Immigration into Western Societies*, London: Pinter.

——(2002) *Bitmeyen Göç* (Unfinished Migration), Istanbul: Bilgi Üniversitesi.

Abadan-Unat, N. and Kemiksiz, N. (1986) *Türk Dış Göçü: 1960–1984* (Turkish External Migration: 1960–1984), Ankara: Siyasal Bilgiler Fakültesi.

Akın, K. (1988) "Yurttaşlık Nasıl Korunur?" (How to Protect the Citizenship), *Yeni Birlik*, 11: 3–7.

Brubaker, R. W. (1989) "Introduction," *Immigration and Politics of Citizenship in Europe and North America*, Lanham MD: German Marshall Fund of the United States.

——(1990) "Immigration, Citizenship, and the Nation-State in France and Germany: A Comparative Historical Analysis," *International Sociology*, 5 (4): 379–407.

Brubaker, R. W. (ed.) (1989) *Immigration and Politics of Citizenship in Europe and North America*, Lanham MD: German Marshall Fund of the United States.

Çağlar, A. "Citizenship Light: Paradoxical State Policies and Multiple Rules of Membership," paper presented to the CRTS International Conference on Citizenship, State and Identity in a Globalizing World, Bilkent University, Ankara, June 2000.

Castles, S. and Davidson, A. (2000) *Citizenship and Migration*, London: Macmillan.

Council of Europe (1991) *Report on Political Participation*, Strasbourg: Council of Europe.

Delanty, G. (1997) "Models of Citizenship: Defining European Identity and Citizenship," *Citizenship Studies*, 1 (3): 285–306.

Dodd, N. (1999) *Social Theory and Modernity*, Cambridge: Polity Press.

Faist, T. (2000) *The Volume and Dynamics of International Migration and Transnational Social Spaces*, Oxford: Oxford University Press.

Giddens, A. (1996) *Beyond Left and Right*, Oxford: Polity Press.

Hammar, T. (1989) "State Nation and Dual Citizenship," in R. W. Brubaker (ed.) *Immigration and Politics of Citizenship in Europe and North America*, Lanham MD: German Marshall Fund of the United States.

——(1990) *Democracy and the Nation-state*, Aldershot: Avebury.

İçduygu, A. (1994) "Unintended Turkish Immigrant Settlement in Australia," *International Migration*, 32 (1): 71–93.

——(1996) "Citizenship at the Crossroads: Immigration and the Nation-state," in E. Kofman and G. Youngs (eds) *Globalization: Theory and Practice*, London: Pinter.

İçduygu, A., Çolak, Y. and Soyarık, N. (1999) "What is the Matter with Citizenship?," *Middle Eastern Studies*, 35 (4): 189–208.

Kofman, E. and Youngs, G. (eds) (1996) *Globalization: Theory and Practice*, London: Pinter.

Kymlicka, W. and Norman, W. (1994) "Return of the Citizen: A Survey of Recent Work on Citizenship Theory," *Ethics*, 104: 352–81.

——(2000) "Citizenship in Culturally Diverse Societies: Issues, Contexts, Concepts," in W. Kymlicka and W. Norman (eds) *Citizenship in Diverse Societies*, Oxford: Oxford University Press.

——(2000) *Citizenship in Diverse Societies*, Oxford: Oxford University Press.

Mason, A. (1999) "Political Community, Liberal-Nationalism, and the Ethics of Assimilation," *Ethics*, 109: 261–86.

Miller, M. J. (1989) "Dual Citizenship: A European Norm?" *International Migration Review*, 23 (4): 945–50.

OECD (2001) *Trends in International Migration, SOPEMI 2001*, Paris: OECD.

Safran, W. (1995) "Conclusions," in J. Lopance and W. Safran (eds) *Ethnicity and Citizenship,* London: Frank Cass.

Sayarı, S. (1986) "Migration Policies of Sending Countries," *Annals*, 485: 87–97.

Soyarık, N. (2000) "The Citizen of the State and the State of the Citizen: An Analysis of the Citizenization Process in Turkey," unpublished Ph.D. thesis, Bilkent University, Department of Political Science.

Young, C. (1993) "The Dialectics of Cultural Pluralism: Concept and Reality," in C. Young (ed.) *The Rising Tide of Cultural Pluralism*, Wisconsin: University of Wisconsin Press.

Part IV

Identity claims and the politics of recognition

10 Citizenship and the hyphenated Germans

German-Turks

Ayhan Kaya

Introduction

Germany-bashing, always a good sport in academic circles, has found particular justification with regard to immigration and citizenship. Germany's political leaders have, until recently, refused to accept that their country has become a "country of immigration" (*Einwanderungsland*). This resistance flies in the face of the fact that Germany is home to approximately 8 million foreign residents, 30 percent of whom are of Turkish origin. Moreover, Germans have traditionally defined citizenship (*Staatsangehörigkeit*) in terms of *jus sanguinis*, that is, a *Volksgehörigkeit* based on descent from German ancestors. Mysteriously, German authorities have continued to uphold such a definition despite its racist overtones and despite the Nazi policies with which it came to be tragically associated. This *Volk* obsession sets limits on what policy-makers can do in order to incorporate foreigners into German society, despite revisions to the law in the year 2000. Nearly 2,500,000 persons of Turkish origin live in Germany. Should they still be treated as "migrants," "foreigners," "settlers," and "denizens,"[1] or is it time to begin calling them "citizens"?

This chapter aims to investigate the linkages between nation, culture, identity and citizenship in the context of German-Turks. After presenting the migratory processes of Turkish migrants in Germany, I shall describe the legal and political aspects of citizenship laws in Germany, with particular emphasis on the hyphenated German-Turkish identity. Subsequently, I shall outline the main parameters of the two antithetical notions of culture, which play a significant role in our denomination of cultural phenomena and citizenship. Additionally, I shall also delineate the main parameters of what we call "third space," or "rhizomatic space" where transnational migrants, or contemporary diasporic subjects, construct and reconstruct their identities. Consequently, I shall combine the debates on citizenship and national identity, and argue that contemporary laws of citizenship should not be based on prescribed cultural, religious, linguistic and ethnic qualities.

The migratory process

Migration into post-war Germany started as labor recruitment to mitigate shortages in specific industries. Between 1955 and 1968, the Federal Republic of Germany concluded intergovernmental contracts with eight Mediterranean countries: first Italy (1955), then Spain and Greece (1960), Turkey (1961 and 1964), Morocco (1963), Portugal (1964), Tunisia (1965) and Yugoslavia (1968). The German Federal Labor Office (the *Bundesanstalt für Arbeit* or BFA) set up recruitment offices in the countries concerned. Employers seeking workers had to apply to the BFA and pay a fee. The BFA then selected suitable workers, tested their work skills, gave them medical check-ups and checked their police and political records.[2] Migrants were recruited at first for agriculture and construction, and later by all branches of industry, where they generally had low-skilled manual jobs (Castles and Kosack 1973). Guest-worker programs were designed to solve immediate labor shortages in Germany by recruiting workers on temporary, short-term residence and work permits (Castles *et al.* 1984). The Turkish population in the FRG rose from 6,700 in 1961 to 605,000 in 1973 (see Table 10.1).

Table 10.1 Germany's non-German population and Turkish minority

Year	*Non-German population*	%	*Turkish minority*	%
1961	686,200	1.2	6,700	1.0
1970	2,600,600	4.3	249,400	16.5
1973	3,966,200	6.4	605,000	15.2
1977	3,948,300	6.4	508,000	12.9
1987	4,240,500	6.9	1,453,700	34.3
1989	4,845,900	7.7	1,612,600	33.3
1990a	5,342,500	8.4	1,675,900	32.0
1991b	5,882,300	7.3	1,779,600	30.3
1992	6,495,800	8.0	1,854,900	28.6
1993	6,878,100	8.5	1,918,400	27.9
1994	6,990,510	8.6	1,965,577	28.1
1995	7,173,900	8.7	2,014,311	28.1
1996	7,314,000	8.9	2,049,060	28.0
1997	7,365,800	9.0	2,107,400	28.6
1998	7,319,600	9.0	2,110,223	28.8
1999	7,343,600	8.9	2,053,600	27.9
2000	7,296,800	8.8	1,998.500	27.3
2001	7,318,600	8.7	1,947,900	26.6

Source: Statistisches Jahrbuch für die Bundesrepublik Deutschland, 2002.

Notes:

a Data from 1961–1990 for the 'old Länder'

b Data from 1991 for the 'old' and 'new' Länder

In the early stages of the migration, Turkish migrants were mainly men between the ages of 20 and 39, relatively skilled and educated in comparison to the average working population in Turkey, and originating from the economically more developed regions of the country (Abadan-Unat 1976; Kemiksiz and Abadan-Unat 1986; Martin 1991). The proportion of rural migrants at this stage was just 17.2 percent. In the second half of the 1960s, recruitment primarily consisted of rural workers (Gökdere 1978). Berlin was relatively late in recruiting Turkish workers. Since the textile and electronics sectors demanded cheap female labor, it was accordingly women who first migrated to Berlin in 1964. Turkish workers who had migrated to Berlin by 1973 were primarily from the eastern provinces and from economically less-developed regions of Turkey. As shown in Table 10.1, there has been a continual increase in the non-German population through the post-war period. The exceptions are the figures for 1977, because the entry of non-European Community workers was banned in November 1973 by the German government due to the oil crisis and its consequent economic stagnation and political considerations. Since 1973, the composition of the Turkish migrant population has tended to become a more general population migration in the form of family reunification and political asylum rather than mainly labor migration.

Contemporary Turkish-origin migrants and their descendants in Germany can no longer be simply considered temporary migrant communities who subscribe to the "myth of return." Rather they have become permanent settlers, active social agents and decision-makers constructing a distinct space that combines Germany and Turkey. They have formed transnational communities by means of the contemporary circuitry of transportation and communication. Today's German-Turks have little in common with the "guest-worker" stereotypes of the past. Today they are a recognized and highly active section of the population. For instance, around 55,200 Turkish businesses in Germany currently employ approximately 293,000 workers in ninety different fields of activity, 71.7 percent of whom are Turkish origin, 18.4 percent German, and 9.9 percent others. Only 24.2 percent of Germany's Turkish businesses are in the traditional strongholds of the restaurant and catering industries; 44 percent are involved in trade; and 19.8 percent in the services sector. They form a dynamic and flexible business sector that benefits the whole country. To give an example, the total amount of investment made by German-Turks in 1999 reached the level of DM12.4 billion, and their total annual revenue DM50.3 billion.

Despite the significant transformation that they have undergone, the Turks of Germany have been continually misrepresented, both in Germany and Turkey. The labels attached to them include derogatory terms such as "in between," "foreigner," "German-like" (*Almancı*), "degenerated," "conservative," "radical," "nationalist" and/or "lost generations." All these problem-oriented representations have acquired wide popularity in both countries. It seems that the popularity of these labels springs from the traditional notion of culture, which has a wide usage in both countries – a point to which I shall return shortly.

As I explained elsewhere (Kaya 2001), the Turkish workers have generally been addressed in the official German discourse as *Gästarbeiter* (guest-workers), *Ausländer* (foreigners), and/or *Mitbürger* (co-citizens) – terms which underline their "otherness" and/or "displacement." On the other hand, they are officially defined in Turkey as either *gurbetçi* or *Almanya'daki vatandaşlarımız* ("our citizens in Germany"). German-Turks are stereotypically defined by their compatriots in Turkey as either *Almanyalı* or *Almancı*. Both terms carry rather negative connotations in Turkey. The German-Turks are depicted as being rich, eating pork, having a very comfortable life in Germany, losing their Turkishness, and becoming increasingly Germanized. Implicitly derogatory in its markedness, in its explicit differentiation from a non-emigrant Turk, the labels correspond to a combination of difference, lack of acceptance, and rejection. Their Turkish and the way they dress also contribute to the construction of an *Almancı* image in Turkey. "Here we are called *yabancı* [foreigner], and there in Turkey they call us *Almancı*" is a refrain one hears frequently, especially among German-Turkish youth. If the labels given these groups are problematic, then how could one define them without being essentialist? Can they be called German-Turkish? If so what are the cultural and legal aspects of such a term? I will try to draw a general framework in which the legal and cultural pillars of the hyphenated identity, "German-Turkish," are outlined.

Toward a limited hyphenated citizenship: German-Turks

The Federal Republic of Germany's constitution, the Basic Law (*Grundgesetz*), recognizes two categories of rights: general and reserved. General rights apply to all individuals in the FRG and include freedom of expression, liberty of person, and freedom of conscience (Arts 2, 3, 4 and 5). Reserved rights are restricted to German citizens, and include the right of peaceable assembly, freedom of movement, freedom of association, and freedom of occupation (Arts 8, 9, 11 and 12). The Basic Law does not prescribe how citizenship is recognized or conferred, but the criteria are based first and foremost on ethnic nationality. The rules governing the acquisition of citizenship are defined by the Basic Law's Article 116, the preamble to the Basic Law, and the 1913 Imperial and State Citizenship Law (*Reichs- und Staatsangehörigkeitsgesetz*), and provide that citizenship is passed by descent from parent to child.[3] Article 116 of the Basic Law reads as follows:

1 A German within the meaning of this Basic Law, unless otherwise regulated by law, is a person who possesses German citizenship, or who has been received in the territory of the German Reich as of 31 December

1937 as a refugee or expellee of German stock or as the spouse or descendant of such a person.

2 Former German citizens who, between 30 January 1933 and 8 May 1945, were deprived of their citizenship on political, racial, or religious grounds and their descendants shall be granted citizenship on application …

The Imperial Naturalization Law of 1913 was designed to make the acquisition of German citizenship difficult for aliens for fear that the Reich was being invaded by immigrants from the east, especially Poles and Jews. At the same time, the law sharply reduced the barriers to the repatriation of ethnic Germans (*Aussiedler*) from outside the Reich (Brubaker 1992: 114–19; Klusmeyer 1993: 84; Marshall 1992).

A claim to naturalization has always been difficult for non-EU "foreigners" in the FRG, and has required repudiation of the citizenship of the country of origin. Non-EU "foreigners" have usually been denied the right to dual citizenship; even the children of migrants born and raised in Germany could not automatically receive the rights of citizenship until January 2000.[4] "Foreigners" who are willing to renounce their previous citizenship can be naturalized only after they have lived in Germany for at least fifteen years. In contrast, the *Volksdeutschen* (ethnic Germans defined by Article 116 of the Basic Law) – primarily Poles and Russians who can prove German ancestry – have a constitutional right to naturalization.

However, the current German government, the so-called Red-Green coalition of Social Democrats and Greens, recently established two mechanisms that, for the first time, endow migrants with the right to acquire citizenship. According to the new *Ausländergesetz* (1991) and the *Gesetz zur Änderung Asylverfahrens, Ausländer- und staatsangehörig-keitsrechtlicher Vorschriften* (1993), two groups of *Ausländer* have been legally entitled to naturalization (paragraphs 85 and 86 of the *Ausländergesetz*). Paragraph 85 declares that "foreigners" between the ages of 16 and 23, who have been residents of Germany for more than eight years, attended a school in Germany for at least six years and who have not been convicted of serious offences, have the right to be naturalized. On the other hand, paragraph 86 allows that those "migrants" who have been residents of Germany for at least fifteen years and possess a residence permit, have the right to naturalization. The absence of any serious criminal conviction, as well as the financial independence of the applicant, are also crucial for the acquisition of citizenship according to this paragraph.

Non-European Union immigrants, or resident aliens, have mostly been given what T. H. Marshall (1992) defined as social and civil rights, but not political rights. The immigrants built a very real political presence in Germany, where their political participation in the system was not legally allowed. The legal barriers to political participation provided the ground for Turkish immigrants in Germany to organize themselves politically along collective ethnic lines. As a response to the German insistence on the exclusionary *Ausländerstatus*, Turkish migrant communities have tended to develop strong ethnic structures and maintain ethnic boundaries. The lack of political participation and representation in the receiving country made them direct their political activity toward their country of origin. In fact, this home-oriented participation has received encouragement from the Turkish government, which has has set up networks of consular services and other official organizations (religious, educational and commercial). Homeland opposition parties and movements have also forged an organizational presence in Germany.

The new law, in force since 1 January 2000, partially changes the principle of descent (*jus sanguinis*) that has so far been the country's traditional basis for granting citizenship. Now, it will also be possible to acquire German citizenship as a result of being born in Germany (*jus soli*). According to the new law, children who are born in Germany to foreign nationals will receive German citizenship when one of the respective child's parents has resided lawfully in Germany for at least eight years and holds entitlement to residence, or has an unlimited residence permit for at least three years. Under the new law, such children acquire German citizenship at birth. The new law has introduced a transitional arrangement for children up to the age of ten, who were born in Germany before the "Act to Amend the Nationality Law" was enacted. Accordingly, those children may be automatically naturalized if they apply. In most cases, they will also acquire their parents' citizenship under the principle of descent. Such children will have to decide within five years of turning eighteen – before their twenty-third birthday – whether they want to retain their German citizenship. They must opt for only one of their two nationalities.

It is apparent that the number of "foreigners" applying for naturalization has remarkably increased since the introduction of the new citizenship laws. In the wake of the new laws the number of naturalizations rose by around 30 percent in the year 2000 compared with 1999. According to the information provided by the *Länder* (state) governments, 186,700 foreigners were granted German citizenship in the course of the year 2000, compared with 143,267 in 1999. Subsequently, a total of 178,100 foreigners were naturalized in 2001. That was a decline of 8,600 or 4.6 percent over the year 2000. Contrary to the increase in naturalization of foreigners in general, the rate of naturalization of Turks in 2000 fell by around 20 percent compared with 1999. This trend remained the same in 2001, decreasing by around 9 percent compared with 2000 (see Table 10.2).

Concerning Table 10.2, there are two essential points to be raised. The first point is the decline in the number of people of Turkish descent being naturalized between 2000 and 2001. In 2000 the new citizenship law took effect. In general, naturalization became easier. There was a rule that children of foreign descent between birth and ten years of age could be naturalized right away, without any waiting period. This rule was limited to

Table 10.2 Naturalization of the German-Turkish population

Year	*Number of naturalizations*
1972–9	2,219
1980–9	10,361
1990	2,034
1991	3,529
1992	7,377
1993	12,915
1994	19,590
1995	31,578
1996	46,294
1997	42,240
1998	59,664
1999	103,900
2000	82,800
2001	75,600
Total	505,106

Source: Germany, Federal Statistical Office, press release, 20 June 2002.

one year. Hence, the naturalization rate was higher than in 2001. The second point is a more complex one and needs further inquiry: I shall briefly touch on it as I have no substantial evidence to demonstrate my hypothesis. As can be seen in the table, there is a considerable increase in the rate of naturalization in 1999 compared with 1998, and a significant decline in 2000 compared with the previous year.[5] The general trend for foreigners to naturalize was upward: from 143,267 in 1999 to 186,000 in 2000. Yet, German-Turks posed an exception in contrast to Greeks, or ex-Yugoslavs, although the new citizenship law was more liberal and inclusionary (see Table 10.3).

There may be several reasons for such a decline. It may be that German-Turks are already content with their "denizenship" status, which gives them civil, social, and cultural rights but no political rights. Another reason may be that German-Turks had expected a more democratic citizenship law to be put into effect without any limitation for dual citizenship; but perhaps their expectations diminished, and they did not see any further benefit in acquiring German citizenship. A third possible reason may be that Turks, who are mostly urban residents, preferred to ignore the new nationality law, which required a relatively more complicated bureaucratic process in city-states such as Berlin. This may have had a discouraging impact on German-Turks in the process of naturalization. A fourth reason may be that there is already a decline in the voting habits of German-Turks, who have not been given the right to vote in Turkish general elections. The right to vote in their own residential areas is an important issue for Turkish citizens living abroad.[6]

Table 10.3 Naturalization of foreigners between 1980 and 2001

Year [1]	*Greece*	*Italy*	*Yugoslavia* [2]	*Croatia* [3]	*Poland*	USSR [4]	*Spain*	*Turkey*	*Hungary*
1980	376	1,010	3,475	–	3,303	4,138	217	399	1,868
1981	281	972	3,131	–	4,206	3,583	181	534	1,895
1982	235	1,084	3,201	–	7,807	3,243	211	580	1,669
1983	350	1,134	3,117	–	7,182	2,446	261	853	1,570
1984	264	946	3,334	–	5,988	1,704	323	1,053	1,432
1985	246	797	2,815	–	5,925	1,146	191	1,310	1,200
1986	173	597	2,721	–	7,251	945	171	1,492	1,105
1987	199	551	2,364	–	9,439	1,111	135	1,184	1,203
1988	191	618	2,119	–	13,958	4,810	155	1,243	1,157
1989	179	548	2,076	–	24,882	13,557	108	1,713	1,556
1990	158	437	2,082	–	32,340	33,339	103	2,034	1,532
1991	194	679	2,832	–	27,646	55,620	107	3,529	1,178
1992	285	1,947	1,947	269	20,248	84,660	168	7,377	1,425
1993	301	1,154	1,988	2,196	15,435	105,801	224	12,915	1,663
1994	341	1,417	4,374	3,695	11,943	164,296	185	19,590	1,902
1995	428	1,281	3,623	2,695	10,174	214,927	189	31,578	1,305
1996	493	1,297	2,967	2,391	7,872	194,849	152	46,294	1,027
1997	418	1,187	2,341	1,914	5,763	179,601	172	42,240	911
1998	427	1,156	2,881	2,373	5,151	170,381	141	59,664	652
1999	375	1,185	3,608	1,648	2,865	89,372	152	103,900	537
2000	1,413	1,036	9,776	3,316	1,604	11,358	190	82,861	561
2001	1,402	1,048	12,000	3,931	1,774	12,254	183	76,573	593

Source:Statistisches Bundesamt V II B – 175, 2002.

Notes:

1 1980–90 in Federal Germany; since 1991 in Germany.

2 1980–91 Yugoslavia; from 1992 Serbia/Montenegro.

3 Since 1992.

4 1980–91, the USSR; since 1992 the Commonwealth of Independent States.

The last, but not the least, explanation would be the processes of "globalization from below" (Brecher *et al.* 1993), which sets up the pillars of modern diasporic identity (Clifford 1992; 1994; 1997; Hall 1991; 1994; Gilroy 1987; 1993; 1994; 1995; Kaya 2001). The wide networks of communication and transportation between Germany and Turkey play a crucial role in the formation and maintenance of a diasporic identity among transnational communities. The modern circuitry connects the diasporic subjects both to the homeland and to the rest of the world. This is the reason why it becomes much easier for German-Turks to live on "both banks of the river" at the same time. German-Turks exemplify an increasing trend of what Brecher *et al.* (1993) have called "globalization from below." This constitutive entanglement has become a characteristic of modern diaspora networks. The expansion of economic, cultural and political networks between diaspora and homeland, for instance, points to this growing phenomenon. In the context of the diasporic condition, "globalization from below" refers to an enhancement in the access of transnational migrants and their descendants to those social, cultural, political and economic mechanisms enabling them to transcend the exclusionary conditions imposed upon them by the German nation-state. To put it differently, diasporic identity symbolically enables diasporic subjects to overcome the limitations and oppression of the country of settlement. In this context, traditional national citizenship discourse loses its accuracy and legitimacy for contemporary diasporic subjects. Therefore, this obsolete rhetoric should be replaced with new forms of citizenship such as double citizenship, multiple citizenship, post-national citizenship, transnational citizenship, or diasporic citizenship.

The question here is, do the new laws leave space for such progressive forms of citizenship in Germany? The new citizenship laws permit the descendants of the Turkish migrants to acquire dual citizenship for at least a certain period of time. The present legal reforms equip German-born "foreigners" with the capacity to go beyond their previously defined "denizen" status. They can thus enjoy political rights as well as civic, social, cultural and environmental ones. Hence, the present German citizenship laws open up a new room for the introduction of a kind of limited, "hyphenated" citizenship for the non-European "foreigners" as well as for the Turkish-origin population. The partial introduction of the principle of *jus soli* clearly indicates that the definition of Germanness is no longer limited to ethnic descent. It also suggests that ethnically non-German and non-European members of the Federal Republic can be incorporated into the political sphere through civic channels. These legal changes, in a way, refer to the transformation of the culturally defined national project towards a rather Habermasian "post-national society" project, which requires the political recognition of newcomers.[7] In other words, the new laws partially distance us from the hegemony of once-essentialized ethnic identities such as "German," "Turkish," "Kurdish," "Iranian," etc. They hold the potential to open the way for the construction of hyphenated civic identities such as

"German-Turkish" (in the Turkish language it literally means a Turk from Germany, *Almanyalı Türk*), "German-Kurdish," or "German-Iranian."

Yet, it should be pointed out that those hyphenated civic identities and/or hyphenated citizenships are distinct from their equivalents in the American case. In the North American experience, when the hyphenated identities are spelled out the emphasis is put on the ethnic origin of individuals, as in Irish-American, or Italian-American. The fact that the emphasis is on ethnic origin does not imply that Americanness is undervalued. On the contrary, what is implicitly celebrated is the Americanness into which the particularist ethnicities are embedded. Hence, the explicit celebration of ethnic origins implicitly implies a celebration of Americanness. In contrast, in the German experience the emphasis is on the "German" component of the hyphenated identity. Therefore, it seems that the precondition of granting a hyphenated identity such as "German-Turk" in Germany is integration into the German way of life. In the United States of America, on the other hand, the granting of the hyphenated identity is relatively less unconditional, since the USA is by definition an immigrant nation. The usage of the German-hyphenated identity in both official and public discourse is an indication of the discursive shift in the perception of Germany as an immigration country by the German authorities. This has actually been confirmed by the changes in the citizenship laws as well as by the report prepared by the Independent Commission on Migration to Germany.[8] Citizenship laws do not only spring from legal concerns, they are also culturally formed. Thus, in what follows the cultural elements defining the nature of citizenship laws in Germany must be depicted. In doing so, I shall also briefly touch upon the changes in academic discourse, or paradigm shift, in respect to research on German-Turks. The reason why I outline the paradigm shift is to address the similarity of changes in both citizenship laws and related scientific research.

Notions of culture

There are two principal notions of culture that I will briefly summarize: the first is the holistic notion and the second is the syncretic notion of culture. The former treats culture as a highly integrated and comprehended static "whole." This is the dominant paradigm of modernity, of which territoriality and totality were the main characteristics. The latter notion is the one which is most obviously affected by increasing interconnectedness in space; this syncretic notion of culture has been put to use by contemporary scholars to demonstrate the fact that cultures can also emerge in hybrid forms beyond national territories.

The term "culture" came to the fore in Europe during the construction of cultural nationalist identities, particularly in the nineteenth century. Since the main constituent of the age of nationalism (the nineteenth century) was territoriality, culture was defined as the cumulative of "shared meanings and values," which manifested itself in that particular territory throughout history. This is the holistic notion of culture that has provided the essential fabric for the emergence of the myth of distinct national cultures. To quote Eric Wolf,

> The demonstration that each struggling nation possessed a distinctive society, animated by its special spirit or culture, served to legitimate its aspirations to form a separate state of its own. The notion of separate and integral cultures responded to this political project.
>
> (Wolf 1982: 387)

The idea that cultures exist as separate and integral entities corresponds to the former notion of culture. The holistic notion of culture resembles the usage of the German Romantics, as in "*Volk* culture," imprisoning cultures within distinct social compartments containing separate sets of "shared meanings and values." This understanding attributes a time, context, territoriality, space, unity and memory to culture. Accordingly, modernity, which appears in the form of electronic communications, transportation, deterritorialization and cultural imperialism, has disrupted the "unity and authenticity of culture" (Smith 1990; 1995; Bell 1978).

The main claim of the holistic approach is that "shared meanings and values" are the principal constituents of each "distinct" culture. The focus on "shared meanings and values" may sometimes make culture sound too unitary, homogeneous, holistic and too cognitive. The fracturing of this unity and totality is considered to result in crisis, breakdown, or degeneration. The themes of "identity crisis," "in-betweenness," "split identities" and "degeneration" raised by some scholars in the study of ethnic minorities are the products of such an assumption. This assumption claims that culture emerges along distinct ethnic lines, and holds no place for syncreticism and mixture. Syncreticism could merely be considered, in this approach, as an impurity that pollutes the "authentic culture."

Although some researchers who work on Turkish migrants' culture in Germany note emergent syncreticisms, they dislike these "cultural impurities." The common trend among these scholars in the context of Turkish migrants in Germany is either to label the cultures of mixture as "degenerate" or to diagnose the situation as a "fragmented cultural world leading to a crisis of identity" (Kağıtçıbaşı 1987; Mushaben 1985; Nauck 1988). These scholars regard the Turkish migrants as the victims of a transnational capitalist process. This is why those "victims" have been considered to be incapable of coping with their new circumstances and the obstacles they face in the diaspora. This approach negates a subject-centered analysis. Ironically, this notion of culture also provides the ground for the formation of multiculturalist polities. Multiculturalism assumes that cultures are internally consistent, unified and structured wholes that belong to distinct ethnic groups (Kaya 1998; 2001; Radtke 1994; Russon 1995; Rosaldo 1989; Kuper 2000; Kymlicka 1995).[9]

Most of the studies on Turks and the Turkish culture in Germany are based on a notion that links ethnicity and culture. This approach mainly rests on the assumption that Turkish migrants carry their own distinct cultural baggage all the way from home to their country of settlement. Underestimating the situational and instrumental nature of ethnicity, these scholars went back to the place of origin of migrants to discover or figure out the main parameters of the Turks' social, cultural and ethnic identifications. These analysts took the "traditional culture" of Turkey as their basis to ascertain the migrants' social and cultural identities in their new social milieu. The emphasis is usually placed on the norms, values and codes that predominate in rural areas of Turkey (Abadan-Unat 1976; 1985; Kağıtçıbaşı 1987).[10] Islam comes to the fore in these studies as the core element of this "traditional culture." Islam has been primarily used in culturalist German academic circles to label the German-Turks in a way that reduces their culture to religion (cf. *inter alia* Nauck 1988; Mushaben 1985; Heitmeyer *et al.* 1997). Moreover, this group of scholars approached the issue through the lens of an "identity" framework in which identity is considered to be stable, fixed, centered and coherent.

The syncretic notion of culture, on the other hand, claims that mixing and bricolage are the main characteristics of cultures. According to this approach, culture does not develop along ethnically absolute lines but in complex, dynamic patterns of syncreticism (cf. *inter alia* Vassaf 1982; Schwartz 1992; Mandel 1996; Zaimoğlu 1995; 1998; Faist 2000; Tertilt 1996). Cultural identity is viewed as the outcome of a constant process of "becoming." From this perspective, migrant cultures mix their newly available set of tools, which they acquire in their migration experience, with their previous lives and cultural repertoires. The syncretic notion of culture embodies a ground whereby a third space can be constructed by the descendants of transnational migrants. The major challenge to those scholars who are bound to the holistic notion of culture comes from those who reject the idea that ethnic groups are preordained, unchangeable social units. Bearing in mind these two opposing notions of culture, how should we name the Turkish migrants and their descendants in Germany? Should they still be compartmentalized as distinct cultural entities with sharp boundaries; or should they be considered as constructing a separate space where different cultural traditions, discourses and practices juxtapose with each other?

A third culture: cultural bricolage

In its 14 April 1997 issue, *Der Spiegel*, a prominent liberal weekly magazine, denounced the "foreigners" in the country as "dangerously alien" and as the cause of the failure of "multicultural society" in Germany. In the magazine, Turkish youths in Germany were represented as "criminals," "fundamentalists," "nationalists" and "traumatized." An approach similar to this type of media coverage of the Turks in Germany has also been observed in academia. Wilhelm Heitmeyer, a scholar cited in the *Der Spiegel* article, is a controversial academic figure. In his book on the German-Turkish youth, *Verlockender Fundamentalismus* (*Enticing Fundamentalism*), Heitmeyer (1997) concluded that it is the Turks who resist integration and incorporation into the political system. His main criterion for unearthing the self-isolationist tendency of the Turkish-origin youths was their contentment to live with Islam and Turkishness. What was missing in both the journalistic piece and the book was any consideration of the structural constraints of Germany, which shaped the survival strategies of migrants and their descendants to a considerable extent. Such an approach does not consider the impact of the institutional structure of the receiving country on immigrant political mobilization, and is therefore quite essentialist and exclusionist. Moreover, this kind of representation of Turkish-origin migrants may mislead the majority society into reducing culture to religion.

It is true that German-Turkish youngsters, at first glance, look as if they are practicing a conventional and essentialist form of cultural identity that they have taken out of the ready-made package of cultural attributes carried over from the homeland by their parents. This is an erroneous conclusion. The formation and articulation of cultural identity are part of a process, one which is intimately related to the constant intercourse between various social groups, classes and cultures. As Czarina Wilpert accurately states:

> The significance of the concept of cultural identity within this framework derives from the assumption that, in the construction of a collective ethnic identity, culture becomes a resource. It is not that culture, which may be in continual transformation, is viewed as something static and fixed, nor that an immigrant "community" is considered to live as a homogeneous closed cultural entity within a foreign society. Rather, elements of culture, its signs and symbols, may be transformed or filled with new meaning and take on a new significance in this process.
> (Wilpert 1989: 21)

Wilpert reminds us of two significant points. The first point to be considered is that the reification of culture in the diaspora is a vital instrument to be employed in the process of identity formation. The second point to bear in mind is that the community culture that is being shaped in the new environment is not immune to the attraction of the culture of the wider society. It is far from being unchanging, or always clear and unambiguous.

In this sense, there are at least three main dimensions shaping the cultural identification of German-Turkish youth in particular:

(a) "Authenticity," that is, the expression of an "imagined" Anatolian culture;
(b) German culture, which refers to the life styles of German peer groups to which the German-Turkish youngsters desire to adapt themselves to; and

(c) Global culture, which is mainly the imitation of urban American symbols.

To take an example, the language used by German-Turkish youth in Berlin reflects a mixture of their Turkishness, Germanness and cosmopolitan identity. This refers us to the "multiple cultural competence" of the descendants of migrants. Modern diasporic communities should learn to inhabit at least two identities, "to speak two cultural languages, to translate and negotiate between them" (Hall 1993: 310). People belonging to such cultures of bricolage tend to gravitate either toward "tradition" or "translation." Gravitating toward tradition is an attempt to restore the former purity and authenticity of the culture that is feared to have been lost. Choosing translation, on the other hand, acknowledges that identity is subject to the play of history, politics, representation and difference rather than being perpetuated in its purity (Hall 1993: 309).

The remarks of Wilhelm Heitmeyer and his approach do not go unchallenged. There are other voices proclaiming the multicultural competence of German-Turkish youth. The Berlin rapper Azize-A tries to shatter the traditional image of the Turkish-origin migrants and their children in Germany, and wants to show that the second and third generation youngsters have become very "multi-kulti" and cosmopolitan. She also rightfully highlights her own multicultural capital in order to be accepted by the majority society:

> I attempt to erase the question "are we Turkish or German," and announce that we are multi-kulti and cosmopolitan. I want to show that we are no more sitting between the two chairs, we have got a "third chair" between those two.
>
> (cited in Kaya 2001: 202)

Negating the so-called state of "in-betweenness," Azize-A presents a new picture of the transnational youth. Her insistence on multiculturalism seems to be the main pillar of her politics of identity. She does not invest in cultural boundaries in any way that would help define culture as a distinct, self-contained and essentialist form. By stating her wish to erase the question: "Are we Turkish or German?" she challenges the holistic understanding of culture, and reconfirms that cultures are learned, not genetically encoded.

What Azize-A calls the "third chair' illustrates how the transnational subject crosses cultural borders and constructs a syncretic cultural identity. In his poem *Doppelmann*, Zafer Şenocak writes of his Germany as follows:

> I carry two worlds within me
> but neither one whole
> they're constantly bleeding
> the border runs
> right across my tongue.
>
> (cited in Suhr 1989: 102)

The transnational subject who is defined in this poem is someone who experiences a constant tension between roots and routes. "The split," as Şenocak states, "can give rise to a double identity. This identity lives on the tension. One's feet learn to walk on both banks of the river at the same time" (cited in Suhr 1989: 102). Having to learn to walk on both banks of the river, the German-Turks develop a multiple cultural competence. Thus, when they gravitate toward tradition by increasingly getting closer to homeland, religion, ethnicity and culture, German-Turks do not necessarily become nationalist, fundamentalist, racist, or xenophobic. Contrary to what Wilhelm Heitmeyer argues, this is rather a rightfully chosen survival strategy developed by the youngsters in response to a structural outsiderism led by the legal, political and economic limitations of the German state. Thus, encountering a more inclusionary and integrative political system, German-Turks may opt out of gravitating toward tradition, and prefer to move toward translation.

Thus these youngsters display a unique subjectivity, a third position, where one may abstain from the Cartesian duality. The third culture is a bricolage in which elements from different cultural traditions, sources and discourses are constantly intermingled with and juxtaposed with each other. The third space is what Homi Bhabha (1988; 1990) called a "differential communality," and what Felix Guattari (1989) referred to as the "processes of heterogenesis." By the "processes of heterogenesis" Guattari suggests that "our objective should rather be to nurture individual cultures, while at the same time inventing new contracts of citizenship: to create an order of the state in which singularity, exceptions, and rarity coexist under the least oppressive conditions" (1989: 14). He describes this formation "as a logic of the 'included middle', in which black and white are indistinct, in which the beautiful coexists with the ugly, the inside with the outside, the 'good' object with the bad," and the self with the other.

Guattari's proposal of "new contracts of citizenship ... in which singularity, exceptions, and rarity coexist under the least oppressive conditions," suggests this third culture (1989: 14). The third culture does not invest in essentialist positioning that imprisons cultures and identities in their strictly defined boundaries. Rather, it requires the existence of a third space in which both "Germanness" and "Turkishness" may coexist.[11] Like all the other transnational migrants, German-Turks constitute a unique experience in the sense that they expose a cultural identity-formation process which is a critique of the Cartesian binary oppositions. They construct and reconstruct their cultural identities in a process whereby the conjunctions of "either" (Turkish) and "or" (German) have been consciously rejected. Instead, they employ the conjunction "and ... and ... and ... " in the process of identity formation, as in "German *and* Turkish *and* global *and* ... and ... and ... " As quoted above, Azize-A phrases this state of mind as follows: "I want to show that we are no more sitting between the two chairs, we have got a 'third chair' between those two."

The term *rhizome*, for instance, coined by Deleuze and Guattari (1987), corresponds to this phenomenon which is displayed by many modern diasporic subjects in general, and German-Turkish youngsters in particular: *rhizome* is a root-like underground stem that produces roots below and sends up shoots from its upper surface. In defining rhizome, Deleuze and Guattari provide us with a convincing standpoint:

> A *rhizome* has no beginning or end; it is always in the middle, between things, interbeing, and intermezzo. The tree is filiations, but the rhizome is alliance, uniquely alliance. The tree imposes the verb "to be," but the fabric of the rhizome is conjunction, "and...and...and..." This conjunction carries enough force to shake and uproot the verb "to be." Where are you going? Where are you coming from? What are you heading for? These are totally useless questions. Making a clean slate, starting and beginning again from ground zero, seeking a beginning or a foundation – all imply a false conception of voyage and movement ... American literature, and already English literature, manifest this rhizomatic direction to an even greater extent; they know how to move between things, establish a logic of the AND, overthrow ontology, do away with foundations, nullify endings and beginnings. They know how to practice pragmatics. The middle is by no means an average; on the contrary, it is where things pick up speed.
>
> (Deleuze and Guattari 1987: 25)

The "middle" does not refer to "caught betwixt and between," it rather connotes a separate space in itself where, for instance, diasporic subjects, *bricoleurs*, cosmopolitans, and hybrids dwell. Thus, knowing that such new cosmopolitan forms spring from the third space, we might open ourselves up to a relationship that transcends us, that exists beyond and apart from us, instead of fully explaining and assimilating the other, thereby reducing her/him to our world. The third space in the case of Turkish migrants and their descendants dwelling in Germany can emerge only if political rights are granted and the hyphenated identity of "German-Turk" is accepted.

Cultural identities cannot be prescribed, because they are socially constructed and subject to change. So are nations. Nations also cannot be prescribed. To give an example, the member nations of the European Union have been going through a process whereby they have to question previously defined norms and codes of nationhood. This process requires the transformation of the traditional conceptions of citizenship and national identity.

National identity and citizenship

A question often heard when any revision of citizenship is suggested is: "What about our national identity?" In fact, citizenship and nation are two imbricate institutions. National identity, like all the other identities, is dynamic, and should not be prescribed. Our identity, be it national, individual, political, communal, or ethnic, is shaped by the acts of *recognition*, *unrecognition* or *misrecognition* of "others" (Taylor 1994: 25). The human mind develops in a dialogical sense, not a monological one. We can construct our identities only if we are able to experience others' reactions to our attitudes and behavior. Thus, it is impossible to build an identity without a dialogue with the "other." If a nation prescribes a holistic notion of culture, then it would be remarkably difficult for newcomer groups to incorporate themselves into the existing social system without major resistance from the majority society. Prescribing, thus essentializing, the nation may inevitably lead its members not to recognize newcomers whom they consider to be culturally distinct. Not recognizing newcomers may result in the construction of radical and centrifugal identities, and thus in conflict. In other words, as Kymlicka and Norman have remarked, "immigrant groups that feel alienated from the larger national identity are likely to be alienated from the political arena as well" (2000: 39). Traditional citizenship rhetoric is inclined to advance the interests of the dominant national group at the expense of migrants. Hence, it is unlikely that the classical understanding of citizenship can resolve issues of the co-existence of "culturally discrete" entities. In order to avoid potential conflict and alienation, there is an essential task to be undertaken: citizenship laws should not be based on prescribed cultural, religious, linguistic and ethnic qualities. This linkage between citizenship and a predefined national identity has actually brought about numerous examples of interethnic conflict and violence around the globe.

The idea of the nation-state, originating from the wholistic notion of culture, is essentially rooted in a "name," a common ancestry, a set of common historical memories and myths, a national anthem, a common territory for which the "forefathers" have died, a national economy, and a set of common legal rights and duties (Smith 1986). Accordingly, foreigners such as "guest workers," asylum seekers or refugees, who have immigrated to the West in large numbers during the post-war era, have been generally excluded from civil, social, political, and cultural rights. The model of national citizenship, which is linked to territorialized notions of cultural belonging and primordial loyalty, has been dominant during the period of massive migration since the turn of the twentieth century. However, the recent experience of transnational migrant workers reflects "a time when national citizenship is losing ground to a more universal model of membership, anchored in *deterritorialized* notions of persons' rights" (Soysal 1994: 3, my italics).

The introduction of European Union Citizenship is an interesting example of how citizenship and nation have been in some way disentangled. One of the most important challenges here is that a cardinal tie of citizenship to a predefined national identity is under dispute. Article 8e of the Maastricht Treaty refers to the "dynamic" and "evolutionary" nature of citizenship rights. The Maastricht Treaty inserted to the amended Treaty of

Rome a new Part Two ("Citizenship of the Union"), Article 8. The article declares that "Every person holding the nationality of a Member State shall be citizens of the Union." Besides, it adds that "Citizens of the Union shall also enjoy the rights conferred by this Treaty and shall be subject to the duties imposed thereby." The term "Community Citizenship" actually became a debated issue after a letter from Felipe Gonzales, the former Spanish premier, to the Office of the European Council, proposing that citizenship should be made one of the three pillars of European political union (the other two being the European Monetary Union and a common foreign and security policy).

Although the Maastricht Treaty's notion of European citizenship originates from the "dynamic" and "evolutionary" rights, which are not prescribed, and thus subject to change, some of the earlier problems remain. These criticisms concentrate on the debates around the political inclusion of *extracommunitari* from non-EU countries, such as Turkish migrants in Germany.[12] As Chris Shore (2000: 66–86) rightly observes, there are four major difficulties. First, the EU concept of citizenship focuses exclusively on rights without outlining a set of corresponding duties. Second, the treaty provides legal basis for granting voting rights to any citizens from a member state, regardless of his/her residence. However, *extracommunitari* residents from EU countries, such as Euro-Turks, are not granted such rights. Third, the very idea of a "community national" is problematic: that is, one can be an EU citizen only by virtue of being a citizen of a member state. Hence, the status of EU citizenship is subordinate to the framework of the nation-state. This is again particularly relevant in the context of German-Turks. Finally, there are also criticisms arguing that EU citizenship is raising the prospect of a more exclusionist "Fortress Europe" discriminating against non-EU nationals.

Then again, one should bear in mind that the drafters of the Maastricht Treaty expected that EU citizenship would be developmental, expanding beyond civil and economic rights to include political and social rights. This perspective is clearly indicated in Article 8e of the Maastricht Treaty, with an emphasis on the "dynamic" and "evolutionary" nature of citizenship rights. Article 8e, in a way, provides us with a ground whereby we could be optimistic in the sense that the treaty shortly may embody more inclusionary principles for the non-EU citizens residing in the European Union. Germany's recent effort, along with the institutionalization of European citizenship and the introduction of the new citizenship law during the Red-Green coalition government, testifies to the rupture of the previously established linkage between citizenship and prescribed national identity.

Conclusion

This chapter has been an attempt to give an account of the debates on citizenship, nation, culture and identity regarding the German-Turks.

Germany's new citizenship law is more inclusionary, although still limited, in the sense that it provides the immigrant-origin settlers with opportunities in civil, social, political, cultural and economic rights greater than before. However, the general requirement of having to relinquish one's Turkish nationality continues to prevent many German-Turks from integrating. For this reason, as the Independent Commission on Migration to Germany proposed, at least the immigrants who entered Germany before the ban on recruitment in 1973, and their spouses, should generally be allowed to hold multiple citizenship. Since the number of German-Turks possessing German citizenship is limited to approximately 650,000, such a new policy formation could be an opportunity for German politics to prompt German-Turks to acquire German citizenship. We are now in a position to implement those forms of citizenship in Germany that allow diversity to flourish. Those new forms could be multiple, multicultural, dual, hyphenated, and cosmopolitan citizenships. They should be seen as inclusionary, cohesive institutions for nations. Furthermore, these forms of citizenship have recently become inevitable in a context whereby transnationality has turned out to be one of the principal characteristics of modern societies, especially of the transnational migrant communities and their descendants.

Transnational communities have lately become visible in the contemporary global order. German-Turks clearly constitute such a set of communities. Nevertheless, both traditional German and Turkish academic circles, which are imprisoned in antithetical, culturalist discourses, still perceive these cultures as "in-between," "problematic" and "degenerative." Attempts to label these transnational subjects are mostly irrelevant. In the last forty years these people have constructed a separate space combining Germany and Turkey, bringing various political, social and cultural undertones together. Their cultural products in music, painting, dance and literature clearly display the fact that they have developed something anew *en route*. Newly emerging transnational communities cannot be studied solely with culturalist and nationalist paradigms, notions and methodologies. Thus scholars, politicians and entrepreneurs should realize that something new is happening in the process of being and becoming. To paraphrase Paul Gilroy, "it is not the roots, but the routes you take" that define you.

Acknowledgments

I want to thank Bianca Kaiser, Jacqueline Stevens, Thomas Faist, Fuat Keyman and Ahmet İçduygu for their stimulating and sustained intellectual remarks.

Notes

1 "Denizen" is a concept introduced by Thomas Hammar (1990) to refer to those migrants in the West who enjoy social and civic rights, but not political rights.

2 The story of migration from the "developing" countries to the FRG was successfully told by John Berger *et al.* (1975) in the book *A Seventh Man*. The photographs in the book, taken during the journey from home to Germany, among other things express the difficulties which the immigrants had to experience during their migration. Pictures taken during the medical check-ups, for instance, evidence the degrading manner in which workers were selected by the "experts" of the recruiting country.

3 Until 1974, the father determined a child's nationality, but now either parent is sufficient.

4 It was common for Turkish applicants to re-apply immediately after their German naturalization for their temporarily-lost Turkish citizenship. Turkey allows dual citizenship once the military service of the applicant has been resolved.

5 The main reason for the higher naturalization rate of Turks in 1999 compared to previous years is the shortening of the required duration of residence from 15 to 8 years by law.

6 There are some exceptions, of course, regarding voting in Turkish general elections. Turkish citizens residing abroad have the right to vote in the Turkish ports of departure such as airports and border control stations. Sometimes, some ethnic/religious organizations in Germany transport their members to the Turkish ports before the elections to make them vote for their affiliated political parties. To give an example, the religious based *Milli Görüş* Association based in Berlin transported its supporters to Turkey to vote for the Islamic-oriented Refah Partisi (Welfare Party) in the 1995 early general election. The flight was free of charge, and the traveling voters were paid extra on top of their travel expenses (Kaya 2001: 117).

7 For a broader explanation of the "post-national society" discussion, see Habermas (1999).

8 The Independent Commission on Migration to Germany was chaired by Rita Süssmuth, MP; and the report prepared by the Commission was submitted to the Federal Minister of the Interior on 4 July 2001.

9 "Multiculturalism as an ideology" should be distinguished from "multiculturality as a phenomenon." The ideology of multiculturalism functions as a mode of governmentality in the Foucauldian sense; and it also operates as a politics of identity exercised by minorities. The former corresponds to "multiculturalism as an official ideology," and the latter to "multiculturalism as a demotic ideology." For further discussion on the ideology of multiculturalism in Germany, see Kaya (1998; 2001).

10 Although Nermin Abadan-Unat previously deployed a holistic notion of culture in her early works, she has been recently demonstrated a great paradigm shift. Her recent book (Abadan-Unat 2002) displays very well an historical account of paradigm shifts in the studies on German-Turks.

11 The progressive nature of the "third culture" does not necessarily apply to all the diasporic youth groups. It is evident that the Turkish diaspora in Germany is not homogeneous, it is rather composed of different diasporas. For instance, the Islamic diaspora is one among many others. Turkish religious communities (*cemaat*) such as *Milli Görüş*, *Süleymancis*, *Nurcus* and *Kaplancis* having fundamentalist beliefs are built around what Salman Rushdie (1990) calls "the absolutism of the Pure." "The apostles of purity," he argues, are always moved by the fear that "intermingling with a different culture will inevitably weaken and ruin their own." They believe that communicating with the "unbelievers" does not strengthen their spiritual belief system. Hence, these religious groups prefer sticking together within their own closed religious communities, and distancing

themselves from the Christian society. For more on *Süleymancis*, *Nurcus* and *Kaplancis*, see Schiffauer (1997).

12 OECD figures published in 1994 estimated that the foreign population living in the member states amounted to 14 million out of an EU population of 320 million. Of these, only 5 million were EU citizens residing in other member countries; and the remaining 9 million were *extracommunitari* residents from non-EU states (cited in Faist 1997).

References

Abadan-Unat, N. (1976) "Turkish Migration to Europe 1960–1975: A Balance Sheet of Achievements and Failures," in N. Abadan-Unat (ed.) *Turkish Workers in Europe 1960–1975*, Leiden: Brill.

——(1985) "Identity Crisis of Turkish Migrants," in I. Başgöz and N. Furniss (eds) *Turkish Workers in Europe*, Bloomington: Indiana University Turkish Studies.

——(2002) *Bitmeyen Göç: Konuk İşçilikten Ulus-ötesi Yurttaşlığa* (Unending Migration: From Guestworker to Transnational Citizen), Istanbul: Istanbul Bilgi University Press.

Bell, D. (1978) "Modernism and Capitalism," *Partisan Review*, 45: 206–22.

Berger, J., Mohr, J. and Blomberg, S. (1975) *A Seventh Man*, Harmondsworth: Penguin.

Bhabha, H. (1988) "The Commitment to Theory," *New Formations*, 5 (summer): 5–23.

——(1990) "The Third Space," in J. Rutherford (ed.) *Identity: Community, Culture, Difference*, London: Lawrence and Wishart.

Brecher, J., Childs, J. B. and Cutler, J. (1993) *Global Visions: Beyond the New World Order*, Boston MA: South End Press.

Brubaker, R. (1992) *Citizenship and Nationhood in France and Germany*, Cambridge MA: Harvard University Press.

Castles, S. and Kosack, G. (1973) *Immigrant Workers and Class Structure in Western Europe*, London: Oxford University Press.

Castles, S., Booth, H. and T. Wallace (1984) *Here for Good: Western Europe's New Ethnic Minorities*, London: Pluto Press.

Clifford, J. (1992) "Traveling Cultures," in L. Grossberg, C. Nelson and P. Treichler (eds) *Cultural Studies*, New York: Routledge.

——(1994) "Diasporas," *Cultural Anthropology*, 9, (3): 302–38.

——(1997) *Routes: Travel and Translation in the Late Twentieth Century*, Cambridge MA: Harvard University Press.

Deleuze, G. and Guattari, F. (1987) *A Thousand Plateaus: Capitalism and Schizophrenia*, trans. B. Massumi, Minneapolis: University of Minneasota Press.

Faist, T. (1997) "Migration in Contemporary Europe: European Integration, Economic Liberalization, and Protection," in D. Cesarani and M. Fulbrook (eds) *Citizenship, Nationality and Migration in Europe*, London: Routledge.

Faist, T. (ed.) (2000) *Transstaatliche Räume: Politik, Wirschaft und Kultur in und zwischen Deutschland und der Türkei*, Bielefeld: Transcript Verlag.

Gilroy, P. (1987) *There Ain't no Black in the Union Jack*, London: Hutchinson.

——(1993) *Black Atlantic: Double Consciousness and Modernity*, Cambridge MA: Harvard University Press.

——(1994) "Diaspora," *Paragraph*, 17, 3 (November): 207–10.

——(1995) "Roots and Routes: Black Identity as an Outernational Project," in H. W. Harris, H. C. Blue and E. E. H. Griffith (eds) *Racial and Ethnic Identity: Psychological Development and Creative Expression*, London: Routledge.

Gökdere, A. Y. (1978) *Yabancı Ülkelere İşgücü Akımı ve Türk Ekonomisi üzerindeki Etkileri* (The Flow of Employment to Foreign Countries and Its Influence), Ankara: İş Bankası Yayınları.

Guattari, F. (1989) "The Three Ecologies," *New Formations*, 8 (summer): 131–47.

Habermas, J. (1999) *The Inclusion of the Other: Studies in Political Theory*, Cambridge MA: MIT Press.

Hall, S. (1991) "The Local and the Global: Globalization and Ethnicity," in A. King (ed.) *Culture, Globalization and the World System*, London: Macmillan.

——(1993) "The Question of Cultural Identity," in S. Hall D. Held and T. McGrew (eds) *Modernity and Its Futures*, Cambridge: Polity Press.

——(1994) "Cultural Identity and Diaspora," in P. Williams and L. Chrisman (eds) *Colonial Discourse and Post-colonial Theory*, New York: Columbia University Press.

Hammar, T. (1990) *Democracy and the Nation State*, Aldershot: Avebury.

Heitmeyer, W., Müller, J. and Schröder, H. (1997) *Verlockender Fundamentalismus*, Frankfurt am Main: Suhrkamp Verlag.

Kağıtçıbaşı, Ç. (1987) "Alienation of the Outsider: The Plight of Migrants," *International Migration*, XXV, no. 2 (June): 195–210.

Kaya, A. (1998) "Multicultural Clientalism and Berlin-Alevis," *New Perspectives on Turkey*, 18 (July): 23–49.

——(2001) *Sicher in Kreuzberg: Constructing Diasporas, Turkish Hip-Hop Youth in Berlin*, Bielefeld: Transcript Verlag.

Kemiksiz, N. and Abadan-Unat, N. (1986) *Türk Dış Göçü 1960–1984: Yorumlu Bibliyografya* (Turkish Foreign Migration 1960–1984: Interpreted Biobliography), Ankara: Ankara Üniversitesi SBF Yayınları.

Klusmeyer, D. B. (1993) "Aliens, Immigrants, and Citizens: The Politics of Inclusion in the Federal Republic of Germany," *Daedalus*, 122, 3 (summer): 81–114.

Kuper, A. (2000) *Culture: The Anthropology Account*, Cambridge MA: Harvard University Press.

Kymlicka, W. (1995) *Multicultural Citizenship: A Liberal Theory of Minority Rights*, Oxford: Clarendon Press.

Kymlika, W. and Norman, W. (eds) (2000) *Citizenship in Diverse Societies*, Oxford: Oxford University Press.

Mandel, R. (1996) "A Place of Their Own: Contesting Spaces and Defining Places in Berlin's Migrant Community," in B. D. Metcalf (ed.) *Making Muslim Space in North America and Europe*, Berkeley: University of California Press.

Marshall, B. (1992) "Migration into Germany: Asylum Seekers and Ethnic Germans," *German Politics*, 1, 1 (April): 124–34.

Marshall, T. H. (1992) [1950] "Citizenship and Social Class," in T. Bottomore (ed.) *Citizenship and Social Class*, London: Pluto Press.

Martin, P. L. (1991) *The Unfinished Story: Turkish Labor Migration to Western Europe with Special Reference to the Federal Republic of Germany*, Geneva: International Labor Office.

Mushaben, J. M. (1985) "A Crisis of Culture: Isolation and Integration Among Guestworkers in the German Federal Republic," in I. Başgöz and N. Furniss (eds) *Turkish Workers in Europe*, Bloomington: Indiana University Press.

Nauck, B. (1988) "Migration and Change in Parent-Child Relationships: The Case of Turkish Migrants in Germany," *International Migration*, 26: 33–55.

Radtke, F. O. (1994) "The Formation of Ethnic Minorities and the Transformation of Social into Ethnic Conflicts in a So-called Multi-cultural Society: The Case of Germany," in J. Rex and B. Drury (eds) *Ethnic Mobilisation in a Multi-Cultural Europe*, Aldershot: Avebury.

Rosaldo, R. (1989) *Culture and Truth: The Remaking of Social Analysis*, London: Routledge.

Rushdie, S. (1990) "In Good Faith," *Independent on Sunday*, 4 February.

Russon, J. (1995) "Heidegger, Hegel, and Ethnicity: The Ritual Basis of Self-identity," *The Southern Journal of Philosophy*, XXXIII: 509–32.

Schiffauer, W. (1997) "Islamic Vision and Social Reality: The Political Culture of Sunni Muslims in Germany," in S. Vertovec and C. Peach (eds) *Islam in Europe: The Politics of Religion and Community*, London: Macmillan Press.

Schwartz, T. (1992) "The Turkish Community in Berlin: Youth Cultures in the German Welfare System," in C. Palmgren, K. Lovgren and C. Gohn (eds) *Ethnicity in Youth Culture*, Stockholm: University of Stockholm Press.

Shore, C. (2000) *Building Europe: The Cultural Politics of European Integration*, London: Routledge.

Smith, A. D. (1986) *The Ethnic Origins of Nations*, Oxford: Blackwell.

——(1990) "Towards a Global Culture?," in M. Featherstone (ed.) *Global Culture: Nationalism, Globalization and Modernity*, London: Sage.

——(1995) *Nations and Nationalism in a Global Era*, Cambridge: Polity Press

Soysal, Yasemin N. (1994) *Limits of Citizenship: Migrants and Postnational Membership in Europe*, Chicago: University of Chicago Press.

Suhr, H. (1989) "*Ausländerliteratur*: Minority Literature in the Federal Republic of Germany," *New German Critique*, 46 (winter): 71–103.

Taylor, C. (1994) "The Politics of Recognition," in A. Gutmann (ed.) *Multiculturalism: Examining the Politics of Recognition*, Princeton: Princeton University Press.

Tertilt, H. (1996) *Turkish Power Boys: Ethnographie einer Jugendbande*, Baden-Baden: Suhrkamp.

Vassaf, G. (1982) *Daha Sesimizi Duyuramadık: Avrupa'da Türk İşçi çocukları* (Our Voices Have Not Been Heard Yet: Children of Turkish Workers), Istanbul: Belge Yayınları.

Wilpert, C. (1989) "Ethnic and Cultural Identity: Ethnicity and the Second Generation in the Context of European Migration," in K. Liebkind (ed.) *New Identities in Europe: Immigrant Ancestry and the Ethnic Identity of Youth*, Aldershot: Gower.

Wolf, E. (1982) *Europe and the People without History*, Berkeley: University of California Press.

Zaimoğlu, F. (1995) *Kanak-Sprak: 24 Misstöne vom Rande der Gesellschaf*, Hamburg: Rotbuch Verlag.

——(1998) *Koppstoff: Kanake Sprak vom Rande der Gesellschaft*, Hamburg: Rotbuch Verlag.

11 Citizenship between secularism and Islamism in Turkey

Yılmaz Çolak

Introduction

This chapter aims to provide a map of citizenship-secularism-Islam interactions in republican Turkey. This will be sought through a study of a selection of historical developments and current events. Such a study needs to take into account the cultural dimension of citizenship, focusing on the role of secularism and Islam in determining the boundaries of the public domain in Turkey. In some recent literature on citizenship, the issue of culture has attracted renewed interest, which is true particularly of the debate to expand individual rights to include cultural rights; these would be in addition to formal-institutional rights. These additions would be in order to provide a secure political and social ground for increasing pluralism and diversity via the concept of "cultural citizenship" (Delanty 2002). For example, the current citizenship debate in Turkey has developed around the issue of cultural rights during the last decade. It concerns the new demands of ethnic (Kurdish), religious (Islamic) and sectarian (Alevi) groups for new rights. These demands are the products of a culturally diversifying society and question the claim that Turkish citizenship should be homogeneous, excluding all kinds of differences. Their basic demand here is to be represented "as they are" in the public sphere. This is relevant at first sight to the issue of the cultural dimension of citizenship, although the full settlement of formal (civic, political and social) rights has not been the case in Turkey.

The basic assumption here is that, together with nationalism, Kemalist secularism[1] has played a significant role in establishing the political and cultural basis of Turkish citizenship from the formative decades of the Kemalist regime (1923–45) until today. Thus in this chapter I seek to explore the role of secularism in the formation of Turkish citizenship and the place of Islam in this formation. My main argument is that Kemalist secularism, which has constituted the very meaning of being modern and civilized, and which has operated on the basis of a "specific interpretation of Islam," has played an extremely significant role in the state-centric making of Turkish citizenship. Moreover, it is through the ideology of secularism that the state has always resisted the demands of Islamic groups to expand the scope of

Turkish citizenship in such a way that their cultural identity claims will be included in the public sphere. Here inclusion does not simply mean their prescribed representation in politics, but an official recognition of the Islamic identity and its symbolic and ritualistic practices. Until now Turkey's laic establishment has closed down all political parties that have sought such an inclusion. However, the sociological bases for these Islamic claims and oppositions continue to exist. This is very clear in the recent victory of the AKP (Ak Parti, the Justice and Development Party, founded in 2001 as one of the heirs of the moderate Islamic Welfare-Virtue Party line) in the 2002 elections. It shows us that their emancipating discourse, their endeavor for inclusion, will probably continue.

The making of Turkish citizenship: the clash of Kemalist secularism and Islam?

The making of citizenship was indeed the product of processes of the making of a secular state. Thus secularizing processes shaped Turkish citizens' profile during the early republican era. It is these processes that provide us some basic clues about the decisive factors that determined the status of Turkish citizenship, including to what extent Islam has been essential to that determination. In my view, such an analysis prevents us from making any far-reaching generalization that some reify Kemalist secularism and Islam as two completely hostile, clashing identities. It also requires us to take into consideration the effects of some social dynamics in the context of the state-generated project of modernization from above.

In the years after 1923, although the Ottoman reform movement and ideological formations during the last century of the empire provided a solid background to the sweeping reforms led by the Kemalists (Rustow 1997: 73), the nationalist movement evolved into a movement to construct a modern nation-state with the far-reaching goal of radically transforming Turkish society and culture. The state was proclaimed a republic based on the Turkish nation. It established a new idea of citizenship, first mentioned clearly in the program of the People's Party (Turkey's only political party until 1946) declared in April 1923. It defined its membership to include every person who is born in Turkey or who accepts Turkish culture and citizenship (Tunçay 1992: 58). This idea was adopted in the 1924 constitution, as citizens were defined as all people living within the borders of Turkey. This legal framework was the main part of the nation-building process and provided the first step to establish citizenship as defined by membership of the state and cultural community.

The Turkish reformist rulers formulated the profiles of "new" Turks as "civilized" and "patriotic" citizens (Üstel 1995). This is why these citizens were largely seen as passive subjects who should only perform the "duties" and "responsibilities" expected of them by the state on behalf of the Turkish nation, rather than be seen as having the right to exercise basic individual rights against the state. Each Turkish citizen would be socialized to display a set of civilized manners, a set of "idealized" and "civilized" symbols, images and rituals for a new social personality. That is, Turkish citizenship was primarily based on a "culturalist" approach. This modernist, civilizationist dimension of citizenship was combined with Turkishness, but not simply defined in ethnic terms. The Turks were those who speak Turkish and were Muslim, preferably Sunni Muslim (Kirişci 2000). The Republic inherited a religiously homogeneous society, overwhelmingly Muslim; the Kemalist rulers aimed to transform this population into a "civilized" and "nationalist" whole. The Muslim migrants from the Balkans (Bosnians, Albanians) and the Caucasus were easily naturalized and even accepted as part of the Turkish nation, although non-Muslims (Greeks, Armenians and Jews) living in Turkey were called Turk only in respect of citizenship. Here the rulers attempted to transmute the Muslim millet of the Ottoman Empire into a "civilized" Turkish nation (for such an equation see Karpat 1988: 51–2). For the ruling elite, the transformation of the people's common religious identity into a modern and national one was only possible by means of a secular political and social system.

By defining citizenship status as "patriotic" and "civilized," the republican elites were seeking to form "nationalist" and "secular" citizens. That is why secularism, the outcome of a series of secularization processes, constituted the basis of the official concept of citizenship. Above all else, secularism for the ruling cadre determined the parameters of the formation of "modern" society. It degraded all titles and notions belonging to the traditional, and so it emphasized the secular and the national, rather than religious, affiliation as a legitimizing force. Here secularism, or *laiklik*, implies "lay control over religion" (Davison 1998: 181); and so, for the Kemalist rulers, it was an attempt to control and domesticate Islam by institutionalizing it under state control, which was seen as necessary for the separation of religion from the state. Here lies the uniqueness of Turkish secularism: "The structures and intention exist to use religion in politics (in what elites believe is the interest of the state) as well as to disengage it (for the same reason)" (Davison 1998: 187). Thus, banning the formation of any autonomous association on a religious basis, the ruling cadre put an end to the hegemony of popular notions and practices of Islam. But this does not mean that "Kemalist secularism" opposes religion itself; on the contrary, it even "proposes 'true religion' by seeking to control its content and regulation with a claim to prevent its 'distortions' and 'politicization' " (Mert 2001: 206).

In the quest to eliminate its distorted "reactionary" and "inferior" form, institutional secularization was the first step, which meant to abolish the "traditional strongholds of the institutionalized Islam of the *ulema*." The second was "the secularization of social life and attack on popular Islam." The third was about "the attack on religious symbols and their replacement by the symbols of European civilization" (Zürcher 1993: 194). The first included a set of secularization attempts: the abolition of the Caliphate, the closing of the *medrese* (religious schools) and the unification of education under the secular Ministry of Education, the elimination of both the office of *Şeyh-ül-Islam* and the Ministry of Sheriah (established in 1920) and instead setting up a Religious Affairs Directorate (*Diyanet İşleri Başkanlığı*) under the prime minister, and abolishing the Sheriah courts. All these measures were ratified by the new constitution in 1924. The process was completed with the abolition of religious law and the adoption of *Türk Kanun-i Medenisi* (Turkish Civil Law) in 1926, an adoption of Swiss civil law. By this law, as Bozkurt Mahmut Esat, the minister of justice, stated, "the Turkish nation will be rescued from the false beliefs and traditions which have encumbered our nation during the last thirteen centuries" (quoted in Sherril 1934: 181). It also included the criminal code, outlawing the formation of political parties and social associations based on religion. The next decisive step in the struggle with "ignorant fanaticism" came with a new law (1925) to erase its social roots. By this law, all *tekke* and *zaviye* (dervish lodges and orders) were closed, individuals were prohibited from continuing with all initials (titles and clothes) associated with such institutions, and all *mescid* (small mosques) attached to the orders and all *türbe* (tombs) were closed (*Resmi Gazete* 30 November 1925: 243).

These efforts to secularize society went parallel with the eradication of all symbols belonging to the past, for example the dress code (1925), the adoption of the "international" calendar in place of the Islamic one (1925), the adoption of the Latin alphabet (1928), Turkifying the *ezan* (call to prayer), the ban on *a-la turca* music in the school of music, the adoption of Sunday as the weekly day of rest (1934) and the code on surnames (1934), which were the end products of the cultural crusade against the traditional symbols. One of the most important acts in the symbolic turn was hat reform. The hat was introduced in place of the fez and *sarık* (turban) (*Resmi Gazete* 28 November 1925: 230). This reform was indeed the most significant end product of the Kemalist view that the people's appearance was of utmost importance as a symbol of becoming civilized. The hat was principally valued as an image of modernity. It was part of the official line that the dress of the Turks had to be rooted in the fashions of "civilized" nations. Mustafa Kemal (founder of modern Turkey) on the occasion of introducing the hat in İnebolu proclaimed that if the Turkish people wanted to be modern, they had to be modern in "family life, social life in general, and had to display their being modern by their appearance" (quoted in İmece 1959: 45). Dress lay at the center of the understanding that even private life, with all its forms, should be similar to the social life of the West. These new forms were introduced as the essential symbols of modernity, and had to be followed if one was to access the public sphere and to benefit from the state's facilities.

Women's dress was at the heart of the issue. In the first instance, to be liberated from the chains of "tradition," they had to be freed from the "uncivilized" form of dress, especially from the veil. However, "correction" of the veiling and other elements of women's dress was not carried out in a legislative way as in the case of men's hats. The belief was that, in time, the forward march of culture would bring about the end of the veil and headscarf in social and private realms (Bayur 1939: 264). However, the wives of public servants were requested to be unveiled and dressed like Europeans. Also, it was obligatory for all women employed as officials and all schoolgirls to dress in a "modern" way. In practice, this meant that women dressed in the "traditional" way were deprived of representation at state level and of benefiting from the public sphere.

In 1930, as a result of rising popular reaction to the reforms, the republican rulers realized that the majority of the people, "even in the more advanced parts of the country, did not identify with the new state" (Ahmad 1993: 61). This was the starting point for another phase of secularization and citizenization. To refresh the revolutionary spirit of the Republic, a new ideological orientation began to be used. The name of the ideology was Kemalism.[2] Measures taken at the People's Party congress brought about the merging of state and party; Turkey became a one-party polity. All autonomous organizations were banned. New state-controlled institutions such as the Turkish History Society (which worked to write a history based on a secular past), the Turkish Language Society (which tried to create a value-free Turkish language), and the People's Houses (introducing laic principles and practices to the ordinary people as a nation-wide network of practicing new modes of behavior) were established in 1931. The aim was to gain complete cultural control.

Throughout the 1920s, the ruling elite ended all previous links between religion and socio-political life, especially by putting it under state control. There was little interest in reforming Islam with one exception. A committee of the Istanbul Theology Faculty suggested in 1928 how the prayers and Koran recitation in the mosques could be Turkified (Levonian 1932: 123). After 1930, new ideological regulations "to melt the people's soul into a national whole" were introduced to civilize and nationalize Islam by requiring that the Koran, the ritual and the call to prayer all be in Turkish. This attempt may be considered within the framework of the task of reforming Islam or creating "Turkish Islam." This "enlightened" interpretation of Islam, appearing to be a creation something like Protestantism, was given a role to justify the new reforms at some initial stages of reform.[3] However, in 1932 and 1933 these changes "caused more widespread popular resentment than any of the other secularist measures" (Rustow 1957: 84); so the policy was ended.[4] Nevertheless, the modernizing rulers expected religious beliefs to lose their strength and impact in the course of Westernization. Thus, they did not make any significant reference to Islam in the official discourse until 1945.

İsmet İnönü (1938–50), the successor of Mustafa Kemal Atatürk, maintained his radical secularizing policies during the first half of the 1940s. For example, in 1941 he increased the penalties for violators of the Hat Law and of the prayer call in Turkish (Rustow 1957: 89). Moreover, under his rule there was a large-scale movement to expand secularizing reforms to rural areas by creating the Village Institutes and spreading village schools. These were to turn the peasants into Turkish citizens in their villages by means of establishing strict cultural control (Tonguç 1944).

In sum, initiating such socialization throughout the formative decades of the Republic, the cultural institutions provided the technologies of citizenship formation with a "harmony and unity among different interests." Membership to the Turkish culture meant the internalization of a set of manners manufactured by the institutions. Full citizenship rights were only possible for those who held and internalized these manners. Others were excluded, which means they were deprived of benefiting from the advantages of the state or public services and of participating in the public sphere or democratic representation. Thus rigid boundaries were established between insiders and outsiders. In the official discourse, those who were not able to assimilate into the new culture were deemed as "internal" outsiders (insisting on the norms and manners belonging to the Ottomans, Kurds, Caucasians, Bosnians, Jews, Armenians, *aşiret*s, *tarikat*, etc.). This resulted in a process of internal exclusion; and so "internal" outsiders were pushed away mentally and spatially.

Democratization and the prevailing conservative notion of secularism

In spite of their intentions, the Kemalist ruling cadre during the early republican era (1923–45) failed to provide a widely accepted ethical and cultural base for the formation of their idea of a formal and social citizenship. Instead, the dominant self-understandings of Turkey's citizens were largely determined by the existing sociological conditions. The official ideology failed because at that time Turkish society was still rural-based (only 16 percent of the population lived in towns and cities in 1927) and there was lack of communications and transportation facilities, which prevented the civilizing rulers from mobilizing the masses for the goals of the center. The majority of the population (almost 80 percent) lived within the confines of traditional social relations even in 1945, and remained untouched in large measure by the reformist hands of the state. There then emerged, as Mardin (1998: 219) aptly puts it, a "structural conflict between the secularization of a Kemalist elite and the Islamic everyday life of the provinces and the villages." The democratization process which was initiated in 1946 was an attempt on the part of the civilizing rulers to take into account this everyday reality.

In that sense, during the democratic transition period (1946–50) İnönü, the leader of the ruling party (the RPP), decided to make some changes to official religious policy, primarily on the basis of spreading the "enlightened" version of Islam. These changes were of course more closely related to the campaign of the opposition Democrat Party (DP), emphasizing the idea of religion as the people's beliefs and values. The RPP government introduced an optional religious course in primary schools, established *İmam-Hatip* schools and a Theological Faculty at Ankara University, and opened the mausoleums of the Ottoman dynasty (Ahmad 1993: 107–8). This attempt to liberalize the society and remove constraints over the practice of Islam was not seen as contrary to the official secularist view that preached a "modernist" interpretation of Islam. This interpretation of Islam saw the secular state as a requirement of Islam itself.

Nevertheless, in order to mobilize voters and citizens, the opposition DP made the religious issue a chief item of debate by stressing the significance of local-Islamic traditions and continuities with the Ottoman-Islamic heritage (coupled with a keen interest in the Ottoman Empire among some political and intellectual elites as contrary to the Kemalist history thesis). The DP, when it came to power with an overwhelming majority in 1950, maintained and expanded the scope of the above-mentioned policy. Its first deed was to allow the call to prayer to be in Arabic. Later it made it possible for religious instruction in the primary schools and for religious radio broadcasts. Except for these changes, however, the DP government, devoted as it was to a "correct interpretation of Kemalism," did not depart from RPP policies. This was for three reasons: "the quest for a secure foundation of common morality, the need for a unified front against Communism, and the never-ending competition for electoral success" (Rustow 1957: 97). Consequently, the most important development in this period was the official acceptance of Islam, and even some traditional forms, by both the state elite and the politicians as part of Turkish identity. At the same time the DP rulers and the state officials grew used to the alternative, or counter-hegemonic, Islamic movements and symbols.

Nevertheless, there were some differences in perception of the appropriate role of Islam in society. These became part of the definition of secularism. As mentioned above, the Democrats came to power by utilizing the existing complaints against the previous single party's radical secularizing reforms. They did this by adopting a new, "conservative" interpretation of Kemalist secularism that aimed to reconcile as far as possible the principles of the laic state and the masses' conservative leanings (Mert 2001: 207). For this conservative critique, secularism is not a problem itself. The Turkish state's idea and implementation of secularism seemed to be more akin to French Jacobin laicism. Here the conservative imagination intended to harmonize state and religion once again, which was chiefly necessary to hinder the "communist threat." This was based on the belief that the nationalization of secularism is necessary, because religion is an indivisible part of patriotism and national identity (Mert 2001: 208). The "conservative interpretation" that has put its stamp on Turkish politics until today would make Turkish citizens both "national" and "religious." This intends to foster national unity against both "external" and "internal" threats. This tendency in the 1970s turned into an ideological search for what was called the Turkish-Islamic synthesis. It was first formulated by a group of right-wing intellectuals, the *Aydınlar Ocağı* (The Hearth of the Enlightened) and later in the 1980s, under the guidance of the generals of the 1980 coup, they achieved a semi-official status. Indeed, as Taşkın and Bora (2001: 545) argue, the Turkish-Islamic synthesis that combined traditional elements with the "authoritarian-statist" core of Kemalism is a conservative or "right-Kemalist perspective."

The multi-party politics and the democratization and structural changes in the 1950s gave way to a small Islamic revival, while constituting a very small section of the population. That revival gave rise to the first signs of Islamic intellectuals and of alternative social and communitarian networks in the cities that were accelerated by the mass migrations.[5] So, in response to the laic state and its policies, newly formed Islamic groups developed an Islamic critique of Kemalist secularism. But, as Mert (2001: 207) puts it, the new Islamism treated the Kemalist policies as contrary to "democracy" and "religious freedom."

DP rule was ended in 1960 by the military intervention. One of the reasons highlighted by the initiators of the coup was the Democrats' accommodating attitude and policies toward religious activities. These were judged to be dangerous by the civil and military bureaucrats to Kemalist secularism.[6] Thus, the state elite sought to establish control over the politicians through checking mechanisms: instituting the National Security Council and the Constitutional Court and strengthening the presidency. In such ways, the leaders of the coup aimed to prevent the use of the religion for "political" purposes. At the same time, they again used what they might call "true Islam" to legitimize their military-political regime and also to prevent the spread of communism and religious reactionism. In this regard, believing in the necessity of "enlightened" Islam as delineated during the first decade of the Republic, General Cemal Gürsel, the leader of the junta, said that "the cause of our backwardness is not our religion but those who have misrepresented our religion to us" (quoted in Cizre-Sakallıoğlu 1996: 239). The act of representing (official) Islam, an end product of Kemalist secularism, was indeed the will to shape the soul of the citizens, most of whom lived within the framework of traditional, conservative-Islamic networks. Such an understanding of secularism anticipates the later understanding of "civilized" social groups in a democratic system as being made legitimate by the centralist bureaucratic elite interventions into democratic processes (Çolak and Aydın, 2004). This attitude was also obvious in the reconstruction attempts of the 1971, 1980 and 1997 military interventions.

However, Turkey's age-old cleavage and structural conflict between the secular state elite and the value system of the provincial and peripheral forces made those attempts fail. The "peripheral forces that continued to command an electoral majority" (Özbudun 2000: 35) determined the direction of the democratic process. This is illustrated by the rise of the Justice Party (the JP, 1961–80) as the heir of the DP. It emphasized a more moderate, "conservative" interpretation of secularism that took into consideration some Islamic symbols and rituals of the masses. Therefore, although the JP maintained its loyalty to the state elite's sensitivity on the "political use" of Islam by going beyond state control and propagating its official interpretation of Islam, the party expanded religious education by increasing the number of *İmam-Hatip* schools and established an organic relationship with "illegitimate" religious orders and communities (Cizre-Sakallıoğlu 1996: 239–40). This "double discourse" increased the suspicions of the bureaucratic elite, especially the military, about the JP. This was one of the reasons for the 1971 and 1980 interventions. During the late 1960s and early 1970s, the JP began to lose its binding force on right-wing politics, especially among the more conservative and nationalist factions. Thus, for the first time in the history of the Republic, one faction of the Islamic groups formed a serious political movement, namely Erbakan's National Salvation Party (the NSP). This party became a coalition partner in the governments of the 1970s. These Islamic groups, like the leftist and nationalist ones, benefited more and more from the 1961 constitution's clear recognition of the right of association. Unlike "conservative secularism," its proponents rejected the basic tenets of Kemalist modernization and proposed an "alternative" identity based on Islam, not a secular world-view. In fact, it was the first serious political struggle over the identity of the Turkish citizen.

The 1980 military intervention signified a new stage in the process of secularization. It was in such a manner that the generals of the coup intended to extend the scope of the previous state elite's efforts to spread official Islam. The 1982 constitution brought about compulsory religious courses in primary and secondary schools and also taught the significance of the Turks' historical, secular and moral values. Thus, in their view, it would be possible to avoid a "moral void" that would be filled by Marxism and Islamic fanaticism. These efforts attempted to propagate a depoliticized, Turkish, Islamic culture. It drew on the earlier idea of "Turkish-Islamic synthesis – that is, that Islam was part of Turkish national culture. ... As a result, officially supported Sunni Islam appears to have been co-opted as a pro-status-quo force, acting as a support rather than a threat to state authority" (Hale 1994: 298–9). Thus, state control over religious education and indoctrination in a new doctrine of co-optation based on the Turkish-Islamic synthesis sought to eliminate the effects and importance of the "reactionary" religious currents in education and socio-political life. Indeed, this is not contrary to the general trend of Kemalist secularism; it used "enlightened" or "modern" Turkish Islam to make strong the ties among citizens. The state elite therefore maintained the well-known struggle against religio-social movements and their "alternative" symbolic world in the name of a war on *irtica* (reactionism), i.e. it used its understanding of Islam politically against what it called "political Islam." It was evident in President Evren's (head of the 1980 coup) insistence on the ban on women wearing headscarves because that was seen as a significant sign of the public reality and visibility of Islamic groups.

In defining the boundaries of citizenship at the official level, Islam had become most important before 1980, with its functional and pragmatic areas as social cement. This importance was confirmed in the post-1980 period by the efforts of the military and the Motherland Party (MP) under the leadership of Turgut Özal. Özal, the initiator of neo-liberalism in the 1980s, embarked on a new plan to integrate some of the religious and nationalist extremists into the center and to moderate them with center-right politics. It was based on a wide ideological spectrum under which conservative, nationalist, liberal and even some left-liberal inclinations would come together. The most important implication for secularism and citizenship in the MP's formulation was its effort to make the conservative "silent majority" (previously on the cultural periphery) part of mainstream politics (Taşkın and Bora 2001: 541). Here it seems possible to claim that Özal's MP went beyond the official recognition of Islam as part of Turkish culture in terms of a specific, "enlightened" form (free from traditional elements). His synthesis expressed the combination of political and economic rationality on the one hand and traditional, Islamic cultural forms on the other. In this regard, though he stressed that "our state is secular," he also said that "what holds our nation together, what serves in a most powerful way in our national cohesiveness and what plays the essential role is Islam" (quoted in Waxman 2000: 17).[7] It seems obvious that the meaning Özal attributed to Islam was that it belonged to the realm of civil society. Next he strove to bridge the gap between the state and civil society.

Attributing a positive role to faith in a modern society and to the revival of religious feeling, Özal writes:

> The Turk is aware that faith, in itself, is not necessarily in conflict with secularism, does not prevent him from being rational. ... In life today, there is no difference in this respect between a European Christian and a Turkish Muslim. Thus a synthesis has been realized between the West and Islam, a synthesis which has put an end to the identity crisis of the Turk. I am a believer and yet I can afford to be open to all changes.
>
> (Özal 1991: 297)

There was no longer any necessary conflict between being Muslim and being a citizen of the secular state. To set an example, he was the first president of the Republic publicly to attend Friday prayers at the mosque and fast during Ramadan. This attitude was also very apparent in the policies of some ministers of his cabinet who introduced Friday prayers and the closing of staff restaurants during Ramadan. These acts attracted harsh criticism from the secular Kemalists throughout the 1980s.

The MP under Özal also took a different attitude to the banning of headscarves worn by female university students from the secular Kemalist elite. Rejecting the view of the secular Kemalists that the headscarf is simply a symbol of rising Islamic "reactionism" against the secular regime, Özal saw it as a matter of individual rights: "At a time when Turkey, as a democratic country, has applied for full membership in the EC, blowing the issue of what people should wear out of all proportion disturbs me very much" (quoted in Dağı 2001: 36). Özal's policies, evolving to some extent around democratic freedoms and human rights, aimed to expand the scope of official notions of both secularism and citizenship through the search for ways to integrate the religiously conservative masses and Kurdish ethnic groups into mainstream politics. That is why the death of Özal, who "symbolized the integration of Islamically-oriented groups into the centre and co-optation by the secular state" (Toprak 1995: 95), in 1993, and the general crisis of center-right politics in a globalizing context, gave way to a void that began to be filled by political Islam developing around the Welfare Party (*Refah Partisi*, the WP), the successor of the pro-Islamist NSP of the 1970s, under the leadership of Necmettin Erbakan.

Globalization and the rise of Islamism as a counter-hegemonic movement

The economic and political liberalization of the Özal era gave way to a form of a religious renaissance that was apparent in the grand gesture of new urban social, political and economic networks and institutions, based on Islamic affiliation. It is actually synchronic with processes of globalization in which transnational forces from above and identity politics from below have brought about an erosion of ideas of nation and citizenship based on a unique identity rooted in national sovereignty. It has given rise to wars between cultures dominating political and social life all over the world. For Turkey the result was an extensive crisis of the state's official ideology, Kemalism, which intended to form a homogeneous and secular nation (Yavuz 2000). Thus the group identity-based social and political movements, namely Islamic, Kurdish and Alevi, in the late 1980s and the early 1990s began to question the basic assertions of Kemalism.[8] In this period the citizenship debate was essentially related to the effects of globalization on Turkey, and the rise of identity politics that occurred especially around constitutional citizenship, to provide a common identity based on the constitution (İçduygu and Keyman 2000). In the sense of Turkey's Islamist movement, as Gülalp (2001) puts it, the rise of Islamism as a political critique of modern universal principles and a search for authentic religious identity was the outcome of the "global crisis of modernism." In these processes, not only the legitimacy crisis of Kemalist secularism, but, perhaps most importantly, that of its "conservative" variants promoted by "right Kemalism," accelerated on the part of the Islamists the questioning of the official notion of citizenship that excludes those who deviate from the secular "mainstream."

Globalization is an ongoing process, creating both losers and winners all over the world. In Turkey, Islamism rose as a movement that represents new provincial businessmen, intellectuals and poor segments of society who are excluded from economic, social and political power (Öniş 2001). What was happening at this point in Turkey, in the context of the weakening of the welfare state and the state's official ideology, was the rejection of the conventional understanding of citizenship by socially and economically marginalized groups who were also not allowed to exercise full social and political rights. Under such circumstances, it appeared very easy for the Islamically-oriented groups, by using its emerging social base, to turn various traditional religious positions (largely represented previously by the center-right parties) into a more effective political tool for action in the 1990s. There has emerged a set of social networks of Islamic groups in which religious traditions are reinterpreted and disseminated and young people learn "real Islam." They accomplish the role of social insurance institutions, and these are coupled with the growth of business and "counter"-elite organizations that can use mass communications effectively. The major end product of this trend has been the emergence of "alternative" public spaces in which many of the conservative masses have begun to socialize within a very different set of values and forms. In these spaces, new bodies politic, new kinds of eating, new fashions and artistic styles, are displayed and disseminated (Göle 2000: 30). It is indeed a real challenge to the modernist ideology and state policy that only the "Westernized" way of life woven around "legitimate" (i.e. modern) cultural codes is a necessary precondition for public visibility. To the extent that the Islamic sectors maintain their autonomous communal life, they are seeking ways to push the state to recognize and institutionalize their view of "Islam," even to "conquer" the state as a counter-hegemonic movement.

The Welfare Party during the mid-1990s became the political voice of the excluded, especially the traditionalist religious segments of the society that were closely linked to the religious renaissance stimulated by the liberalization and globalization that occurred during Özal's time. It successfully mobilized these segments for the sake of its political and cultural program. The social base the WP relied on comprised a wide spectrum: "Islamic institutions including newspapers and publishing houses, numerous Islamic foundations, an Islamist labor union, and an Islamist businessmen's association" (Gülalp 2001: 434). Using a much more populist rhetoric with a cross-class demands, the WP tried to unite the peripheral businessmen and urban poor and workers around a "common Islamic identity."[9] Thus, by combining religious, class, and social interests, the WP's ideology aimed to challenge the secular establishment. It promoted a form, as Tuğal (2002) argues, of "religio-moral populism," articulating different social interests and religious enthusiasms, with a "moral criticism of modernity." Beside its emphasis on a just order and equality for the excluded, it promised to make legitimate their "religious" symbols and rituals (such as clothing, including the headscarf) and to arrange official working days in accordance with Islamic worship. In other words, the promise was mainly to restore the Turks' real, Islamic, identity. This message was effectively launched with the help of the party's nation-wide grassroots organization. Their goal in the long run was to transform people's way of life and to pave the way for a new "Islamic" society (Gülalp 2001: 434).

So WP leaders presented themselves as representatives of the true "values," not simply the "interests," of "the society" currently dominated by the "authoritarian," laic state. They saw themselves as the carriers of faith and morals against the faithless state's oppressive rule.[10] In this way they strove to "re-institute" the people's values and symbols, to reshape Turkish citizens as members of a religious-moral community. Although its ideology aims at establishing "Islamization" processes in social and political life, it is ambiguous in its program, as Özbudun (2000: 87) writes, as to "whether the WP seriously intends to establish an Islamic state based on the *Shari'a* or would be satisfied with [merely] symbolic [changes] in some areas of social life." If we look at the nature of WP supporters, many seem to be very pragmatic, willing to use populist policies to gain support among the masses. Surveys (in 1995 and 1996) conducted among WP supporters show that almost half of the voters voted for the WP for non-ideological reasons.[11]

28 February: a secularist restoration of citizenship

When the WP won the 1995 elections and became the leading party in the WP-TPP (True Path Party) coalition government in 1996, one of the most serious political crises of the Republic occurred. It was a crisis between the elected regime on the one hand and the state elite and secular social groups on the other. The WP pragmatically promised to obey the rules of the game, even before the 1995 elections. Its leaders voiced their support of "right Kemalism." However, their different view of secularism insisted on the use of some symbols, symbols that Kemalists see as harmful to "civilized" and laic citizens, for their own identity. Thus, WP ministers maintained a responsible attitude toward government affairs. However, they were also seen to make some provocative symbolic acts, especially to please the party's radical supporters.

In fact, what is significant for the Kemalist establishment is that for the first time in the Republic's history, a political leader with Islamic inclinations became prime minister and put into practice a number of measures not desired by the Kemalists. When the WP was in government, a Kemalist bloc – including the military, the judiciary, a large group of intellectuals, the mainstream secular media and some civil societal elements more sensitive on the issue of "Islamic reactionism" – began to work together to resist the threat they considered to be posed by the WP's policies, for example the

WP's emphasis on removing the ban on headscarves, the project to build a mosque at Taksim, the attendance of religious leaders in religious dress to Ramadan dinner at the residence of the prime minister, and the prohibition on alcoholic beverages in municipalities controlled by the WP.[12]

Indeed, it seemed there was a chance that the secularist groups would revitalize their Kemalist spirit, one that had faced a serious legitimacy crisis in the post-Cold War era. Unlike the previous period, after the Cold War the Kemalists decided to organize vertically (i.e become deep-rooted in the society), as well as horizontally, on the basis of a political program aimed to "save modern, secular and national Turkey." This was indeed a turning point for Kemalism. Once again, the Kemalism that the secular establishment prefers to call "Ataturkism" became more visible around a simple symbolism that turned into an excercise of re-identification for the Kemalists, not only among the ruling secular circles, but also among secular social groups outside the state's structure (Yeğen 2001: 70–1). In the context of processes of neo-liberal globalization necessitating democracy, human rights and freedoms, and as a reaction to the claims and demands of various social and communal identities, in the 1990s the Kemalist elite put into use a large-scale social engineering program on the bases of the early Kemalist reforms, to transmute Kemalism into a social identity. However, in the end, such an act poses a dilemma for them, especially "in times of crises when the priority shifts from a Western style government to 'protection and safeguarding of the state and Kemalist reforms', during which the Westernization project can temporarily be postponed for the future" (Dağı 2001: 30).

Once again the military, by launching a nation-wide campaign on behalf of the Kemalist bloc and effectively using the National Security Council (NSC), intervened in the democratic process in 1997. This was publicly known as the 28 February process. This process again militarized Turkish politics and resulted in the "indirect" intervention against the Islamic groups, dubbed a "postmodern intervention" by its initiators (*Milliyet*, 15 January 2001). The initiators of 28 February claimed that they were restoring Western/modern ways through saving democracy and protecting young's "fresh brains" from reactionaries (Gökmen 2002). The NSC's decisions announced on 28 February 1997 returned secularization to every aspect of public and social life. The decisions included legislation and other measures to reduce the political and social visibility of the Islamic-oriented groups (for the decisions see Şahin 1997). They re-instituted state control over especially religion and education, which would protect the citizens of the Republic from "anti-secular" forms of life.[13] In the eyes of the civil and military bureaucrats who denied they were "anti-Islamic" (Şahin 1997: 123), the WP with its emphasis on an "archaic" interpretation of Islam and its traditional symbols was the source of all reactionary movements (*irtica*).

Therefore, that "national threat" (Bora 1999: 132) to the integrity and unity of the state and the nation they attempted to eliminate by the spread of official Islam. Here lies the search for an enlightened religion suited to the

Turkish citizens. The hope that schoolchildren would internalize it via compulsory state-sponsored Islamic religious and moral instruction in public 8-year primary schools and high schools. It seeks to teach Islam in a way that would support the secular state. In the 28 February process, there was significant official support for the attempts by Yaşar Nuri Öztürk (a popular, modernist professor of the Istanbul Theology Faculty) to make Islam "more simple," "contemporary" and "Turkish." One of his traditionalist-conservative critics calls him "a quasi-official modern *mehdi*" (the Muslim messiah) with a mission to spread "true Islam" (Mete 2001). He brought about a new interpretation of the Koran on the basis of "reason" and "science" by attacking many of the traditional religious institutions (the *tarikat* – dervish orders) and traditional symbols, for example stressing that wearing the headscarf was not a religious obligation, and decreasing the number of prayers per day (for his recent views see Sazak 2002). During the mid-1990s, the efforts to join the Alevi sect with Turkish nationalism or take its support in the name of the state may be regarded as a similar thing. Being interested in Alevilik due to its openness to secularism, the Kemalist perspective defines it as Turkish Islam ("Anatolian Islam") free from Persian-Arabic influence and befitting real Turkish people's culture (Bora 1999: 120; and also see Aktay 1999). Nevertheless, Sunni Islam, the official sect, has maintained its influence on Turkish secularism. The Alevis, whose interpretation of Islam is excluded by the Religious Directorate as being "heretical" and "deviant" have always been critical of the state's Sunni nature and the rise of Islamic politics in the last decade. Thus, the Alevis began to refuse compulsory religious instruction in primary and secondary education. In the campaign against Islamic groups through the second half of the 1990s, the Alevis took an active role by participating in social and public rallies and in organizations led by the Kemalist bloc. In fact that participation gave a little bit of official recognition and visibility for the Alevi groups and organizations, for example the *Cem Evi* (the Alevis' place of worship).

The measures of the 28 February process under the guidance of the civil and military bureaucracy brought about a series of political bans lasting to this day. First the WP-TPP government was ended by pressure from the military-led coalition in June 1997 and then accused of being at the center of all anti-secular activity. The Constitutional Court closed down the Welfare Party in January 1998 and its leading cadre, including Erbakan, was banned from politics for five years. The Virtue Party (*Fazilet Partisi*, the VP), the successor of the WP, became the third party in the 1999 elections. It was closed down in January 2001 mainly because it defended the wearing of the headscarf in public. The reason behind the closure of the two parties becomes more meaningful in relation to the general tendency of the Turkish Constitutional Court's decisions in political party cases. As Aslan (2002: 11) aptly argues, the dominant approach is "ideology-based" in all decisions that express a "positivist, one-dimensional, monolithic, and authoritarian outlook" and ignore individual rights. In the decision regarding the WP, it was seen as the center of reactionary activity. In that decision the Court defined secularism as the guarantor of contemporary political, social and cultural life, and thus it cannot be sacrificed for "the sake of liberties" (Aslan 2002: 16–17). This legal framework represents the will to protect the secular state and society from "reactionary movements" and also sets the limits for Turkish citizens' exercise of civil, political and cultural rights. It therefore restricts the possibility of people with different religious understandings and practices being represented in the state. The current state elite, in the name of speaking for the people, maintains a very narrow policy of representation.

The re-secularization process launched on 28 February 1997 aimed to regulate public and social life. It enforces some restrictions on "non-authorized" religious appearances and expressions in state offices and state-run institutions, including the universities. In 1998 Turkey's Higher Educational Board expanded the ban on Islamic dress and symbols in educational institutions by new regulations.[14] The NSC and the military sought to revive the ban on participation in dervish orders and religious communities and other quasi religio-social orders that had been banned officially since the 1920s, but which had become largely tolerated. To this end the activities of many of religious foundations have been inspected and controlled periodically.[15] All acts of controlling and monitoring are very clearly documented in a report on the "Strategies of Struggle with Reactionism" presented to the NSC in June 2001 (*Radikal*, 30 June 2001). This report also documents the state's interactions with leading figures of the dervish orders (*tarikat*) and sects to keep their loyalty to the state. All these groups were persuaded to accept the rules of the state or to become "statist." This move to monitor religious citizens sometimes led to mass arrests. For example, in May 2002, a group of people were arrested while engaged in making *zikir* (the mystical practice of repeating, silently or loudly, the word Allah). They were accused of being members of a banned mystic order called *Hakikat* (*Radikal*, 15 May 2002). The scope of monitoring was even expanded to include how photographs should be stamped on the ID card. For example, the Prime Ministry General Directorate of Population and Citizenship in November 2001 required all local governments to report ID numbers of those with "turbaned" (*sarıklı*) ID cards (*Hürriyet*, 20 November 2001). The elimination of such types of "alternative," "illegitimate" religious practices and symbols is part of the official quest to form a "modernized" Islam.

The transformation in Islamic perspectives on secularism and citizenship

Unlike the Welfare Party, its heir, the Virtue Party adopted more moderate rhetoric. It emphasized democratization, individual rights and liberties, and the necessity of EU membership. In fact such an attitude might be seen as a form of tactical discourse to survive under the political system of a Kemalist regime that also drew its legitimacy from an idea of democracy, however limited. The difference between the two parties, particularly regarding the issues of secularism and citizenship, is very evident in the programs of the WP (1995) and the VP (1999) (Öniş 2001: 288). The WP program emphasizes mainly social rights and the freedom to practice religion. It sought a collective identity for all citizens, but not individual civil rights. Islamic sensibilities and practices took an important place in its program by defining Turkey as primarily a Muslim country. Though rejecting the Kemalist secular formulation of Islam, the WP with counter-hegemonic premises seemed to adopt its notion of the collective as a whole, but in much more religious terms. Nevertheless, in the Virtue Party program, a major emphasis was placed on individual and human rights. The primary motive for extending democratic rights was to defend religious freedoms. The VP's view of secularism, associated with a liberal interpretation of Islam, appeared to be more close to the Anglo-Saxon formulation of secularism based on the strict separation between religion and the state. The VP began to work according to a new strategy to co-exist with the secular state (Öniş 2001). Nevertheless, in February 2001 it was closed down by the Constitutional Court, which relied on the charge that it was only a continuation of the Welfare Party, given its support for the right to wear headscarves. Its two successors – *Saadet Partisi* (the Felicity Party) founded by Erbakan's close friends in 2001, and the AKP, founded under the leadership of Recep Tayyip Erdoğan, the former mayor of Istanbul – also adopted this strategy of co-existence. Although the AKP in particular seems to be undistinguishable from other center-right parties, both new parties see secularism as necessary to guarantee religious freedoms and individual rights (*Hürriyet*, 9 August 2001). In a general sense, "co-existence" envisions the emergence of multiple and alternative social forms including different life styles, different patterns of consumption and diverse modes of behavior based on different moral principles. At first glance, all these policies appear to work as co-existence strategies. But it has not been so easy for the secular establishment to believe that they are genuine, given its understanding of the past, if we take into account the previous interventions, especially the events of 28 February 1997. The main reason for 28 February was the public presence of new Islamic groups and the expansion of new social and public spaces over which the existing secular state claims authority.

The above transformations seem to be intimately associated with globalization processes and the nature of group-identity politics. They also follow from the emancipating discourse stimulated by the 28 February process. It stems from the changing "realities of the globalizing world" that make "*identification*, a never-ending, always incomplete, unfinished and open-ended activity in which we all, by necessity or by choice, are engaged" (Bauman 2001: 482). In the case of Turkey, as a result of these globalization processes and their democratizing effects, the diverse attempts to find an

Islamic identity have given rise to a cultural movement that also accepts a kind of secularization process (Kahraman 2001a; 2001b). Nowadays, almost all Islamic groups defend the separation between state and religion and look for safe, suitable spaces in the country's civil society.[16] The Islamic movement is moving from a conflict-centered view of communal identity to more privatized life-politics of integration. This is very evident in the case of the AKP (Bayramoğlu 2001). At this point one might argue that this movement is linked to the "neo-Islamic" claim that there is a right to a separate identity considered within the framework of human rights and global values. Relying on that claim, Islamic circles are calling more loudly for the right to active political participation and more toleration of their symbols and rituals.

After its establishment, the AKP became gradually the voice of "neo-Islamic" demands, placing a strong emphasis on the synthesis between democratic values and traditional-Islamic ones. In fact, that characteristic brings it closer to Özal's MP. In the 2002 elections it received 34 percent of the votes and gained an overwhelming majority, with 363 seats in the 550-member parliament. It seems clear that AKP's victory was partly the result of past failures of all center-right and center-left political parties to cope with Turkey's major economic and political problems. AKP leaders have promised to solve problems caused by widespread corruption, decadence and poverty on the one hand, and to guarantee effective human rights for each citizen on the other. While its pragmatic leaders seem to have adopted a discourse of loyalty to the limits set by the secular establishment for the hegemony of the Kemalist regime, they are dealing with the headscarf issue and the state's control over religion instead on the basis of tolerance and individual rights. Rejecting an exclusive "Islamic" identity diminishes the possibility of a social and political cleavage developing. Instead they see the AKP as a "conservative democratic" party. In this respect, they claim to have the mission of combining Islam both with democracy and modernity, a "Turkish model" for the rest of the Islamic world in the wake of the 11 September 2001 attacks on the United States. According to the AKP's program, all issues relating the state to religion should be settled by a public consensus that is only possible through democratic practices. Thus, Turkey's proposed EU membership is of great importance for the AKP's leadership. It is seen as an emancipatory mechanism to establish a consolidated democratic regime and to help to expand the democratic rights to be enjoyed by Turks. That is why the AKP government immediately initiated a state-wide and international campaign to receive a clear date for membership negotiations with the EU.

The "multi-judiciary order debate" and the question of headscarves: an Islamic dilemma of multiculturalism?

Generally speaking, the Islamism of the 1990s seemed to defend "communal" rights of the "Muslims" *vis-à-vis* the secular state. At first glance it appeared as a question of multiculturalism. The "Islamic" demand for communal rights indeed finds its clear expression in a project called the "multi-judiciary order" that denotes an Islamic view of multiculturalism. The WP leaders, both in opposition and in government, supported that project, which was mentioned as one of the reasons behind the closure of the WP; "to justify its judgment, the Court cited Erbakan's public statements, such as 'you shall have the right to opt for whatever law you want' (legal pluralism)" (Aslan 2002: 17). The idea of a "multi-judiciary order" was first developed on the basis of the "Medina Document" by a group of Islamic intellectuals, especially Ali Bulaç, as an alternative political project, or more particularly an alternative model of citizenship to both Kemalist monism and liberal democracy. It is mainly about the Islamic communitarian view of multiculturalism in the age of identity politics, which envisions the emergence and survival of autonomous, legal communities (Muslim, Christian, Jewish, and atheist) with their own "religious" or "secular" laws. These laws would protect and maintain the collective cultural identity of each individual seen as member of the community chosen by each individual. So freedoms would be meaningful within these autonomous, homogeneous bodies. In fact, a hierarchical ordering among different communal bodies is proposed. Some communities are seen as inherently more virtuous, or faithful than others – as is Islam over secular or other non-Muslims. But nowadays, as Akyol (2001) notes, even Ali Bulaç, the main theoretician of this proposed perspective, is placing less emphasis on "living as a community" and thus also having a "multi-judiciary system." Leaving aside that exclusionary system of formal pluralism, there is more and more talk using the liberal notion of multiculturalism.

In the 28 February process, there was a widespread move to ban the wearing of religious dress in state institutions and services, including universities. For the Kemalist rulers, right from the beginning there has been no place for any kind of religious or traditional garb in a "modern" way of life. But since the early 1980s, the debate on the headscarf has plagued Turkish politics. On this issue there are two dominant views: first, common among the state elite and some secular intellectual circles, the headscarf is a symbol of "challenge" to the principles of the Republic and a rejection of "civilized" forms (e.g. women's emancipation, a secularized public, freedom); that is why it is divisive. This attitude seems to have been shaped by the Constitutional Court's judgment on the closure of the VP. It pointed out the party's emphasis on the freedom to wear headscarves. It saw women with headscarves in the public realm as contrary to the Kemalist principle of secularism, and also took the view that a party that defends the freedom to wear headscarves must also be seen as acting against secularism (Berkan 2001).[17] According the second view, offered by liberal and Islamic groups, headscarves provide a way for traditional women to participate in both social and public life. Religious women also use it as a cultural marker to differentiate themselves from the rest. As part of the search to "expand the public space allowed to Islam," Islamic feminists seek to "work in public services and attend universities with their head covered" (Arat 2000: 119).

At that point, as Keyman (2000: 35) aptly argues, the question of headscarves becomes part of the "citizenship debate." He argues that the conventional wisdom of citizenship based on a separation between public and private spaces cannot meet the demands of some new social movements and of some changing socio-political structures. Thus, "when we say that different cultural identities may show themselves off in the public realm (e.g. by wearing a headscarf), we should regard it as the rights of citizenship" (Keyman 2000: 35). Like the "multi-judiciary order" debate, it may be considered as a demand for a right to a collective cultural identity within the confines of existing, but blurred, "religious communities." However, like all new re-articulations of Islamic demands in "neo-Islamic discourse," the headscarf issue is coming more and more to be seen as an individualized or privatized matter, as a human right to articulate different cultural identities and forms.

Conclusion

One of the most debated issues regarding the consolidation of democratic government in Turkey throughout the 1990s is the representation of ethnic groups and religious communities. The official attitude, signifying the exclusion of groups with alternative cultural claims from the political sphere, might be defined as a hegemonic policy of representation largely inspired by Jacobin logic. Kemalist secularism coupled with the passive and obedient, rather than rights-bearing, notion of republican citizenship, has been at the center of the problem of democratic representation. Secularism here turns into a mechanism for preaching about what constitutes a good ("civilized") life and also for an "enlightened Turkish Islam" that would strengthen ties among citizens. It is apparent that the internalization of these center's values and their religious perspective until recently provided the way for any individual to receive the full benefits of citizenship (civil, political, and cultural) rights. In fact it is this view that has hindered the provision of inclusive policies that would also address the needs of religious groups with different understandings of Islam. Without a doubt, such internal exclusion is the main reason for the age-old tension and division between the secular state and the religious masses.

The debate was stimulated in the 1990s by Islamist claims to collective rights, which challenged the Turkish state's conventional idea of citizenship. The struggle between Islamic and secular groups has dominated the Turkish political scene during the last decade, and has evolved over the question of who shall control the statecraft for the formation of their own notion of citizenry. Intolerant of the public visibility of religious groups who introduced alternative symbolic and organizational forms to the country's public sphere, Kemalist secularism became the prime motive for 28 February's restoration movement. It launched another tide of internal exclusion. As in the case of the headscarf, public policies control the access of religious women to some public services. Such cultural preferences have set the limits of equitable access and opportunities. At the beginning of the millennium, the trend among Islamic groups and politicians is to adopt the basic rule that the needs of the individual should be protected against the state. In a new form of life politics, more privatized and individualized than the previous counter-hegemonic demands, that quest for democratic (mainly political and cultural) rights includes the recognition and representation of their symbols and socio-cultural organizations. This tendency might be seen as a starting point for the mutual secularization of both Islamic groups and the Kemalist state. In fact, what is needed for the consolidation of today's Turkish democracy is a more mature, democratic secularism that includes tolerant religious groups.

Notes

1 The Turkish word for secularism is *laiklik*, drawn from the French *laicisme*. Turkish *laiklik* has its own peculiarities, and differs from both Anglo-Saxon secularism and French laicism (see Davison 1998). In this study I prefer to use the term "secularism," as in Kemalist or Turkish secularism, to express its official understanding, while emphasizing its uniqueness.

2 Kemalism came into existence first at the Third Republican People's Party Congress in 1931 and continued to be developed throughout the 1930s. As a "political discourse" it both described the boundaries of politics and provided the standard for judging attitudes in every sphere of social life.

3 Mustafa Kemal was opposed, as one of the foreign observers reported, "only to those features of the religion which he regards as backward or as interfering with the complete dedication of the citizen to his nation. … If religion can help in achieving this goal (the establishment of an enlightened modern state), well and good. If not, let it step aside" (Allen 1934: 117–18).

4 This is also observed in education: *İmam-Hatip* (Imam-Preacher) schools and the Istanbul Theology Faculty were closed in 1933; and, although optional courses in religion existed in primary schools until 1935, there was no compulsory public religious teaching in the public primary and secondary schools (Reed 1957: 111, 122).

5 For the role of democratization in the emergence of new localized networks of communities, see Aktay (1999).

6 For Özbudun (2000: 31–2) this reaction was the result of the "conflict between the DP and public bureaucracy." Beside this, the other two reasons for the breakdown of democracy were the nature of the DP as a coalition of anti-RPP forces (leaving little room for the opposition) and the diminished social status and political influence of the civil and military bureaucracy under DP rule.

7 For modern societies he therefore underlined three main freedoms as necessary for being a civilized nation: "freedom of thought and speech, freedom of religion together with secularism as its guarantee, and freedom of enterprise" (Özal 1991: 311).

8 Identity politics dominated the Turkish political scene in the 1990s. This was clearly seen in the 1995 and 1999 general elections:

> The three parties representing three different identities – the Welfare Party, representing the Islamic identity; the Nationalist Action Party, representing the ultranationalist Turkish identity; and the People's Democracy Party, representing the Kurdish identity – gained a combined total of approximately one-third of the votes. There is also a growing identity consciousness among the Alevis, who do not have their own party but play an important role within the RPP.
>
> (Özbudun 2000: 142)

This type of trend is also to a greater extent true of the 1999 elections.

9 For example, a voluntary association of rising peripheral businessmen, "MÜSİAD," writes Gülalp (2001: 439), "attempts to provide its members with services that they would be unable to obtain from the state. These services include organizing conferences, establishing periodicals, and disseminating technology and market-related information. It uses the Islamic identity at both the domestic and international levels as a basis for cooperation among businesses. It turns 'peripheral' status from a disadvantage into a network of solidarity."

10 For an evaluation of the equation of the exploiters and the faithless and of the dominated and the faithful, see Tuğal (2002: 95).

11 Almost half of the voters "seem to vote for the party for non-ideological reasons. ... Thus, a substantial number of WP voters cited economic problems as Turkey's most important problem" (Özbudun 2000: 90–1).

12 The secular groups have always been more concerned with such types of symbolic acts. For example, as Toprak (1995: 93) writes, in the late 1970s, "the legislation that the National Salvation Party introduced to classify beer as an alcoholic beverage and therefore limit its sale to businesses with a liquor license turned into a major controversy as the new law was interpreted as a serious assault on the secular state."

13 The policy makers of 28 February saw the existing Directorate of Religious Affairs (which today "controls" almost 80,000 mosques) to be ineffective in taming existing Islamic ways of life by propagating official Islam. They saw it as leaving a void that was filled by reactionary religious orders and organizations such as *Milli Görüş* (National Outlook) (Şahin 1997: 112).

14 These regulations vested university administrators with authority to "fire those who 'acted against the republic and its values'. Violators also could 'lose their pensions and face a life-long ban in state sector employment' " (Yavuz 2000: 35).

15 One of the leading moderate Islamic leaders, Fethullah Gülen, in August 2000 was accused of violating the secular principles of the regime. In June 2001, a Sufi Muslim preacher, Aydoğan Fuat, was arrested on "charges of causing religious enmity, conducting illegal religious activities that threaten the secular State, and wearing banned religious clothing." In May 2001, an Islamic leader began serving a 2-year sentence for "inciting religious hatred." Mehmet Kutlular, leader of a branch of the Nur Cemaati religious community, had published a statement in October 1999 claiming that "the August 1999 earthquake (which killed over 17,000 people) was 'divine retribution' for laws banning headscarves in state buildings and universities." For these cases see International Religious Freedom Report, released by the Bureau of Democracy, Human Rights and Labour (http://www.gov/g/drl/rls/irf/2001/5694.htm 2–4).

16 That trend finds its apparent expression in the views of an Islamic critic, Hayrettin Karaman. For him, the last point in Islamism or political Islam is that it has been gradually evolving into a movement seeking to attain religious freedom by searching for suitable social and public spaces to allow for their differences (Karaman 2001).

17 The measures against the wearing of headscarves include dismissing those civil servants wearing headscarves and supporting them, and forbidding them to register as university students. This move also includes some measures to check whether or not some civil servants' spouses and daughters wear headscarves. For example in July 2000, "Deputy Prime Minister Bahçeli confirmed a circular issued by the State Planning Organization barring any civil servants or family members wearing a headscarf from entering the organization's rest and recreation facilities" (see International Religious Freedom Report, released by the Bureau of Democracy, Human Rights and Labour, online at http://www.gov/g/drl/rls/irf/2001/5694.htm: 2–3). A similar rule was introduced in university residential apartments under a directive of the Higher Education Board on 15 September 2000.

References

Ahmad, F. (1993) *The Making of Modern Turkey*, London: Routledge.

Aktay, Y. (1999) *Türk Dininin Sosyolojik İmkanı* (The Sociological Possibility of Turkish Religion), Istanbul: İletişim.

Akyol, T. (2001) "Erbakan çekilsin" (Erbakan must Withdraw), *Milliyet*, 28 June.

Allen, H. (1934) "The Outlook for Islam in Turkey," *The Moslem World*, XXIV/2.

Arat, Y. (2000) "From Emancipation to Liberation: The Changing Role of Women in Turkey's Public Realm," *Journal of International Affairs*, 54 (1): 107–23.

Aslan, Z. (2002) "Conflicting Paradigms: Political Rights in the Turkish Constitutional Court," *Critique*, 11 (1): 9–25.

Bauman, Z. (2001) "Identity in the Globalizing World," in E. Ben-Rafael and Y. Sternberg (eds) *Identity, Culture and Globalisation*, Leiden: Brill.

Bayramoğlu, A. (2001) "Kavganın Altındaki" (Reason behind the Struggle), *Sabah*, 7 July.

Bayur, H. (1939) "Atatürk," *Belleten*, III/10: 247–86.

Berkan, İ. (2001) "Türbanı Tartışmak" (Discussing the Headscarf), *Radikal*, 27 June.

Bora, T. (1999) *Türk Sağının üç Hali: Milliyetçilik, Muhafazakarlık, İslamcılık* (Three Dimensions of the Turkish Right: Nationalism, Conservatism, Islamism), Istanbul: İletişim.

Cizre-Sakallıoğlu, Ü. (1996) "Parameters and Strategies of Islam-State Interaction in Republican Turkey," *International Journal of Middle East Studies*, 28: 231–51.

Çolak, Y. and Aydın, E. (2004) "Dilemmas of Turkish Democracy: The Encounter Between Kemalist Secularism and Political Islamism in the 1990s," in D. W. Odell-Scott (ed.) *Democracy and Religion: Free Exercise and Diverse Visions*, Kent OH: Kent State University Press.

Dağı, İ. D. (2001) "Human Rights, Democratisation and the European Community in Turkish Politics: The Özal Years, 1983–87," *Middle Eastern Studies*, 37 (1): 14–40.

Davison, A. (1998) *Secularism and Revivalism in Turkey: A Hermeneutic Reconsideration*, New Haven: Yale University Press.

Delanty, G. (2002) "Two Conceptions of Cultural Citizenship: A Review of Recent Literature on Culture and Citizenship," *The Global Review of Ethnopolitics*, 1 (3): 60–6.

Gökmen, Ö. (2002) "28 Şubat: Bir 'Batılılaşma Restorasyonu mu?'" (February 28: A 'Restitution of Westernisation'?), in T. Bora and M. Gültekin (eds) *Modern*

Türkiye'de Siyasi Düşünce: Modernleşme ve Batıcılık, Cilt III (Political Thought in Modern Turkey: Modernization and Westernism, vol. III), Istanbul: İletişim.

Göle, N. (2000) *Melez Desenler* (Hybrid Patterns), Istanbul: Metis.

Gülalp, H. (2001) "Globalisation and Political Islam: The Social Bases of Turkey's Welfare Party," *International Journal of Middle East Studies*, 33: 433–48.

Hale, W. M. (1994) *Turkish Politics and the Military*, London: Routledge.

İçduygu, A. and Keyman, F. (2000) "Globalleşme, Anayasallık ve Turkiye'de Vatandaşlık Tartışması" (Globalisation, Constitutionalism and the Citizenship Debate in Turkey), in E. F. Keyman and A. Y. Sarıbay (eds) *Global Yerel Eksende Türkiye* (Turkey in a Global-Local Axis), Istanbul: Alfa.

İmece, M. S. (ed.) (1959) *Atatürk'ün Şapka Devriminde Kastamonu ve İnebolu Seyahatleri, 1925* (Atatürk's Trips to Kastamonu and İnebolu during the Hat Revolution 1925), Ankara: TTK Basımevi.

Kahraman, H. B. (2001a) "Demokrasinin İslamı," (Democracy's Islam), *Radikal*, 8 June.

——(2001b) "İslamcılık" (Islamism), *Yeni Şafak*, 1 July.

Karpat, K. (1988) "The Ottoman Ethnic and Confessional Legacy in the Middle East," in M. J. Esman and I. Rabinovich (eds) *Ethnicity, Pluralism, and the Middle East*, Ithaca NY: Cornell University Press.

Keyman, E. F. (2000) "Globalleşme Söylemleri ve Kimlik Talepleri: 'Türban Sorunu'nu Anlamak'" (Globalisation Discourses and Identity Claims: Understanding the "Question of the Headscarf"), in E. F. Keyman and A. Y. Sarıbay (eds) *Global Yerel Eksende Türkiye* (Turkey in a Global-Local Axis), Istanbul: Alfa.

Kirişçi, K. (2000) "Disaggregating Turkish Citizenship and Immigration Practices," *Middle East Studies*, 36 (3): 1–22.

Levonian, L. (ed. and trans.) (1932) *The Turkish Press, 1925–1932*, Athens: School of Religion.

Mardin, Ş. (1998) "Some Notes on Normative Conflicts in Turkey," in P. L. Berger (ed.) *The Limits of Social Cohesion: Conflict and Mediation in Pluralist Societies*, Boulder: Westview.

Mert, N. (2001) "Cumhuriyet Türkiye'sinde Laiklik ve Karşı Laikliğin Düşünsel Boyutu" (Intellectual Dimension of Secularism in Republican Turkey and Counter-Secularism), in A. İnsel (ed.) *Modern Türkiye'de Siyasi Düşünce: Kemalizm, Cilt II* (Political Thought in Modern Turkey: Kemalism, vol. II), Istanbul: İletişim.

Mete, Ö. L. (2001) "Yarı Resmi Mehdi Buyuruyor!" (Semi-official Mehdi is Commanding!) *Binyıl*, 1 January.

Öniş, Z. (2001) "Political Islam at the Crossroads: From Hegemony to Co-existence," *Contemporary Politics*, 7 (4): 281–96.

Özal, T. (1991) *Turkey in Europe and Europe in Turkey*, Northern Cyprus: K. Rustem and Brothers.

Özbudun, E. (2000) *Contemporary Turkish Politics*, Boulder: Lynne Rienner.

Poulton, H. (1997) *Top Hat, Grey Wolf and Crescent: Turkish Nationalism and the Turkish Republic*, London: Hurst and Company.

Reed, H. A. (1957) "Religious Life of Modern Turkish Muslims," in R. N. Frye (ed.) *Islam and the West*, Gravenhage: Mouton & Co.

Rustow, D. A. (1997) "Atatürk as an Institution Builder," in A. Kazancıgil and E. Özbudun (eds) *Atatürk: Founder of a Modern State*, London: Hurst and Company.

——(1957) "Politics and Islam in Turkey 1920–1955," in R. N. Frye (ed.) *Islam and the West*, Gravenhage: Mouton & Co.

Sazak, D. (2002) "Deniz Bey Tuzağa Düştü" (Mr Deniz Falls into a Trap), interview with Yaşar Nuri Öztürk, *Milliyet*, 7 October.

Sherril, C. H. (1934) *A Year's Embassy to Mustafa Kemal*, New York and London: Charles Scribner's Sons.

Şahin, M. (ed.) (1997) *MGK 28 Şubat Öncesi ve Sonrası* (MGK Before and After 28 February), Ankara: Ufuk Kitabevi.

Taşkın, Y. and Bora, T. (2001) "Sağ Kemalizm" (Right Kemalism), in A. İnsel (ed.) *Modern Türkiye'de Siyasi Düşünce: Kemalizm, Cilt II* (Political Thought in Modern Turkey: Kemalism, vol. II), Istanbul: İletişim.

Tonguç, İ. H. (1944) "Köy Eğitimi ve Öğretiminin Amaçları" (The Goals of Village Education and Instruction), in *Köy Enstitüleri: 2* (The Village Institutes: 2), Ankara: Maarif Matbaası.

Toprak, B. (1995) "Islam and the Secular State in Turkey," in Ç. Balım (ed.) *Turkey: Political, Social and Economic Challenges in the 1990s*, Leiden: Brill.

Tuğal, C. (2002) "Islamism in Turkey: Beyond Instrument and Meaning," *Economy and Society*, 31 (1): 85–111.

Tunçay, M. (1992) *T. C.'nde Tek Parti Yönetiminin Kurulması (1923–30)* (The Establishment of the Single Party Regime in T. R. (1923–30)), Istanbul: Cem Yayınevi.

Üstel, F. (1995) "Cumhuriyet'ten Bu Yana Yurtaş Profili" (Profile of Citizens throughout the Republic), *Yeni Yüzyıl*, 24 April.

Waxman, D. (2000) "Islam and Turkish National Identity: A Reappraisal," *The Turkish Yearbook of International Relations*, 30: 1–22.

Yavuz, H. (2000) "Turkey's Fault Lines and the Crisis of Kemalism," *Current History*, January: 33–8.

Yeğen, M. (2001) "Kemalizm ve Hegemonya?" (Kemalism and Hegemony?), in *Modern Türkiye'de Siyasi Düşünce: Kemalizm, Cilt II* (Political Thought in Modern Turkey: Kemalism, vol. II), Istanbul: İletişim.

Zürcher, E. J. (1993) *Turkey: A Modern History*, London: I. B. Tauris.

12 Articulating citizenship and identity

The "Kurdish question" in Turkey

E. Fuat Keyman

Introduction

Antonio Gramsci's famous statement that "the old is dying and the new cannot be born: in this interregnum a great variety of morbid symptoms appear," though penned as early as the 1930s, captures and expresses eloquently the transformative and the ambivalent nature of the world in which we live. One of the sites at which such transformation and ambivalence has occurred is that of "the political," where particularistic identity claims have begun to increasingly dictate the mode of articulation of political practices and ideological/discursive forms in national and global relations. This politics has a name: the politics of identity. Debates over multiculturalism and citizenship in the West and North America, call for democratic and humane governance, but at the same time the rise of Islamic fundamentalism and meta-racism, and ethnic conflicts in various places in the world, to name a few, while constituting different manifestations of the politics of identity, are also indicators of the transformative and the ambivalent nature of the present.

In this sense, to talk about world affairs today is to recognize the increasing importance of identity politics without assuming that it is conducive to the democratic rearticulation of the political. Identity politics could constitute a ground for what William Connolly (1996) calls "the ethos of pluralization" as the ineradicable dimension of democracy. Yet it is through political claims to identity that the (communitarian) attempts at renouncing a democratic vision of society operate and assume self-referential legitimacy, as in the cases of etnonationalism, meta-racism and religious fundamentalism. It is in this sense that a critical analysis of the transformative nature of the present is of utmost importance, in order to reconstruct the relationship between the universal and the particular in a way that makes the democratic rearticulation of the political possible.

This chapter attempts to analyze critically the transformative and the ambivalent nature of the present by focusing on one specific case where it has taken the form of "the dilemma of cultural identity on the margin of Europe," namely Turkish social formation (Keyder 1993). Since the 1980s, especially in the 1990s, Turkish politics has increasingly been marked by the tension between the universal and the particular, where at stake is the clash between the secular national identity as the bearer of cultural homogenization, and the revitalization of the language of difference through the resurgence of Islam, the reemergence of Kurdish nationalism in organized form, the minority question and the increasing importance of civil society. Despite significant differences among them, especially within the context of their political agendas,[1] all these movements directly challenge the unifying discourse of Turkish modernity on the basis of which secularist Turkish nationalism reproduces itself. These movements have made identity-based claims, initiated calls for "recognition" and played a significant role in the creation of political polarizations and ideological oppositions, that have served only as unnecessary impositions on and effective restrictions to the possible democratization of state-society relations in Turkey.

Of these movements, the "Kurdish question" has been most politically troublesome and challenging. The Kurdish question has placed ethnicity at the center of Turkish politics in a very effective way; it has made its mark on almost every aspect of the domestic and foreign policies of the Turkish state in the 1990s. It has also caused a very bloody and violent ethnic conflict, or "low-intensity war" between government forces and the PKK (the Kurdish Workers Party) which has left more than 30,000 people dead. In this sense, the Kurdish question has involved not only "a growing Kurdish ethnic assertiveness" in the form of an identity politics which calls for the "recognition" of difference, but also and more importantly and devastatingly, "a campaign of violence" and terrorist activity by the PKK "to achieve its objective of establishing an independent Kurdish state in southeastern Turkey" (Kirişci 1998: 227). Thus, the politics of recognition has gone hand-in-hand with violence and death, making it almost impossible to separate discursively and politically the politics of identity/recognition from the politics of war for territory. As Cizre correctly puts it,

> The harshness of the present armed conflict between the state security forces and the Kurdish Workers Party (PKK) reinforces the belief that Kurdish nationalism is not a simple expression of discontent, but a movement that demands changing the boundaries of the Turkish entity to make room for an independent Kurdish state.
>
> (2001: 124)

The embeddedness of identity claims in violent ethnic conflict has also rendered impossible a critical and problem-solving analysis of the Kurdish question. Instead it has become an effective heuristic device for Kurdish and Turkish nationalist discourses to establish themselves as hegemonic in the political arena and to present themselves as the "absolute truth" about the question. Thus, rather than theoretical efforts aiming at providing an historical and critical analysis of the Kurdish question, the political polarizations and the binary oppositions have dictated the *modus vivendi* of Turkish politics in the 1990s. Hence, disciplinary impositions are placed on the political imagination, effective restrictions are set in front of demands for democratization, and talks aimed at possible solutions are deferred in the name of stability and normalization. The politics of identity has become the politics of ethnonationalism, generating violent ethnic conflict and transforming itself into a low-intensity war, which has resulted in the creation of a no-win situation in which ethonationalism once again has served very effectively for the escalation rather than the solution of an identity-based conflict.

In this chapter, I will argue that one way to better understand and analyze critically the Kurdish question in Turkey might be to approach it historically and sociologically, by situating it in Turkish modernity as a hegemonic ground for the construction of a secular and homogeneous discourse of national identity. In doing so, not only will I provide an historical analysis of the way in which the Kurdish question was constructed at the time of the nation-state's construction as the "other" of Turkish national identity, but I will also demonstrate the transformation of the question into the politics of identity in the "late-modern and post-national stage" of Turkish modernity in the last two decades. This will allow me to put forward and substantiate the argument that a feasible and effective solution to the Kurdish question should be sought not in "ethnic terms," but by exploring "with an emphasis on the practice of democracy" (Isin and Wood 1999: 4) possible ways of articulating identity-claims to citizenship-rights. Of course, such an articulation requires first abandoning a false dichotomy drawn between identity and citizenship, second an attempt to go beyond the purely legal-universal conception of citizenship, and finally, by following Isin and Wood, approaching citizenship and identity "from a perspective that sees modern citizenship not only as a legal and political membership in a nation-state but also as an articulating principle for the recognition of group rights" (Isin and Wood 1999: 4).

Seen in this way, citizenship involves not only legal obligations and entitlements which frame the boundary of the "membership-based relations" of individuals with their states, but also "the practices through which individuals and groups formulate and claim new rights or struggle to expand or maintain existing rights." Therefore, as Isin and Wood correctly point out (1999: 4–5), citizenship is neither purely sociological nor purely legalistic, but refers to a "relationship" whose discursive and political conditions of existence are constituted sociologically and legalistically by a set of practices which makes the claims of individuals or groups for new rights both possible and limited to the existing regime of modernity in a given country. In this sense, citizenship contains in itself both enabling and conditioning relationships between individuals/groups and their states. It provides a ground for the possibility of new right-claims to challenging and expanding the existing model of citizenship in a given country, but at the same time acts as a conditioning practice by framing, situating and limiting those claims within the regime of modernity. This implies first that there is no need to think of identity-claims and citizenship-rights as necessarily antagonistic or incommensurable: instead they should be seen as sociologically interlinked claims involving possible tensions, conflicts and antinomies. Second, it should be pointed out here that, as Turner (2000: 23) has suggested, citizenship could be both "(1) an inclusionary principle for the distribution and allocation of entitlements, (2) an exclusionary basis for building solidarity and maintaining identity." In other words, the conditioning and limiting practice that citizenship exercises on new right-claims could generate both negative (exclusionary) and positive (inclusionary) results, for it might be used as a practice of silencing and limiting right-claims, but at the same time it might function as a solution to the politics of identity by preventing its transformation into ethnonationalism or religious fundamentalism.

As for the Kurdish question in Turkey, articulating identity-claims to citizenship-rights means then trying to seek democratic solutions to ethnonationalist conflict and violence not in terms of the politics of recognition, initiated by ethnic claims for group rights, but by attempting to reconstruct the republican model of Turkish citizenship in such a way as to make it more flexible, differentiated and constitutional. In so doing, it becomes possible to transform ethnic assertiveness into "claims for group rights as a challenge to the *modern* (and republican) interpretation of universal citizenship, which is itself a form of group identity" (Isin and Wood 1999: 4). In this way, we recognize the omnipotence of Kurdish identity not as the dangerous Other that makes its realm of existence an "environment of insecurity" for the territorial integrity of Turkish society, but as a social and historical fact "that cannot be wished away, that cannot be phantasmatically made to disappear" (Yeatman 2000: 103). Thus, we become able to attempt both sociologically and historically to articulate ethnic identity-claims to citizenship-rights as a solution to the Kurdish question within the context of a constitutional citizenship which operates "not only as a legal and political membership in a nation-state but also as an articulating principle for the recognition of group rights."

The historical and discursive context in which we should embed the Kurdish question in Turkey and attempt to develop a solution to it on the basis of constitutional citizenship, is Turkish modernity and its recent governability and representation crisis. For this reason, I will first focus on the foundation of Turkish Republic in order to show that the Kurdish question has been "internal" to the construction of the modern secular Turkey as a modern nation-state. In this sense, to discuss the Kurdish question is in fact to speak of Turkish modernity with respect to the making of modern Turkey as an organic, homogeneous national society. Second, I will delineate the ways in which Turkish modernity has entered a serious governability and representation crisis since the 1980s, and especially in the 1990s; a crisis in which the changing nature of the Kurdish question as the politics of identity has involved ethnic violence and terrorism, claims of recognition and political efforts for parliamentary representation. Finally, I will try to make a theoretically and politically convincing case that the concept of constitutional citizenship as founded on the articulation of identity-claims with citizenship-rights could provide an effective basis for the solution of the Kurdish question.

Rethinking Turkish modernity

As Feroz Ahmad (1993) correctly observes, "Turkey did not rise phoenix-like out of the ashes of the Ottoman Empire. It was 'made' in the image of the Kemalist elite which won the national struggle against foreign invaders and the old regime." The making of modern Turkey raises an interesting question for students of social change, since neither the class-based understanding of revolution nor the (post-colonial) state-oriented development theory can be used as an explanatory model. This is precisely because Turkey had never experienced "colonialism" in the real sense of the term; nor had its national independence been carried out by a social class. However, just as with other post-colonial states, the history of the making of modern Turkey has been that of Westernization, conditioned by what de Ferro calls "the will to (Western) civilization" (de Ferro 1995). In the process of "making," the primary aim of the Kemalist elite was to "reach the contemporary level of civilization" by establishing its political, economic, and ideological prerequisites, such as the creation of an independent nation-state, the fostering of industrialization, and the construction of a secular and modern national identity. The Kemalist elite thus accepted the universal validity of Western modernity as *the way* of building modern Turkey. In this sense, the making of Turkey was based upon both an independence war against Western imperialism and an acceptance of its epistemic and moral dominance.

Two paradigms of Turkish modernization

The embeddedness of the Kemalist will to civilization in Western modernity requires a new theoretical framework that "goes beyond" the existing paradigms of Turkish modernization, since it provides with us a significant clue for understanding the increasing strength and importance of the politics of identity since the 1980s, especially in the 1990s. With a certain degree of generalization, one can discern in the available literature on Turkish modernization the dominance of two paradigmatic readings of Kemalism: namely those of *modernization* and *identity*. The modernization paradigm situates the Kemalist will to civilization into a teleological and typological understanding of historical development as a transition from Gemeinschaft ("community") to Gesellschaft ("society"). However, how to think of this transition produces two different positions in this paradigm. Political modernization sees this transition as a process of nation-building, in which the nation-state is taken to be the unfolding essence of modernization. The making of modern Turkey does then refer to the process of political modernization which aims at creating through nation-state building a modern nation *vis-à-vis* the Ottoman past as representative of a backward, traditional society. Whereas political modernization sees this transition as a positive break from the past and a move forward, economic modernization in line with dependency theory considers it to be a new form of "peripheralization" and dependent capitalist development which started with the integration into the world capitalist system of the Ottoman economy in the nineteenth century. In this respect, nation-state building does not alter the condition of economic dependency as the unfolding essence of modernization, even though it means the recognition in *de jure* manner by the international community of modern Turkey as a politically independent state.

However useful it is in accounting for the making of modern Turkey, the modernization paradigm, as a mode of an analysis of the processes of political and economic modernization, operates as a theoretical framework which is limited in its scope and reductionist in its methodological procedures. It is limited, as it attempts to analyze its subject-matter by privileging a certain type of social interaction as "the prime mover" of social change. Thus, either nation-state building or economic development is considered to be a process that produces a *system-transforming effect* in the formation of social interactions, which results in a lack of attention paid to the role of other processes, thereby neglecting their transformative capacity. The modernization paradigm also proves to be reductive insofar as it attributes in a Hegelian fashion to the concept of society a quality of being an expressive, constituting totality in which the conditions of existence of various social interactions are regarded as necessarily linked to and determined by the unfolding essence. As a result, the making of modern Turkey is analyzed as a process of modernization, the multi-dimensionality of which is reduced to what is conceived of as the essence, the political level or the economic level.

Contrary to the modernization paradigm, the paradigm of identity attempts to discover the essence of the manner in which Kemalism approaches the question of national identity. Two alternative accounts of the essence are produced in this paradigm, which are derived from two different interpretations of what the notion of "Turk" connotes in cultural practices that were put into service in the process of the making of modern Turkey. On the one hand, there is a tendency to interpret Kemalism as a nationalist discourse whose understanding of national identity was "cultural" in its essence. In this sense, the notion of "Turk" is referred to as a "metaidentity," that is situated above and beyond "the difference principle," and thus operates as a point of sameness at which the claim to the impartiality and the universality of the state is constructed. On the other hand, there is an interpretation of Kemalism on the basis of the difference principle, claiming that the notion of "Turk" is framed to a large extent by and within an ethnic-based understanding of national identity. In this sense, Kemalism is regarded as an ethnonationalist discourse whose aim was to impose a secular and ethnically-essentialist vision of modern Turkey on "the other but real Turkey."

Despite the fundamental difference between them, these two modes of interpretation however share in their *modus operandi* two sets of highly problematical epistemological and methodological gestures. The first concerns the *historicist* nature of the paradigm of identity, insofar as its search for the true essence of the Kemalist vision of national identity rests upon an attempt to *read the past in terms of the present* (Dean 1994: 9). This is so, since what is at stake in this paradigm is not to analyze Kemalist nationalism in its own right or in its own context, but to find a legitimizing ground for the competing political discourses of the present political landscape over such issues as the Kurdish question, political Islam, laicism, the question of minorities, ethnonationalism or the crisis of representation in state/society relations. The second problem concerns the *essentialist* nature of the paradigm. The notion of identity employed in the claim that the Kemalist understanding of national identity is constituted by and operates as a cultural or ethnic identity, assumes that each individual or collectivity possesses a fixed, coherent, and totalizing self. This means that each identity involves an unfolding essence which makes it a self-contained, self-referential and self-propelling presence, and therefore that the variations that occur historically in terms of the identity formation of individuals or collectivities do not alter the essence of their identities. The paradigm of identity thus acts as an essentializing gesture that ignores the relationality, multiplicity and historically constructed nature of identity formation, and presents the Kemalist understanding of national identity as a universalizing discourse of what is in fact a fixed, unchanging and original identity.

As for the Kurdish question, both paradigms employ limited and reductionist methodologies by approaching it either as a problem that originates from the "pre-modern and the tribal" nature of the southeastern region of Turkey, or a reactionary politics whose essence should be sought in the feudal and backward economic structure of the region, or as primarily an identity problem that stems from the assimilationist nature of Turkish modernity which has resulted in the exclusion of Kurds from the national identity. Thus, political modernization reduces the Kurdish question to a reactionary politics of the tribal type, economic modernization to economic backwardness, and an identity paradigm to the problem of exclusion and otherness. While focusing on only one dimension or aspect of the Kurdish question and making use of it as the explanatory basis for their analyses, each paradigm ignores the historical context in which the question is embedded.

Kemalism as a project of modernity

The problematic nature of the paradigms of modernization and identity therefore occurs as they ignore the complex link between the Kurdish question and Turkish modernity. Here the crucial point is modernity, articulated by the Kemalist elite as the will to civilization. However, the Kemalist elite's will to civilization was not simply an economic or a political modernization. Nor was it based essentially upon an attempt to create a national identity. As will be apparent later, it was much more complex and at the same time ambiguous than presented by these paradigms. To understand this, however, requires regarding the Kemalist will to civilization as a project of modernity which was premised on the equation of modernity with progress, that is, on the making of a modern nation through the introduction and the dissemination of Western reason and rationality into what were regarded as traditional and backward social relations. It is in this sense that the connection between Kemalism and modernity, which has been ignored by these paradigms, is what needs to be explored, in order to provide an adequate account of, and a feasible solution to the Kurdish question.

In his analysis of the making of modern Turkey, Şerif Mardin (1994a) argues that the meaning of Kemalism lies in "the conceptualization of the Turkish Republic as *a nation-state in its fullest form,*" and finds its expression in its constant effort to create a modern nation. Mardin's seemingly straightforward and commonsensical argument in fact carries with it a number of crucial insights for a more adequate understanding of Kemalism. Firstly, to think of Kemalism as "an act of conceptualization" is to present it as a "project" of creating a nation on the basis of a set of epistemological and normative procedures. Secondly, to argue that Kemalism means the conceptualization of the Turkish Republic as a nation-state in its fullest form is to recognize that it constitutes a project of modernity; a project of creating a *modern* nation that "accepts the claim to universality of the "modern' framework of knowledge" (Chatterjee 1986: 11). Thirdly, to think of Kemalism as a project of modernity is to recognize its *modus operandi* as a social engineering project that aims at creating a modern nation in a social formation where the material and institutional availability of the conception of modern nation as a nation-state in its fullest form was absent. These three points also indicate that Kemalism is a nationalist discourse that operates as a "will to civilization" by producing at the conceptual level a boundary between what is civilized and what is uncivilized. Thus, by accepting rational thinking and rational morality as the way of becoming modern, Kemalist nationalism attempts to "reach the level of civilization," that is, the making of modern Turkey as nation-state in its fullest form.

Kemalism and the will to civilization

According to Mardin (1994b), the conceptualization of the Turkish Republic as nation-state manifests itself in: (i) the transition in the political system of authority from personal rule to impersonal rules and regulations; (ii) the shift in understanding the order of the universe from divine law to positivist and rational thinking; (iii) the shift from a community founded upon the "elite-people cleavage" to a "populist-based" community; and (iv) the transition from a religious-community to a nation-state. These transitions were regarded by Mustafa Kemal as the pre-condition for the possibility that "Turkey would live as an advanced and civilized nation in the midst of contemporary civilization" (Ahmad 1993: 53). It is in this context that the Kemalist elite attempted to remove from political discourse the notion of an Islamic state, the existence of which was regarded as the main cause of the perpetuation of the backwardness of Turkey. Thus, the foundation of a modern nation-state was seen as the key element of the will to civilization. For the Kemalist elite, modern Turkey could thus possess secularity and rationality; employ reason to initiate progress, and establish a modern industrial economy, thereby fostering the processes of industrialization and modernization. In a Weberian fashion, the purpose of political power was considered as being to "carry out a social and economic revolution without which the political revolution would dissipate" (Ahmad 1993: 72). This means that for the Kemalist elite political power was "not reducible but interrelated to the economic." The rationalization of the political and the rationalization of the economic were seen to be relational processes whose reproduction could be made possible through the construction of a national identity as a modern rational self. In this respect, the Kemalist will to civilization was based upon an articulation of modernity (reason) and capitalism (capital) into Turkish society through the construction of a modern nation-state.

As Metin Heper (1985) points out, the idea of the state employed by the Kemalist elite was by no means abstract: rather it was derived from a reaction to two fundamental problems which they saw as the key to the decline of the Ottoman Empire. First, the Ottoman state was identified with the personal rule of the sultan, which eventually led to its inability to compete with the European nation-state system (Heper 1985: 49). Second, the Islamic basis of the Ottoman state was regarded as the primary obstacle to progress in Ottoman society. For the Kemalist elite, there was therefore a need to create a nation-state distinct from the person of the sultan and secular enough to reduce Islam to the realm of individual faith. This meant a reconstruction of the idea of sovereignty as a national rather than popular sovereignty. Underlying this, as Heper argues, is the association of the Kemalist elite with the Durkheimian conception of the state as the agent of rationality. The state is thus viewed not as an arbitrary institution nor an expression of class interest, but as an active agent that, while taking its inspiration from the genuine feelings and desires of the nation, shapes and reshapes it to "elevate the people to the level of contemporary (Western) civilization" (Heper 1985: 50). Therefore, the Kemalist idea of the state was embedded in the question of how to activate the people toward the goal of civilization, that is, how to construct a national identity compatible with the will to civilization.

Gellner considers the Kemalist idea of the state to be a commitment to "political modernity," which sees "the modernization of the polity and society" as "linked to the state." This commitment "constitutes its legitimation and is itself in turn justified by the strength which it bestows on the state" (1994: 83). However, it would be wrong to view the Kemalist idea of the state as institutional. As Bobby Said has correctly pointed out, the Kemalist elite

> took seriously the Weberian answer to the riddle of the "European miracle"; that is, that the reasons behind Western advancement could be located precisely in Western cultural practices. Kemalism understood modernization not just as a question of acquiring technology, but as something that could not be absorbed without a dense network of cultural practices which made instrumental thought possible.
>
> (1994: 269)

This means that the commitment to political modernity has to be supplemented with a set of cultural practices in order to ground "the articulation of reason and capital via the nation-state:" that is, the institutional and discursive construction of national identity. It is for this reason that the Kemalist elite initiated a set of reforms which needed to be *imposed from above* to "enlighten the people and help them make progress" (Heper 1985: 51). These reforms were designed to equate the general will with the national will, thereby creating a vision of society not as an aggregation of different interests, but almost in a Platonic vision as an organic totality organized around the principles of division of labor and the reciprocity of needs.

Republicanism, nationalism, etatism, secularism, populism, and revolutionism-reformism (from above) were the six principles of the act of governmantality. Republicanism defined the nation-state as "impersonal rule," which was contextualized as national sovereignty through nationalism. Thus, these two principles constituted the political image of the Kemalist elite. Etatism was designated to foster capitalist industrialization through import-substitution policies carried out by the state, and gave expression to the politico-economic logic of the Kemalist elite. These three principles indicate the acceptance of the dominance of the West and its determination of the Kemalist elite's will to civilization. They also indicate the significance of nation-state building for nationalist discourse. What gave specificity to Kemalist nationalism, however, was its populist character, its rejection of the West as a class-based social formation. Populism meant, in the Turkish context, the affirmation of the non-class character of Turkish society. As Toprak put it,

> Kemalist populism defined "people" as an organic unit composed of professional groups rather classes. As opposed to class solidarity, populism emphasized the solidarity of the whole nation. There were no classes, hence no privileges based on class differences, and hence no class conflict.
>
> (Toprak 1987: 218)

In this sense, Kemalist nationalism was an attempt to base its will to civilization on populism rather than liberalism, whose reflection on the economic level was the replacement of laissez-faire with etatism. The last two principles, secularism and reformism from above, served to construct a national identity compatible with republicanism, nationalism, and etatism, and at the same time to concretize populism and its appeal to organic unity into the identity of the individual subject. They were also central to the practice of inclusion/exclusion, that is, to the determination of who is included in and who is excluded from the organic unity. It is through secularism that Kemalist nationalism initiated its boundary-producing performance between the self and the Other, thereby giving a concrete form to its populist-based creation of the national identity. Hence, the national identity was meant to be an organic unity of the secular non-class based identity which necessarily involved the subjugation of its Other, i.e. the Kurdish identity, Islamic identity, and various minorities. This identity was the citizen as the symbol of secularism and civilization, virtuous enough to privilege state interest over his or her own interest, and the Other was expected to accord primacy to citizenship over difference.

To the degree that the Kemalist will to civilization acted successfully as a project of modernity, employed a discourse of nation as an organic unity between state and people (constructed discursively as citizen-subject) and operated at the theoretical level with a non-ethnicist notion of national identity whose Other was mainly the Ottoman past and Islam, the Kurdish question did not appear as the politics of identity (Mango 2000: 22). Even the Shaikh Said rebellion of 1925, which was the major reaction to the newly founded republic, contained references to religion, the economic backwardness of the region and the centralizing policies of the state (Kirişci and Winrow 1997: 104). In this period, the Kurdish question was "silenced," "frozen into history as the Other" and "assimilated" into the Kemalist elite's theoretical discourse of nation as "consisting of a group of people who inhabited the same piece of land, who were bound by the same laws, and shared a common morality and language" (Kirişci and Winrow 1997: 97). As Yeğen (1996: 216) points out, the exclusion of Kurdish identity from the modernity project takes the form of "concealment" which finds its clear expression in

> the striking silence of the Turkish state as to the "Kurdishness" of the Kurdish question: Whenever the Kurdish question was mentioned in Turkish state discourse, it was in terms of reactionary politics, tribal resistance or regional backwardness, but never as an ethno-political question.

It is in this sense that in the period from the 1920s to the 1980s, the Kurdish question remained not a question of identity nor an ethno-political act for recognition, but as a "regional problem" stemming from the pre-modern and tribal formation of that region's economic and cultural backwardness: a regional problem whose solution should be sought in the assimilation of the Kurdish question into the discourse of political modernity as a unity between the state and its people. It can be argued, therefore, that the emergence of the Kurdish question as the politics of identity involving an ethnic claim to recognition occurs in the 1980s, and especially in the 1990s. In other words, in the last two decades Turkish modernity has witnessed the transformation of the Kurdish question into the politics of identity, which can no longer be concealed, silenced or frozen into history as a regional question. In what follows, I try to explain the main reasons for this transformation.

The crisis of Turkish modernity[2]

If Turkish modernity provides a discursive and historical ground for the concealment of the Kurdishness of the Kurdish question, it also constitutes the ground on which the transformation of the question into the politics of identity occurs and takes the form of an ethnic assertiveness for recognition. More concretely, the Kurdish question both as a language of (ethnic) difference and the politics of identity is situated in the legitimacy and the representation crisis of Turkish modernity in maintaining its state-centric discourse, which claims that modernity is directly linked to the ability of the state to create a modern nation as a unity between state and people. It is in this sense that to talk about the transformation of the Kurdish question is to speak of the crisis of Turkish modernity, especially in the 1990s, in general, and of the internal and external (global) reasons for this crisis in particular.

In the most general sense, the legitimacy and the representation crisis of Turkish modernity has occurred as its state-centric character has become unable to cope effectively or efficiently with societal changes and transformations that Turkish society has been going through since the 1980s, especially with respect to economy and culture. These changes and transformations can be located in three fundamental shifts that have emerged in state-society relations in Turkey. By following Delanty's (1998) terminology, we may identify these shifts as (a) the shift from ideology to identity; (b) the shift from state to society; and (c) the shift from structure to agency. The shift from ideology to identity refers to the emergence of "the fragmentation of political culture" in which the crisis of the state-centric and monolithical political culture which, as noted, operates on the basis of secular reason, the organic vision of society and the republican (duty-based) model of citizenship has given rise to different claims to identity and recognition. In this sense, political culture becomes a site where each identity/recognition claim justifies itself by resisting state-centricism. Mapping the developments of the last two decades in Turkish politics illustrates this shift to fragmentation. In this period, one can observe an increasing gap between state and society, in which the simultaneous developments of (a) the "increasing dominance of economic liberalization" in economic life, whose laws of motion are, to a large extent, dictated by economic globalization; (b) the resurgence of Islam as a strong political and cultural actor; and (c) the revitalization of the Kurdish question which involved both ethnic assertiveness and violent acts, have initiated radical changes and transformations in social relations which cannot be captured, coped with or regulated by the state-centric discourse of Turkish modernity. In other words, the crisis of Turkish modernity since the 1980s has been increasingly marked by the co-existence of economic liberalization and the resurgence of traditionalism and its appeal to the "return to ethnic authenticity."[3] It is in this context that the shift from structure to identity has provided a momentum or a discursive space for a redefinition of the Kurdish question with a strong and ethnonationalist emphasis on identity, and thus the "Kurdishness" of the question emerged as a claim not for economic or political development but for ethnic recognition. Moreover, the historical context in which this momentum has occurred is not only national but global, in the sense that both economic liberalization and the politics of identity have been embedded historically and discursively in an increasingly globalized world economy and politics. Neoliberal economic globalization, the end of the Cold War, the Gulf War, the regional integration in Europe, Turkey's application to the EU for the full membership status: all have made significant contributions to the shift from ideology to identity, which has given rise to the Kurdish question as the politics of identity/recognition (Keyman 1995; 2000).

Cizre (2001: 234) argues in this context that

> Kurdish nationalism since 1987 owes much of its militancy to the transformation of official Turkish nationalism in the same period. In contrast with the cold war times when the physical conflict dimension of Kurdish nationalism was almost non-existent, the post-cold war momentum for Kurdish nationalism came from two sources: the force of the official redefinition of the Turkish nation with a strong dose of ethnic homogeneity and the process of global change. The official response to the radicalism of Kurdish nationalism has been to narrow the political space to Kurdish demands, which are now organized on the basis of an "identity claim".

More importantly, continues Cizre,

> this has led to a vicious circle: the political space for the expression of Kurdish identity, interests and ideas is restricted by the failure of traditional political parties in conveying and processing Kurdish demands, and by the closing down of exclusively Kurdish parties by the Constitutional Court.

At the beginning of the 1990s, first the People's Labor Party, then the Democracy Party was closed down, and in the latter case the parliamentary members of the party were jailed. Now, the People's Democracy Party is threatened with closure by the Constitutional Court. Thus, the more Kurdish demands were not articulated by existing parties, and did not find parliamentary expression, the more Kurdish radical etnonationalism found a space for initiating its ethnically essentialist claims for recognition, as well as for attempting to legitimize its violence and terrorism.

As for the shift from state to society, a mapping of the literature on the crisis of Turkish modernity indicates that since the 1980s we have been witnessing the increasing "decoupling of the nation from the state" (Delanty 1998: 30), which has resulted first in the emergence of the governing crisis of "the strong-state tradition," and second in the reopening of the political to new conflicts beyond the "left-right axis." In this shift, society is mobilized against the strong-state tradition, and this mobilization has taken the form of "cultural contestation" articulated both by democratic civil society organizations and the politics of identity having claims for either religious or ethnic recognition (Keyman 2000). Moreover, the mobilization of society, especially in the 1990s, has gained an important institutional and economic characteristic with the creation of new economic and civil society organizations voicing the language of difference and recognition (Özbudun and Keyman 2002). In this sense, the shift from state to society has given rise to both "the changing meaning of modernity," that is, "the emergence of alternative modernities," and "the governing crisis of the strong-state tradition."

Today in Turkey, economic actors, civil society organizations and intellectuals agree that since the 1980s, the process of Turkish modernization has involved new actors, new mentalities of development and new identity claims. This means, first, the emergence of the critique of the status of secular-rational thinking as the exclusive source of modernity in Turkey; second, the increasing strength of Islamic discourse both as a "political actor" and as a "symbolic foundation" for identity-formation; and third the revitalization of the Kurdish question, not only as ethnic assertiveness but also as a "regional problem" whose solution requires both cultural recognition and economic development and distributive justice (Göle 1991; 1994; Özbudun and Keyman 2002). Thus, during the 1990s, there have emerged new and alternative claims to modernity, such as Islamic modernity and conservative modernity. The Kurdish question in this context was voiced by regional business and economic organizations, as well as by municipalities, as a developmentalist (conservative) claim to modernity and regional development. Although so far it has not been very successful, an attempt has been made by these organizations to link ethnic identity claims to economic development with the intention of discussing the Kurdish question outside ethnic terror and violence. This development is also very important in order to transform the politics of identity based on a strong claim for recognition into a citizenship claim demanding both recognition and redistributive justice and initiating a democratic call for "constitutional, differential and multicultural citizenship" (Özbudun and Keyman 2002; Ong 1999).

The second process, embedded in the shift from state to society, is related to "the governing crisis of the strong-state tradition" in Turkey since the 1980s. As noted before, Turkish modernity, since the beginning of the Republic, has been characterized by and has given rise to the "strong-state tradition." This tradition means, first, that the state has assumed the capacity of acting almost completely independently of civil society; second, that the state, rather than the government, has constituted "the primary context of politics;" and third, that as a moral/ethical actor, the state has intervened in the cultural domain with the aim of transforming societal affairs into a secular, civilized and rational national identity. The strong-state tradition has thus functioned as the organizing "internal variable" of Turkish politics up until the 1980s. However, since the 1980s, the emergence of new actors, new mentalities and the new language of politics, as well as democracy as a global point of reference in politics, has made culture and cultural factors an important variable in understanding political activities. Thus, the state has faced a governing and a legitimacy problem in maintaining its position as the primary context for politics, as a result of the shift toward civil society and culture as new reference-points in the language and the terms of politics. The momentum for the redefinition of the Kurdish question as the politics of identity emerged in this context, as Kurdish ethnonationalism found for itself a discursive space for its claim for recognition in the increasing gap between state and society in Turkey.

The third shift is from structure to agency, which refers both to the increasing inability of the state-centric model to legitimize its representation of Turkish society as an organic, unitary and monolithic unity, and to the emergence of new actors aiming to unleash their discourses and strategies from the strong-state tradition and mediating their ontologies and histories with culture. In this context, the shift from structure to agency means, first, that the mediation between agency and culture, which also indicates that culture, can no longer be taken as secondary to politics and economics. Second, it means that culture makes it possible for us to think about politics and political actors outside of the strong-state tradition, and for hitherto silenced identities to create a change in the meaning of modernity. The Kurdish question in this sense appears to be an important point of reference for the calls for a more liberal, multi-cultural and pluralist Turkey, in which citizenship is defined on the basis of the language of rights rather than that of duties to the state. Kirişci and Winrow (1997: 203) argue that on the basis of the recognition and the maintenance of the unitary structure of Turkey, fostering a multicultural society would be a solution to the Kurdish question: "Acknowledging the Kurdish reality by granting additional rights to the Kurds, moving towards the further democratization of Turkish society, and beginning a dialogue with certain Kurdish political groups would help to lessen ethnic tensions in the country." The call for multiculturalism without "threatening the territorial integrity of the state" would also transform ethnic agency into an identity-claim with demands for citizenship-rights. Of course, here the Kurdish question is considered by making a distinction between the politics of identity-claims for cultural rights and a politics of recognition initiating ethnic violence and terror in its act of ethnic assertiveness. Although both claims (identity and recognition) demonstrate the "return of agency" and bring about the importance of culture as a crucial heuristic device for political contestation, it is important to make a distinction between them, in order to explore solutions to the Kurdish question within the unitary structure of Turkey.

The Kurdish question and the possibility of democracy

In this chapter, I have tried to provide an historical account of the Kurdish question by linking it with Turkish modernity as a hegemonic and state-centric discourse of society. In doing so, I have argued:

(i) first that although the Kurdish question is usually presented as a "geopolitical question," or the "southeast problem," or the "economic backwardness problem associated with the premodern tribal politics," the question in essence is a "governing question," that is, the question of "the governance of those people inside the territory of Turkey who identify themselves as Kurds" (Robins 2000: 65). The question of governance is an historical question and is deeply embedded in the establishment of republican Turkey as a modern nation-state in its fullest form. In this sense, Turkish modernity constitutes an historical and discursive context for a sociological and analytical analysis of the Kurdish question;

(ii) second that locating the Kurdish question in its historical context helps us understand the continuities and changes that the question involves, thereby allowing us to see that the enduring nature of the question in the history of Turkish modernity does not mean that it remains fixed and static. On the contrary, as noted, the Kurdish question has evolved over time and its challenges to the Turkish state have taken different forms. In the 1920s and 1930s, the Kurdish challenge was organized on the basis of Islam, whereas in the 1960s and especially the 1970s, it was mainly a left-wing reaction to the state employing the terms of Marxist-Leninist discourse. This brings about two crucial points for an analytical understanding of the Kurdish question: (a) First, to the extent that the state-centric discourse of Turkish modernity was successful in dealing with the Kurdish question by erasing its "Kurdishness" and thus approaching it as a problem of traditional, tribal and premodern reaction to modernity, the question was assimilated in the organic vision of Turkish society and did not appear as an "identity claim" to political and cultural recognition; and (b) Second, it was only in the 1980s and especially the 1990s that the Kurdish question was transformed into the politics of identity/recognition, involving a violent ethnic assertiveness, thereby becoming/becoming perceived as a serious threat to the territorial integrity of the Turkish state. Robins (2000: 66) explains the shifting goals, claims and discourses of the Kurdish challenge as follows:

> In the 1920s and 1930s, the challenge from the Kurdish areas to the new state of Turkey was made in the name of Islam, with tribal affiliation also being exploited to mobilize opposition. In the1960s and 1970s, the challenge was couched in terms of Marxism-Leninism, a convenient ideological mechanism that legitimized both struggle against a national security state and the Kurdish clients of the state.

These challenges in these periods have different goals:

> During the 1920s and 1930s the uprising in the southeast aimed at restoring Islam as the central organizing principle of a state that would embrace both Kurds and Turks mixed with a tendency among the tribes of the periphery to want to circumscribe the power of the state. During the 1960s and the 1970s revolutionary politics preached solidarity between the oppressed among both Kurds and Turks for the transformation to a single socialist state for all. It is only in the 1980s and the early 1990s that the maximalist aim of full secession for the southeast of Turkey has come to the fore, an objective that would divide Kurds from Turks irreparably.

and

(iii) Third that it is very important for us to recognize the changing nature of the Kurdish question and its claims and goals. This allows us not only to come to terms with the historical and discursive construction of the politics of identity, but also to search for solutions to the question by going beyond an ethnonationalism that regards identity as a "fixed" entity assuming an "essentially unchanging quality." It is also important for us to recognize that the historical context in which the Kurdish question becomes a claim to identity/recognition is the crisis of Turkish modernity, in which the legitimacy, the representation and the governing crisis of the state-centric discourse creates a gap (or a discursive void) between state and society, and between structure and agency, and this gap, or void, creates a space for the revitalization of the language of difference and recognition. If we recognize this crisis, we should be able to see that the solution to the Kurdish question should be sought in attempting to fill the emerging and increasingly widening gap between state and society through a more democratic, pluralist, multicultural and constitutional vision of Turkey.

Similarly, von Bruinessen (2000: 108) argues that "Like many other states, Turkey may find that its long-term interests are best served by adopting new forms of cultural and political pluralism." Today, there is a possibility and in fact a need for a serious attempt to solve the Kurdish problem on the basis of restructuring state-society relations through cultural and political pluralism. There is a possibility, (a) because of the disarray of the PKK since its terrorist activities were successfully contained and weakened by the Turkish military in the late 1990s; (b) because of the capture of the leader of the PKK, Abdullah Öcalan, on 15 February 1999 in Kenya, and his repatriation, trial and sentencing to death on 29 June 1999; (c) because of the fact that "Most important, on 2 August 1999, Öcalan ordered the PKK to end its armed struggle and to withdraw its fighters from Turkish territory," (Robins 2000: 62) which also meant the beginning of the process of what has come to be known as "the politicization of the PKK," especially in Europe; (d) because the politicization of the PKK has created a diasporic discourse, mainly in Europe, of ethnic identity, that initiates the language of (cultural and political) rights as the basis of its claim for recognition, and finally, (e) because of Turkey's attempt to become a full member of European Union, which involves the required constitutional and institutional changes for making Turkey a democratic, plural society in which individual and cultural rights are constitutionally secured and protected.

There is also a serious need to solve the Kurdish question through a cultural and political pluralism, because of the fact that, as Robins noted, "the costs of continuity" in the Kurdish question have been, and will be, enormous. Not to mention the drastic and tragic scale of human loss in a conflict that has killed 30,000 people, we could talk about the serious costs to Turkey of the Kurdish insurgency, costs with internal and external dimensions. In exploring the internal costs, Robins (2000: 70) refers to the political, economic and physiological turmoil the Kurdish question has created in Turkish society. This turmoil involves not only a serious economic cost in which "the annual bill is substantial, the equivalent of approximately 15 percent of GNP." It also involves political scandals, corruption, illegal drugs and arms trafficking, black money laundering and extra-judicial killings. Internationally, the cost to Turkey involves problems and even crises in EU-Turkish relations and Middle East-Turkey relations. In both cases, Turkey's relations with its neighbors have faced difficulties because of the Kurdish question, which has brought about a series of problems ranging from human rights violations to terrorism. In addition to the human loss, these enormous costs to Turkey, too, have brought to the fore the need to solve the Kurdish problem politically.

I argue that this solution should be sought not in identity but in an attempt to articulate identity-claims to citizenship-rights within the context of a democratic and pluralist vision of Turkish modernity. To substantiate this argument, I will first suggest making two important and necessary demarcations: the first concerns the problem of identity, in this case ethnic identity. By focusing on identity-based conflicts, as in the case of Rwanda, or Bosnia, as well as Turkey, we can see that in each case the possibility of democracy has been impeded by essentialist and ethnonationalist claims to identity. The more identity remains both the cause and the solution to the conflict, the more the result will be escalation and reinforcement of the conflict rather than a democratic solution to it. In our case, to the extent that the Kurdish problem results in ethnic assertiveness and violence, in which identity becomes essentialized as fixed and unchanging, the solution to the question with an emphasis on the practice of democracy should be based on an attempt to recognize "the limits of identity." This recognition helps us to resist the essentialist operation of ethnonationalism, and also to create a space beyond the politics of identity to deal effectively with the claims for recognition. The second demarcation concerns Turkish modernity. By taking the question of the Turkish modernity project as a theoretical and historical object of inquiry, and by acknowledging that "Turkey has been and continues to be made," we are able to recognize the crisis-ridden and changing nature and formation of Turkish modernity. This helps reconstruct the modernity project on the basis of political and cultural pluralism, and in doing so it becomes possible to create a new historical and discursive context for transforming the Kurdish question into a citizenship-demand for individual and cultral rights. Both demarcations are necessary to search for a solution to the question by considering identity-claims within the context of citizenship-rights as a way of breaking with ethnonationalism.

Articulating identity-claims to citizenship-rights as a solution to the Kurdish question allows us to shift our focus from ethnonationalist assertiveness to the domain of citizenship. The break with ethnonationalism as an identity-claim for recognition and a call for citizenship is a very important move, insofar as it provides an opportunity to create egalitarianism, an inclusive political culture, and a thin conception of consensus in social and cultural life. Moreover, locating the Kurdish question in the domain of citizenship without ignoring its "Kurdishness" enables one to rethink one's loyalties and sense of belonging in terms not of identity and community but of the rule of law and constitutionalism. However, the call for citizenship, as noted, should be post-national, differential and constitutional: (a) post-national in the sense that it should not reduce the meaning of citizenship to the legal and political membership of a nation state; (b) differential in the sense that it should recognize not only individual rights but also cultural group rights, and thereby function as a point of articulation between identity and citizenship; and (c) constitutional in the sense that it should function as a common language or ground for the constitutional guarantee and protection of both individual and group rights. Thus, we could create the possibility of preventing an identity claim for recognition from being articulated by ethnonationalist discourses whose basic aim is to denounce democracy. This possibility is also one for coping effectively with the recent legitimacy, representation and governing crisis of Turkish modernity by democratizing its state-centric operations.

As Kramer (2000: 52) has pointed out,

> Turkey's Kurdish problem is more than just socioeconomic underdevelopment or the separatist terrorism of the PKK. It has to do with the difficult question of how to politically organize a multiethnic and multicultural society without endangering the legitimacy of the polity and its state. Even after the defeat of the PKK, the question will not go away as long as the state answers it in an unsatisfactory manner. The solution will not come in the southeastern and eastern Anatolian provinces unless it starts in the minds of Turkey's elites.

In this paper, I have attempted to demonstrate in a convincing way that the possibility of politically organizing a multiethnic and multicultural society beyond ethnonationalist lines and with a strong emphasis on the practice of democracy lies in the possibility of restructuring state-society relations on the basis of a differential and constitutional citizenship which functions as a point of democratic articulation between identity-claims and citizenship-rights.

Notes

1 Whereas the rise of Islam and the reemergence of Kurdish nationalism appear to be reactionary in terms of their essentialist appeal to political identity, civil society organizations aim at democratic reconstruction of civil society on the basis of the recognition of difference.

2 These reforms include "the hat revolution," "the reform of attire," "the adaption of a civil code," "the alphabet reform," and "the religious reform."

3 This section and those that follow are based upon three years' research I have carried out on the impacts of globalization on Turkey, which was a part of the research project on "cultural globalization" conducted by Professor Peter Berger of Boston University. For the written results of that research, see Özbudun and Keyman 2002.

References

Ahmad, F. (1993) *The Making of Modern Turkey*, London: Routledge.

Birtek, F. and Toprak, B. (1993) "The Conflictual Agendas of Neo-Liberal Reconstruction and the Rise of Islamic Politics in Turkey: The Hazards of Rewriting Turkish Modernity," *Praxis International*, 13: 192–211.

Bruinessen, M. V. (2000) "Shifting National and Ethnic Identities: the Kurds in Turkey and Europe," in G. G. Özdoğan, and G. Tokay (eds) *Redefining the Nation, State and Citizen*, Istanbul: Eren Yayınevi.

Chatterjee, P. (1986) *Nationalist Thought and The Colonial World: A Derivative Discourse,* The United Nations University: Zed Books.

Cizre, Ü. (2001) "Turkey's Kurdish Problem: Borders, Identity and Hegemony," in B. O'Leary, I. S. Lustick and T. Callaghy (eds) *Right-Sizing the State*, New York: Oxford University Press.

Connolly, W. (1996) *Identity/Difference*, Ithaca NY: Cornell University Press.

Dean, M. (1994) *Critical and Effective Histories*, London: Sage.

de Ferro, C. (1995) "The Will to Civilization and Its Encounter with Laissez-Faire," *Alternatives*, 27: 89–103.

Delanty, G. (1998) "Redefining Political Culture in Europe Today: From Ideology to the Politics of Identity and Beyond," in U. Hedetoft (ed.) *Political Symbols, Symbolic Politics*, Aldershot: Ashgate.

Foucault, M. (1979) "Governmentality," *Ideology and Consiousness*, 6: 5–21.

Gellner, E. (1994) *Encountering Nationalism*, London: Routledge.

Göle, N. (1991) *Modern Mahrem* (Modern Privacy), Istanbul: Metis.

——(1994) "Toward an Autonomization of Politics and Civil Society in Turkey," in M. Heper and A. Evin (eds) *Politics in the Third Turkish Republic*, Boulder: Westview.

İçduygu, A., Romano, D. and Sirkeci, I. (1999) "The Ethnic Question in an Environment of Insecurity: The Kurds in Turkey," *Ethnic and Racial Studies*, 22: 6.

Isin, E. F. and Wood, P. K. (1999) *Citizenship and Identity*, London: Sage

——(2000) "Introduction: Democracy, Citizenship and the City," in E. F. Isin (ed.) *Democracy, Citizenship and Global City*, London: Routledge.

Heper, M. (1985) *The State Tradition in Turkey*, North Humberside: Eothen Press.

Keyder, Ç. (1993) "The Dilemma of Cultural Identity on the Margin of Europe," *Review*, 16: 19–33.

Keyman, E. F. (1995) "On the Relation between Global Modernity and Nationalism: The Crisis of Hegemony and the Rise of (Islamic) Identity in Turkey," *New Perspectives on Turkey*, 13: 95–121.

——(1997) *Globalization, State, Identity/Difference*, New Jersey: Humanities Press.

——(2000) "Global Modernity, Identity and Democracy: The Case of Turkey," in G. G. Özdoğan and G. Tokay (eds) *Redefining the Nation, State and Citizen*, Istanbul: Eren Yayınevi.

Kirişci, K. and Winrow, G. M. (1997) *The Kurdish Question and Turkey*, London: Frank Cass.

——(1998) "Minority/Majority Discourse: The Case of The Kurds in Turkey," in D. G. Gladney (ed.) *Making Majorities*, Stanford: Stanford University Press.

Kramer, H. (2000) *A Changing Turkey*, Washington DC: Brookings Institution Press.

Mango, A. (2000) "Atatürk and the Kurds," in S. Keduri (ed.) *Seventy-five Years of the Turkish Republic*, London: Frank Cass.

Mardin, Ş. (1994a) *Türkiye'de Din ve Siyaset* (Religion and Politics in Turkey), Istanbul: İletişim.

——(1994b) *Türkiye'de Toplum ve Siyaset* (Society and Politics in Turkey), Istanbul: İletişim.

Ong, A. (1999) *Flexible Citizenship*, Durham NC: Duke University Press.

Özbudun, E. and Keyman, E. F. (2002) "Globalization and Turkey: Actors, Discourses, Strategies," in P. Berger and S. Hungtinton (eds) *Many Globalizations*, Oxford: Oxford University Press.

Robertson, R. (1992) *Globalization*, London: Sage.

Robins, P. (2000) "Turkey and the Kurds: Missing Another Opportunity?," in M. Abramowitz (ed.) *Turkey's Transformation and American Policy*, New York: The Century Foundation Press.

Steinbach, U. (1984) "The Impact of Ataturk on Turkey's Political Culture since World War II," in J. M. Landau (ed.) *Ataturk and the Modernization of Turkey*, Boulder: Westview Press.

Toprak, B. (1987). "The Religious Right," in I. C. Schick and A. E. Tonak (eds) *Turkey in Transition*, New York: Oxford University Press.

Turner, B. (2000) "Liberal Citizenship and Cosmopolitan Virtue," in A. Vandenberg (ed.) *Citizenship and Democracy in a Global Era*, New York: St Martin's Press.

Yeatman, A. (2000) "The Subject of Democratic Theory and the Challenge of Co-existence," in A. Vandenberg (ed.) *Citizenship and Democracy in a Global Era*, New York: St Martin's Press.

Yeğen, M. (1996) "The Turkish State Discourse and the Exclusion of Kurdish Identity," *Middle Eastern Studies*, 32 (2): 216–30.

13 Citizenship and the minority question in Turkey

B. Ali Soner

Introduction

When he was developing an innovative approach to the question of nationalism, Ernest Gellner (1993) suggested that the socio-political and economic dynamics of the modern age fostered the congruence of political and cultural realms. This view implied that the modern state was the state of a territorially and ethno-culturally bounded society. It was through the consolidation of this modern tendency that the demarcation lines between the notions of state-membership (citizenship) and ethno-cultural membership (nationality) gradually disappeared. The connotation of "nation-state" symbolized the political extension of a cultural community. Although a clear-cut distinction was drawn between "western" (civic) and "eastern" (ethnic) models (Kohn 1965; Brubaker 1992), nationalism, as an ideology and political project, has sought an ideal fusion between citizenship and nationality. Both civic and ethnic models, implicitly or explicitly, have situated ethno-cultural identity at the core of the linkage between citizens and the state (Özdoğan 2000). It has been generally believed that a state's citizens should be composed of its nationals, both civic and ethnic members of the state (Oommen 1997).

However, nationalism as a theoretical and political project has largely run counter to the diverse circumstances of modern times. Only a few of the world's existing states have accomplished the homogeneity of a nation-state. Ethno-cultural diversity, instead, has remained an integral feature of modern conditions (Connor 1994). It has become evident that notions of citizenship and nationality are not synonymous but inherently refer to two different sources of identity, that is, legal-political and ethno-cultural. In these circumstances, the possibility of developing genuine equality between the "national" and "non-national" citizens of a country has depended on the capacity to create a complete disassociation between the two concepts. Otherwise, it is argued, the concept of citizenship would come to relinquish its inclusive substance and begin to operate as an instrument of exclusion for those sections of the state's population who remain outside the "imagined" category of ethno-cultural designation (Schnapper 1998).

Nevertheless, ethno-cultural neutrality, as Kymlicka and Norman (2000) have recently demonstrated, has remained a myth even for the liberal democracies of the Western world, where a dominant ethno-cultural substance has frequently violated the legal-political inclusiveness of citizenship. The rhetoric of citizenship has, in most cases, been historically advanced at the expense of ethno-cultural diversity. There has existed a potential tension between the notion of universal citizenship and ethno-linguistic and religious particularities of minority groups. Because of this, notwithstanding universal premises of the concept of citizenship, the practice has tended to create a duality between two categories of citizens, those who belong to the majority and those who are outside the category of mainstream identification.

The traditional position of non-Muslim minorities in Turkey has presented a good example of the citizenship duality inherent in the practices of a multi-cultural context. Thus, despite the fact that the republican state adopted a legal-political neutrality in conceptualizing Turkish citizenship, Turkish practices have often made a clear distinction between "national" and "formal" citizens of the country. In so doing, universal implications of citizenship status have been narrowed by the exclusivist conceptualization of nationality. The Turkish citizenship practices have, therefore, created a constant stalemate, blocking the building of a true compromise between the universal implications of citizenship status and the "non-national" position of the non-Muslim minorities.

I will review this republican duality as it relates to the citizenship status of non-Muslim minorities in Turkey, focusing merely on Turkish political culture and the Muslim-inclusive formulation of Turkish nationalism. Therefore, this chapter will, first, briefly examine major aspects of Ottoman rule relating to the issue of minority-majority classification and the ways of minority treatment. Second, in connection with the former, the constitution of minority and majority categories of the republican state will be discussed. Here, the eventual emergence of the legal-political status of minorities, both in the context of the Peace Treaty of Lausanne and the Turkish constitutional settings, will be reviewed. Third, by looking at the republican treatment of minorities, the practice of this legal-political background will be elaborated. Finally, taking into consideration that the traditional basis of minority citizenship has recently began to lose effect, I will point out some current trends which have begun to transform the classical practices and parameters of the established regime.

The Ottoman legacy

Although Western politicians and travelers used to designate the Ottoman Empire as "Turkey" and its rulers as "Turks," this European ethnic categorization was no more than a misrepresentation of the Ottoman reality (İnalcık 1996: 19). The Ottoman Empire was not a Turkish state in the modern sense of the word, but a multi-ethnic, multi-religious and multi-lingual Islamic empire. Its socio-political, economic and judicial system rested largely upon the instructions of Islamic law (Berkes 1998: 14). It was because of this that, although ethno-lingual differentiation was not unknown to the Ottoman world, religious belief signified the prime source of identity, both before the state authorities and in the eyes of the general public (Davison 1954: 844). The imperial order (*nizam*), hence, incorporated a policy of ethno-lingual indifference and governed religious diversity exclusively with a long-established Islamic instrument, the *millet* system. Accordingly, while granting official recognition to the corporate existence of the Greek Orthodox, Armenian-Gregorian and Jewish subjects, the Muslim population was totalized within a uniform category of Muslim *millet*. Non-Muslim communities were accorded a privilege of spiritual and temporal autonomy on questions of taxation, education, religious practices, and judicial proceedings that facilitated the protection and promotion of their ethno-cultural characteristics (Braude and Lewis 1982).

However, communal autonomy in the Ottoman context did not mean equality. The functioning of the Ottoman *nizam* depended not upon the principle of equality but on an inegalitarian version of justice (*adalet*) which recognized equality neither between the rulers and the ruled nor among the different sections of the ruled. The meaning of *adalet*, instead, prescribed for each of the communal groups a legal status no less and no more than they deserved (Berkes 1998: 11). Immunities and the privileges of the *millet* system relied on an ontological inequality formulated in the Islamic maxim of *dhimma* in which believers (*Muslims*) and non-believers (*dhimmis*) were strictly separated from each other in terms of civil, political and legal status (Gibb and Bowen 1962: 207–8). Thus, notwithstanding the fact that they were members of the same political community, non-Muslim *millets* received different, if not discriminatory, treatment, among others, in the affairs of public employment, military obligation, judicial proceedings and taxation, and even regarding styles and colors of dress (Bozkurt 1996: 7–32; Peters 1999).

Thus, state-membership and ethno-cultural membership were constituted in the Ottoman context within two different realms. Legal status was grounded not in the accomplishment of the former, but it was the latter which decided peoples' socio-political and legal position in the state. Peoples were considered, first and foremost, as members of *millet* communities, outside of which none could claim legal existence (Gibb and Bowen 1962: 211–12). In this form, the classical system displayed more the characteristics of a "federation of *millets*" or of "*umma* communities" having no common identity and legal status independent of religiously delimited communal affiliations. Administrative organization incorporated inward-closed and strictly separated communities of religion which lived side-by-side but separate from each other. As a result, neither the concept nor the practice of citizenship, involving equal rights and obligations, appeared in the Ottoman Empire before the nineteenth century (Davison 1954: 845).

Nevertheless, the classical *millet* system, despite its inegalitarian ramifications, functioned well as long as religion remained the dominant source of identity for all Ottoman subjects. Neither did the communities challenge its premises nor did the imperial administration trouble itself with the creation of a universal status of citizenship. However, after the influence of the French Revolution, the principles of liberty, equality and "nationality" had infiltrated the Ottoman lands by the early nineteenth century, the classical *nizam* began to lose its legitimate grounds. A dramatic transformation occurred in the non-national *millet* identities and loyalties toward ethno-linguistic and territorial particularities. Non-Muslim minority nationalism came to preoccupy administrative minds in the empire. It was in this context that the Sublime Porte began to feel an urgent need to substitute inegalitarian aspects of the classical system with a substantive equality of Ottoman citizenship cutting across ethno-linguistic, religious and sectarian affiliations (Lewis 1965).

At this stage, the Ottoman rulers adopted the reformist policy of *ittihad-ı anasır* (union of elements) which aimed at substituting the classical *millet* system with an egalitarian project of *Ottomanism*. To this end, leading documents of the reform process in the nineteenth century, the so-called *Tanzimat* era, addressed the civil, political and legal equality of Ottoman subjects. Discriminatory practices in the affairs of judiciary, taxation, military obligation, public employment and those relating to peoples' everyday circumstances were gradually renounced.[1] The first Ottoman Constitution (1876) affirmed that apart from religious matters, Muslim and non-Muslims had identical rights and obligations. The same constitution stipulated that all of the Ottoman peoples, whether Muslim or non-Muslim, were to be considered "Ottoman" in terms of national affiliation, irrespective of religious and sectarian origins (Kili and Gözübüyük 1985: 31–44). Depending on this egalitarian articulation of the law and the legal-political formulation of nationality, citizenship and national affiliation converged. From the political point of view, therefore, the traditional discrepancy between state membership and communal membership, in principle, was eliminated to a considerable degree in the Ottoman context.

The reform period attempted to dissolve ethno-religious and legal compartmentalization within an inclusive formula of citizenship and nationality. However, what Ottoman authorities would not see, if they wanted to see, was the fact that the non-Muslim minorities were not seeking equality within, but political liberation without, the state. This is why civil and political liberties brought neither an integrated Ottoman society of citizens, nor did it halt the non-Muslim minorities' nationalist aspirations. The traditional duality between the notion of Ottoman citizenship consisting of equal individuals and the corporate structures of the *millet* system remained unsolved. The political project of *ittihad-ı anasır* which marked the Ottoman policies of modernization, therefore, culminated in a great failure. The Christian communities moved out of *millet* consciousness directly into a national consciousness without ever accepting Ottoman citizenship (Davison 1963: 407–8). Once touched by the winds of nationalism, traditional *millet* compartmentalization resulted not in the emergence of an integrated "Ottoman nation" but national states of non-Muslim minorities. Greece, Serbia, Romania, Montenegro and Bulgaria ultimately declared their independence. Moreover, even some of the Muslim elements, including Albanians and Arabs, had joined in this ethnic dismemberment by the turn of the century. When the final collapse came with the Treaty of Sèvres (1920) in the aftermath of World War I (WWI), the disintegration of the empire along the lines of minority identities was almost complete.[2]

The failure of the politics of *ittihad-ı anasır* aroused much resentment among the Muslim people and the rulers of the empire, prominently the Turks, who had invested great hopes in the principle of citizenship equality as a means of saving the state from collapse. Non-Muslim minorities and the persistence of *millet* divisions, hence, came to be considered one of the major causes behind the dissolution of the empire. As a result, minority issues lost their naivety in the eyes of the Turkish statesmen, who came to see minority rights not as a matter of respect, freedom, liberty or equality within the borders of a shared polity, but more as the instrument of ethnic dismemberment and as a pretext for external interference. It was this legacy that aroused a general distrust, suspicion and hatred against minority claims in Turkey that greatly constrained the issue of minority rights and the citizenship position of minorities in the republican period.

The republican regime

The Treaty of Sèvres marked the final partition of the country among minority nationalities aided by the diplomatic and armed support of the Allied powers. Against this state of affairs, nationalist leaders, led by Mustafa Kemal Atatürk, fought a war of national liberation between 1919 and 1922, during which time Turkish politics underwent a process of transition from a multi-national empire to a relatively homogeneous nation-state. It was in this period, having learned much from the fact that the universalist project of Ottoman citizenship had lost meaning in the nationalist aspirations of the non-Muslim minorities, that the founding leaders came to favor the creation of a secular minority policy, on the one hand, and a religiously delimited national vision, on the other.

In doing this, unlike the *millet*-system-like formulations, the Turkish authorities affirmed the then prevailing standards of minority treatment outlined in the Minorities Treaties of the post-WWI European context.[3] As is well-known, while extending the concern of minority protection from religious groups to linguistic and racial (ethnic) elements and from state-to-state practices into a limited international regime vested in the discretion of the League of Nations, the treaties brought innovative changes to the traditional framework of minority rights in Europe. Apart from group-specific regulations of differential treatment, minority peoples were provided with universal principles of citizenship status (Rosting 1923). In the aftermath of the liberation war, the founding leaders also agreed on the equal accommodation of minority distinctions in Turkey. To this end, articles 37–45 of the Peace Treaty of Lausanne (24 July 1923), that is the Turkish equivalent of the Minorities Treaties, were assigned to the issue of minority protection (Hurewitz 1956: 119–27).

It is significant to note here that, though an open commitment was declared within the framework of the Minorities Treaties, the Turkish treaty drifted from its contemporaries in specifying its beneficiaries. In the view of the Turkish authorities, ethnic and linguistic classification could not be reconciled with the traditional form of socio-political and legal divisions that had hitherto rested in the Turkish context on peoples' religious distinctions. The Turkish leaders insisted that Turkey involve no minority on the basis of ethno-linguistic or racial distinctions except those of the historically constituted non-Muslim communities (Rıza 1999: 103).[4] The Lausanne document, hence, specified that the wording "minorities" incorporated in the Treaty indicated nothing but the "non-Muslim minorities" resident in Turkey. Consequently, following the religious legacy of the classical *millet* system, only the Greeks, Armenians and Jews were allowed to benefit from the effect of minority provisions. Turkish-Muslim peoples, whatever their ethno-lingual and sectarian differences, were totalized under an imagined unity of national category.

Unlike minority/majority classification, the scope of rights, nevertheless, was almost completely detached from the imprints of traditional Turkish practices. Aware of the fact that the political, legal and administrative grounds of a national formation would necessarily seek the establishment of a direct linkage between citizens and the state, the founding leaders were convinced that corporate aspects of the *millet* system could no longer be maintained. Primarily, minority provisions of the Lausanne document considered members of the non-Muslim communities individual citizens of the republican state, independent of their religious or sectarian affiliations. In the new regime, therefore, communal membership, if it ever existed, remained secondary in deciding the legal status of the non-Muslim peoples. Unlike the dual application of the late Ottoman system, the citizenship status of minorities was expected to dominate their communal membership. It was for this reason that rights and freedoms specified in the document directly addressed the religious, linguistic and cultural peculiarities of "Turkish nationals belonging to non-Muslim minorities."

The minority section of the Lausanne Treaty, therefore, aimed first at protecting and reproducing the distinct identities of non-Muslim Turkish citizens. To this end, the Turkish government undertook to grant positive measures of differential treatment for members of non-Muslim minorities in education, religious practices and charitable foundations. It was affirmed that non-Muslim citizens would establish, manage and control their own charitable, religious and social institutions and schools in which they would freely use their own language and exercise their own religious instructions (Art. 40). Provided that teaching of the Turkish (official) language remained obligatory, it was recognized that minorities would receive primary instruction in those regions or districts where they constituted a considerable proportion of the resident population. In the same areas, the government also undertook to give financial support, particularly to their educational activities (Art. 41).

After group-specific concerns were secured, minority provisions assured that the act of differential treatment would by no means be understood against the principle of citizenship equality. In order to avoid the emergence of an adverse development, minority-specific rights were substantively supplemented in the Turkish treaty with those egalitarian measures of civil and political equality grounded in the citizenship status of minority individuals. In this respect, the provisions guaranteed full and complete protection of life and liberty to all inhabitants of the country without distinction of birth, nationality, language, ethnicity or religion (Art. 38). In other articles, it was affirmed that "Turkish nationals belonging to non-Muslim minorities will enjoy the same civil and political rights as Muslims ... shall be equal before the law ... [and in] admission to public employment, functions and honors, or the exercise of professions and industries." Notwithstanding the existence of official language, the Treaty further stipulated that "no restrictions shall be imposed on the free use by any Turkish national of any language in private intercourse, in commerce, religion, in the press and publications of any kind or at public meetings ... [and] before the courts" (Art. 39).

Having guaranteed both the individual and group-specific dimensions of minority existence, the republican state established legal diversity without violating universal premises of citizenship status. The new framework affirmed that minority individuals would freely enjoy the benefits of equal Turkish citizenship as well as their particular characteristics. Although they might have lost the protective function of communal organizations, non-Muslim minorities, being equal members of the Turkish citizenry, obtained, henceforth, effective guarantees pertinent to the protection and promotion of their ethno-cultural identities. However, even after the reception of the Lausanne regime, centuries-old cleavages, confrontations and prejudices continued to jeopardize possible grounds for creating an egalitarian coexistence between Turkish-Muslim and non-Muslim sections of population. Primary reflections of this foundational continuity appeared merely in the dual formulation and practices of citizenship policies.

Legal-political delimitation of the republican nationhood

The Ottomanist citizenship of *ittihad-ı anasır* projected an abstract Ottoman nationhood superior to sub-national particularities of ethno-linguistic and religious groupings. While considering each member of the population as "Ottoman," the imperial authorities devised no distinction between citizenship and nationality. Once one received Ottoman citizenship, one was secured membership in the Ottoman national category. However, under the constraints of the failure of Ottomanist citizenship, the republican leaders became convinced that it was no more than a dream to include non-Muslim minorities in the national category of the new state. In their eyes, the national struggle itself had partly been staged against the nationalist aspirations of non-Muslim minorities (Oran 1997: 125–8). Because of this, the republican authorities ceased to produce a political definition of nationality and citizenship. The Ottomanist ideal of *ittihad-ı anasır* was by no means replaced by an ethnic Turkism, but with a strong policy orientation of *itthad-ı anasır-ı İslamiye* (union of Muslim elements). Adherence to a common religion was placed in the foundational basis of the Turkish national identity. The historical and cultural unity of the Muslim peoples, resident within the borders of the new state, delimited also the majority characteristics of the republican population.[5]

In conformity with this policy turn, Ziya Gökalp, the prominent ideologue of Turkish nationalism, formulated a Muslim-inclusive concept of Turkish citizenship and nationality. He believed that the main reason for the failed development of Ottoman citizenship within an integrated nationhood lay in the persistence of religious distinctions among subject peoples. The religious diversity of the imperial population, for him, prevented development of a national unity, which, in turn, culminated in the failure of its citizenship policies (Berkes 1981: 78). A coherent nation, in his view, would be established on the basis of a cultural community speaking one language and professing one religion (Berkes 1981: 136–7). In so doing, Gökalp closely connected the notions of citizenship and nationality and believed that a workable citizenship policy would successfully be created, in the Turkish context, only on the basis of the cultural community of the Turkish-Muslim peoples of the country.

Similarly, in bringing a secular approach to the question of Turkish national identity, Atatürk intended first to develop a comprehensive formula of Turkish nationalism inclusive of all of the inhabitants of the country. In doing this, he explicitly denied the constitutive function of religious substance and promoted a common language, culture and history as the bases of Turkish nationhood (Afetinan 1998: 18–25). However, his definition still concealed a religious implication in the sense that traditional practices had hardly produced a cultural unity between Muslim and non-Muslim citizens. If there was any cultural, historical or linguistic affinity, it had been generated among the members of the same religious community. The designation of the "cultural community of citizens," therefore, indicated a national category consisting of the Muslim community of citizens. Having been aware of this historical background, Atatürk, in another definition, limited membership of Turkish nationality to those citizens who had participated in the founding process of the Republic, in which non-Muslim citizens had been completely excluded (Afetinan 1998: 18).

Thus, Turkish practices, by the early years of the republican regime, came to articulate a close association between citizenship and nationality based on the Muslim characteristics of the population. The same rationality also affected the formal definition of Turkish citizenship. The parliamentary elaboration of the 1924 constitution, in this sense, stipulated that formal membership of the Turkish citizenry was not sufficient to guarantee the full-fledged scope of citizenship status. Although the constitution (Art. 88) laid down that "the name Turk, as regards to citizenship, shall be understood to include all citizens of the Turkish Republic without distinction of, or reference to, race or religion," the drafting authorities denied formulating an identical citizenship status equally applicable to Turkish-Muslim and non-Muslim sections of the population.[6] While articulating a civic definition of Turkish nationality, contrary to what the principles of civil and political equality might imply, the inclusive concept of the name "Turk" was limited to the cultural community of Turkish-Muslim peoples. A strict distinction between possession of "Turkish nationality" (*milliyet*) and "Turkish citizenship" (*tabiiyet*) was preserved. In doing this, non-Muslim minorities were included in the formal definition of Turkish citizenship, but excluded even from the legal-political content of Turkish nationhood (Toker 1979: 361–4).

Depending on this nationality/citizenship differentiation, citizenship practices lost their neutrality in the Turkish context in terms of ethno-cultural particularities. Following the same differentiation, the republican regime instead opted to create two categories of citizens: "national citizens" (citizens by nationality) and "formal citizens" (citizens by law). In this case, notwithstanding the civic features of the legal definition, the distinction of nationality carried two significant implications for Turkish citizenship practices as they related to the issue of minority treatment. On the one hand, with the Muslim-inclusive formulation of nationality, which superseded the ethno-lingual and sectarian differences of Muslim citizens, the Ottoman Muslim *millet* was culturally, legally, politically and practically reproduced within the borders of the new state. The full-fledged scope of citizenship was largely identified with ethno-cultural membership of the Turkish nation. This Muslim-inclusive nationality provided legal equality for Turkish-Muslim citizens irrespective of their sub-national characteristics. But, since the uniform designation of national citizenship denied public expression of the Muslim population's ethno-cultural distinctions, the socio-political and legal ramifications of equal treatment were reflected in an understanding and practice of unanimous treatment. Second, since the ratification of the Lausanne Treaty, the republican state has extended official recognition and measures of differential treatment to members of non-Muslim minorities.

However, because of their national "otherness," in contravention of the Lausanne commitments, almost no compromise could be accomplished between the principles of citizenship equality and differential treatment on the part of the non-Muslim minorities.

Dual practices of Turkish citizenship

The dual formulation of Turkish citizenship has operated in an assimilationist manner with respect to the Turkish-Muslim elements. Since they have historically represented ethno-cultural others of the Turkish-Muslim population, the same formula has shown an exclusivist attitude toward members of the non-Muslim minorities. The demographic, linguistic, cultural and economic policies of nationalism, which marked, in particular, the single-party period of the new state (1923–50), have, therefore, advanced at the expense of non-Muslim minorities' ethno-cultural, demographic and economic presence in the country.

In fact, the official reception of the Lausanne commitments was accompanied by an act of national homogenization in terms of religious affiliation. Unwilling to live with a larger minority population, the Turkish and Greek governments agreed in 1923 on the exchange of kin groups living on the land of the other country. By the time it was completed, toward the end of the 1920s, more than 1.5 million people of minorities had been relocated.[7] Interestingly, in conformity with the premises of Turkish national formation, throughout the implementation of the exchange, citizenship status was bestowed upon religious kin resident in the Greek state. A person's creed determined their national and citizenship position as well. The population exchange, hence, resulted in "two deportations into exile, of Christian Turks to Greece and of Muslim Turks to Turkey" (Lewis 1968: 355). Apart from Greek-speaking ones, the Turkish government exchanged its Turkish-speaking Orthodox citizens with many non-Turkish-speaking Muslims who were granted full and complete Turkish citizenship (Psomiades 1968: 60–8).

Coinciding with the years of "demographic nationalization," the government initiated a new process of exchange, particularly in the personnel of those companies owned by non-Muslim minorities or foreign residents. The companies were compelled to exchange their foreign and non-Muslim staff with Muslim-Turkish citizens (Alexandris 1992: 111). It is estimated that by the year 1926 approximately 5,000 employees from the Greek minority had already been replaced with Muslim-Turks (Alexandris 1992: 110). Indicating the inegalitarian effect of "formal citizenship," the government blocked their capacity in public employment as well. The *Law of Public Employment*, dated 1926, conditioned public employment on "being Turk" and not on "being a Turkish citizen." Hence, since non-Muslim minorities were considered Turkish only in terms of citizenship, the law, in practice, excluded non-Muslim peoples from the state sector while reserving it exclusively for the benefit of Turkish-Muslim citizens (Aktar 2000: 118–21).

Hence, despite the fact that it ran counter to the principles of civil and political equality, incorporated both within the Lausanne commitments and subsequently adopted form of the republican citizenship, the employment facilities of non-Muslim minorities were to a large extent curtailed. Nevertheless, the dual version of republican citizenship had its most enduring impact on the linguistic rights of minority citizens. Free use of minority languages, both in public and private, had been guaranteed at Lausanne. However, the task of liquidating minority languages was considered one of the immediate objectives of the Turkish national project. To this end, from the early years of the republic, Turkish was emphasized as an essential criterion not only for Turkish nationality but also of the legal-political category of Turkish citizenship. The political and intellectual circles of the country came to believe that if one desired to have equal and full access to Turkish citizenship, one must have adopted the Turkish language (Bali 2000: 107). Consequently, instruction in minority languages was greatly limited, even in minority educational establishments (Sezer 1999: 17–35). Several municipalities subsequently agreed to discourage minority citizens from speaking a non-Turkish language in public places (Bali 2000: 108). In this context, a widespread campaign of "Citizen! Speak Turkish" was instigated in 1928 in the Turkish press, political circles and the general public against both private and public use of minority tongues (Galanti 2000).

The "Citizen! Speak Turkish" campaign was practiced in the form of a mass movement in which predominantly intellectual circles and ordinary people took the lead. In that sense, it remained largely a "civil" act focusing mainly on the non-Muslim residents of big cities. However, anti-minority measures obtained an official and nation-wide characteristic when the Turkish Grand National Assembly (TGNA) enacted a new settlement law in 1934 (*Official Gazette* 1934). Having found the shortcomings of Ottoman cosmopolitanism dangerous to the country's national and territorial unity, creating a homogeneous nation integrated in "one language, one sentiment and one ideal" was stated as the main objective of the law (TGNA 1934: 69–70). To this end, the law, in conformity with its inherent duality, divided Turkish citizens into two categories: those belonging to the Turkish cultural and linguistic group and those who remained outside the borders of this ethno-cultural designation. It was affirmed that the latter group of citizens would be relocated based on the political, cultural and security considerations of the state. Although the act aimed at relocating all non-Turkish speaking citizens, its immediate effect fell on the "formal citizens." Certain parts of the country were closed to minority settlement. In the aftermath of the legislation, for example, approximately two thirds of the regional Jews were forced to evacuate Turkish Thrace (Karabatak 1996).

The overwhelming emphasis of the Turkish nationalism had shifted, by the early 1930s, from common culture to ethnic cores (Oran 1997: 200–7). However, this transformation by no means affected citizenship practices of the republican state based upon the Muslim/non-Muslim duality of national classification.[8] On the contrary, the increasing effect of nationalist feeling further crystallized the foundational distinction between "national" and "formal" citizens. At this stage, the implementation of the Capital Tax presented the extreme example of the new tendency. From the legal point of view, the law was enacted in 1942 in order to levy extraordinary wealth earned by exploiting the then-prevailing wartime conditions (Ökte 1987: 1–14). However, as Akar (2000: 166–7) has explained, the law entailed also the implicit goal of achieving capital transfer from non-Muslim hands to Turkish-Muslim citizens. As Prime Minister Saraçoğlu is reported to have stated:

> The law carries, at the same time, a revolutionary nature in the sense that it will create an opportunity to achieve our economic independence. Because, in doing this, on the one hand, we will be able to hand over the Turkish economy to Turks while eliminating the non-Turkish elements from the Turkish economy. On the other hand, with this law, we will be able to transfer immovable estates in Istanbul to Turkish peoples. ... In short, this law will put a final end to the economic superiority of non-Turkish elements in the country.
>
> (Barutçu 2001: 594)

The prime minister had given assurances on several occasions that the government recognized no distinction between citizens of the country (Yalman 1997: 1253–4). But the implementation of the tax proved the reverse. The law, in practice, drifted from the principle of citizenship equality, and classified taxpayers into two separate groups, Muslims and non-Muslims (Ökte 1987: 19). The latter were arbitrarily assessed at a rate ten times higher than the amounts levied on their Turkish-Muslim equivalents. When they failed to pay, the assessed amount, along with movable and immovable properties belonging to the defaulters, were confiscated and sold at auction, 98 percent of which were bought out by Turkish-Muslim peoples and companies (Aktar 2000). Most significantly, those defaulters who declared that they were unable to pay were sent to labor camps where they were expected to pay their taxes by working for the state. Although liability to forced labor was, in principle, applied to Turkish-Muslim defaulters as well, the government refused to dispatch Muslim citizens to the labor camps (Ökte 1987: 71–2).

Toward the end of World War II, the Turkish government abolished both the capital tax and the labor camps. In the aftermath of the war, Turkey aligned itself with the Western world, which was preaching democratic governments and individual human rights. Hence, the Turkish political system began to transform autocratic structures into liberal-democratic models of politics. Democratic transformation of the political system raised hopes among the members of minority groups as well. Minority citizens came to believe that religious, linguistic and cultural distinctions would no longer prejudice government policies and that the doors were being opened wide to equal and non-discriminatory ways of minority treatment (Bali 1998).

However, by the middle of the 1950s it became evident that the democratic context had by no means eradicated imprints of the foundational duality rooted in the practical and legal basis of Turkish citizenship. Political authorities and the general public continued to rank non-Muslim Turkish citizens within exclusivist categories of "unreliable" and "foreign" residents of the country. Yet, unlike the previous decades, the position of non-Muslim minorities in Turkey began to be shaped this time not by nationalist aspirations of internal politics but by diplomatic crises in external relations. The first example of this attitude appeared in the mid-1950s when Greek-Turkish relations became strained over Cyprus. With Turkey and Greece disagreeing on the future status of the island, the position of minority citizens in Turkey once again came under question. In particular, instead of being viewed within the terms of Turkish citizenship, members of the Greek minority came under suspicion as "foreign" and "dangerous" elements of the country (Benlisoy 2000). Inflamed by the Cyprus crisis, on the night of 6 September 1955 angry crowds destroyed many shops, houses, factories, cultural centers and cemeteries belonging to the Greek, Jewish and Armenian minorities in Istanbul and Izmir.[9] The total amount of damage assessed in Istanbul alone was estimated at $60 million (Alexandris 1992: 259). Official sources stated that during the night three people were killed and thirty injured (Dosdoğru 1993: 100). Helsinki Watch subsequently reported that fifteen people had been killed (Human Rights Watch 1992: 8).

September 6–7 was officially evaluated as the "expression of national feelings" and a "national upheaval of the Turkish youth" (Birand *et al.* 1991: 124–5). From this point of view, leaving aside the damages, the affair underlined the vulnerable position of non-Muslim citizens. Despite the protective framework of the Lausanne commitments and constitutional guarantees, they indeed continued to constitute internal victims of an external crisis. The persistence of diplomatic tensions between Greece and Turkey culminated in the curtailment of minorities' educational rights as well. The Theological Seminary of Khalki was closed down in 1971. As the seminary had been the centre of Orthodox ecclesiastical learning for centuries, the decision badly affected the educational capacity of the Greek Orthodox Patriarchate. Because of this, the restoration of the institution to its original position still occupies a prominent place in the issue of minority treatment in Turkey (Özyılmaz, 2000). Also, during the 1970s and 1980s, attacks on Turkish institutions and diplomats by the ASALA (Armenian Secret Army for the Liberation of Armenia)[10] made the social position of the Armenian minority rather vulnerable. Although social unrest never turned into a real violence, members of the Armenian minority increasingly found themselves in an insecure situation, and eventually many opted to emigrate.

Inconvenient circumstances created by inegalitarian practices of the Turkish citizenship resulted in the gradual homogenization of the Turkish population in terms of religious affiliation. Though the first republican census had counted 2.8 percent non-Muslim citizens in 1927, the proportion declined to 2 percent in 1935, 1.6 percent in 1945, 1.1 percent in 1955, 1 percent in 1960 and 0.8 percent in 1965 (Dündar 2000: 138). The 1992 estimates showed that, apart from earlier migrations, during the previous three decades more than 20,000 Armenians, 23,000 Jews and 55,000 Greeks had emigrated from Turkey (Franz 1994: 331). Although there are now thought to be 1.2 million non-Muslims in Turkey (Courbage and Fargues 1998: 115), community sources recently counted no more than 50,000 Armenians, 27,000 Jews and 3,000 Greeks (Dündar 2000: 138).

To sum up, Turkish citizenship practice, with its "national"/"formal" classification, can be seen to a great extent to have followed the Muslim/*dhimmi* compartmentalization of the imperial administration with its latent aspects of inequality. Almost no compromise would be achieved between the principle of civil and political equality of universal citizenship and the group-specific dimension of minority rights. In practice, the notion of full citizenship has been reserved exclusively for the Muslim sections of the Turkish population. A minority intellectual recently remarked that though minorities have formally been considered equal citizens of the country, practice has proved the reverse. This person observed that non-Muslim minorities had come to believe today that only Muslim nationals were full citizens of the republican state, and that they were not regarded as "citizens" even within the limited meaning of the concept (Kaplan 2000).

Toward a system of substantive equality

Two major transformations that had gradually occurred in Turkey by the middle of the 1980s greatly challenged the traditional parameters of republican citizenship practices relating to the official treatment of minority concerns. On the one hand, the imagined unity of the *anasır-ı İslamiye* entered into a process of ethno-linguistic and sectarian disintegration. It was quite evident by the early 1990s that the monolithic formulation of the "national citizenship" would no longer satisfy identity claims of the Turkish-Muslim population in which ethnic Kurdish, Alevi sectarian and fundamental Islamist sections began to seek ways for official recognition and legal-political accommodation. The Turkish citizens of Kurdish origin, for example, came to take an increasing interest in the issue of the official recognition and free expression of their ethno-linguistic characteristics, in particular in the fields of education, broadcast media and cultural activities (Ekinci 1997).

On the other hand, the end of the Cold War unleashed minority problems all over Europe that had been frozen within the ideological confrontations of the previous decades (Liebich 1996). The issue of the equal accommodation of minority differences within a pluralist configuration of legal-political settings began to preoccupy national and international circles for both security and humanitarian considerations. Dedicated to this end, as well as the United Nations (UN), the Council of Europe (CoE), the Organization for Security and Cooperation in Europe (OSCE), and the European Union (EU) gave greater significance to the protection and promotion of cultural, linguistic and religious characteristics of minority peoples. The Copenhagen Summit of the EU Council announced in 1993 that a candidate country must have achieved, before accession to the EU, among others, "stability of institutions guaranteeing democracy, the rule of law, human rights and respect for and protection of minorities" (Verheugen 2000: 440).

The two processes evolved simultaneously in Turkey. With the intensification of EU-Turkey relations, Turkish governments became more prone to increasing international pressure on those issues of democratization and minority protection that strengthened, in turn, the effect of minority claims within the country. Starting from 1998, for example, the EU Commission's annual reports have included a comprehensive assessment of the prevailing conditions of minority treatment and the legal-political grounds of the peaceful coexistence of sub-national differences in Turkey. Generally speaking, referring directly to the traditional shortcomings of minority protection in Turkey, the reports have insisted on the extension of official recognition of the three non-Muslim communities (Armenians, Greeks, and Jews) to the Kurdish, Alevi and Assyrian groups. Furthermore, it has been recommended that Turkish governments facilitate the cultural and political expression of minority differences whether Muslim or non-Muslim. In doing this, the reports suggested that Turkey should undertake appropriate steps in the direction of adopting its constitutional system to the contemporary standards of minority protection specified in the latest documents of the CoE (European Commission 1998; 1999; 2000a; 2001). It is well known that these documents have laid down a number of group-specific rights and freedoms pertinent to facilitating the free use of minority languages in education, press and broadcast media. Accordingly, Turkey's EU *Accession Partnership* agreement has conditioned Turkish membership on the removal of "any legal provisions forbidding the use by Turkish citizens of their mother tongue in TV/radio broadcasting" in the short-term and in the field of education in the medium-term (European Commission 2000b).

Thus, by the 1990s, internal and external changes had compelled Turkey to revise its traditional practices with regard to citizenship issues. At this stage, the question for the Turkish authorities was how to integrate various ethnic, linguistic and religious groups without endangering the national and territorial integrity of the state. The view in official circles was that the EU standards would open a "Pandora's box" in the country, paving the way to the national and territorial disintegration of the republican state (Mete 1998: 18). More specifically, the act of granting public recognition to group-specific rights was considered an attempt destined to restore the conditions of the Treaty of Sèvres that had been defeated at Lausanne (Demirel 1998a).

Nevertheless, this did not mean that the dualistic conceptualization and practices of Turkish citizenship, which had excluded non-Muslim minorities from the benefits of genuine equality and denied the ethno-linguistic and sectarian identities of Turkish-Muslim citizens, could still be maintained. Partly under the impact of EU integration, and partly because of growing identity claims from within Turkey, the Turkish authorities, in the past decade, have come to admit group-specific particularities of both Muslim and non-Muslim peoples on the grounds of "individual freedoms."[11] It was in this context that the notion of constitutional citizenship was introduced and began to be widely discussed by the Turkish public, intelligentsia and state (İçduygu *et al.* 2000).

It is argued that the notion of constitutional citizenship would disassociate citizenship status from particularistic identities of peoples while causing legal-political ramifications related to the concept of a neutral source of identification for the whole of the population. In this view, it is expected that the constitution would operate as an integrative mechanism through which nationals of the country develop into a common polity without divorcing themselves from their ethno-linguistic, sectarian and religious particularities (İçduygu *et al.* 2000: 192). In other words, situated within the rights and obligations of an all-inclusive constitution, full and equal citizenship is associated not with membership of an ethno-cultural grouping but with the neutral framework of a legal setting. Thereby, it is believed that the state would cease to act as the representative institution of a single ethno-linguistic and religious community of citizens, but would make room for the free expression of all the particular distinctions. In the name of constitutional equality, thus, the state would take responsibility for all of its citizens in protecting and promoting their ethno-cultural, religious and linguistic interests.

The principle of constitutional citizenship, in this form, presented a possibility not only for overcoming the traditional duality rooted in Turkish citizenship practices, but also for meeting claims of social diversity brought forth both by different sections of the Turkish population and the EU standards. Aware of this fact, Süleyman Demirel, the former president, remarked on several occasions that the Turkish system would find a way to accommodate its social diversity without violating the uniform image of Turkish citizenship. While defending the development of a democratic response to the prevailing problems of ethno-cultural diversity, the Prime Minister Demirel remarked in 1992 that:

> differences in culture, thought, belief, language and origin are natural among our citizens. Such diversity is not a weakness in a democratic and unitary state. In a unitary structure, various ethnic, cultural and linguistic characteristics can be freely expressed, preserved and easily developed. This does not weaken the unity of the nation, but strengthens it. Everyone is equal and has the same status. The right to

> search for, preserve and develop one's mother tongue, culture, history, folklore and religious beliefs falls within the framework of human rights and freedoms. The law will ensure these rights.
>
> (Demirel 1992: 33)

"The law," in Demirel's view, is associated with the concept of constitutional citizenship. The former president subsequently suggested that "while granting universal citizenship equally to every individual member of the state, constitutional citizenship would, at the same time, recognize their ethnic and sectarian differences" (Demirel 1998b). This approach signaled the substitution of the dualistic conceptualization of Turkish citizenship with a legal diversity of Turkish nationals united only in respect to a formal connection stipulating the same rights and obligations. Putting the matter differently, it was believed that constitutional affiliation to the republic would not necessarily make a "Turk," even in the formal sense of the word, but he or she would continue to claim his or her particular identity. In this sense, the discourse of universal citizenship would no longer be used as a neutralizing instrument over the particular identities of the Turkish peoples. More specifically, in the words of Demirel (1998b), "a Turkish citizen of Kurdish origin would freely express his or her ethno-cultural identity provided that he or she proved loyal to the constitution and the essential principles of the republic."

While Demirel was concerned with examples of internal constraints on the traditional parameters and practices of republican citizenship, the High Board of Human Rights (HBHR 2000) and the Ministry of Foreign Affairs (MFA 2000) instigated similar debates for the sake of Turkey's EU integration. Under the influence of EU standards, both public institutions recently conceded that the persistence of a monolithic national identity had blocked free expression of particular differences in religion, sect, language and ethnicity. In order to improve Turkey's human rights standards in the contemporary world, the HBHR accordingly reported that social diversity and national unity must be reconciled within an inclusive framework of a "comprehensive constitutional citizenship." The universal equality of citizenship status, in other words, should not exclude peoples' right to difference without which those citizens who differ from the majority in ethnic, linguistic, religious and cultural terms would be less equal in enjoying contemporary standards of human rights. In so doing, it was suggested, the indivisible unity of the country with its nation and territory would continue to remain a constitutional principle and no threat would arise from the official recognition of minority differences.

Although there is little compromise among the different departments of the state,[12] these reports indicated the emergence of a new trend in Turkey's citizenship policies, one inclined toward a system of socio-political and legal equality within ethno-cultural diversity. Several steps have already been taken in this direction. The ban on speaking Kurdish in public and using it in press and publications was canceled in 1991. Subsequently Demirel declared, in a speech delivered in one of the Kurdish-populated cities, that the state recognized existence of the "Kurdish reality." In a similar manner, though closed down several times after having been convicted of engaging in separatist activities, a pro-Kurdish political party had eventually taken a secure place in Turkish democracy by the middle of the 1990s. Tens of municipalities have been governed for almost a decade by those mayors who were elected from among the ranks of this pro-Kurdish party. Similarly, the Supreme Court of Appeals passed a judgment on 31 March 2000 which confirmed the freedom of individual citizens to give their children any names of their choosing, including Kurdish names.

Furthermore, unlike the legal-political practices of the previous decades, the republican state has undertaken several other steps to guarantee the equal status of non-Muslim citizens. In this respect, public policies began for the first time to disregard the traditional parameters of Turkish citizenship and treat non-Muslim minorities on the same grounds as Turkish-Muslim citizens. In December 1999, an official circular, for example, recognized that non-Muslim minorities would no longer be required to seek permission from the state in order to restore churches and other buildings belonging to minority foundations. In the following year, the Turkish presidency issued a message on the eve of the year 2000 to non-Muslim minority groups on the occasion of Christmas and Hanukah (*Radikal* 2000b). The message carried a symbolic significance in the sense that it confirmed the equal position of non-Muslim citizens in the eyes of the authorities. Similarly, the Ministry of Education, for the first time, attempted to eliminate prejudices about Gypsy citizens from the national educational texts. To this end, the ministry issued a circular in 2001 in order to cancel pejorative words used about Gypsies from the dictionaries published by the same ministry.

Without doubt, recent political trends indicate the emergence of a substantive transformation in the classic duality of Turkish citizenship practices. While non-Muslim minorities came to be treated with genuine equality of citizenship, sub-national identities of the Muslim population began to find an implicit recognition in the public realm of the state. Yet it seems too early to talk about the consolidation of a comprehensive constitutional citizenship expressed in a system of substantive equality tolerant of ethno-linguistic, religious and sectarian differences between both Muslim and non-Muslim members of the Turkish citizenry. It is significant to note here that, at the time of writing this chapter, the TGNA has enacted progressive reforms allowing the free use of minority languages and dialects, whether Muslim or non-Muslim, in education and broadcast media. The same reforms accord corporate-communal rights to non-Muslim pious foundations relating to the issue of obtaining and disposing of real estate. The policy implementation of the enacted laws and regulations indicate that deepening innovative changes have occurred in Turkish citizenship practices. This would be an appropriate topic for subsequent studies.

Notes

1 The Imperial Rescript of Gülhane (1839) and the Reform Edict (1856) are the pioneers of the Ottoman reform process in creating legal grounds of civil and political equality between Muslim and non-Muslim subjects of the empire (see Hurewitz 1956: 113–16, 149–53).

2 According to the provisions of the Treaty of Sèvres, of European Turkey only Istanbul was to be left to Turkey; in Anatolia, an Armenian state and a Kurdish state were to be created; part of western Anatolia was to be ceded to Greece (see Hurewitz 1956: 81–7).

3 The fifth article of the National Pact (*Misak-ı Milli*), the provisions of which outlined minimal objectives of the nationalist struggle, drawn up in 1920:

> The rights of minorities as defined in the treaties concluded between the Entente powers and their enemies and certain of their associates shall be confirmed and assured by us -in reliance on the belief that the Muslim minorities in neighboring countries will also be given the benefit of the same rights.
>
> (see Macfie 1996: 124–5)

4 The Turkish delegate indicated at Lausanne, in the Sub-Commission of Minorities, that Turkish political culture limited minority status exclusively to the case of the religious minorities, and that political expression of ethnic and linguistic particularities remained alien to Turkish political history. Under these circumstances, it was stated, the Turkish state should not be expected to grant official recognition to ethnic and linguistic distinctions that existed among the Turkish-Muslim population (see Meray 1969: 154, 160).

5 Concluding documents of the nationalist congresses of Erzurum and Sivas proved that the "national" component of the Turkish national struggle connoted Muslim residents of Anatolia whatever the ethno-linguistic and sectarian distinctions (see Gologlu 1968: 201–3; İğdemir 1969: 113–15).

6 The civic wording of the citizenship clause of the constitution remained intact both in the 1961 (Art. 54) and the 1982 constitutions (Art. 66).

7 Toward the end of the Turkish national struggle, approximately 1,350,000 Anatolian Greeks migrated to Greece (Tekeli 1990: 61). With the implementation of the Turkish-Greek population exchange, this number reached to an amount exceeding 1,500,000 (Geray 1970: 10).

8 The Gagauz Turks of Romania, who spoke Turkish but were Orthodox Christian in religion, were not allowed to migrate to Turkey in the mid-1930s. Because of religious distinction, they were not considered within the conceptual borders of Turkish national identity. In the same period, however, large groups of Balkan Muslims, from different ethnic and linguistic backgrounds, were able to take Turkish citizenship as equal members of the Turkish national category (see Kirişçi 2000).

9 The damage in Istanbul included 1,004 houses, 4,348 shops, 27 pharmacies and laboratories, 21 factories, 110 restaurants, cafes and hotels, 26 schools, 5 athletic clubs and 2 cemeteries (Alexandris 1992: 259). In Izmir, the mass attacks resulted in the destruction of 14 houses, 6 shops, 1 pavilion, the Greek consulate, and a Greek church. It was reported that fifty-seven persons were wounded in the same city (Kılıçdere 2000).

10 It was reported that between 1973 and 1985 ASALA staged 86 attacks against Turkish nationals, killing 47 Turkish citizens, 32 of whom were officials, and injuring 19 officials (Franz 1994: 327).

11 The Turkish National Programme submitted to the EU Commission considered cultural and linguistic rights not within the terms of minority protection, but as

"individual freedoms" to be granted to the benefit of all Turkish citizens irrespective of language, race, color, sex, political opinion, and philosophical or religious belief (TNP 2000).

12 The National Security Council, which is one of the most influential constitutional institutions in Turkish politics, has denied any deviation from the scope of the Lausanne regime and the monolithic understanding of Turkish citizenship on the grounds of preserving the territorial and national integrity of the republic (*Radikal* 2000a).

References

Afetinan, A. (1998) *Medeni Bilgiler ve M. Kemal Atatürk'ün El Yazmaları* (Civil Knowledge and Ataturk's Unpublished Notes), Ankara: TTK.

Akar, R. (2000) *Aşkale Yolcuları: Varlık Vergisi ve Çalışma Kampları* (Passengers to Aşkale: The Capital Tax and the Labour Camps), Istanbul: Belge Yayınları.

Aktar, A. (2000) *Varlık Vergisi ve Türkleştirme Politikaları* (The Capital Tax and the Policies of Turkification), Istanbul: İletişim Yayınları.

Alexandris, A. (1992) *The Greek Minority of Istanbul and Greek-Turkish Relations: 1918–1974*, Athens: Center for Asia Minor Studies.

Bali, R. N. (1998) "Resmi İdeoloji ve Gayri Müslim Azınlıklar" (Official Ideology and Non-Muslim Minorities), *Birikim*, January-February: 170–6.

——(2000) *Cumhuriyet Yıllarında Türkiye Yahudileri: Bir Türkleştirme Serüveni (1923–1945)* (The Jews of the Republican Turkey: A Venture of Turkification), Istanbul: İletişim Yayınları.

Barutçu, F. A. (2001) *Siyasi Hatıralar: Milli Mücadeleden Demokrasiye* (Political Memoirs: From National Struggle to Democracy), vol. 1, Ankara: Yüzyıl Yayınları.

Benlisoy, F. (2000) "6/7 Eylül Öncesinde Basında Rumlar" (Greeks in the Press before the Affair of 6/7 September), *Toplumsal Tarih*, 81: 28–38.

Berkes, N. (1981) *Turkish Nationalism and Western Civilisation: Selected Essays of Ziya Gökalp*, Westport CT: Greenwood Press.

——(1998) *The Development of Secularism in Turkey*, New York: Routledge.

Birand, M. A., Dündar, C. and Çaplı, B. (1991) *Demirkırat: Bir Demokrasinin Doğuşu* (Iron Horse: Emergence of a Democracy), Istanbul: Milliyet Yayınları.

Bozkurt, G. (1996) *Gayrimüslim Osmanlı Vatandaşlarının Hukuki Durumu: 1839–1914* (Legal Status of the Non-Muslim Ottoman Subjects), Ankara: TTK.

——(1996) *Batı Hukukunun Türkiye'de Benimsenmsesi* (The Reception of Western Law in Turkey), Ankara: TTK.

Braude, B. and Lewis, B. (eds) *Christians and Jews in the Ottoman Empire: The Functioning of a Plural Society*, New York and London: Holmes & Meier.

Brubaker, R. (1992) *Citizenship and Nationhood in France and Germany*, Cambridge MA and London: Harvard University Press.

Bulaç, A. (1992) "Sözleşme Temelinde Toplumsal Proje" (A Social Project on the Basis of a Contract), *Birikim*, 40: 53–62.

Connor, W. (1994) "A Nation is a Nation, is a State, is an Ethnic Group, is a … ," in J. Hutchinson and A. Smith (eds) *Nationalism*, Oxford: Oxford University Press.

Courbage, Y. and Fargues, F. (1998) *Christians and Jews Under Islam*, London and New York: I. B. Tauris.

Davison, R. H. (1954) "Turkish Attitudes Concerning Christian-Muslim Equality in the Nineteenth Century," *The American Historical Review*, LIX (4): 844–64.

——(1963) *Reform in the Ottoman Empire: 1856–1876*, Princeton: Princeton University Press.

Demirel, S. (1992) "Creating a Community of Equals: The Democratic Response to Ethnic Diversity," *Harvard International Review*, XV (1): 32–3.

——(1998a) "Güneydoğuda Sevr Deneniyor" (The Treaty of Sevres is Being Tried in the Southeast), *Milliyet*, 22 August.

——(1998b) "Sigorta, Anayasal Vatandaşlık" (Constitutional Citizenship is the Insurance), *Milliyet*, 22 August.

Dosdoğru, H. (1993) *6/7 Eylül Olayları* (The Affair of 6/7 September), Istanbul: Bağlam Yayınları.

Dündar, F. (2000) *Türkiye Nüfus Sayımlarında Azınlıklar* (Minorities in the National Censuses of Turkey), Istanbul: Çiviyazıları.

Ekinci, T. Z. (1997) *Vatandaşlık Açısından Kürt Sorunu ve Bir Çözüm Önesrisi* (The Kurdish Question from the Perspective of Citizenship and a Proposed Solution), Istanbul: Küyerel Yayınları.

European Commission (1998) *Regular Report from the Commission on Progress Towards Accession of Turkey*. Online. Available at http://europa.eu.int/comm/enlargement/turkey/rep_11_98/b12.htm (accessed 15 February 2001).

——(1999) *Regular Report from the Commission on Turkey's Progress Towards Accession*. Online. Available at http://europe.eu.int/comm/enlargement/report_10_99/pdf/eng/turkey (accessed 15 February 2001).

——(2000) *Regular Report from the Commission on Turkey's Progress Towards Accession*. Online. Available at http://europa.eu.int/comm/enlargement/report/11_00/pdf/en/tu (accessed 15 February 2001).

——(2001) *Regular Report from the Commission on Turkey's Progress Towards Accession*. Online. Available at http://europa.eu.int/comm/enlargement/report2001/tu (accessed 15 February 2001).

——(2000b) *Accession Partnership for Turkey*. Online. Available at http://europa.eu.int/comm/enlargement/turkey/pdf/ap_turk_en.pdf (accessed 15 February 2001).

Franz, F. (1994) *Population Policy in Turkey: Family Planning and Migration Between 1960 and 1992*, Hamburg: Deutsches Orient-Institut.

Galanti, A. (2000) *Vatandaş Türkçe Konuş Yahut Türkçe'nin Ta'mimi Meselesi: Tarihi, İçtimai, Siyasi Tetkik* (Citizen, Speak Turkish! or the Question of Dissemination of the Turkish Language: A Historical, Social and Political Analysis), Ankara: Kebikeç Yayınları.

Gellner, E. (1993) *Nations and Nationalism*, Ithaca NY: Cornell University Press.

Geray, C. (1970) "Türkiyede Göçmen Hareketleri ve Göçmenlerin Yerleştirilmesi" (Migratory Movements in Turkey and the Settlement of the Migrants), *Amme İdaresi Dergisi*, 3 (4): 8–36.

Gibb, H. A. R. and Bowen, H. (1962) *Islamic Society and the West: A Study on the Impact of Western Civilisation on Moslem Culture in the Near East*, London and New York: Oxford University Press.

Gologlu, M. (1968) *Erzurum Kongresi* (The Congress of Erzurum), Ankara: Nüve Matbaası.

HBHR(High Board of Human Rights) (2000) "İnsan Hakları Koordinatör Üst Kurulu Raporu" (The Report of the High Board of Human Rights), *Radikal*, 19 June.

Human Rights Watch (1992) *The Greeks of Turkey*, New York and London: Human Rights Watch.
Hurewitz, J. C. (1956) *Diplomacy in the Near and Middle East: A Documentary Record*, New York and London: D. van Nostrand.
İnalcık, H. (1995) "Political Modernization in Turkey," in R. E. Ward and D. A. Rustow (eds) *Political Modernization in Japan and Turkey*, Oxford: Clarendon Press.
——(1996) "The Meaning of Legacy: The Ottoman Case," in L. C. Brown (ed.) *Imperial Legacy: The Ottoman Imprint on the Balkans and the Middle East*, New York: Columbia University Press.
İçduygu, A., Çolak, Y. and Soyarık, N. (2000) "What is the Matter with Citizenship? A Turkish Debate," in S. Kedourie (ed.) *Seventy-five Years of the Turkish Republic*, London and Portland OR: Frank Cass.
İğdemir, U. (1969) *Sivas Kongresi Tutanakları* (Records of the Sivas Congress), Ankara: TTK.
Kaplan, P. (2000) "Azınlıklar Konuşmaz" (Minorities Do Not Speak), *Radikal*, 26 March.
Karabatak, H. (1996) "Türkiye Azınlık Tarihine Bir Katkı: 1934 Trakya Olayları ve Yahudiler" (A Contribution to the History of Minorities in Turkey: The 1934 Thracian Affairs and the Jews), *Tarih ve Toplum*, 146: 68–80.
Karpat, K. H. (1982) "Millets and Nationality: The Roots of Incongruity of Nation and State in the Post-Ottoman Era," in B. Braude and B. Lewis (eds) *Christians and Jews in the Ottoman Empire: The Functioning of a Plural Society*, New York and London: Holmes & Meier.
Kılıçdere, A. 2000. "İzmir'de 6/7 Eylül Olayları" (The Affair of 6/7 September in İzmir), *Toplumsal Tarih*, 74: 34–41.
Kili, S. and Gözübüyük, Ş. (1985) *Türk Anayasa Metinleri: Sened-i İttifak'tan Günümüze* (Constitutional Documents of Turkey: From the Deed of Alliance to Today), Ankara: Türkiye İş Bankası Kültür Yayınları.
Kirişçi, K. (2000) "Disaggregating Turkish Citizenship and Immigration Practices," *Middle Eastern Studies*, 36 (3): 1–22.
Kohn, H. (1965) *Nationalism: Its Meaning and History*, Princeton, New York and London: D. van Nostrand.
Kymlicka, W. and Norman, W. (2000) "Citizenship in Culturally Diverse Societies: Issues, Contexts, and Concepts," in W. Kymlicka and W. Norman (eds) *Citizenship in Diverse Societies*, Oxford: Oxford University Press.
Lewis, B. (1965) "The Impact of the French Revolution on Turkey," in G. S. Métraux and F. Crouzet (eds) *The New Asia: Readings in the History of Mankind*, New York and Toronto: New American Library.
——(1968) *The Emergence of Modern Turkey*, New York and Oxford: Oxford University Press.
Liebich, A. (1996) "Getting Better, Getting Worse," *Dissent*, summer: 84–9.
Macfie, A. L. (1996) *The Eastern Question: 1774–1923*, London and New York: Longman.
Meray, S. L. (1969) *Lozan Barış Konferansı: Tutanaklar-Belgeler* (The Peace Treaty of Lausanne: Records and Documents), vols 1–2, Ankara: Siyasal Bilgiler Fakültesi Yayınları.
Mete, N. (1998) "Azınlıklar Azar Mı?" (Would Minorities Get Out of Control?), *+Haber*, 12 (7–13 March).

MFA (Ministry of Foreign Affairs) (2000) "Raporlar Savaşı" (A War of Reports), *Radikal*, 19 June.

Official Gazette (OG) (1934) Law no. 2510, *Resmi Gazete* (Official Gazette), 21 June.

Oommen, T. K. (1997) "Introduction: Conceptualising the Linkage Between Citizenship and National Identity," in T. K. Oommen (ed.) *Citizenship and National Identity: From Colonialism to Globalism*, London: Sage.

Oran, B. (1997) *Atatürk Milliyetçiliği: Resmi İdeoloji Dışı Bir İnceleme* (Kemalist Nationalism: A Non-Official Approach), Ankara: Bilgi Yayınevi.

Ökte, F. (1987) *The Tragedy of the Turkish Capital Tax*, London and New Hampshire: Croom Helm.

Özdoğan, G. Göksu (2000) "Civic Nation vs. Ethnic Nation: Transcending the Duality?" in G. Göksü Özdoğan and G. Tokay (eds) *Redefining the Nation State and Citizen*, Istanbul: Eren Yayıncılık.

Özyılmaz, E. (2000) *Heybeliada Ruhban Okulu* (The Seminar of Khalki), Ankara: Tamga Yayıncılık.

Peters, R. (1999) "Islamic Law and Human Rights," *Islam and Christian-Muslim Relations*, 10 (1): 5–14.

Psomiades, H. J. (1968) *The Eastern Question: The Last Phase*, Institute for Balkan Studies.

Verheugen, G. (2000) "The Enlargement of the European Union," *European Foreign Affairs Review*, 5: 439–44.

Radikal (2000a) "MGK 180 Derece Ters" (The View of the National Security Council is 180 Degrees in Reverse), 19 June.

——(2000b) "Gayrimüslime Köşk Mesajı" (A Presidential Message to non-Muslims), 23 December.

Rıza, N. (1999) *Lozan Hatıraları* (The Lausanne Memoirs), Istanbul: Boğaziçi Yayınları.

Rosting, H. (1923) "Protection of Minorities by the League of Nations," *American Journal of International Law*, 17 (4): 641–60.

Schnapper, D. (1998) *Community of Citizens: On the Modern Idea of Nationality*, New Brunswick and London: Transaction Publishers.

Sezer, A. (1999) *Atatürk Döneminde Yabancı Okullar: 1923–1938* (Foreign Schools in the Atatürk Period: 1923–1938), Ankara: TTK.

TGNA (Turkish Grand National Assembly) (1934) *TBMM Zabıt Ceridesi* (TGNA Records), 4 (23): 67–160.

Tekeli, İ. (1990) "Osmanlı İmparatorluğu'ndan Günümüze Nüfusun Zorunlu Yer Değiştirmesi" (Forced Migration From the Ottoman Empire to Today), *Toplum ve Bilim*, 50: 49–71.

TNP (Turkish National Programme) (2001) *National Programme for the Adoption of the Acquis*. Online. Available at http://europa.eu.int/comm/enlargement/turkey/pdf/npaa (accessed 15 February 2001).

Toker, Y. (1979) *Milliyetçiliğin Yasal Kaynakları* (The Official Sources of Nationalism), Istanbul: Tekin Yayınevi.

Yalman, A. E. (1997) *Yakın Tarihte Gördüklerim ve Geçirdiklerim* (Memoirs of the Recent Past), vol. 2, Istanbul: Pera Yayınları.

Index

For Product Safety Concerns and Information please contact our EU representative GPSR@taylorandfrancis.com
Taylor & Francis Verlag GmbH, Kaufingerstraße 24, 80331 München, Germany

www.ingramcontent.com/pod-product-compliance
Ingram Content Group UK Ltd.
Pitfield, Milton Keynes, MK11 3LW, UK
UKHW020019200926
475702UK00014B/1970
* 9 7 8 0 4 1 5 6 4 6 6 5 9 *